Blackball Stars

Blackball Stars
Negro League Pioneers

John B. Holway

Meckler Books
the trade division of
Meckler Corporation

Earlier versions of some of the chapters previously appeared in the following publications: *Bullet Joe and the Monarchs*, Capital Press, Washington, DC, 1984; "The Cannonball" (Dick Redding), *SABR Research Journal*, 1980; "Charleston No. 1 Star of 1921 Negro League" (with Dick Clark), *SABR Research Journal*, 1986; "Charlie 'Chino' Smith," *SABR Research Journal*, 1979; "Cuba's Black Diamond" (Jose Mendez), *SABR Research Journal*, 1981; "Dandy at Third: Ray Dandridge," *The National Pastime*, 1982; "Dobie Moore," *SABR Research Journal*, 1982; "'I Never Counted My Homers Unless They Won Games;' Turkey Stearnes Tells His Story," *Detroit News Sunday Magazine*, August 15, 1971; "Jud (Boojum) Wilson," *Baltimore Sun Magazine*, June 24, 1979; "Judy Johnson, A True Hot-Corner Hotshot," *SABR Research Journal*, 1987; "Louis Santop, The Big Bertha," *SABR Research Journal*, 1980; "Not All Stars Were White" (Mule Suttles), *The Sporting News*, August 2, 1983; "One Day at a Time" (Leon Day), *SABR Research Journal*, 1983; "The One-Man Team—Cristobal Torriente," *SABR Historical Review*, 1983; "Oscar Charleston," *Black Sports Magazine*, March, 1976; "Rube Foster, Father of the Black Game," *The Sporting News*, March 13, 1982; "Rube Foster, The Father of Black Baseball," Pretty Pages, Washington, DC, 1981; *Smokey Joe and the Cannonball*, Capital Press, Washington, DC, 1983; and "Turkey Stearnes, 'A Humdinger of a Hitter,'" *Black Sports Magazine*, April, 1976.

FIRST EDITION

Library of Congress Cataloging-in-Publication Data

Holway, John.
   Blackball stars.

   1. Afro-American baseball players—Biography.
2. Baseball—United States—Records. I. Title.
GV865.A1H614   1988   796.357'08996073'0922   87-12078
ISBN 0-88736-094-7 (alk. paper)

Meckler Books, a division of Meckler Corporation, 11 Ferry Lane West, Westport CT 06880
Meckler Ltd., Grosvenor Gardens House, Grosvenor Gardens, London SW1W 0BS, UK

Printed on acid free paper.

Manufactured in the United States of America.

To
Frances I. Holway,
without whom this book
would not have been possible

There were many Satchels, there were many Joshes.

Satchel Paige

Contents

Foreword

John Holway has produced scintillating profiles of a collection of the most superior players in the history of baseball. They had magic hands, feet that literally flew, muscles of steel, the eyes of eagles, hair-trigger savvy—and black skin.

It was the latter, of course, that permitted old racial custom to relegate them to the shantytown of the national pastime. It is not news that bigotry and blind prejudice for too many years kept the major leagues the exclusive province of the white man.

In his dedication to the cause of better baseball, John Holway is serving both races. He is an indefatigable researcher, articulate historian and graceful author. The stories he presents here are enlightening, thrilling, and inspiring. I feel fortunate to have him for a friend. I'm certain my life was changed by articles he published in 1981 in *The New York Times* and the *Christian Science Monitor.* He recalled anew the significant role I played as high commissioner of baseball in authorizing Branch Rickey to transfer Jackie Robinson to the Brooklyn Dodgers. That action, of course, broke the color line that had barred black players from donning major league uniforms.

Except for those articles being noted by the veterans committee, the Baseball Hall of Fame might not have gotten around to inducting me during my lifetime.

John Holway presents cogent and forceful arguments for granting blacks greater representation as directors and committeemen in the Hall of Fame. His points are valid and I feel corrective action is long overdue.

I found this book brilliantly written and engrossing. With pleasure and pride, I commend the author and his work.

Albert B. Chandler
Versailles, Kentucky
October, 1987

Introduction:
Before You Could Say
Jackie Robinson . . .

. . . America had not two but four major leagues, two white and two black.

For every Babe Ruth there was a Josh Gibson or Mule Suttles. For every Walter Johnson there was a Smokey Joe Williams or Bullet Joe Rogan, just as today there are Mike Schmidts and Reggie Jacksons, Roger Clemenses, and Luis Tiants.

Black baseball gave us shin guards (Bill Monroe), the batting helmet (Willie Wells), night games (J. L. Wilkinson), and the hit-and-run bunt (Rube Foster).

It also gave us Jackie Robinson, Roy Campanella, Larry Doby, Don Newcombe, Satchel Paige, Willie Mays, Hank Aaron, and Ernie Banks, all of whom learned their baseball from veteran teachers and coaches of the Negro leagues. Without black baseball, it is fair to say, when the white game was ready to open the doors, there might not have been any black players ready to enter.

"You were the pioneers," Mays once said to a panel of Negro league old-timers. "You were the ones who made it possible for us."

When Jackie Robinson's signing with Brooklyn was first announced, Jackie was playing in Venezuela and confided to his roommate, outfielder Gene Benson, that he was nervous that he might not make the grade. "Just remember," Benson told him, "that where you're going is not going to be half as tough as where you've been."

Yet neither our newspapers of those days nor our history books of these days have told us much about the black half of the pre-1950 majors.

Which half was the better half? Suppose Willie Mays, Hank Aaron, Ernie Banks, Jackie Robinson, Roy Campanella, Willie McCovey, Reggie Jackson, Jim Rice, Juan Marichal, Bob Gibson, Luis Tiant, Vida Blue, Dwight Gooden, Joe Morgan, Ozzie Smith, Tony Gwynn, Ricky Henderson, and so on, were taken out of the present major leagues and put into two separate leagues. Would they be major leagues?

Would the National and American Leagues still be "major"

leagues without them? Each fan may answer these questions for himself.

Larry Doby, who played in both worlds, said of the Negro National League: "It was—no question in my mind—a great league. The only difference between it and the [white] major leagues was bench strength." The whites carried 25 men on each team, the black teams only 16 (and at one time 14). "But you put nine men out there on the field, you had a good ball club. I went from Newark direct to Cleveland, so I must have had pretty good training."

How well would the blacks have done in the white major leagues? Actually, we can just as well turn the question around: How well would Babe Ruth, Ty Cobb, and others done in an integrated league?

As Satchel Paige said, "If I had been pitching to Ruth and Gehrig, you could knock a few points off those big lifetime batting averages."

Could Ruth have hit 60 home runs if Paige had been pitching in 1927? The Babe hit no less than 34 of his homers against just 12 pitchers. If those 12 had been replaced by the best black pitchers of that year—Paige, Smokey Joe Williams, Bill Foster, Bullet Joe Rogan, Rats Henderson, Nip Winters, Luther Farrell, Webster McDonald, Chet Brewer—how many home runs would he have lost? We can't even be sure that he would have led the league if black sluggers Mule Suttles, Turkey Stearnes, and John Beckwith had been competing with him.

In 1930 Bill Terry hit .401 with a record total of 254 hits. If he had lost only two hits that year, he'd have ended with a .398 average. And who would have been the real batting champ—Terry, or Chino Smith, who hit .429 for the New York Lincoln Giants? If Ty Cobb had lost only one hit in 1922, he'd have hit .399 instead of .401. No man has ever hit .400 since the major leagues were integrated. It is not a coincidence.

When Joe DiMaggio was in the Pacific Coast League, he got an infield hit against Satchel Paige and exulted that he was ready for the majors. Would he have hit in 56 straight games in 1941 if he had had to face Satch—or Leon Day, Hilton Smith, or Raymond Brown?

We suggest that every citation for a record set before 1950 should bear an asterisk, with the following explanation: *Set before the American and National Leagues became the major leagues.

We do know that the two halves of baseball played each other dozens of times each year in the autumn and winter; we have scoured newspaper files, both black and white, from 1900 to 1950 and uncovered 436 interracial games. The whites won 168. The blacks won 268.

These are revolutionary numbers. They wrench and tear decades of mental habits of millions of fans, particularly those whose baseball attitudes were set before 1946. How can we account for these numbers? Perhaps Earl Weaver answered it best when he was asked why the National League wins so many All Star games.

"The only answer I can give you," Weaver said thoughtfully, "is that they score more runs."

Baseball is, after all, a simple game. All it takes to win is to cross home plate more often than the other team. Why couldn't the Ty Cobbs and Jimmy Foxxes, the Grover Alexanders and Lefty Groves do it? The most quoted excuse is that the whites were loafing and skylarking and not really trying hard, while the blacks had something to prove. Yet the image of Cobb stomping off the field after being thrown out by a black catcher and of John McGraw shouting at his New York Giants after losing to a Cuban team dispel this easy explanation. If one asks a white veteran today about this or that game he lost to a black team, he looks evasive and says he can't remember. If they are embarrassed to be reminded of it now, how much more embarrassed were they half a century ago when they played and lost the game in front of a grandstand full of white—or black—fans?

Even granting the argument that the whites could have won more if they had really wanted to, then one must wonder: How many more? Twenty more? Thirty? Fifty? If they had won 50 more than they did, they would have won 218 and lost 218. Could they still argue that the blacks were not their equals on the field?

Yet, ironically, the membership in baseball's national Hall of Fame is heavily weighted in favor of the losers. To date some 160 men who were active before 1950 have been elected to the Hall. Of these, some 150 are white; only 11 are black.

Nine black veterans—a symbolic all-star team—were admitted by a special Negro league committee, which, as columnist Dick Young revealed in a Cooperstown speech, had been given a quota at its creation. When the quota was filled, the committee was disbanded.

A vigorous fan protest succeeded in preventing the heavy oaken doors of Cooperstown from closing forever on the many other great black stars of the past. Their fate was put in the hands of a new veterans' committee of 17 whites and one black, all from the pre-Jackie Robinson generation of players or writers. They operated under a set of rules that required 14 votes to elect. Gradually, two more blacks were added to the committee, making the balance 15–3. but the rules remained the same: Five negative votes could blackball a candidate.

In its nine years of existence, the committee has elected 19 men—17 whites and two blacks—Rube Foster, a symbolic manager for the symbolic team, and Ray Dandridge, possibly the best third baseman of all time, black or white. Ray knocked on the door for three years, watching others leapfrog over him, before he was finally elected in 1987.

Cooperstown is a white memory bank. No blacks sit on the board of directors. The numbers illustrate the situation:

	white	black
board of directors	14	0
veterans committee	15	3
pre-1950 inductees	150	11
pre-1950 games won	168	268

Thus the game's Hall of Fame itself perpetuates the old mind set of the pre-1946 generation. A stroll through the museum in Cooperstown confirms the bias. The black half of baseball history is tucked away in a small corner display case, half as big as the space devoted to the white minor leagues and about the same space given over to American Legion (that is, high school) ball.

However, a new generation of leaders has moved onto the board of directors. Where once the local townsfolk had a majority, baseball men and women now have the controlling vote. And a new commissioner, Peter Ueberroth, plus new presidents of both the American and National leagues, Dr. Bobby Drown and Dr. A. Bartlett Giamatti—all products of the post-Jackie Robinson generation—now sit on the board. The opportunity exists for a more liberal policy.

Slowly the earlier view of our history is being chipped away. Scholars in the Society for American Baseball Research (SABR) and others are peeling off the layers of myth and ignorance.

Authors A. S. "Doc" Young, Robert Peterson, Ocania Chalk, Donn Rogosin, Quincy Trouppe, Jim Riley, Charles Whitehead, Larry Hogan, Janet Bruce, and Art Rust, Jr., as well as TV producer Craig Davidson, have begun to popularize the "other half" of baseball history.

Historians such as Jim Bankes, Mike Stahl, and this author are taping miles of oral histories to bring to life the color, the drama, and the poetry of the past.

Scholars, led by Dick Clark, Paul Doherty, Bill Plott, Jerry Malloy, Merl Kleinknecht, and others of SABR's Negro league Committee, are assiduously squinting at miles of newspaper microfilm to resurrect batting averages and other data from newspaper box scores, black and white, of the past. It is a monumental job. Jorge Figueredo provided Cuban league statistics, and Bob Hoie and his SABR committee, minor league records. Thanks are due to all who have participated:

Terry Baxter, Gene Benson, John P. Bourg, Harry Brunt, C. Baylor Butler, Harry Conwell, Dick Cramer, Debbie Crawford, Garrett Finney, Bob Gill, Troy Greene, Richard Hall, Jim Holway, John Holway, Jr., Merl Kleinknecht, Larry Lester, Joe McGillen, Mona Peach, Mark Presswood, Susan Scheller, Addie Suehsdorf, Lance Wallace, Edie Williams, and Charles Zarelli.

The job is far from over. The data cited in these pages are the most up-to-date available. Almost daily, as new box scores are tabulated, the totals change. Most of the effort so far has been centered on the 1920s. Gradually, the work is shifting to the 1930s, and then the 1940s.

Black baseball has been a victim of its own, as well as white, myths—the invincibility of Satchel Paige, 72 home runs in one year by Josh Gibson, the superhuman speed of Cool Papa Bell, and so on. Research is now giving us a truer picture. Paige was a splendid pitcher. But there were black pitchers who could beat him and black hitters who could hit him. Several years Gibson's home-run figures were topped by others. And in any given year, there were other black runners who stole more bases than Bell. (In fact, blacks didn't steal an inordinate number of bases then; their speed was manifest in stretching hits, the hit-and-run, and taking extra bases.)

The stories of the 26 men herein are a result of this scholarship. For most, the stories will be new. The same thrill awaits us as that we felt as kids when we first began to discover the white heritage of the game. Here are tape-measure homers, brilliant no-hitters, World Series duels, fun times and tragic times to match anything in the white half of baseball history.

The 26 men we have chosen are not the 26 greatest before 1946. We have left out Paige and Gibson, whose stories are too voluminous to include and who already have books of their own in print. We have also skipped Bell, Buck Leonard, Willie Wells, Bill Foster, and Hilton Smith, whose stories were told in their own words in *Voices From the Great Black Baseball Leagues* (Dodd, Mead, 1975).

We could, of course, include more than 26 men—pioneer Ed Bolden; pitchers Nip Winters, Chet Brewer, Rats Henderson, Raymond Brown, Schoolboy Johnny Taylor, and Ramon Bragana; catcher Bruce Petway; infielders Ben Taylor, George Giles, Home Run Johnson, Bingo DeMoss, George Scales, Sammy T. Hughes, and John Beckwith; and outfielders Pete Hill, Spotswood Poles, Jimmy Lyons, Rap Dixon, Wild Bill Wright, Gene Benson, and Willard Brown, as well as others. Perhaps some day their stories will be fully told as well.

By bringing these 26 stories to today's fans, we hope to bring pleasure to our readers, as well as justice to our subjects. We also hope to make a plea for historical accuracy.

One by-product of the research is the revelation that white men have shared key roles in the history of black baseball. J. L. Wilkinson, owner of the Kansas City Monarchs, was one of the fathers of night baseball, as well as the man who gave Jackie Robinson his springboard to the Dodgers.

Happy Chandler, on the very day he was named commissioner, gave the green light to admit blacks to the major leagues. Without it, Branch Rickey could not have made his move with Robinson. Chandler then defied all 15 of the remaining club owners and approved Rickey's action. He would later lose his job, partly as a result of that courage.

Ted Williams raised the first eloquent voice urging that Cooperstown honor the Paiges and Gibsons who had been kept outside for so long.

But, like the opening of the West, the story of the opening of baseball's doors has its villainous side as well. From one point of view, Rickey was a saint, who gave the black man a chance. From another, he was a thief, who stole Robinson and dozens of other valuable stars from their rightful owners. The real meaning of the Jackie Robinson Revolution was not to get black players into major league baseball—we hope the following stories will make clear that they had already been playing "major league baseball" long before 1946. The real meaning of the revolution was to get black owners out.

A corollary is that baseball has also driven black fans out. The next time you go to a game, look around. The only black faces in a stadium of 50,000 persons will probably be either playing center field or selling beer. Nor will you see many—if any—blacks in the front offices, even as typists. And none in the public relations offices. There are only three black baseball writers that we know of covering major league teams. Even SABR, with its 6,000-plus members, can count less than half a dozen black members, all former players.

Blacks have deserted the game they once loved and thronged to see. Even in the depression, the Negro leagues had filled Comiskey Park with black fans for the annual East-West, or All Star, games. Washington saw 30,000 black fans fill Griffith Stadium for a Homestead Grays night game hours after 3,000 white fans had drifted home from a Senators afternoon game in the same park. Now those black fans have turned their backs on the sport. Bringing them back can only enrich the game.

We hope that, by recognizing black baseball history as the legitimate equal of white history, the game will take the first step toward wooing back those millions of potential fans. If so, baseball will become again what it had been before Jackie Robinson—America's national game.

1

Sol White:
White on Blackball

Nowhere in American life is the color line more firmly drawn than in baseball.

Sol White
History of Colored Baseball
1906

If Rube Foster was the father of black baseball, then Sol White was the grandfather.

His life, 1868–1948, encompassed the beginning and the end of baseball's 60-year apartheid. White was a 19-year-old second baseman in 1887, when Chicago star Adrian "Cap" Anson stomped off the field rather than play a black, thus slamming the door on integrated teams. Sixty years later Sol was a spry little man of 79, when Jackie Robinson stepped on the field in a Brooklyn uniform, thus pushing the creaking oaken door open once again.

More than most other men, Sol White had dreamed and labored so that, when the door was ready to be opened, there would be a Jackie Robinson ready to step through.

Sol was born June 12, 1868 (some accounts say June 27), three years after Lee's surrender at Appomattox, in Bellaire, Ohio, an industrial town across the Ohio River from Wheeling, West Virginia. When Sol was 15, in 1883, an Oberlin College graduate, Moses Fleetwood Walker, joined Toledo in the white Northwestern league. That same summer Sol was hanging around the Bellaire Globes, a white amateur club, when the second baseman got a finger smashed just before a game with Marietta, and White was rushed into the lineup. Captain and second baseman of the Mariettas that day was Bancroft "Ban" Johnson, who would later go on to become president of the American League.

In 1884 White was 16, and Moses Walker and his brother Welday Walker were playing for Toledo, at that time a member of the American Association, one of three major leagues that year. Thus they became the first blacks to breach the color barrier in the majors—and also the last, until Jackie Robinson. That same summer Bud Fowler,

from Cooperstown N.Y., became the third known black to play in a
white organized ball league, when he joined Stillwater, Minnesota,
according to Bob Peterson in *Only the Ball Was White.* Meanwhile, Sol
White was playing every position on the field, as the Globes barnstormed around the Ohio valley. Researcher William Akin says little
was made of the fact that Sol was black: "This is not to say that people
were color blind, but there is no mention of his color in the local
papers."

Sol was still with the Globes in 1885, when the first black professional team was formed from among waiters at the Argyle Hotel on
Long Island. They talked gibberish on the field, hoping it would be
taken for Spanish, and called themselves the Cuban Giants.

In 1886 the Cuban Giants were strong enough to beat a major
league team, the Cincinnati Red Stockings, who finished fifth in the
American Association. White, meanwhile, joined the professional
Wheeling Green Stockings.

The next season the Cuban Giants almost beat the National
League champion Detroit club, losing, 6–4, in the ninth on an error.
But in April Anson, muttering, "Get that nigger off the field," had
taken his famous walk, rather than face George Stovey, a light-skinned
Canadian Negro who had won 30 games with Newark the year before. Since Anson was the biggest star in the National League, his walk
pretty well brought the curtain down on integrated baseball in the
United States. That same spring the Green Sox entered the Ohio
league in organized ball, and White was left off the roster. The team
included three players who would go on to the major leagues—Jake
Stenzel, Sammy Nichol, and Sam Kimber. But they "struggled to
avoid the cellar," Akin said, and in June brought in T. M. "Parson"
Nicholson of the Globes as manager and White as third baseman. In
his first game, Sol pounded four hits and by season's end had helped
raise the club to fourth. There were several other blacks in the league,
including Welday Walker and Robert Higgins, the first great black
pitcher. White ended up with a .381 batting average, second to Stenzel's .390. (Stenzel would go on to hit .339 in his big-league career.
Kimber would pitch a no-hitter with Brooklyn.)

That October the Ohio League decided to prohibit its clubs from
using blacks, and though it later rescinded its order, White had
already decided he had better make other plans.

He joined the Pittsburgh Keystones in a seven-team black league
that included Louisville, Washington, the New York Gorhams, Philadelphia Pythians, Boston Resolutes, and the Lord Baltimores. He
made one triumphant return to Wheeling on opening day 1888 in a
game against his old club, the Green Stockings. Wheeling fans turned
out to present him with flowers before the game in recognition of his
play the previous year.

The black league folded mid-way through the season, but when White tried to rejoin the Wheeling club, the manager refused to use him. So he hopped to the Gorhams as catcher, first baseman, and second baseman at a salary of ten dollars a week, to play semipro ball against white clubs and other black teams such as the Cuban Giants, Norfolk Red Stockings, Long Island City, Hoboken, and other teams. In 1889 the Gorhams beat the Cuban Giants two games to none and claimed the black championship of the world.

White, however, jumped to York in the Eastern Interstate League, one of the few white leagues still accepting blacks. Frank Grant, just fired from Buffalo of the International League, played for rival Harrisburg. Since both White and Grant were second basemen, a personal rivalry sprang up. Grant hit .349 and brought Harrisburg in second. White hit .356, second best in the league, as the York team finished first.

In 1891 White was with the Cubans. We're not sure why, but presumably the Interstate League had begun easing its black players out. When the Cubans fell behind with their paychecks, the Gorhams, under manager Cos McGovern, reraided the Cubans, signing the

Sol White (center) with Smokey Joe Williams (left) and Dick Redding (right).

entire team back, plus Grant and Stovey. Grant moved to shortstop, where he and White starred on double plays. Sol called that one of the finest teams ever assembled, black or white. They played over 100 games and lost only four. Financially, however, they floundered and broke up after only a year.

So Grant landed back with the Cuban Giants, as well as the revived Keystones, the Hotel Champlain team in upstate New York (where he also waited tables), and the (black) Boston Monarchs.

In 1895 White snuck in ten games with Fort Wayne in the white Western Tri-State League. He made $80 a month and batted .452. When the league disbanded, he went west, to Adrian, Michigan, and the Page Fence Giants, organized by Bud Fowler and sponsored by the company that invented the barbed wire that really tamed the West. Sol teamed on double plays with a young fellow named Grant "Home Run" Johnson. In the off-season he enrolled at Wilberforce University.

From then on, White had an odd career. Almost every team he played on claimed the black world championship, and each time they won the title, the loser promptly stole White and won the flag itself the following year. When, in 1896, Page Fence beat the Cuban X-Giants, an offshoot of the original Cuban Giants, the X-Giants grabbed White and beat the "original" Cuban Giants in 1897.

Then came one of the pivotal dates in Eastern blackball history— 1902. H. Walter Schlichter, sports editor of the white Philadelphia *Item,* decided to organize a new team, the Philadelphia Giants, and recruited White to manage it. Sol's first decision was to get Grant, third baseman Bill Monroe, and outfielder Andrew "Jap" Payne. Sol himself played shortstop and second base. The Phils' record was 81–43, and they claimed the black championship of the East, a claim disputed by the X-Giants.

White's club was cocky enough to challenge the Philadelphia Athletics, kings of the American League that year. The A's won both games, 8–3 and 13–9, though White drilled three hits in the second game against Howard "Highball" Wilson (7–5 with the As).

In 1903 White put his players on salary, from $60 to $90 a month. Along with the X-Giants, they joined the white Independent League (Harrisburg, Williamsport, Altoona, and Lancaster). White's Giants again claimed the black championship, though the X-Giants protested loudly again, and they did have a powerful club. Home Run Johnson played shortstop; flamboyant George "Chappie" Johnson, who loved to dress in cane and spats, was the catcher; rookie Preston "Pete" Hill was in left (*real* old-timers put him on their all-time black team); and pitching were little lefty Danmny McClellan and a strapping Texas right-hander named Andrew "Rube" Foster.

On September 12, at Trenton, New Jersey, White's Phils met the X-Giants to settle the black championship of the world. They thus beat the Boston Red Sox and Pittsburgh Pirates by three weeks for the honor of playing the first world series in the new century. The first game was a shock for White. His proud Giants lost, 3–1, as the upstart Foster pitched a three-hitter. They beat McClellan in game two. But in the third contest, Foster did it again, beating them, 12–3, and the X-Giants went on to take the series five games to two.

So what did White do? Naturally, he hired Foster, McClellan, Hill, and Chappie Johnson away from the champions. With two New York Irishmen, Eddie and Jess McMahon, bankrolling the team, Sol also replaced Frank Grant at second with Charlie "Cincy" Grant, the fabled "Chief Tokahoma," who had almost crashed the American League as an "Indian" in 1902 with John McGraw's Baltimore Orioles. Now White could boast the best team in black baseball—and one of the best in the world. His infield was especially brilliant, with himself at first, Grant at second, and Monroe at third. They played several games against clubs in the white New England League and didn't lose a game. They also played four games against the Newark Bears of the International League, managed by future Yankee owner Ed Barrow, and won all four of them.

Still, the team was struggling financially. They played on the "co-op" plan, divvying up receipts among the players after paying off the expenses. Writing of himself in the third person, he would complain that, "with the many complaints of players and threats of quitting ringing in his ears day after day, he passes many a sleepless night." Years later he would reminisce that he often gave up his own share of the receipts in order to hold the team together.

That September, in Atlantic City, the team took on the X-Giants again. "Both players and spectators were worked to the highest fever of excitement," he wrote. "Never in the annals of colored baseball did two nines fight for supremacy as these teams fought." The Phils nipped the X-Giants two games out of three, thanks mostly to Foster. Sol White was champ again.

That winter he took the team to Cuba and won the title there as well.

White completed the humiliation of the X-Giants in 1905. He took their last remaining star, Home Run Johnson, thus giving the Phil's an infield of four superstars—himself, Charlie Grant, Johnson, and Monroe. Johnson particularly was one of the great hitters of his era. In 1910 in Cuba he would outhit Ty Cobb. He contributed a chapter on hitting to White's 1906 *Negro Baseball Guide,* which sounded as if it had been written 70 years later by Ted Williams—like Ted, Johnson preached waiting for a good pitch to hit. (Johnson also had a beautiful singing voice, according to Ted Page, who played for him 20 years later, and enlivened long trips harmonizing with the other players.)

In his 1906 *History* White surveyed the first three decades of black baseball history with the color line firmly drawn between the races. He wrote:

> The colored ball player suffers a great inconvenience at times while traveling. All the hotels are generally filled from the cellar to the garrett when they strike a town. It's a common occurrence for them to arrive in a city late at night and walk around for several hours before getting a place to lodge. . . .
> With the color question uppermost in the minds of the people at the present time, such proceedings on the part of hotel keepers may be expected, and will be difficult to remedy.

Pay was also a sore point. The average white big leaguer made $2,000 in 1905; the average minor leaguer, $500, and the average black, $466.

In 1906 White lost his star hitter when Home Run Johnson left to manage the Brooklyn Royal Giants under John W. Connors, black owner of the Royal Cafe in Brooklyn. Jess McMahon started a rival Philadelphia club, the Quaker Giants, and took Monroe and Chappie Johnson. So White recruited Nate Harris and Bill "Brodie" Francis at short and third. The team claimed a record of 134–21 and clinched the black championship on Labor Day before a record 10,000 fans. They issued a challenge to the winners of the white World Series, between the Cubs and White Sox, "and thus decide who can play baseball best, the white or black Americans." The challenge went unanswered.

White received another blow in 1907. Foster jumped to the Chicago Lelands, taking Hill and others with him. But White obtained catcher Bruce Petway from the Brooklyn Royals; Petway just might have been one of the best catchers of all time—real old-timers say he *was* the best; G. A. "Georgia" Rabbit pitched. But the best of the newcomers was John Henry Lloyd, who went on to become one of the best shortstops ever and a member of the Hall of Fame.

In 1908 White took his club out West to meet Foster's Lelands. He beat them four straight in Detroit. The final games were scheduled for Chicago, but Rube refused to play them.

But as usual, to the losers belonged the spoils. In 1909 Foster grabbed Lloyd and Petway away from White. But the resourceful Sol had one more jewel to unveil, a deer of an outfielder named Spotswood Poles, who was soon being called "the black Cobb." Poles would compile a .610 batting average in games against white big leaguers. Still, the once great Philadelphia Giants had been riddled.

In 1911 White and Poles moved to the New York Lincoln Giants, a team that had originated in Lincoln, Nebraska, in 1891 and was being reorganized by the McMahon brothers. White's star catches were a couple of rookies—pitcher Cannonball Dick Redding and catcher Louis Santop.

The team, however, broke up by July 4, and Sol went home to Bellaire for the next eight years.

When Foster organized the Negro National League in 1920, Sol came out of retirement to serve as secretary of the Columbus club. In 1922 he briefly managed the short-lived Fear's Giants of Cleveland, a black minor-league team. Catcher William "Big C" Johnson calls him "the best educated man I ever played with. Sol wanted what they never were able to get—a reporter to keep records. They never had enough money to hire a man to do that," and with only 14 men on the roster, they didn't have any spare players who could do it.

In 1926 Sol helped coach Newark of the Eastern Colored League. Rookie Ted Page said Sol used to give signals with his scorecard. Holding the card down, for instance, meant the hit-and-run. One day Sol dozed off, and his hand dropped, still firmly clutching the score-card. "Man," Page laughed, "everyone was running wild on the bases."

Finally, White retired completely, haunting the libraries in search of good books and writing a column for the New York *Amsterdam News*.

Two decades later, at the age of 79, Sol White would see his dream finally come true, when Jackie Robinson stepped onto the grass at Ebbets Field in a Brooklyn Dodger uniform. Along with a handful of other men—Foster, J. L. Wilkinson, Cum Posey, and others—White had held black baseball together throughout 60 years of apartheid, making Robinson's debut possible. "I don't think he ever got his just desserts," "Big C" Johnson said.

As Sol wrote in his 1906 *History of Colored Baseball:* "Baseball is a legitimate profession. It should be taken seriously by the colored player. An honest effort of his great ability will open the avenue in the near future wherein he may walk hand in hand with the opposite race in the greatest of all American games—baseball."

2

Rube Foster:
The Father of Black Baseball

With the election of Andrew "Rube" Foster to baseball's Hall of Fame in 1981, the heavy doors of Cooperstown opened at last to one of the five or six most towering figures in the history of American baseball.

White baseball has never seen anyone quite like Rube Foster. He was Christy Mathewson, John McGraw, Connie Mack, Al Spalding, and Kenesaw Mountain Landis—great pitcher, manager, owner, league organizer, czar—all rolled into one.

Foster has been called "The Father of Black Baseball." This is an understatement. Through much of the long years of baseball apartheid, 1887–1947, Rube Foster *was* black baseball, as Winston Churchill *was* Britain in World War II, inspiring his people, keeping their spirits alive, imbuing them with his own strength and genius.

Foster organized one of the early great black teams, the Chicago American Giants. He organized the first viable black league in 1920, for the first time assuring black players a regular pay check, and urged blacks to maintain a high level of play so that when the white doors were open at last, they would be ready. That day came in 1945, and Jackie Robinson, who had been a baby of two in 1920, was ready. Without Foster, it is fair to say, there might never have been a Robinson—or a Willie Mays or a Hank Aaron, also products of Foster's league. All baseball, black and white, is in his debt.

Big, genial Andrew Foster, the pistol-packin' preacher's son from Texas, won his nickname "Rube" by beating Connie Mack's pitching ace, Rube Waddell, 5–2, in 1902. It was one of 51 contests Foster is said to have won that year, when he just may have been the best pitcher, black or white, in America. Honus Wagner, John McGraw, and Frank Chance admired him, and Rube even taught Mathewson how to throw his famous fadeaway.

It was Rube Foster who invented the hit-and-run bunt. Even big league managers used to go out to the games to see how he did it. Yet it has never been used in the white leagues, though it worked miraculously well for the American Giants. The play was simplicity itself. With a "race horse" on first, the batter dropped a bunt down the third baseline. The runner was off with the pitch and almost to second by the time bat touched ball. He didn't stop but kept charging around toward third, which was left unguarded as the third baseman came in to pick up the ball. It was practically impossible to defend against the play. If the third baseman played back on the bag, the batter got an automatic hit. If he came in, the runner slid safely into third. The play also worked with a man on second. If the infielder tried to throw the batter out at first, the runner was expected to keep flying past third and not stop until he had crossed the plate. Some men, like Cool Papa Bell, were even known to score from first on it.

"Rube knew the value of speed, and he knew the value of being able to fit into a directed play," said Dave Malarcher, Foster's long-time third baseman and understudy on the American Giants. Take Ty Cobb, for instance. If Cobb had had a manager like Rube Foster, Malarcher believed the Detroit Tigers never would have lost the pennant. Rube would have had Cobb running and the rest of the Tigers bunting and placing their hits until the opposition was worn to a frazzle. Instead, the Tigers were fanning the air with strikeouts or banging into double plays. In 24 years Cobb played on only three pennant winners and no world champions. Said Malarcher: "If Cobb had had a smart manager like Rube Foster to make him fit into the plays, they would have won pennant after pennant after pennant."

Malarcher yearned to see Rube Foster orchestrating a team with Maury Wills and Lou Brock on it. "Those managers are not using those men to spark the whole team," he said. "You notice what happened with Jackie Robinson in Brooklyn? Sparked the whole team. During the 1967 World Series, you remember that Lou Brock got all of the hits, got all of the stolen bases, and some of those great sluggers didn't do one thing. Orlando Cepeda and Tim McCarver didn't do anything. If they had been taught Rube Foster's diversified system of play, they wouldn't have gone down hitless." Foster had a few sluggers—Pete Hill, Cristobal Torriente—but everyone, including the hard hitters, could also bunt or hit-and-run. "If they couldn't hit one pitcher, they would bunt him, be just as effective. That's what good baseball is. That's what good management is. And that's what Rube taught."

Andrew Foster was born in Calvert, Texas, between Dallas and Houston on September 17, 1879. He was the son of the presiding elder of the AME church in southern Texas. Foster was an asthmatic child. He went faithfully to church every Sunday morning and just as faithfully to the ball field every Sunday afternoon. When his mother died and his father remarried and moved to southwest Texas, Andy quit school after the eighth grade and ran away to Fort Worth to devote his life to baseball. The game would bring some "bitter, heart-breaking memories," he would reminisce later. He rode freight trains, and he was often barred from homes because blacks then considered baseball "low and ungentlemanly," he wrote, but he never stopped loving the game and never worked at anything else for the rest of his life.

By the time he was 17 he was a strapping six-footer playing for the Fort Worth Yellow Jackets and pitching batting practice against big-league clubs doing their spring training in Texas.

In 1901, at the age of 21, Andy was pitching against Connie Mack's Philadelphia Athletics in Hot Springs, Arkansas. He received a

Rube Foster.

bid to pitch semipro ball in Iowa. Instead, he joined the black Leland Giants, owned by Frank Leland, and traveled with them to Oswego, Michigan.

The following year, 1902, Foster jumped to E. B. Lamar's so-called Cuban Giants (actually a Philadelphia club of American blacks). As Foster would recall years later, he pitched for $40 a month, plus 15 cents a meal eating money and confidently called himself "the best pitcher in the country." Perhaps he was. The cocky Texan took quite a ribbing about his six-shooters but defiantly declared that he feared no team anywhere. He was beaten badly in his first game, Rube says, but he got a new catcher and won his next 44 straight. By his own recollection, that's the year he met and whipped the great Rube Waddell, who was 25–7 with the pennant-winning Athletics. Other reports say the Waddell game was in 1903 or 1905. No box score has yet been found. However, since there was no Sunday baseball in those years, the Athletics were in the habit of playing exhibitions outside the city every Sunday, and it is not unlikely that they played Rube's club on one or more of those occasions. Foster's final 1902 victory came against the Philadelphia Giants, the black champions of the year before.

In 1903, according to another persistent legend, John McGraw, skipper of the New York Giants, hired Rube to teach his screwball to Christy Mathewson, Iron Man McGinnity, and Red Ames. Whether the legend is true or not, Matty suddenly jumped from 14 wins in 1902 to 34 in 1903; McGinnity also won over 30 for the first time in his life, and the Giants leaped from last place to second.

That year, Rube jumped across town to the Cuban X-Giants, also an American black club based in Philadelphia, which, in addition to Rube, boasted little Danny McClellan pitching, second baseman Grant "Home Run" Johnson, and outfielder Andrew "Jap" Payne. Their big rivals were the crosstown Philadelphia Giants, managed by Sol White and featuring a fine double play combination in shortstop Bill Monroe and second baseman Charlie Grant. (Two years earlier Grant had been on the roster of John McGraw's American League Baltimore Orioles masquerading as an Indian, "Chief Tokahoma." He was unmasked when hundreds of blacks in Chicago turned out to cheer the "Chief"—a little too lustily, a suspicious White Sox owner Charlie Comiskey thought.)

In the fall of 1903, the X-Giants challenged the Philadelphia Giants to black baseball's first world series—the same year, incidentally, that the Red Sox were challenging the Pirates to white baseball's first modern classic. Foster hit clean-up and won the opening game, 3–1, on a three-hitter. After the Philadelphia Giants tied it, Rube came back and won the third game, 12–3, collecting three hits. including a triple. In all, he won four games in the series as the X-Giants easily won the championship, five games to two.

The next year, Rube and virtually the entire X-Giants squad jumped to the Philadelphia Giants. The world series that fall against their former club should have been a walkover, but Rube turned up sick just before the games opened. While the X-Giants sneered that Foster was afraid of them, manager White pleaded with his star to start the series. Rube did, winning, 8–4, with 18 strikeouts. The X-Giants won the second game, but Rube came back to win the third and deciding game, 4–2, on a two-hitter.

We have no other data on Foster for 1904, but the following year he reportedly won 51 games against five losses, according to black baseball historian Norman "Tweed" Webb.

By 1905, Foster was at the height of his powers. Pittsburgh's great shortstop, Honus Wagner, reputedly called him "the smoothest pitcher I've ever seen."

Rube pitched with his head as much as with his arm. He liked to throw the curve on the 3–2, knowing that most hitters wouldn't be expecting it. The real test of a pitcher, he wrote for Sol White's black baseball guide, comes when the bases are filled.

"Do not worry," he counseled. "Try to appear jolly and unconcerned. I have smiled often with the bases full with two strikes and three balls on the batter. This seems to unnerve them." Foster continued: "In other instances, where the batter appears anxious to hit, waste a little time on him, and when you think he realizes his position and everybody's yelling at him to hit it out, waste a few balls and try his nerve; the majority of times you will win out by drawing him into hitting at a wide one."

Rube and the X-Giants played in the otherwise all-white Philadelphia city league against such former or future big leaguers as Turkey Mike Donlin and Harry McCormick of the Giants, Jake Stahl of the Red Sox, and Topsey Hartsel of the Athletics. In one game Foster found himself in a tight squeeze with Hartsel at bat. Foster was leading by one run with the tying run on third, the winning run on second, and the count 3–0 on Hartsel. Catcher Pete Booker hollered to Foster to walk the hitter. Rube replied with a quick pitch over the plate for strike one. Again Booker called to Foster to walk Hartsel; again Rube surprised Topsy with another over the plate. Strike two. As the crowd stamped and shouted, Foster suddenly called to the umpire to make Hartsel get in the batter's box. Topsy looked down to confirm that his feet were well inside the chalk lines, and before he could look up, strike three had whistled past. Rube would do anything to win. They say he was laughing as he walked off the mound.

Foster could hit too. A semipro catcher in Scranton was riding the

Rube until Foster turned and growled, "Watch this!" He hit the next ball so hard that—the legend insists—the ball literally fell apart in mid-air somewhere behind second base.

In 1906, White lost his star author. Foster wanted more pay and, not getting it, walked off the team. He walked clear to Chicago, figuratively, listening to the lure of his old boss, Frank Leland, who wanted a manager for the Leland Giants. With him, Rube brought seven Philadelphia teammates—Grant "Home Run" Johnson, Pete Hill, Pete Booker, Nate Harris, Mike Moore, Bill Gatewood, and Bill Bowman. Rube insisted that Leland fire his other players and hire Rube's. That year they won the Chicago city semipro league title and capped the season with a series against the City All Stars, who included several big leaguers playing under assumed names. Rube pitched four of the games and won them all, says his biographer, Charles E. Whitehead, in *A Man and His Diamonds* (Vantage Press, 1980).

The Lelands played at Auburn Ball Park at 79th and Wentworth Avenue and advertised primly that "the best of order is maintained at all times." General admission was 25 cents, grandstand 35 cents, and boys' seats 15 cents. Leland and Foster floated $100,000 worth of stock

The 1905 Philadelphia Giants. Front (left to right) are Danny McClellan, Pete Hill, two unidentified players, Bill Monroe, and, rear (left to right), Grant "Home Run" Johnson, Rube Foster, unknown, Schlicter, Sol White, unknown, and Charlie Grant. In 1902, Charlie Grant tried out for the American League Baltimore Orioles as an Indian.

and laid big plans for an amusement park and ball field with roller rink, grill room, and bowling alley. Foster did the booking and ran the team on the field as well. In 1907 the Lelands won 110 games (48 in a row), lost only 10, and walked off with the pennant in the otherwise white Chicago city league.

Frank Chance, the manager of the Cubs, wistfully called Rube "the most finished product I've ever seen in the pitcher's box." The Cleveland *Post* added: "There have been but two real pitchers who have put their feet in the Cleveland ball yard. They are Addie Joss and Rube Foster."

The Chicago *Inter-Ocean* was also impressed by the big black hurler from Texas. "Rube Foster," it wrote, "is a pitcher with the tricks of a Radbourne, with the speed of a Rusie, and with the coolness and deliberation of a Cy Young. What does that make him? Why, the greatest baseball pitcher in the country; that's what the greatest baseball players of white persuasion who have gone against him say. He would be a priceless boon to the struggling White Sox or the Highlanders (Yankees) just now."

Young Willie Powell, peering through a knothole, remembered that "Rube had a way to grip that ball, throw underhand, and he could hum it. And he was a trick pitcher, always tried to trick you into doing something wrong. If you were a big enough fool to listen to him, he'd have you looking at something else and strike you out." "He was a superb pitcher," sighed Joe Taylor, a teenager in Louisville at the time. "Every time he came to Louisville those Leland Giants used to walk right away from those Louisville teams—white and colored. Whatever he was pitching, they weren't hitting it. That big joker could fall off that mound!"

In 1908, Rube was offered a $650 raise to go back east and play, but he refused; he was afraid the Lelands would fold without him, he said. With Rube back at the helm, the club climbed into its own private Pullman to go south for spring training, the first black club ever to do so. For the season the team won 64, lost 21, and tied one. Thirteen of their wins were shutouts.

Rube broke his leg the following July and didn't pitch the rest of the year, but that October he challenged the Chicago Cubs to a series to determine the real city champion. Frank Chance and second baseman Johnny Evers refused to play, though they watched the games from the stands.

The Cubs had finished second in the National League that year, but they didn't take any chances against Foster's club. In the first game they opened with their ace, Mordecai "Three-Fingered" Brown, 27–9, with a 1.31 earned run average against National League teams. Brown handcuffed the Lelands on five hits. The Lelands' Joe Green slid into third on a steal as the ball got away from the Cubs' Harry Steinfeldt. Green broke his leg on the slide but gamely got up and tried to hobble home. Of course he was out, but a young reporter named Ring Lardner was impressed at the spectacle of a man trying to score with a broken leg.

Foster himself pitched the second game—his first outing since his own broken leg three months earlier. He faced Orval Overall, 20–11 that season. The Rube was in command early, as the Lelands took a five-run lead in the third. The Cubs got one in the fourth when Joe Tinker (.256) hit the short left-field fence for a double. In the eighth the Cubs scored again on three hits, but Pete Hill's good throw choked off the rally, and Foster went into the ninth still ahead, 5–2. Then he started to weaken.

According to Lardner, this is what happened next: Foster got Tinker for the first out, but Pat Moran (.220), Overall, and Heinie Zimmerman (.273) all singled to load the bases, and Jimmy Sheckard (.255) walked to force in a run and make it 5–3. Outfielder Frank Schulte (.264) forced Overall at the plate for the second out, leaving the bases filled. First baseman Del Howard (.197) then singled off the right-field fence, scoring two runs to tie the game and send Schulte to third.

At this point, Foster called time and walked to the dugout in order, as he said afterward, to get someone to come out and relieve him. As he left the field, Schulte dashed for home, the umpire called him safe, and exuberant Cubs and their fans swarmed onto the field.

Rube Foster (standing, far right) with the 1909 Chicago Leland Giants. Also pictured is Pete Hill (standing, far left).

Foster was fit to be tied. He insisted that the run did not count, but the umpire refused to reverse himself, and the game went into the record officially as a 6–5 victory for the Cubs.

The next day, Brown returned to the mound and beat Lefty Pat Dougherty of the Lelands, 1–0, when Tinker doubled and scored on Brown's single on a very close play. It gave the Cubs a three-game sweep. Foster would try and try for years afterward, but he never got a rematch.

That winter, Foster and John Schorling, a white saloon keeper and brother-in-law of White Sox owner Charlie Comiskey, wrested control of the team from Leland in a bitter court fight. The team moved from its former park at 69th and Halstead into the old White Sox park at 39th and Shields, though some warned that it was too close to the Sox' new park on 35th Street. Rube dismissed the fears. He changed the team's name to the American Giants, and thus was born perhaps the greatest team in the history of black baseball.

The pitching staff was Foster and Dougherty, plus newcomers Bill Lindsey and Frank Wickware, who came from Walter Johnson's hometown of Coffeeville, Kansas, and once beat his illustrious towns- man, 1–0. The outfield was Hill, Payne, and rookie Frank Duncan. Catching was Bruce Petway, whom many regard as one of the greatest receivers in the history of black baseball. That winter in Cuba he would stun the great Ty Cobb by throwing him out stealing three straight times. In the infield, Pete Booker was on first, Home-Run Johnson on second, Wes Pryor played third, and the great John Henry Lloyd arrived from Philadelphia to play short. They were soon calling Lloyd "the black Wagner," and there are many who insist that he was the finest black shortstop of all time. The double-play combination of Lloyd and Johnson was the most potent in black baseball for that day and probably rivaled Tinker and Evers of the Cubs as the best in the country, period.

The American Giants traveled to Fort Worth for spring training, and thousands of people turned out to welcome them, thronging to town by wagon, carriage, streetcar, and horseback. While there, Rube picked up a hard-throwing prospect, Cyclone Joe Williams, and brought him back north with the club.

Foster would later call that the greatest team he ever assembled. They must have been. In 129 games in 1910 they won 123 and lost only six. The American Giants proudly advertised their star-studded lineup, which could be seen in person for the bargain rate of only 50 cents for a box seat, including free ice water. For special promotions heavyweight champion Jack Johnson, a former first baseman himself, would be on hand to give souvenirs to the ladies. In fact, Johnson later masqueraded as an American Giants player to flee prosecution under the Mann Act. When the team crossed the Canadian border on a barnstorming trip, Johnson jumped off and escaped to Europe.

In the fall of 1910 Foster took his team to Seattle, playing white teams on the way out and back. They wintered in Cuba, playing tough Cuban clubs. The American Giants' fame was spreading far and wide.

White Sox-owner Charlie Comiskey was apparently worried about the rival only two blocks from his new park. He urged Foster to play only when the White Sox were out of town and predicted failure for the black team if he didn't. Rube ignored the warning. In 1911 he deliberately challenged both the Cubs and White Sox to an attendance war. On one Sunday when all three teams were in town, the Cubs drew 6,000, the Sox 9,000, and Foster's American Giants 11,000.

That fall, Foster also challenged the Cubs on the field. The Cub manager, Johnny Evers, replied that it all depended on whether the players wanted to stay in town or not. Apparently they didn't; the series was never played.

The American Giants won the Chicago city semipro crown in 1911 and again in 1912. In the latter year Foster hooked up against the great Cuban pitcher, Jose Mendez, conqueror of Christy Mathewson. The two fought to a 12-inning tie in what the papers called "the duel of the decade."

In the spring of 1913, Rube took his club to the West Coast by Pullman. Later that summer the great Cy Young, then 46 years old and pitching for Benton Harbor, Michigan, faced the Giants and got beat, 6–1. In the fall the Giants journed east to meet the New York Lincoln Giants in the black world series, but the Lincolns won it on the pitching of Steel Arm Johnson.

In 1914, Rube had gathered another fine club—Dougherty, Gatewood, and Dicta Johnson pitching; Petway catching; Judy Gans, "Uncle" Bill Monroe, John Henry Lloyd, Candy Jim Taylor, and Brodie Francis in the infield, and the slugging Pete Hill in center field. Cy Young returned for a rematch, and Rube beat him again, 7–6. (Chicago's Lee Wade beat Cy a third time, 9–1.) The Giants challenged Joe Tinker's Federal League club, but the challenge went unanswered.

After the season was over, Rube and his Giants embarked for the West again on their private Pullman car to play in the California winter league. Among their victims was the San Bernadino club, starring Honus Wagner, whom they beat, 6–3.

The next year, 1916, the American Giants wintered in Cuba, returning home via the West Coast, where they won five out of six against the Portland Beavers, champions of the Pacific Coast the previous year.

By now Rube was 36 years old and putting on weight. He appeared less and less on the mound, although pitcher Bill Drake of the multiracial All Nations team recalled that Foster had a sensational pick-off move to second base. According to Drake, the Rube could flip the ball underhanded behind him without turning around and still get his man. In May he also put himself in as a pinch runner and stole second and third to the cheers of the crowd.

That fall, the American Giants met the Brooklyn Royal Giants for the "colored world series" and swept it in four games straight. Wickware opened with a three-hit, 3–0 victory; Wade followed with a two-hitter, 7–0; and Horace Jenkins won the last two, 7–4 and 3–1.

Foster was in Cuba for the winter again and just missed pitching a no-hitter when outfielder Judy Gans misjudged Cristobal Torriente's fly, which fell for a double.

The Giants barnstormed through the South in the spring of 1915 on their way back to Chicago. They traveled in style in private Pullman cars hooked onto the regular trains. Dave Malarcher, then a student at New Orleans University, recalls his first youthful look at the Foster men:

I never shall forget the first time I saw Rube Foster. I never saw such a well-equipped ball club in my whole life! I was astounded. Every day they came out in a different set of beautiful uniforms, all kinds of bats and balls, all the best kinds of equipment.

The American Giants traveled everywhere, as you know. No other team traveled as many miles as the American Giants. When Rube gave them the name American Giants, he really selected a name. That was a good idea, because it became the greatest ball club that ever was. That's right; the way he played, the way he equipped his team, the way he paid his men, the way he treated his men, the miles that they traveled.

One time—I wasn't with them then, but Rube told us about it later—Rube traveled down South. They were in a private car and for some reason or another they had switched his car off of the main track, you know, and he said one of the workmen, the brakeman around the yard, saw all of these big Negroes getting out of that car and he said, "Hey there. hey there, what are you Negroes doing getting out of Mr. Rube Foster's car?" He had heard about Rube Foster being a great promoter and a great baseball man, but he didn't know that Rube was a Negro. And you know what Rube said? "I just happen to be Mr. Rube Foster."

The American Giants were the class of the West again in 1915 and met the New York Lincoln Stars for the colored championship. The Stars were indeed a formidable club. Pitching was Cannonball Dick Redding, who had reputedly won 20 straight games that year, the last one against the Philadelphia Athletics' Andy Coakley just one week earlier. Redding's battery mate was slugging Louis Santop, who hit the old dead ball almost as hard as Josh Gibson would hit the lively ball 20 years later. Pop Lloyd, who had left Chicago, was holding down shortstop for the Stars. And their center fielder leading off was Spotswood Poles, a black deer on the bases and often called "the black Ty Cobb." The Stars were an excellent match for Foster's men, and the two clubs battled for ten games, each winning five. For some reason no tie-breaker was played, and so the series ended in a deadlock.

Meanwhile, another rival was forming in the West—the Indianapolis ABCs, managed by C. I. Taylor and starring center fielder Oscar Charleston and second baseman Elwood "Bingo" DeMoss, each usually rated the best black player ever at his position. They beat Foster's American Giants two out of three in the 1916 playoffs.

The World War I draft pretty well broke up the ABCs in 1917, and Foster claimed the western pennant that year. He had another powerful lineup, including Lloyd, who had returned, and two fine new pitchers, Dick Whitworth and Padrone, a Cuban lefty. That August they met the Lincoln Stars for the national black championship. Whitworth and Wickware won their starts to give Chicago a two-to-one lead, but the New Yorkers bounced back to go ahead three games to two with two left to play. Padrone tied the series for Chicago with a four-hit shutout, and in the finale the Giants spotted New York three runs, then exploded for a 17–7 victory and the championship.

Foster would do anything to win. New York infielder Frank Forbes, later a member of Mayor Fiorello LaGuardia's New York boxing commission, conceded that Rube was "a mastermind" but insisted that he was also "a thieving son of a bitch." Forbes said:

> He built his ball club with speed. We'd go out there to play those son of a bitches—excuse me—and you know what he does? We don't wise up until the end of the ball game, but he had drowned the goddam infield the night before. Those suckers lay down a bunt, it rolls nine feet and stops. The man's on. My God, by the time you got to the ball the man was on.
>
> Something else he pulled on us: He and the umpires were working together. The balls we were getting when we came to bat were frozen. Now Santop was about 6'2" or 3", 200-some odd pounds. Goddam, he hit a ball 999 miles. He hits this damn ball, should have gone out of the ball park, and the ball drops in short left field. Right away Jess McMahon, our owner, hollered, wanted to know what was going on. Come to find out it was those damn balls. You could feel them. If you held one long enough, your fingers stuck to the ball!

(Foster had another little trick, according to speedster James "Cool Papa" Bell. He built almost imperceptible ridges along the foul lines to insure that any bunted ball would stay fair while his race horses streaked across first base safely.)

Foster played on his immense prestige to lure young players to his team. If you sign with us, he told a young Texan, pitcher Jesse Hubbard, you'll live in Chicago, travel by Pullman, "and play with the great Rube Foster."

The next year, the once great Giants were decimated. Pitcher Tom Williams was fired for breaking Rube's strict rule against drinking. Lloyd refused to leave his temporary defense job to go south for spring training. Gans and pitcher Frank Wickware were drafted. Still, the Giants won the city semipro crown and the black world series as well.

Dave Malarcher, an excellent third baseman for Indianapolis, was in the army in France when Rube wrote to him, offering him a job after the war. When Dave got back to Indianapolis, he asked C. I. Taylor of the ABCs for an advance so he could go home to New Orleans and see his fiancee. When C. I. hesitated, Dave hopped a train to Chicago to look up Foster, or "Jock," as the players called him. Rube quietly reached into his rolltop desk, took out a roll of bills, and handed it to Malarcher without a word. A contract followed that winter.

"That's the difference," Malarcher shrugged. "Rube was just a great guy."

That spring Rube also signed Oscar Charleston, hailed as the best black player of all time. The year 1919 saw great race riots erupt in several American cities. Thirty-eight persons died in Chicago alone. The Giants were on the road when the riots broke out, and on their return they found their park occupied by the tents of National Guardsmen.

Foster also faced another problem, the threat of raids from the eastern black clubs. He warned against an all-out bidding war. In 1902, he wrote, the X-Giants had a total payroll of $700 a month. The next year the Philadelphia Giants paid their players $850 a month but had to disband when they couldn't meet the payroll. Later, the Lincoln Giants were paying $900 month. "At this enormous figure, they wrecked the other clubs," said Foster. But they too couldn't meet the payroll, and when their players sued them, they went under. Foster said that in 1910 he had paid the Leland players $1,000 a month, but though the team won 126 games, it lost $2,000 for the season. Rube wrote that he raised the American Giants' payroll to $1,500 a month, and in 1918 the total had reached $1,700 a month. The lowest paid men on the Giants were making more than a mailman or schoolteacher, though some couldn't even write their names. Still, he complained, the players were looking for "fat lambs"—owners who would pay and pay "until they cannot." Players jumped so much, he said, even their new owners couldn't trust them.

With the end of the war, white semipro baseball in the Chicago area began to fall apart. Top teams like the Logan Squares, which sent Phil Cavaretta and others to the big leagues, lost their drawing power. And since the black clubs depended heavily on income from playing against them, the effect was felt by the American Giants too.

So, in the winter of 1919, Foster made a revolutionary decision. He called together the owners of the best black clubs in the Midwest and proposed a Negro National League. (One of those attending, Elisha Scott, would later argue the historic *Brown* v. *Board of Education* case desegregating schools before the Supreme Court.) They met in a Kansas City YMCA on Friday, February 13, 1920, and drew up a constitution that barred raids on each other, outlawed jumping by instituting the white leagues' reserve clause that bound players to their clubs, and provided fines for ungentlemanly conduct on and off the field. Rube envisioned a completely black league—he wanted to keep black money in black pockets, he wrote—but reluctantly admitted one white owner, J. L. Wilkinson of Kansas City.

The result was an eight-team league: The American Giants, Joe Green's Chicago Giants, the peripatetic Cuban Stars, the Detroit Stars, the St. Louis Stars, the Indianapolis ABCs, the Kansas City Monarchs, and the Dayton Marcos.

Rube hoped to bring the eastern and western clubs together under one umbrella and gave associate memberships to the Philadelphia Hilldales and the Atlantic City Bacharachs. Clubs who could afford the long trip east played home-and-home series against them. Foster also dreamed of a pyramidal structure, much like the white major and minor league system. Eventually, he hoped, the black and white champs would play each other in a real world series. Paradoxically, he wanted black baseball to develop, so that when the white leagues were ready to integrate, "we would be ready." That integration did come 25 years later, and Jackie Robinson, a one-year-old infant when Foster formed his league, would be the first black to show that he was indeed ready.

"We are the ship," Rube told his colleagues, "all else the sea." From his offices at Indiana and Wentworth, according to SABR's Jerry Malloy, Foster kept his fragile ship afloat, running the league virtually as a benevolent autocrat. To balance the teams, he sent his own star, Charleston, back to Indianapolis. When teams ran out of money on the road, he wired some to them so they could get home. He advanced loans so they could meet their payrolls. He financed the Dayton franchise out of his own pocket. When catcher William "Big C" Johnson wrote to him, complaining that the Marcos were not giving him a regular's pay, Rube wrote curtly, "Either give the man what you promised him or let him go."

He also dug into his pocket to help players in need. He once explained to a sports writer, "It will be August before that fellow pays me back all he owes me, but I guess he's got to live." He'd even advance money to a man on a rival club if that club couldn't meet its payroll and took his chances on collecting from the club the following year.

Foster may have saved black baseball. He would boast later that total players' salaries jumped from a mere $30,000 a year in 1919 almost ten-fold to $275,000 a year. It wasn't a princely sum, considering the number of players—about 120—cutting up the pie. Still it averaged $2,000 per man per year—not too bad for those days. As Foster said, the secret of putting together a championship team is "brains and money: You can't keep good players without paying them good salaries."

Meantime, Rube also put together a team that would dominate the West for most of the next decade.

The ace of the pitching staff was Dave Brown, an exconvict from Texas who many call the best left-hander in black history.

The rest of the club was built around speed and bunting. Malarcher explained:

We had Jimmy Lyons, Torriente, and Jelly Gardner in the outfield. They're all fast. I was on third, I'm fast. Bobby Williams shortstop, real fast. Bingo DeMoss second, he's fast. We had George Dixon and Jim Brown catching. Brown was fast, could push and bunt, and hit too. Leroy Grant playing first base was the only slow man on the team. He usually hit way down by the pitcher. See, when James Brown was catching, we had seven men in the line-up could run a hundred yards in around ten seconds. All speed, and with Rube directing it, it was something. Rube telling us what to do—push it here, hit it by the first baseman, hit over there. He directed your play all the time.

When you play a diversified game, you don't allow your team to get into slumps, because you are making your breaks. You don't just say, "We got the breaks today." You make your breaks.

Foster would draw a circle in front of home plate and make his players practice bunting into the circle. The American Giants could bunt on third strike and did so against white big leaguers.

"I've seen Foster have his club bunt seven straight innings and then beat you," said Birmingham pitcher Harry Salmon. "Yes, it did put a lot of pressure on the pitcher, on all who were playing the American Giants."

Chicago pitcher Webster McDonald said Foster would have his players "push it to short, push it to second." The infield would edge in, "and sooner or later someone was going to mess up." Foster told them, "If you get your first man on, you ought to get a run." "A ball club don't need but two hitters on it," Mac said. "We had two: Torriente and Jim Brown."

"But you had to listen to what Rube said," continued Mac. "If you didn't, your pay check would be kind of small. He was good to you, but you had to listen, you had to learn, or you'd find yourself with one of the weaker clubs in the league."

Pity the poor infielders when the American Giants came to bat. If the third baseman played in, Gardner would tap the ball over his head, often good for two bases. If he played back, Jelly would drop the ball in front of the plate and streak across first before the throw. Then the fireworks began.

DeMoss was a wizard with the bat. If Gardner broke for second, DeMoss could wait until the last split second before swinging, depending on whether Jelly had the base stolen or not. "He would save you if he thought you were out," Gardner said. "He'd hit behind you. If the second baseman was moving over to cover second, he'd hit by the second baseman." DeMoss was probably the best bunter in black baseball annals. He didn't square around to bunt, but took his natural stance, at the last moment flicking the bat down and virtually picking the ball out of the catcher's mitt. They say it would almost bounce backward when it hit the turf, like a draw shot in billiards. Gardner meanwhile had already left the bag and was rounding second, head down, toward the uncovered third base. It was almost impossible to get either one of them.

Malarcher, the next man up, was equally adept at bat control, and another bunt might easily bring Gardner home and put DeMoss on third.

If you walked a man against Rube, McDonald shrugged, "that was a run."

Torriente, the clean-up man, could hit screamers over the center-field fence as easily as he could drop a bunt into a hat on the base line. Now the infield didn't know what to do. If they played back, Torriente would drop it just beyond the pitcher's reach; if they moved in, he'd swing away and decapitate the first baseman.

Gardner, Lyons, and infielder Johnny Reese could even pull off triple steals, Willie Powell said. "I saw that happen more than one time. You couldn't hesitate with them on base. If you hesitated, you were lost."

Rube often ordered the first man on to steal, just to see the pitcher's move. Even if the runner got thrown out, Powell said, it helped the men behind him when they got on base.

Lyons once complained that he didn't know what it was to stand up and take a full cut at the ball because Foster had him bunting so much.

Rube was one of the first masters of psychological baseball. Malarcher remembered:

> Rube would do a lot of kidding with the other team. He would tell them, "I'm going to do so-and-so and so-and-so-and-so." Just like in prize fighting, get the other guys nervous and thinking and guessing and wondering and doing just the opposite. One thing he used to say: "The element of surprise in baseball is like everything else. We do what the other fellow does not expect us to do." This was his philosophy. This was why we did all of those things, that's why our center fielder Jelly Gardner was great on the bases. We all were, because he taught this: that in order for a man to put you out going from base to base, the other team must make a perfect play. If you can run, if you're fast, he's got to make a perfect play, and if you surprise him, he can't make a perfect play, he can't make it.

J. G. Taylor Spink, editor of *The Sporting News*, baseball's "bible," told his readers:

> Recently, especially in games played in Chicago, the negro teams have shown wonderful speed and skill in their work as well as remarkably good conduct.
>
> They have developed the old happy-go-lucky high score game into regular aggressive, low-scoring contests, with the same wonderful curve pitching, sharp calling of balls and strikes and superb throwing from both the in and out fields that is in evidence in the regular games in the major leagues. . . .
>
> Experts who have seen the negro games in Chicago this year have been astonished at their wonderful progress and development, and now class some of the regular teams with the best there is in the regular major leagues.

Actually, except for Torriente, the rest of the Giants did not boast very high batting averages. Malarcher, DeMoss, Williams and the others usually hit in the low .200s. Their main rivals, Kansas City, boasted five men—Bullet Rogan, Dobie Moore, Oscar "Heavy" Johnson, in the .360s or above. Yet Foster's Giants beat them out for the pennant three years in a row.

Malarcher said:

> From 1920, when the league started, the first three years we had a powerful team, we had a powerful team. Because we had gotten together the speed, the daring, the men that could really hit, a good pitching staff,

good catching. See, Rube was smart enough, a genius, to know how to pick men to fit into his plays, and he used to say all the time, "If you haven't got intelligence enough to fit into this play, you can't play here." That's all there was to it. It isn't generally known, but Rube was so superior in his knowledge of baseball that from 1920 to 1922, the first three years of the league, we were so far out in front of the league by July, they had to break the season up into two halves so there would be interest in the league the second half.

Rube himself once explained another reason for his tactics—to tire the pitcher out. Not only did the hurler have to field the bunts, but the hitters could "work" him, making him throw more pitches. When the pitcher began to tire, about the seventh inning, that's when Rube's hitters suddenly centered their attack.

Rube's younger half-brother, Bill, who joined the team a few years later, had another theory to explain Rube's bunt-and-run tactics. "He didn't believe in beating anybody bad," Bill says. "It would draw the crowd away. If you can beat the ball game, win it, but don't beat the other team so bad that nobody wants to see the team the next time it comes. So he held the runs down a lot by playing a whole lot of fancy stuff."

One fundamental that Rube taught was to make contact with the ball. As Malarcher said:

> Rube used to say the easiest way out is to strike out. And the easiest way to get three outs is to get a man on base and do nothing behind him; the men behind him all strike out. But if you get a couple of men like Jelly Gardner, Torriente, or Lyons on base, you should get some runs. Every time they get on base, the other team is in trouble.
>
> During those times all ball players developed to a high point of professionalism. I look at some of the players that are supposed to be good ball players today, and they are hitting balls down at their toes sometimes, over their heads, way outside. In those days the balls had to be in there for those guys. They would have to be strikes. That's professionalism, and that's what those fellows were then.

That was one of Rube's rules, Powell said: "Never let that last ball go by."

"And Rube could really get his men into shape," Malarcher added. He further stated:

> When I came up to the American Giants, he would hit that ball to me at third. He was a great big man—250 to 300 pounds—a powerful man, and he would stand up there and drive that ball down there to me like a shot. I mean, really conditioning me. For example, he used to

laugh all of the time, winking at some of the players, you know, and he said, "Little man like you, I could knock you down." You know, just kidding. No, he wouldn't really do it, he wouldn't. He was a fine man.

Ball players love the fast life, and the American Giants were no exception. Two of the most notorious night owls were Gardner and Torriente. Recalled Gardner:

> Rube was a nice manager, an even-tempered man. Rube never told me what to do after I left the ball park. You can do what you want to do, but when you came to the ball park he wanted you to play or he'd fine you. Like most ball players go out and have a big night and then didn't feel too good the next day. He'd take it away from you, say, "If you can't play, go back to the hotel." Take a day's pay away from you. It never happened to me though. I could recuperate quick at that time.

Sam Streeter, the left-handed spit-baller, called Foster the best manager he ever played for, but adds: "If he told you to do something, he meant for you to do what he said. If he told you to throw a ball behind the batter, he meant for it to be behind him; don't come throwing it inside close and say, 'I tried.' He'd say, 'You're supposed to do what you try to do.'"

Ted Radcliffe, the American Giants' batboy who would grow up to be pitcher and catcher "Double Duty" Radcliffe, remembers Rube once telling his pitcher to walk Oscar Charleston. "The guy didn't walk him and Charleston hit a home run. When he came in the clubhouse, Rube spit in his face, said, 'That'll cost you $150, you son of a bitch. When I tell you to walk a man, walk him!'"

"All the ball players had to hustle—even the batboy had to hustle," sighed another ex-batboy, Normal "Tweed" Webb. "Rube was a pretty firm type of fellow."

One of his earlier pitchers, Arthur W. Hardy, described Rube's leadership tactics to Robert Peterson in *Only the Ball Was White* (Prentice-Hall, 1970):

> I wouldn't call him reserved, but he wasn't free and easy. You see, Rube was a natural psychologist. Now he didn't know what psychology was and he probably couldn't spell it, but he realized that he couldn't fraternize and still maintain discipline. He wasn't harsh, but he was strict. His dictums were not unreasonable, but if you broke one he'd clamp down on you. If he stuck a fine on you, you paid it—there was no appeal from it. He was dictatorial in that sense.

With youngsters, Rube was less draconian. "He never would holler at you," recalls infielder Lou Dials. "He'd call you aside, say,

'Come here, son,'" and give his advice. Rube had a standing five-dollar fine for being tagged out at first, Dials said. "You're supposed to slide," he told his men.

"Rube had been an underhand pitcher like I was," Webster McDonald said, "and on the three-and-two you better break something. You better break that curve ball. And you better break it over the plate, and not over the heart of the plate either."

Rube didn't rely on his catcher to give the signals to the pitcher. He'd flash the signs himself from the dugout. Said McDonald:

> The catcher'd get down there, waggle his fingers around, don't mean nothing. Rube just told me what to throw. Remember old Jim Brown, the catcher? Mean, ornery guy? He come dragging up to the mound, going to give me hell. I said, "Jim, Rube told me what to throw!" "Damn Rube."
> He'd drag on back behind the plate. After the inning, get in the dugout, Rube said, "Jim, go to the clubhouse, take my uniform off." Jim, you know, was a big strong guy. When he was ready to go in the shower, Rube went in there, told Jim, "Lock the door." He whipped Jim! Rube was tough. He was tough!

When Rube's brother, Bill, 25 years his junior, signed with the Memphis Red Sox as a pitcher in 1924, Rube hit the roof. He didn't want the boy to become a ball player and had told him so some six years earlier. When he found out Bill was with Memphis, Rube ordered Memphis owner Bubber Lewis to send the boy to Chicago immediately. Rube wanted him on the American Giants, under his wing.

Now it was Bill's turn to get mad. He didn't like being ordered around like that and made up his mind that no matter what Rube tried to teach him, he wouldn't listen. Every time Rube put the stubborn boy in to pitch, he promptly got bombed out of the box. Bill refused to pitch for Rube, and Rube refused to trade Bill. "I know you can pitch," Rube told him. "I'm not going to trade you. You can just stay out there and make a fool of yourself, but I'm not going to trade you."

"But," grinned Bill half a century later, "Rube was a shrewd man. The more I think of it, the older I get, I can see Rube's point of view on a lot of things. And whatever he told me stuck." The next year Rube suffered a nervous breakdown and had to leave the bench. Bill walked to the mound, did exactly as Rube had been teaching him— and went on to become perhaps the top left-hander in black baseball history. A photo of him winding up to pitch, hands above his head, is the spitting image of his brother Rube on the mound, Malarcher said.

"I had learned the stuff that he had given me, and didn't know it," Bill said. "I had it, and didn't know that I had it."

McDonald smiled, "Bill thought at first that by being Rube's brother he would get some short cuts. Rube treated him as hard as any other man on the team."

In Powell's debut with the American Giants in 1925, Willie had the Monarchs shut out after six innings. Kansas City had already clinched the flag, and Rube called Powell over. "I want you to do what I say," he said. From then on Foster called every pitch from the bench. "Kansas City whipped my ass off in the seventh inning. Beat me 10–4. Rube called me over to the side, said, 'You'll do.' I got hit to death, but he said, 'You know, if I'd left you alone, you'd have beat the great Kansas City Monarchs, then I'd never be able to tell you nothing.' Years later, I found out he was right."

"Oh Rube was strict," agreed Bobby Williams. "When he got angry with you, he got angry. I've seen him sit on the bench and somebody did something wrong—he smoked a pipe all the time, and he took his pipe and hit you on the head with it. He was fun, though. Wherever you were traveling, you could tell where he was stopping. He would get a chair and sit on the sidewalk in front of the hotel, and people would just listen to him talk."

"Every time Rube Foster would come to Kansas City, he'd draw crowds down there," said George "Never" Sweatt, then a rookie outfielder for the Monarchs. "He liked to tell stories about how he was going to do the Monarchs. He'd just brag and get crowds. They'd have to have the police come so the traffic could move." It was shrewd showmanship: The Giants-Monarchs games were always sell-outs.

Foster had a habit of calling everyone "Darling." He said he probably knew more people than any other man in America. He once called on the new commissioner of baseball, the hard-bitten Kenesaw Mountain Landis, to seek permission to play in big-league parks. Landis immediately greeted him with, "Why, I know you: You're Rube Foster."

When Foster complained to Landis for restricting the games the white big leaguers could play against black clubs, the commissioner replied candidly, "Mr. Foster, when you beat our teams, it gives us a black eye."

"Rube would give signals with his pipe," Gardner said. "He'd hold his pipe at different angles. He didn't care about them stealing his signs." Powell says, however, that the smoke signals were decoys. While everyone was studying Foster's pipe, someone else on the bench was flashing the real sign.

After a while, Foster didn't even bother to hide his signals. Big C Johnson says when a Chicago batter came up in a crucial spot, Rube would sometimes call an audible, like a modern football quarterback, just as the pitcher was about to deliver, shouting "hit it!" to a player squaring to bunt.

Gardner said Foster "would holler and tell the [opposition] pitcher that the next fellow was going to bunt, and they didn't believe him. But that's what would happen. Or he'd tell the third baseman, 'Get ready to pick this one up.' Well, the third baseman wouldn't believe it, and sure enough, there comes the bunt. Sometimes he'd get you out, sometimes he'd throw it by the first baseman."

The result was some of the most exciting baseball seen in America. And the American Giants' park was often filled to overflowing. Bill Foster recalled:

> It was a wood structure. It was as big a playing field as any of the major league ball parks. It was 350-360 feet down the line, something like that. Four hundred or four and a half to left center and center. You had to hit the ball good when you hit it out of there. Thirty-ninth and Wentworth, just across from the White Sox park—they've got a housing project out there now. It seated about 18,000. I don't doubt that Rube's club would outdraw the White Sox and Cubs. When Kansas City came in there, and St. Louis, we packed them in. Yeah, quite a few white fans too. When the Cubs or Sox were playing and we played Kansas City, we didn't miss what the Sox and the Cubs drew. We didn't miss 'em. That place was full.

Bobby Williams agreed:

> Now you couldn't get in our park when we played the [Indianapolis] ABCs. We used to put people in the outfield—3,000 people standing in the outfield. Oh yeah, we got a lot of white fans. Things were so different then. White fans came on the South Side, and nothing was said about it, it was just like everybody else. The White Sox park was in the South Side, right in the heart of the black belt. You would get out of the elevated at 35th and State and walk over to Shields, where the White Sox played. You never ran into trouble. Our park was like two blocks from the White Sox park. You could walk right across a field and be in the White Sox park and go to the ball game in the evening. We all had passes. That was a must to us. We had to go. Rube insisted that we go. He said, "See what you can learn."

Appropriately, the American Giants won the new league's first pennant in 1920.

They went east to play the Bacharachs for the national championship and split four games. No fifth game was ever played, "as the result of some disruptive tactics on the part of an irate female fan," the Chicago *Defender* replied enigmatically.

The following year, on the Fourth of July, the Giants found themselves losing, 18–0, to the Indianapolis ABCs with only two innings left. Foster's response would shock a modern manager. Instead of ordering his men to hit away, Foster stubbornly flashed the bunt sign 11 times in a row. The strategy worked. The ABC defense was demoralized, and twice Torriente and Jim Brown were able to clear the bases with grand slam homers. The Chicagoans, believe it or not, went on to tie the game, 18–18! After such a display, how could any club stand a chance against them? They won the pennant, again, over Kansas City, and boarded their Pullman for the journey east to play the top teams of that still unorganized section, the Philadelphia Hilldales and the Bacharach Giants of Atlantic City.

The Hilldale series opened in Philadelphia's Shibe Park. "Rube was always anxious to play in Philadelphia." Malarcher recalled, "because that's where he had played years ago, you know, and he knew a lot of people there." He didn't waste any time showing the Easterners how the American Giants ran the bases. In the first inning Williams and DeMoss pulled off a double steal, and Torriente's sacrifice bunt scored the first run. In the fourth Torri homered over the right-field fence to make it two runs. In the sixth Lyons singled, stole second, stole third, and stole home. That was the third run. In the eighth Bobby Williams did the same thing. In all, before the bedazzled Hilldales could recover, the Giants had stolen ten bases and won the game, 5–2.

"That evening," said Malarcher, "when we came to the hotel, people always liked to come out and talk to Rube. He was a great showman, and Rube laughed about it. After the ball game, when he went up to settle up with the park, he and Mr. Shibe were in the office together. And you know Shibe had seen all of the major league ball players. Rube said Mr. Shibe said to him, 'Now, Mr. Foster, how do you make 'em *move* so on the bases?' Rube got a great kick out of that." The Hilldales, however, swept the next three games to tarnish the Rube's image.

Still ahead were the Bacharachs, which appeared to be an even stronger team than the Hilldales. In Spottswood Poles they had a center fielder as fast as or faster than anyone the Chicagoans could boast. The infield starred three all-time greats—Lloyd, Dick Lundy, and Oliver "Ghost" Marcelle. Pitching were Cannonball Dick Redding, Jesse "Mountain" Hubbard, and Jesse "Nip" Winters, one of the top left-handers of black history. The series would be a furious one. For it, the Rube reached down into his bag for perhaps his most potent trick of all. Young pitcher Bill Holland, who made the trip with the Americans, recalled:

Marcelle is a great third baseman, everyone knows it. Before the game Foster would walk up to Marcelle and say, "They tell me you're a great third baseman." Marcelle would say, "Well, I do the best I can." Foster would say, "Well, we'll find out today. I got some race horses out there; we'll lay down some bunts. See if you can field 'em." A lot of times that kind of talk will make a guy nervous. And sure enough, Foster would have those guys laying down bunts, and the first one Marcelle missed, Foster would yell, "I told you so."

For eight games the two clubs battled, and at the end it was Bacharachs four, the Americans three, and one tie. Finally, in the ninth game the Chicagoans shut out Redding, 5–0, to tie the series, and that's how it ended, a dead heat.

The American Giants won the pennant again in 1922, and the Bacharachs came west for another showdown. It produced one of the classic games of black baseball history, as the two clubs dueled, 0–0, for 19 innings. Harold Treadwell pitched all the way for the Bs. But to Foster's eagle eye, the game was really decided in the tenth. That's when the Bs lifted right-fielder Warren Duncan for a pinch hitter and replaced him with Cuban Ramiro Ramirez. "There goes the ball game," Rube smiled. He'd already made a note that Ramirez' arm was weak and decided to test it in the 12th inning. With Williams on second, Rube signaled to Malarcher to hit to right. Sure enough, Williams tagged up after the catch and took third easily. In the 20th, it was Torriente on second, and again Foster signaled to Malarcher to hit to right. Dave's hit fell safely in front of Ramirez, and Torriente was waved home with the winning run.

As Foster's league prospered, other sections of the country began thinking of forming leagues. A Southern League was first to follow, and in 1923 the Eastern Colored League was formed. The result was war, as the Easterners raided Foster's West for talent. Among those who made the jump were Raleigh "Biz" Mackey, star catcher of the ABCs; George Scales and McKinley "Bunny" Downs of St. Louis; Dave Brown of Foster's own Giants, and Clint Thomas, Bill Holland, and Frank Warfield of Detroit. Although the West had long been doing the same thing to the East, bad blood flowed. As a result, no world series was played between the two league winners, Hilldale and Kansas City (the American Giants faded to third that year).

The loss of Brown was painful. It almost wrecked Rube's pitching staff. Foster had rescued Brown from jail, posting bond for him and giving him a new start. Two years after jumping, Dave would murder a man in New York in a fight over cocaine, according to one old Lincolns player. Brown fled to the far West, where "he got his throat cut."

Indianapolis had been almost decimated, losing two-thirds of their outfield, including Charleston, half their infield, and catcher Biz Mackey. To keep them going, Rube sent his own first baseman, Leroy Grant. "It is the beginning of the wrecking of a once great machine," Foster wrote, "but I have come to the conclusion that I am forced to do so."

Unlike Foster's league, most of the Eastern clubs were owned by whites—Jim Keenan in New York, Nat Strong in Brooklyn, Charlie Spedden in Baltimore, Tom Jackson in Atlantic City. Only Ed Bolden of the Hilldales and Alex Pompez of the Cubans were black. Calling the Eastern loop "black," Rube sneered, was like calling "a streetcar 'a steamship.'"

In spite of the raids, Rube reported at the end of the season that league attendance was up. But the strain of keeping his ship afloat was intense. "Oft-times I have felt that the task was hopeless," he wrote in the *Defender:* "I felt ready to give up. . . . The strain placed upon me has proved great almost beyond endurance. . . . It is your league. Nurse it! Help it! Keep it!"

The following year, Foster was still wrestling with economic troubles. The white big-league owners are rich men, he sighed. "We have only faith of the weatherman." Only on Sundays could the teams make a profit, and there were only 27 Sundays and holidays a season.

In spite of his problems, Foster took pride in his creation. "We have been severely criticized," but the Giants have done more "to keep a friendly feeling between the Negro and whites than any other institution of its kind in the world."

In addition to his team, Rube owned a barber shop and an auto service shop. They helped enable him to send his son Earl to college.

Wilkinson, whose Monarchs won the pennant again in 1924, outflanked Rube by issuing his own challenge to the East for a world series. When Bolden accepted for his champion Hilldales, Foster played the good sport and traveled to Philadelplhia for the opening game and gave Bolden a symbolic handshake.

It was a thrilling series, going down to the tenth game all tied up, four wins apiece plus one tie. In the final game the Monarch manager, 38-year-old Jose Mendez, one of Cuba's greatest pitchers 15 years earlier, had no one left to start on the mound. "Well, Darling," Foster smiled, "how do you feel yourself?" Mendez gulped. "If you say so," he said, "I do it." Foster called every pitch for him from the bench, and Mendez hurled a three-hitter to beat young Holsey "Scrip" Lee, 5–0, and take the series.

The next year, Rube continued to strip his own team to help Indianapolis, where C. I. Taylor's widow was in desperate trouble. He sent DeMoss and catcher George "Tubby" Dixon to shore up her club.

Rube continued to oversee every detail of both the league and the American Giants. Malarcher recalled:

> Rube had a fine memory. As an owner and a manager, he used to come in the club house in the spring of the year, and I marveled at the mind that he had. He was president of the league, owned our team, and he loved to manage our team, even though he was the biggest man in baseball. He did all of the ordering of all of the uniforms and baseballs for us. I have a baseball somewhere around here with his name and signature on it. We had our own regular National League balls. And he would come in the clubroom in the spring and say, "Well, I'm going down to Spalding's today, let me know what you'd like to get." Maybe Gardner would say, "Get me a jock strap, so-and-so size," and another man would say, "Get me so-and-so glove, so-and-so size," and another man would say, "Get me some featherweight shoes"—we always wore featherweight shoes at bat, very fine shoes. And do you know, he never wrote that stuff down, and when he came back he would have everything. I marveled at it. But I guess he wore himself out. He broke himself down.

Rube began acting erratically. He almost died when he fell asleep in a hotel room and was overcome by deadly heating gas from an open jet. Willie Powell says he saw Rube chasing imaginary fly balls outside his home on Michigan Avenue. Foster backed his car out of a garage and struck a woman pedestrian. Bobby Williams says that in Indianapolis, Rube barricaded himself in a washroom, and a player had to climb to the roof and through a window to get him out.

George Sweatt, by that time playing with Chicago (fulfilling a lifetime ambition), says that when he and Rube were walking home from a game, Foster would suddenly break into a run for no apparent reason. Sweatt lived in the apartment just above Foster's on Michigan Avenue and recalled: "The night he went crazy—1926—we were sitting upstairs and his wife hollered, 'Oh no, don't do that!' So I ran down and knocked on the door, said, 'Mrs. Foster, is there anything wrong?' She said, 'There's something wrong with Rube, he's just going crazy down here. I'm going to have to call the law.'"

It took several men to subdue Foster, but they finally wrestled him into a wagon and took him to the state insane asylum at Kankakee.

Malarcher took over the team and brought it in first, thanks in large part to Bill Foster, who suddenly blossomed into the star that Rube had nurtured. The American Giants whipped the Bacharachs in the World Series in ten games, as Bill won the final game, 1–0, for Rube. To fans who suggested that Malarcher was an even greater manager than Rube, Dave replied, "I'm just doing what the master taught me."

Powell says Illinois Governor Horner tried to get Rube out of the asylum but, according to Powell, Mrs. Foster would not agree to it. Bingo DeMoss and some of the other Giants used to visit him in the hospital, Powell says, and take him out for the day. They brought along Rube's car, an Apperson Jackrabbit, so he could drive himself.

Foster died December 9, 1930, raving about winning one more pennant. He received a mammoth funeral from the crowds he adored—and who so adored him. He was probably the most famous black man in Chicago. After his body lay in state for three days, 3,000 mourners stood outside the church in the falling snow while Rube's casket was carried out to the strains of "Rock of Ages."

Rube's league died with him, a victim of the depression. It was reborn, however, in the mid-thirties. The American Giants had to abandon their Pullmans and bump along the highways in buses, but they remained a formidable club under Malarcher, their new manager.

Foster was elected to Cooperstown in 1981.

Sweatt reminisced:

> That man was a great man. He did a lot of things that people didn't like, but he was a great man. He had to be! He had to be a genius to organize the league like that. I was thinking of the brainwork he had to do and the organizing he had to do to organize six teams of Negroes, because they're hard to organize. People in those days, they'd wait for you to do something, then say, "Here, let me help you." But he started from scratch. He was my idol of a man.

Malarcher agreed:

> Foster had had an opportunity to leave Negro baseball and go into white semipro baseball because he was the leading drawing card outside of the major leagues back in those days when he was pitching. But Rube told me he refused to go because he knew that all we had to do was to keep on developing Negro baseball, keep it up to a high standard, and the time would come when the white leagues would have to admit us. The thing for us to do, he said, was to keep on developing, so that when that time did come, we would be able to measure up.

The time came in 1945, and Jackie Robinson, a product of Rube Foster's dream, was ready to measure up.

Said ex-sportswriter Ric Roberts of the Pittsburgh *Courier:*

> Rube Foster was a creative personality. Way back in the darkest years he walked in and looked bankers in the eye and walked out with a $20,000 loan. That's quite an accomplishment. A black boy would have

thought he was crazy. He tried to get black baseball respectability. Otherwise this reservoir of black talent, which is the backbone of the major leagues today, might not have been there. Just might not have been there. Thirty-six of the boys in the Negro leagues went up to the majors. Through the first 14 years they dominated the Most Valuable Player votes in the National League in 11 of them, plus eight rookie-of-the-year awards.

That's Rube's greatest contribution, the organization, the perpetuation of black baseball.

When Branch Rickey looked in the cupboard in 1945, the talent was thin. The big leagues hadn't had a Hall of Fame pitcher since Carl Hubbell came up in 1928. Wasn't a single 200-game winner in baseball. And for him to find Hall of Famers like Roy Campanella, Robinson, Roberto Clemente—that was another one of his finds [at Pittsburgh]. Almost half the Hall of Famers who have come up since 1946 were blacks.

I don't say the blacks saved baseball, but they did it a hell of a service. Foster produced a miracle to keep baseball respectable for blacks, so that Jackie could go in as a college boy for $500 a month. It was crucial to baseball's continuity. The cupboard was dry, and Rickey got $40 million worth of ball players for nothing.

This pasture, this harvest, this crop was the result of Rube Foster's enterprise.

3

John Henry Lloyd:
The Black Wagner

*They called John Henry Lloyd "The Black Wagner," and I
was anxious to see him play. Well, one day I had an opportunity to go see him play, and after I saw him I felt honored
that they would name such a great player after me.*

Honus Wagner

Honus Wagner and Pop Lloyd were probably the two finest shortstops, white or black, ever seen in America. "You could put
Wagner and Lloyd in a bag together," Connie Mack, the venerable
and kindly owner of the Philadelphia Athletics, used to say, "and
whichever one you pulled out, you wouldn't go wrong."

To Mack, Lloyd was the best black player he'd ever seen.

Lloyd and Wagner faced each other twice, in 1911 and 1915.
Wagner got one hit, and Lloyd got two against Walter Johnson and Pol
Perritt.

Many old-timers believe Lloyd was the finest example of a player,
on the field and off, that black baseball has ever produced. Off the
field, he personified the very best qualities, as a man and as a teacher,
just as Christy Mathewson personified the ideal gentleman of white
baseball. (In an era of rough-neck baseball, Lloyd's strongest oath was
"Dad gum it!" or, if he were particularly angry, "Gosh bob it!")

In his quiet way, Lloyd worked to improve the lot of his people.
He played a crucial role, along with A. Philip Randolph of the
Pullman Porters' Union, in opening Yankee Stadium to black teams in
1930.

Almost everyone loved Pop Lloyd. "He always had a good word
for everyone, a pat on the back," said pitcher Arthur W. Hardy, who
played with Lloyd in 1914. "I never saw him get ruffled."

"He was a gentleman," agreed first baseman Napoleon "Chance"
Cummings. "Everybody who knew him liked him. He was a man
practically everybody could get along with."

Everybody but pitchers. "We dreaded to see him come to bat,"
shuddered pitcher Sam Streeter. "Everything he hit was just like you
were hanging out a clothes line. And hard? Mmmmmm-*hmmmmm!*"

In 1911, at the age of 27, Lloyd hit .475, probably against semi-pro opponents. In 1928, at the age of 44, he hit no less than .458 and led all Eastern hitters in home runs and stolen bases. His lifetime average in the black leagues was .339, though most of the data cover the years 1920 and after, when he was 36 or more. Against white big leaguers he hit .327.

Pop Lloyd's finest hour probably came in November 1910 in Havana in a classic confrontation with the great Ty Cobb himself.

Cobb, the American League batting king with .385, had not been with his team, the Tigers, in 1909, when Lloyd and the Cubans humiliated them, winning seven out of 11 games played. Nor did he report for the beginning of the 1910 tour, although his slugging teammate, Sam Crawford, did, along with most of the rest of the Tigers.

In the first game, Lloyd hit Detroit's Ed Summers (12–12 that year) for three singles in five at bats; however, the Tigers won handily, 10–2.

In the next game, Lloyd cracked a double against Ed Mullin (21–12). Detroit won the third game, 4–2; Lloyd got one hit in two at bats against Ed Willett (16–10).

At this point the great Cobb arrived. But he didn't faze Havana a bit. In the first inning the Georgian dropped a bunt in front of home, but little Bruce Petway, the black catcher, seized it and rifled it to first to beat The Great One.

In the fourth, Cobb walked and decided to show the locals how they stole bases in the American League. Lloyd knew of Cobb's reputation for coming into base with his spikes high, and he was ready. Under his stockings he wore cast-iron shin guards. "Base runners were suckers to slide in there any other way except with the bottoms of their feet out front," Ted Page said. "If you slid in with a hook slide, you'd get your shins torn up, because he'd stick those 'stilts,' as he called them, down between you and the bag, and there was no way to get in there. I've seen him catch a man with one foot and just dash him off to one side." Cobb, unawares, came thundering into second just as Petway's throw reached the bag. Lloyd hooked a "stilt" around Cobb's outstretched leg and practically tossed him into center field.

When the game was over, Cobb had gone 0-for-3 at bat; Lloyd was 2-for-4, as Havana won the game, 3–0. "Detroit," *The Sporting News* wrote, "has been badly beaten by Cuban Negroes."

In all, Ty played five games in Cuba. The Tigers won the last four but Cobb never did succeed in stealing second. He tried twice more but didn't make it either time. As Cummings told it, Lloyd had Petway throw the ball to the first-base side of the bag, about three feet to the right of second. "When Cobb went up in the air, leaping at the base,

Nov. 10, 1910, Havana

Tigers	AB	H	R	Havana	AB	H	R
2B Schaeffer	5	3	1	RF C. Moran	4	1	2
SS O'Leary	3	1	1	CF Hill	3	1	0
CF Crawford	5	3	2	2B Johnson	5	2	0
3B Moriarty	4	3	3	SS Lloyd	5	3	2
1B Jones	4	2	1	LF Hernandez	4	0	0
LF Mullin	4	0	0	1B Parpeti	3	0	0
C Stanage	4	1	0	C Petway	2	0	0
RF Casey	4	2	1	3B Bustamente	3	0	0
P Summers	3	0	1	P Pareda	4	0	0
	36	15	10		33	7	2

Tigers   001 014— 10 15 4
Havana 100 010— 2 7 5

2B: Hill
SB: Moriarty
DP: Havana 1
SO: Pareda 1, Summers 1
W: Pareda 2, Summers 5

Lloyd was standing behind him. When Cobb passed him, all he had to do was tag him. When Cobb went up in the air, that's when Lloyd got him."

Finally even Cobb gave up. On his third attempt, according to third baseman William "Judy" Johnson, Ty saw that the throw had him beat, turned around, and trotted off the field.

In their final game, Lloyd and Cobb each went 2-for-5. For the series Lloyd ended up with 11 hits in 22 at bats for an even .500. Grant "Home Run" Johnson, another American black, hit .412. Even the light-hitting Petway reached .388. Cobb was fourth at .369, followed by Crawford with .360. The Georgia peach was furious. He stomped off the field, vowing never to play against blacks again.

The Cuban fans adored Lloyd. They called him "Cuchara," meaning a scoop or a shovel, perhaps because of his prominent chin, perhaps because of his big hands. Like Wagner, Lloyd had hands "as big as a telephone book," Ted Page said. "He'd come up with dirt and everything when he'd field ground balls. Honus Wagner did the same way."

When Lloyd stretched out his left arm to snatch a hit away from one Detroit batter, one fan was heard to shout: "That's not baseball, that's jai alai!"

"He looked like he was gliding over to the ball," said Judy Johnson. "You could hardly see his feet move." Second baseman

George Scales, later Junior Gilliam's mentor, called Lloyd a better
shortstop than either Joe Cronin or Luke Appling of the white major
leagues.

Pop Lloyd was born in Palatka, Florida, outside of Jacksonville, on
April 25, 1884, ten years later than his white counterpart, Wagner.
John Henry's father died when he was an infant, and the boy had to
drop out of grade school to work as a delivery boy, then as a porter in
the railroad terminal. That's where Cummings first met him; he was
pushing a freight wagon for the Southern Express Company.

Lloyd also played ball for a team called the Jacksonville Old
Receivers. In 1905, at the age of 21, Lloyd, 6'1", journeyed to Macon,
Georgia, to play on the Macon Acmes with such pioneers of southern
black baseball as "The Georgia Rabbit" and "Big Foot Mary." Lloyd

John Henry Lloyd in the 1930s.

was a catcher then. The face mask hadn't been invented yet, and when a foul tip closed both his eyes, he bought a wire wastepaper basket to put over his face and returned to the game.

In the winter, Lloyd joined other players waiting on tables at Florida resort hotels and played baseball on the side to entertain the guests. He must have attracted attention, because in the spring of 1906 he traveled north to play with the famous Cuban X-Giants, a misnamed team of American blacks who played out of Philadelphia and claimed to be the best black team in the world. They brought Lloyd up as a second baseman, where he understudied the great Charlie Grant, the so-called Chief Tokahoma, who five years earlier had tried to pass as an Indian on John McGraw's Baltimore Orioles of the American League.

The X-Giants were good enough to play the Philadelphia As that year, and although they lost, the young Lloyd, hitting lead-off, had a fine day. He got four hits in five at bats against pitcher Andy Coakley (7–8) of the As.

The next year, 1907, Lloyd jumped to the rival Philadelphia Giants, managed by Sol White. An exshortstop himself, White set about teaching the youngster the secrets of playing short. It was a fine investment for White, who had just lost his star pitcher, Rube Foster, and others to the Lelands of Chicago. Lloyd rounded out an excellent infield—White at first, Nux James on second, Lloyd at short, and Bill "Brodie" Francis on third. Bruce Petway caught, and little lefty Danny McClellan pitched. In 1908 they traveled west to meet the renegade Foster and beat him three out of four. The Rube cancelled the rest of the series.

In the fall of 1908, Lloyd and the other Giants faced the Philadelphia As and pitcher Cy Morgan (16–9). Although they lost, 5–2, Lloyd got two hits. The next year Eddie Collins, Frank Baker, and Jack Barry would join the As to form the nucleus of the "$100,000 infield" with first baseman Harry Davis and later Stuffy McInnis. Barry, the shortstop, was the weak link in the foursome, hitting .243 for a lifetime average. Imagine Lloyd playing between Collins and Baker—how much would *that* infield have been worth?

Lloyd journeyed to Cuba in the winter of 1909, along with Petway and outfielder Pete Hill, to help the Havana Reds play the barnstorming Detroit Tigers, the American League champions. Detroit must have thought the games would be a cinch, because they left their two stars, Cobb and Crawford, home. The rest of the champs made the trip, however, including pitchers, George Mullin (29–8), Ed Willett (21–11), and Ed Summers (19–9).

Detroit rookie Bill Lelivelt opened the series before a crowd so thick it overflowed the stands and covered part of the outfield. For nine innings the two teams deadlocked, 2–2, before the Tigers scored three in the tenth. In the last of the tenth, with one man on, Lloyd drove one into the crowd for a triple to make it 5–3, but he died on third, as the Reds failed to bring him home.

The Reds played six games against the Tigers, winning four and losing two. Lloyd got five hits in 24 at bats, not a very impressive beginning. But the Tigers were humiliated. In all, they could win only four times in Cuba while losing seven. One of their losses was a 10-inning no-hitter by Eustaquio Pedroso. Even the *Reach Guide* the next spring shook its editorial head and lamented the Detroiters' "disastrous artistic results."

The Tigers were followed into Havana by an all-star squad boasting such big leaguers as Sherry Magee, Fred Merkle, and Jimmy Archer, plus a magnificent pitching staff of Mordecai Brown (26–9), Howard Camnitz (24–6), and Addie Joss (13–14). In the first game Lloyd got one hit in three at bats to help beat Joss, 2–1. He went 1-for-4, as Joss and Brown lost the second game, 5–0. Joss finally won the third game, 7–2, although Lloyd clipped him for one hit in two at bats. In all, he had hit the big leaguers for a .546 average (18-for-33) that winter.

The next spring, 1910, Rube Foster enticed Lloyd to join his Chicago Leland Giants, along with Hill, Petway, "Jap" Payne, and "Home Run" Johnson.

Lloyd and Johnson became probably the best double-play combination in America, as good as—maybe better than—the Cubs famous duo of Joe Tinker and Johnny Evers. Probably they hit better than the Cub combo (Tinker was .288 that year, Evers .263). Altogether, it may have been Rube Foster's greatest team. Their won-lost record for the year was 123–6.

That autumn Lloyd returned to Havana for his showdown with Cobb.

The world champion Philadelphia As followed the Tigers to Havana, and Lloyd's bat remained as hot as it had been against the Tigers. He got a single in two at bats against the As Chief Bender (22–5) as Havana beat the Chief, 2–0. Lefty Eddie Plank (17–10) shut Lloyd out, 0-for-4, in the next game, although Havana won it, 5–3. In his last game, an 8–6 rout of Bender, Lloyd chipped in with a double and single to help give Havana a clean sweep.

For the winter Lloyd's batting average was .429 (12-for-28) against some of the best pitchers in the American League. He stayed on for the regular Cuban league schedule, and hit .400.

In 1911, Lloyd went back east with the New York Lincoln Giants. The Lincolns had a powerhouse. Spotswood Poles, "The Black Cobb," played center and led off. Jimmy Lyons, another mercury on the bases, was in left. Lloyd himself hit clean-up, ahead of slugging Louis Santop, the catcher. Pitching was one of the best right-handers ever to play black baseball—Cannonball Dick Redding. Altogether they boasted no less than four .400 hitters—Poles .400, Lyons .450, Santop .470, and Lloyd, the best of all at .475. Playing mostly white semipros, they won 105 and lost only 17. That included splitting a double header with the Jersey City Skeeters of the Eastern (now International) League.

At last the Lincs were ready to take on the best in the country— Walter Johnson and Honus Wagner themselves. Johnson was the best pitcher in the American League that year with a 25–13 record and an earned run average of only 1.89. He brought along his Washington Senators catcher, Gabby Street, to do the receiving. Wagner had just won his eighth National League batting crown with a .334 mark. For the first time in baseball history, the two greatest shortstops of all time, one white, the other black, would face each other on the same field.

For some unknown reason Redding didn't get the call to pitch against Johnson. Perhaps he had already returned home to Georgia after the end of the regular season. Instead, little lefty Danny Mc-Clellan, a hero of the black World Series eight years before, got the nod. Johnson came off the winner, 5–3. In the personal duel between the game's greatest shortstops, Wagner emerged with the edge. Against Johnson, Lloyd went 0-for-4; against McClellan, Wagner got one hit, a triple.

Manager Sol White had left the Lincolns in mid-season, and Lloyd, the field captain, was given the top job. Apparently there was friction with some of the other stars, for at season's end Lloyd sent in his resignation. Some of the players would not play for him, he said, and he vowed never to manage again for any amount of money.

In 1912, however, Lloyd was apparently mollified, for he did return as field manager, hitting .376. That fall the Lincolns played two more games against the big leaguers. They beat the Yankees, or Highlanders, 6–0 and the Giants, the National League champs, by the same score, as Smokey Joe Williams hurled both shutouts. No box score has been found for the Yankee game, but against the Giants, Lloyd cracked out two hits, a double and a single. In Cuba that winter he hit .388.

In 1913, under Lloyd, the Lincolns boasted 101 victories and only six defeats. Again they were ready to challenge the best of the white big leaguers. Lloyd got two hits, as the Lincolns defeated Earl Mack's All Stars, 7–3, then lost, 1–0, as Mack threw out Lloyd at home in the ninth. Finally, they beat Chief Bender, who was 21–13 with the As, by a score of 2–1.

But the biggest game of all came against the Philadelphia Phils, the second best team in the National League, and their pitching phenom, Grover Cleveland Alexander (22–8). The game was a rout. Joe Williams beat Alex, 9–2; Lloyd collected two hits and, more important, swiped four bases.

Lloyd went back to Chicago in 1914 to rejoin Petway, fastball pitcher Frank Wickware, Brodie Francis, and others. That fall they claimed the National Negro championship, sweeping a challenge series against the Brooklyn Royal Giants, the eastern kings.

A year later, 1915, Lloyd was back in New York as playing manager for the Lincoln Stars, an offshoot of the old Lincoln Giants. Besides Lloyd, they starred Santop and Redding. They met the American Giants in the fall to settle the black championship of the land and played to a marathon ten-game tie. According to figures compiled by researcher Merl Kleinknecht, Lloyd led both clubs at bat with a .393 average. An eleventh game, the bottom of a double header, ended in darkness after four innings with the Lincolns ahead by a run, but officially the final outcome of the series was a draw.

According to the old-time spitballer, Frank "Doc" Sykes, Lincoln owner Jess McMahon drank up the gate receipts. Lloyd was so mad, he stomped off the team and back into the happy arms of his old boss, Foster.

That winter Lloyd went with Foster's Lelands to the West Coast.

John Henry Lloyd (seated, center) with the New York Lincoln Giants in 1912. Also pictured are Spotswood Poles (standing, far right), Dick Redding (seated, far left), and Louis Santop (seated, far right).

That's where he met Wagner in their second *mano a mano* showdown. Of course, Wagner was 41 years old and his batting average had fallen to .274. He failed to get a hit in four at bats against the Lelands' Dizzy Dismukes. Lloyd got two hits against Pol Perritt (12–18) of the Giants, as the Fosters won 6–3.

Lloyd enjoyed another splendid year in Cuba, which attracted the best players in the U.S. Negro leagues, plus current and future major leaguers. Lloyd led the league with a .393 average.

In 1917, Lloyd's batting average dropped to .266, but he had a good year afield. Foster snatched young second baseman Bingo DeMoss from the ABCs. Considered by many the finest black second baseman in history, DeMoss joined Lloyd in what must have been the best double-play combination in black baseball annals, and—who knows?—perhaps in all baseball, black or white. In September the Chicagoans challenged the eastern champions, the Lincoln Stars, and whipped them three games to two.

That winter Lloyd and DeMoss joined most of the other American Giant stars at Florida's Poinciana Hotel, where they waited tables and played baseball against their rivals, the Breakers Hotel club, made up mostly of New York and Brooklyn standouts.

The following spring, 1918, the Brooklyn Royals enticed both Lloyd and Redding to return to the East, Lloyd as playing manager. A year later Pop agreed to manage the Bacharach Giants, a new club that was being put together with players recruited from Lloyd's hometown of Jacksonville.

In 1921, Lloyd was on the move again. His old mentor, Foster, had organized the nation's first black league and asked Pop to take charge of the new club in Columbus, Ohio. The team was one of the weakest in the circuit, but Pop hit .337 before the club folded and he traveled east again to rejoin the Bacharachs.

The Eastern Colored League was born in time for the 1923 season, and Ed Bolden, diminutive owner of the Philadelphia Hilldales and founder of the league, brought Lloyd to his club as manager. The Hilldales had a powerful club. Santop and Raleigh "Biz" Mackey caught. The pitching staff featured fork-baller Red Ryan, knuckle-baller Phil Cockrell, and lefty Jesse "Nip" Winters. The infield was particularly formidable; Lloyd and Frank Warfield sparkled as the double-play combination, Judy Johnson handled third base slickly, and big George "Tank" Carr was at first. Lloyd hit .333 as they easily outclassed the rest of the league.

Lloyd was a patient developer of young talent. "He was like a father to me," rookie shortstop Bill Yancey would recall years later. "I was just a kid, and he was the great Lloyd I'd heard so much about, and he's the one who taught me to play shortstop." Yancey remembered his first time at bat against the legendary Cyclone Williams. It gave Bill the shakes until Lloyd gently reminded him that Williams had to get the ball over the plate just like any other pitcher. It calmed the boy down considerably.

One Hilldale player, however, did not get along with Pop. Outfielder Clint Thomas hit .310 and asked for a raise of $150 a month, and, according to Thomas, Bolden agreed. Lloyd reportedly blocked it. "Lloyd thought he owned me," Thomas said. "I never had much use for him from that time on."

That winter Lloyd was dismissed as manager. Pitcher Holsey "Scrip" Lee thought Bolden could hire Warfield as playing manager at half Lloyd's salary.

So in 1924 Lloyd returned to the Bacharachs, switching to second base to make room for an acrobatic young shortstop named Dick Lundy. Many veterans insist that Lundy was as good or better than Lloyd at shortstop. But in 1924 there was no question. Lundy hit .360; Lloyd, belying his 40 years, hit .400. The Bs, however, could finish only fourth, while Warfield brought the Hilldales to the pennant.

In 1925, the Bs added Oliver "Ghost" Mardelle at third base. With flashy Chance Cummings at first, they now had perhaps the finest defensive infield of all time. Pop hit .328, as the Bs finished fourth again.

Lloyd was on the move again in 1926, returning to the Lincolns. He hit .342, but the Lincolns finished fifth. Meanwhile Lundy took over as manager of the Bs and led them to the pennant.

Playing third for the Lincolns was George Scales, one of the best right-handed hitters of black baseball. Years later he would pass his lessons on to a Baltimore youngster named Jim Gilliam. "When I first met Lloyd, he was an old man," Scales said. "He was a line drive hitter, a big ol' batter who just laid on the ball. The older he got, the better he knew how to play. You'd think he was still a young man."

"I thought Lloyd was one of the scientific hitters," said Page. "He hit the ball where it was pitched. He would hold the bat on his arm and he could just lay it out that way or over here, hit to this field or that. I never saw Lloyd hit 'skyrockets' [long home runs], although he must have. But he hit line drives. He could lay that bat on his shoulder and just lean on it. He was a terrific old man. I'd like to have seen him back in 1910–1915. He was terrific then, so they tell me."

In 1928 John Henry Lloyd, then 44 years old, enjoyed one of the finest seasons at bat ever recorded in big league baseball. He walloped pitchers for a .564 average to far out-distance Lundy, who finished second with a .410. In 37 games, Lloyd smacked 11 home runs to lead all hitters—equal to about 50 in a 161-game schedule. He also stole ten bases, good enough to tie for first place.

The next year pitchers held him to only .383 at the age of 45.

Meantime, Lloyd was strengthening the Lincolns. By 1930, he boasted a powerful lineup. Little Chino Smith, perhaps the best black hitter of all time, played right field. Speedy Fats Jenkins, a basketball star in the winter, was in center. Larry Brown, an excellent defensive man, caught. Bill Holland, Broadway Connie Rector, Red Ryan, and Nip Winters pitched. Lively Dick Seay or Walter "Rev" Cannady were at second, Orville Riggins at short, and moody John Beckwith, who could hit the ball a mile, played third. Lloyd, several steps slower afield, shifted himself to first base.

This was the lineup on July 10, a historic day in black baseball history, when the Lincolns trotted onto the field at Yankee Stadium to open the first game ever played by black teams in "the house that Ruth built." Lloyd himself had been instrumental in getting the game, played before 18,000 fans, as a benefit for A. Philip Randolph's Union of Pullman Porters. The Lincolns won the game, 13–4, over the defending champion Baltimore Black Sox.

Lloyd, 46, ended the year with a .295 average.

That fall his Lincolns challenged Cum Posey's Homestead Grays in a clash for the black championship of the East. The Grays were a powerhouse. Josh Gibson was an 18-year-old rookie. All-time greats Oscar Charleston and Smokey Joe Williams added experience. Lefty Charlie Williams was undefeated. New York's batting star, Chino Smith, went into a severe slump, and Lloyd had to fill the void. He did, hitting .367, just one point less than Gibson. The series opened at Yankee Stadium, and Lloyd weighed in with a triple against Joe Williams. With the Grays leading two games to one and ahead in game four, 2–0, Lloyd started an eighth inning rally with a single to tie the game, though the Grays won it in ten innings. Coming down to the final double header, the Grays were ahead five games to three, and New York had to sweep to stay alive. Pop got three hits in the first game against Joe Williams, as the Lincs won, 6–2. The Grays took the second game however, to clinch the championship.

Pop returned to Cuba for one final time. "He was so tired," said old-time second baseman Rogelio Crespo. "He went to the park one or two hours before the game, because he used so much adhesive around his legs, then would go out and exercise to get in shape." He hit .236.

By the following year the depression had settled in, and the Lincolns were no more. Dancer Bill "Bojangles" Robinson formed a new club, the Black Yankees, who survived by passing the hat and splitting the meager receipts among the players. Pop played 20 games for them, hitting .185.

Lloyd went back to the Bacharachs in 1932 before finally calling it a career at the age of 48. He still played semipro ball, though, appearing with the Atlantic City Johnson Stars well past the age of 50. How long could he go on? "Until a left-hander strikes me out," he would laugh. That day apparently came in 1942, when he was 58 years old, and he finally decided to stop.

He went to work as a janitor in an Atlantic City high school, where he was a favorite of the kids and a familiar figure along the boardwalk. "Pop's greatness was passed on to every youngster he came in contact with," his widow Nan said. "They loved him so, they just hated to leave him." His name still lives today in that resort city in John Henry Lloyd Stadium.

Pop Lloyd died in 1964, just before his 80th birthday, bequeathing to Yancey his scrapbooks, filled with a lifetime of rare newspaper clippings, which now repose in the National Baseball Library at Cooperstown. His funeral was a big one. Old protégés Yancey, Arthur "Rats" Henderson, Judy Johnson, and Cummings were there. So were some of the top politicians in New Jersey, who opened a campaign to put Lloyd in the Hall of Fame. Cummings himself, who as a boy in Jacksonville had once carried Lloyd's glove, was the last to leave the cemetery, and threw the last handful of dirt onto the grave.

Lloyd was elected to the Hall of Fame in 1976.

Was Pop Lloyd born too soon? "No," he once said, "I don't consider that I was born at the wrong time. I feel it was the right time. I had a chance to prove the ability of our race in this sport, and because many of us did our best for the game, we've given the Negro a greater opportunity now to be accepted into the major leagues with other Americans."

How good was Pop Lloyd? Many of the oldest black veterans, who saw him at his prime, insisted that he was the best black shortstop of all. (Younger ones vote for Lundy or Willie Wells.) At least one white sports writer, Ted Harlow of St. Louis, called Lloyd "the greatest player of all time, including Ty Cobb and Babe Ruth."

And it may be apocryphal, but one of the legends of black baseball is that back in the early days of radio, pioneer sportscaster Graham McNamee was interviewing Babe Ruth and asked the Babe whom he regarded as the greatest player of all time. "You mean major leaguers?" Ruth asked. "No," said McNamee, "the greatest player anywhere." "In that case," Ruth is supposed to have replied, "I'd pick John Henry Lloyd."

John Henry Lloyd

Year	Team	G	AB	H	2B	3B	HR	BA	SB
1908	Cuba	—	102	26	2	1	0	.255	—
1910	Cuba	—	53	18	2	0	0	.400	—
1912	Cuba	28	103	40	3	2	0	.388	14
1913	Cuba	—	135	46	5	2	1	.341	20
1915	Cuba	15	61	24	1	1	0	.393*	—
1917	Chicago	27	94	25	6	2	0	.266	5
1919	Brooklyn	6	25	7	—	—	—	.280	—
1920	Brooklyn	9	36	13	—	—	—	.361	—
1921	Columbus, OH	63	246	83	17	3	1	.337	17
1922	Cuba	—	131	45	4	8*	0	.344	—
1923	Philadelphia	13	57	19	—	—	—	.333	—
	Cuba	—	303	82	9	5	0	.270	5
1924	Atlantic City	32	130	42	7	5	3	.400	4
	Cuba	—	196	73*	7	6*	0	.372	—
1925	Atlantic City	55	201	66	6	1	0	.328	0
	Cuba	—	134	50	8*	4	3*	.373	—
1926	New York	40	152	52	7	3	1	.342	—
1927	New York	28	116	40	7	1	2	.345	1
	Cuba	—	109	40	3	3	1	.365	0
1928	New York	37	149	84	4	1	11*	.564*	10*
1929	New York	36	128	49	8	2	2	.383	1
1930	New York	37	146	43	4	0	1	.295	0
	Cuba	—	51	12	1	1	0	.236	1
1931	New York	11	35	7	0	0	0	.200	0
Totals			2,893	988	111	51	26	.342	78

Post Season

Year	Team	G	AB	H	2B	3B	HR	BA	SB
1930	New York	8	33	12	0	1	0	.367	0

* Led league.
Note: Against semipro teams in 1911 and 1912, Lloyd reportedly hit .475 and .376.

John Henry Lloyd vs. White Big Leaguers

Year	AB	H	2B	3B	HR	Pitcher	(W-L)
1906	5	4	—	—	—	Coakley	(7-8)
1909	(4)	2	—	—	—	Morgan	(18-15)
	5	1	0	1	0	Lelivelt	(0-1)
	4	2	0	0	0	Lelivelt	
	4	2	0	0	0	Lelivelt	
	3	0	0	0	0	Willett	(21-11)
	4	0	0	0	0	Willett	
	4	0	0	0	0	Mullin	(29-8)
	3	1	0	0	0	Joss	(13-14)
	4	1	0	0	0	Joss, Brown	(26-9)
	2	1	0	0	0	Joss, Brown, Camnitz	(24-6)
1910	5	3	0	0	0	Summers	(12-12)
	2	1	1	0	0	Mullin	(21-12)
	5	2	0	0	0	Mullin	
	2	1	0	0	0	Willett	(16-10)
	4	2	0	0	0	Willett	
	2	1	0	0	0	Bender	(22-5)
	4	2	0	0	0	Bender	
	4	0	0	0	0	Plank	(17-10)
1913	(4)	1	0	0	0	Chalmers (McRubie)*	(3-10)
	(4)	1	0	0	0	Chalmers	
	(4)	2	0	0	0	Alexander	(22-8)
1914	(4)	0	0	0	0	Marquard	(12-22)
1915	(4)	0	0	0	0	Ragan	(15-12)
1918	(4)	1	—	—	—	Thormahlen	(7-3)
1923	4	0	0	0	0	Dibut	(0-0)
	1	0	0	0	0	Fuhr	(0-6)
1925	3	0	0	0	0	Cooney	(19-14)
	4	1	0	0	0	Cooney	
Totals 29 games	106	34	1	1	0	Average: .321	

*Not a major leaguer.

4

Jose Mendez:
Cuba's Black Diamond

Jose Mendez is better than any pitcher except Mordecai Brown and Christy Mathewson—and sometimes I think he's better than Matty.

John McGraw

L ittle Jose Mendez, the wiry 20-year-old Cuban fast-baller, startled the baseball establishment in November 1908 when the fifth-place Cincinnati Reds arrived on the island and faced him for the first time. Showing them a hopping fast ball "that looked like a pea," in the words of one old-timer, and a curve "that looked like it was falling off a pool table," Mendez struck out nine Reds, walked only two, and went into the ninth with a no-hitter. He got pitcher Jean Dubuc and center fielder Jim Kane (.213). Then little second baseman Miller Huggins (.239) hit a slow roller between first and second, which neither infielder could reach. Jose pounced on it and raced Huggins to the bag but arrived too late. Hug got a hit, and Mendez lost his no-hitter. He had to settle for a one-hitter and beat the major leaguers, 1–0.

Then, to prove it wasn't a fluke, two weeks later he blanked the Reds again in seven innings of relief, according to historian Jorge Figueredo. Four days after that he shut them out for nine more innings on a five-hitter with eight strike outs and no walks. That made 25 straight innings without giving up a run. No wonder the Cubans hailed Mendez as "El Diamante Negro"—The Black Diamond—and the Reds limped out of Cuba after winning only four games and losing seven.

In the next three winters Mendez would beat touring big leaguers six more times, including Eddie Plank, Howard Camnitz, and the great Christy Mathewson himself.

In 1909 Mendez' Almendares teammate, Eustaquio Pedroso, threw an 11-inning no-hitter against the American League champion Detroit Tigers. Thus, Mendez and Pedroso together made dramatically clear that the upstart Cuban game was the equal of the best in the U.S. big leagues.

Havana, Nov. 15, 1908

Reds	AB	H	R	Almendares	AB	H	R
CF Kane	3	0	0	RF A. Marsans	3	1	1
2B Huggins	4	1	0	LF Valdez	2	0	0
3B Lobert	3	0	0	C Gonzalez	3	2	0
LF Mitchell	4	0	0	1B Garcia	3	0	0
1B Hoblitzel	4	0	0	3B Almeida	3	0	0
C McLean	3	0	0	CF Hidalgo	3	1	0
SS Hulsmitt	3	0	0	SS Cabrera	3	1	0
RF Spade	2	0	0	2B Cabanas	3	0	0
P Dubuc	2	0	0	P Mendez	3	1	0
	29	1	0		26	6	1

Reds   000 000 000—0 1 1
Almendares 100 000 000—1 6 2

SB: Huggins
DP: Cincinnati 1, Almendares 1
SO: Mendez 9, Dubuc 6
W: Mendez 2
HB: Mendez 1

"Pedroso was good," shrugged Arthur W. Hardy, who played against both men in the United States in 1909, "but I wouldn't put him in a class with Mendez. The first time I met Mendez was in Chicago, and boy, could he throw a ball! He had developed tremendous shoulders and biceps from chopping sugar cane. That ball was hopping. It looked like a pea coming up there." To Hardy, Mendez was even faster than Smokey Joe Williams.

In the early 1920s rookie outfielder George "Never" Sweatt would play under Mendez, who was then managing the Kansas City Monarchs in the Negro National League. "He was a small man," said Sweatt, "about 155–160 pounds, about five-eight. But he could burn that ball. It was so heavy you hated to catch it. He'd only warm up a few minutes. He'd throw about ten balls right fast, and was warmed up."

Sweatt, a college graduate and a schoolteacher, was shocked by the rowdy behavior of many of the players of that day. But he was drawn to Mendez. "That's the fellow I copied" Sweatt says. "He was quiet, unassuming. But he did the job."

"Mendez was smart," adds third baseman Judy Johnson, who played against him in the black world series of 1924 and 1925. "He was a small guy, a Bobby Shantz sort of pitcher. He had everything, and he knew how to use it."

Jose de la Caridad Mendez was born in humble circumstances in

Havana, Nov. 18, 1909

Tigers	AB	H	R	Almendares	AB	H	R
CF Jones	2	0	0	RF Marsans	4	1	0
2B O'Leary	5	0	0	2B Cabanas	3	2	1
3B Moriarty	4	0	0	C G. Gonzalez	3	1	0
LF McIntire	4	0	1	1B Castillo	4	0	0
C Schmidt	4	0	0	3B Almeida	4	1	0
RF Mullin	4	0	0	CF Hidalgo	4	1	0
1B Beckendorf	3	0	0	SS Cabrera	4	0	0
SS Hopke	3	0	0	P Pedroso	4	1	0
P Lelivelt	4	0	0	LF R. Valdez	4	0	1
	33	0	1		34	7	2

Tigers   000 000 100 00—1 0 3
Almendares 100 000 000 01—2 7 2

Cardenas, Cuba, in 1887, while Cuba was still in Spanish hands. The Yankee game was already well established, transplanted by white Cubans, who had been educated in the United States, and by Yankee sailors, who visited Cuba. In fact, Cuban championship records go back to 1879. Jose was a barefoot kid of 11 when Teddy Roosevelt charged up San Juan Hill. The boy had musical ability, played the cornet, clarinet, and guitar. But he preferred a baseball career and at 13 was already playing on adult teams.

By 1908 Mendez was pitching for the Almendares Blues with a 9–0 record in the Cuban League when the Reds arrived and innocently walked into his one-hitter.

After Mendez' 25 straight shutout innings against the big leaguers, Figueredo said, Jose added 20 more. He shut out a visiting Key West team for nine innings, then went to Florida to play them again in what may have been the first integrated baseball game in Florida history. To mark the historic game, Mendez pitched a no-hitter. Finally, he threw two hitless innings against arch-rival Havana in the Cuban league before finally giving up a run.

That winter Mendez compiled a league mark of 15–6. He led the league in victories, complete games (18), and shutouts (5).

In 1909 Jose barnstormed in the United States with the Cuban Stars. Figures obtained by Merl Kleinknecht of SABR show Mendez with 44 victories and only two defeats, presumably mostly against semipro teams.

That October he returned to Havana and beat the touring Indianapolis club of the American Association, 2–1, with 11 strikeouts.

Then the American League champion Detroit Tigers arrived. The president of Cuba led a jam-packed crowd to the Havana Stadium to see Jose go against Ed Willett (21–10 that season). And Mendez was humiliated. Even without Ty Cobb and Sam Crawford, the Tigers socked him for 11 hits and a 9–3 drubbing, "the worst beating of his career," one Havana newspaper wrote.

In his next game, Mendez would face Ed Mullin (29–8), the biggest winner in the majors. This time Jose pitched like "the heretofore invincible Mendez," as the U.S. *Reach Guide* would call him. He held the Tigers to six hits and one earned run, though four errors gave the Tigers three unearned runs and a 4–0 victory.

A few days later Pedroso would restore the Cubans' lost pride with his no-hitter. The Tigers had never been so humiliated. The Cubans would have won in nine innings, but in the seventh Detroit's Matty McIntyre walked and later scored on an error when umpire

Jose Mendez.

"Silk" O'Loughlin ruled that a spectator helped catcher "Striké" Gonzalez retrieve an errant ball and waved McIntyre home. Pedroso was forced to battle through 11 innings and finally won on a walk, a bunt by future Cincinnati Red Armando Marsans, a wild throw, and a squeeze. The elated fans passed the hat and collected 300 pesos for Pedroso—even the president of Cuba and some of the Tigers contributed. Pedroso was feted and wined so much that he did not pitch again that winter.

It was up to Mendez to carry the burden. This he did in his next start against Detroit, a 2–1 victory on a five-hitter. In all, that winter the Tigers ended with a 4–8 record. Havana's *La Lucha* called their performance "disastrous." The *Reach Guide* called it a "disgrace."

Next to try its luck in Cuba was an all-star big league squad made up of "Circus Solly" Hoffman (.285), Sherry Magee (.270), Germany Schaeffer (.250), Jimmy Archer (.230), Fred Merkle (.191), and pitcher Howie Camnitz (25–6), ace of the world champion Pirates. But they fared little better than the Reds and Tigers, winning two and losing three. In their only game against Mendez, Jose gave them only two hits and two walks, struck out ten, and beat Camnitz, 3–1. No one can say Mendez got any help from a hometown umpire; Hank O'Day of the National League was behind the plate for the whole series.

In the summer of 1910 Mendez posted a perfect 7–0 record in the Cuban league. He held opposing batters to an estimated .172 batting average (compare that to the U.S. major league record of .168 by Luis Tiant in 1968).

That November the Tigers returned for revenge. This time they brought along Sam Crawford, the American League RBI champ, who had hit .289. They started their ace, Mullin (21–12) against Mendez. Jose shut Crawford out without a hit in four tries and gave the Tigers only five hits altogether. But Mullin was even better and beat him, 3–0.

A week later Ed Summers (13–12) went into the pit against Mendez. Again Mendez stopped Crawford without a hit. In fact, he gave only three hits in all, collected two himself, yet could settle only for a 2–2 tie.

At this point the great Cobb arrived with a .385 batting average, tops in the major leagues. In his first clash against Mendez, the Georgian drove out a hit. In his second trip, Jose struck him out to give Ty 1-for-2 for the day. Again Crawford went 0-for-4. The rest of the Tigers were hitting, however, and pinned a 6–3 defeat on their Cuban *bête noir.*

They also split two 11-inning games with Pedroso, losing, 2–1, and winning, 4–3. They left the island much more satisfied this time, with seven victories against four defeats.

Connie Mack's world champion Athletics were next. They won only one of their first three games, as Jack Coombs (31–9) defeated Pedroso, 2–1. Chief Bender (23–5) lost twice.

In the fourth game Mack put in his top lefthander, Eddie Plank (16–10), to stop the slide. The Cubans countered with Mendez. Jose stopped the A's on five hits, 5–2, and would have had a shutout but for six errors behind him. Mendez fanned five, Plank one. In another duel against Plank five days later, Mendez won, 7–5. meanwhile Coombs beat Pedroso again, 7–4, and Bender salvaged the last two games. The A's were happy to get back on board ship with an even split in eight games.

After the big leaguers left, Mendez dominated the 1910–1911 Cuban winter league with an 11–2 record. His 11 victories, 12 complete games, and four shutouts were again tops. According to Figueredo, one of Mendez' victories was a two-hitter in which he faced only 27 men. He picked one man off first; the other, American Spotswood Poles, was out trying to stretch his hit.

That fall (1911) the fourth-place Phils arrived, and Mendez whipped them, 3–1. He slugged a triple of his own off George Chalmers (13–10). He then shut out Eddie Stack (5–5) by a score of 4–0. Finally Chalmers had the pleasure of humiliating his Latin tormentor, 8–1. In all, the Phils won five and lost three, somewhat better than their intercity rivals, the As, had done the year before.

Now it was John McGraw's turn to bring to Havana the famous New York Giants, champions of the National League. They boasted three, .300 hitters—Art Fletcher (.319), Turkey Mike Donlin (.316), and Larry Doyle (.310). Pedroso won the first game, 6–4. In the second contest a white Cuban youngster, Adolfo Luque, also beat the Giants, 3–2.

McGraw was in a rage. "Angry, humiliated, he gave the players a real going over," Mrs. McGraw wrote in her memoirs, *The Real McGraw*. "You'll beat these clowns, or I'll know the reason why." Josh Devore particularly felt McGraw's wrath, wrote Christy Mathewson (*Pitching in the Pinch*). Devore had spent his World Series bankroll in nightclubs, then failed in the pinch on the field. McGraw fined him $25. When Devore gave him some backtalk, McGraw thundered, "Take the next boat home. I didn't come down here to let a lot of coffee-colored Cubans show me up."

The next day, Thanksgiving Day, Mathewson himself went up against Cuba's best, Mendez, setting up the duel the fans had been waiting for. And it was a splendid duel. The chastened Giants gritted their teeth, took up a collection, and bet $800 on themselves to win. Mendez was in great form. According to one story, when he blew his first strike over against Donlin, Turkey Mike laid down his bat, muttered, "Tell him to throw two more," and walked back to the bench. But in view of McGraw's angry outburst, the story sounds unlikely. Anyway, when the duel was over, Mendez had given up only five hits, Matty three. Mendez struck out four batters, Matty two. Mendez allowed two walks, Matty none. But Matty gave up no runs, and Mendez lost another shutout, this one, 4–0. The jubilant McGraw threw a party for his players to celebrate.

In his next game, Mendez faced Otis Crandall (15–5). Jose was fast—he whiffed 11 New Yorkers—and though they clipped him for 11 hits, the game was all tied, 3–3, after ten innings. In the eleventh Mendez put two Giants on base, and Buck Herzog (.267) hit a home run to win it, 6–3. In the United States *The Sporting Life* hailed the Giants' victory over the "Mathewson in black," SABR's John Schwartz reported.

Four days later Pedroso and Matty hooked up. Pedroso went five innings, giving up six hits, before he yielded to Mendez. Jose stopped the Giants with only one hit the rest of the game, and the two Cuban stars had finally done it—they had whipped Christy Mathewson, 7–4. McGraw was mightily impressed. He'd give $50,000 for Mendez, and $50,000 for his battery mate Gonzalez—"if only they were white."

Mrs. McGraw called Jose "the black Mathewson." She stated that, "Without mincing words, John bemoaned the failure of baseball, himself included, to cast aside custom or unwritten law, or whatever it was, and sign a player on ability alone, regardless of race or color." But the Giants trained in Texas, she explained, and McGraw "understood the significance and severity of segregation laws. At no time did he wish to offend the ordinance of people who lived by them 365 days of the year." Thus he "settled for players who were undeniably Cuban."

Outfielder Armando Marsans and third baseman Rafael Almeida had already received tryouts with Cincinnati. Marsans particularly looked impressive. He hit .317 in 1912. In 1914 Luque would get a tryout with the Boston Braves and go on to win almost 200 big league games, including a league-leading 27 in 1923.

Would dark-skinned Cubans like Mendez get a shot at the majors too? Not a chance. Even the Caucasian Luque was sometimes jeered as a nigger. For the next dozen years, while Luque was traveling by Pullman around the National League circuit, Jose Mendez spent his summers bouncing by bus across the prairies and small towns of Missouri, Kansas, Oklahoma, and Nebraska.

The big league jaunts to Cuba ended in 1911. No more U.S. teams would arrive for another eight years. The Cubans, meanwhile, could be excused for their pride. In four years they had played 65 games against the best the U.S. big leagues had to offer. They won 32, lost 32, tied one. As for Mendez, he pitched 18 games, won eight, lost eight, and tied one. Three of his losses were shutouts. For years afterwards it was said, Jose Mendez had merely to walk into a restaurant in Havana and everyone would stand and applaud.

Mendez was at the pinnacle of his career. In seven years he had led the league in victory percentage and shutouts five times. His record against U.S. teams, in both major and minor leagues, was 25–13. In all he had won 62 and lost only 15 for an .805 percentage. He started the 1914–15 season with two more victories.

Then his arm went dead. The brilliant career was cut off. Mendez didn't pitch another game that winter. He tried a comeback the next year, pitched six games, and completed only one. For the next four years he was out of the Cuban campaigns entirely.

He journeyed to the United States as a shortstop—in fact, he played every position except catcher—and managed J. L. Wilkinson's All Nations team. True to their name, they included U.S. Caucasians, U.S. Blacks, Cubans, Hawaiians, Chinese, and even one girl, who was advertised as Carrie Nation. They played all the small towns of the Midwest and met the best U.S. black teams too, often visiting Chicago for games against Rube Foster's Leland Giants. The All Nations traveled with a dance band, wrote historian Janet Bruce of Kansas City. The combination provided both a ball game and a dance for folks in the prairie towns. Mendez doubled as both a pitcher and a cornet player, she reported in the *The Kansas City Monarchs.*

In 1916 Mendez sailed to Puerto Rico as a coach and received a hero's welcome from the enthusiastic citizens of San Juan. He was lionized both as a coach and as a maestro of the guitar. His home was filled to over-flowing every evening with crowds of listeners, Cuban historian Charles Monfort wrote.

Infielder Rogelio Crespo first met Mendez in 1917, when the rookie Crespo was trying out with the Almendares Blues. Mendez encouraged him, "OK, boy, OK, you're going to stay." "I'll never forget it," Crespo says. "He was a beautiful, beautiful friend."

In 1918 Foster enticed Mendez to join the American Giants. A year later the Cuban hopped to the Detroit Stars. In the winter he went to Los Angeles, playing with the L.A. White Sox, made up of Bullet Joe Rogan and other exarmy stars who were about to become the nucleus of the brand-new Kansas City Monarchs.

When the Negro National League was formed in 1920, Wilkinson asked Mendez to return as playing manager of the Monarchs. Mendez played shortstop and third base and spot-pitched on occasion. In fact, he played every position that year but catcher, though his batting averages, in both Cuba and the United States, were never impressive.

Brooklyn Dodger outfielder Babe Herman remembered seeing

Mendez play all nine positions in one game. "He even did a good job catching."

In the fall of 1922 the papers were already referring to Mendez as "methusalah," although he was only 35 years old. The Monarchs played the American Association Kansas City Blues in a postseason series, and Mendez went in to pitch against Stan Baumgartner, who had been 1–1 with the Phils that year and would go back to the majors in 1924 with the A's. Bunny Brief, the American Association home-run champ, struck out twice, singled, and tripled against Mendez. But Dode Paskert, a veteran of the Phils, Cubs, and Reds, could not get a hit in five at bats, as Mendez beat Baumgartner, 6–4.

In 1923 he combined with Bill Drake to pitch a no-hitter, a rarity in the free-hitting Negro leagues. Mendez pitched the first five innings. Drake the last four.

Mendez was considered a good manager. "He spoke English pretty well," said Monarch pitcher Chet Brewer. "Some words would tie him up, but he spoke well enough. He was a very shrewd manager and really a good teacher of baseball." Brewer remembered one clubhouse lecture, when some of the players weren't paying close attention. "Now, what did I say?" Mendez demanded. "I'm just wasting your time and mine if you fellows aren't going to pay attention." "They'd stand there with their mouths agape," Brewer said. "He was really a good teacher of baseball. He was a man of very high character, very neat dresser. Just an all-round class guy."

Mendez was still lionized in Cuba, the Kansas City *Star* reported; his photo was inserted in cigarette packs, along with those of other Monarchs.

Mendez guided the Monarchs to pennants in 1923 and 1924. With the second flag, they won the right to play the Philadelphia Hilldales in the first modern black world series. The struggle went to ten games, including one 12-inning marathon.

In that contest the Hilldales tied the score in the ninth against Hilldales' great Jesse "Nip" Winters (26–4). Mendez had recently undergone surgery and was under doctors' orders to sit out the games, but he put himself in to pitch against big George "Tank" Carr, who had recently jumped from the Monarchs. Mendez threw three strikes past him. Next, Winters, a good left-handed hitter (.333), stepped in. Mendez got him on a fly, and the game went into extra innings. For three more innings, Mendez "was a puzzle to the Easterners," the Kansas City *Call* wrote. Finally, in the bottom of the twelfth, the Monarchs scored on George Sweatt's long triple to win.

By the time the final game came around, each club had won four, and the Monarchs' pitching staff was depleted. So once again, Mendez took the mound on a cold, windy day, to face the young submarine hurler, Holsey "Scrip" Lee.

Mendez was 36 years old and beginning to show some white hairs around the ears and temples. "Gray, gaunt, and grim," as the Philadelphia *Tribune* described him, he matched the younger Lee for seven long innings. In the last of the eighth, Mendez had given only two hits, but the score was still 0–0. Then the Monarchs caught fire. A single, sacrifice, and double brought in one run. A walk and Mendez' single loaded the bases. Two more hits made it 5–0.

In the ninth Mendez trudged back to the mound to nail down the victory. Winters pinch-hit a long drive that the wind carried over to the right-field corner, but the Monarchs' Hurley McNair speared it. Mendez got Otto Briggs (.243) on a ground ball but walked Frank Warfield (.251). With dangerous Biz Mackey (.363) up, Mendez bore down and got Biz on a pop to short, and the Monarchs were champs.

The winter of 1926 was the year of the big hurricane in Havana, when even the Almendares Park blew down. In the championship game that year, Dolph Luque, managing the Almendares, put Mendez in for two innings in relief in a free-hitting contest. It would be Mendez' last game.

About seven months later, pitcher Juanelo Mirabal said, Mendez was dead, probably of tuberculosis. His family had to ask for government help to pay for the funeral.

Just a few years earlier, Mirabal said, Adolfo Luque had returned to Havana in triumph after leading the National League in victories. He was given a parade to the ball park and presented with a new car at home plate. After the ceremony, Luque spotted Mendez sitting quietly on the bench. "You should have gotten this car," Luque told him. "You're a better pitcher than I am. This parade should have been for you."

Jose Mendez' Record in Cuba

Year	G	CG	W-L	Avg.	IP	SO	BB	H
1908	15	6	9-0	1.000	—	—	—	—
1908-09	28	18*	15*-6	.714	—	106	56	—
1910	7	7	7-0	1.000	66	51	16	39
1910-11	18	12*	11*-2	.846	129	68	41	91
1912	19	—	9-5	.643	138	92	36	115
1913	7	2	1-4	.200	41	17	21	47
1913-14	12	7	10-0	1.000	85	38	25	67
1914-15	2	1	2-0	1.000	13	3	1	14
1917-20	Did not play							
1920-21	5	1	1-2	.333	—	—	—	—
1922-23	Did not play							
1923-24	9	1	3-1	.750	—	—	—	—
1924-25	19	2	2-3	.400	—	—	—	—
1925-26	6	1	1-1	.500	—	—	—	—
1926-27	10	1	3-1	.750	—	—	—	—
Totals	157	59	74-25	.747				

* Led league.

Jose Mendez vs. White Major Leaguers

Year	Team	Rank	Score	W-L-SV	Pitcher	W-L	Comments
1908	Reds	(5)	1-0	W	Dubuc	(5-6)	(1-hitter)
	Reds		2-3	—	Campbell	(12-13)	(7 innings relief; no runs)
	Reds		3-0	W	Dubuc		
1909	Tigers	(1)	3-9	L	Willett	(21-10)	
	Tigers		0-4	L	Mullin	(29-8)	(1 earned run)
	Tigers		2-1	W	Lelivelt	(0-1)	
	All Stars		3-1	W	Camnitz	(25-6)	(2-hitter)
1910	Tigers	(3)	0-3	L	Mullin	(21-12)	
	Tigers		2-2	—	Summers	(13-12)	
	Tigers		3-6	L	Summers		
	As	(1)	5-2	W	Plank	(16-10)	
	As		7-5	W	Plank		
1911	Phils	(4)	3-1	W	Chalmers	(13-10)	
	Phils		4-0	W	Stack	(5-5)	
	Phils		1-8	L	Chalmers		
	Giants	(1)	0-4	L	Mathewson	(26-13)	
	Giants		3-6	L	Crandall	(15-5)	(11 innings)
	Giants		7-4	SV	Mathewson		(4 IP, 1H, 0R)

Recap: Won 8; Lost 7; Saved 1.

5

Joe Williams:
Smokey Joe

If I was going to pick a man to throw hard, I'd have to pick Joe Williams. I'd pick him over all of them. They talk about Satchel and them throwing hard, but I think Joe threw harder. It used to take two catchers to hold him. By the time the fifth inning was over, that catcher's hand would be all swollen. He'd have to have another catcher back there the rest of the game. He could throw hard! We were playing the Brooklyn Bushwicks once, and I think I saw Joe strike out 25 hitters in the game—24 or 25, somewhere around there. Yep.

Sam Streeter,
pitcher,
Homestead Grays

He strode out of Texas—lanky, hawk-nosed, half-Indian—and exploded his fast ball with an easy overhand motion. Some hitters swore he could throw it through a wall.

He could beat almost anyone. Between 1912 and 1932 Joe Williams faced the best white big leaguers of his day 30 times. He won 22, lost seven, and tied one. Two of his losses came at the age of 45. Two others were by the score of 1–0. Against Hall of Famers, Williams' record was 8–2–1. Among his victims: Grover Alexander, Walter Johnson, Chief Bender (twice), Rube Marquard (twice), Waite Hoyt, and Satchel Paige. And he didn't start pitching against them until the age of 26. Yet, as of 1987, Williams himself was not deemed good enough to join them in Cooperstown.

In 1952, when the Pittsburgh *Courier* asked a panel of black veterans and sports writers to name the best black pitcher of all time, Smokey Joe Williams was the winner, 20–19, over Satchel Paige.

In October 1917, according to tradition, Williams took the mound against the New York Giants, the best club in the National League. For ten innings the big Texan set the Giants down without a hit, fanning 20 of them, yet losing 1–0 on an error. The game has not been found in either the white or black press, but Oscar Owens, a pitcher for the Homestead Grays, who claimed to have been there that day, described it in an article in the *Negro Baseball Pictorial Annual* of 1945. Owens said the Giants' lineup included outfielders Ross Youngs, George Burns, and Benny Kauff; infielders Walter Holke, Larry Doyle, Art Fletcher, and Heinie Zimmerman, and catcher Bill Raridan. "Williams was the hero," Owens wrote. "The crowds swamped him. During the ovation he looked up and said, 'See that fellow over there? Well, I almost made a mistake in pitching to him.' We turned to see who he was talking about. It was Ross Youngs, the man John McGraw called the best outfielder the Giants ever had." Youngs trotted up, stuck out his hand and exclaimed, "That was a hell of a game, Smokey!"

And that's how Smokey Joe Williams got his name. It may have been the finest game he ever pitched, although he hurled many masterpieces in his long career.

One of them reputedly was a 1–0 victory over his illustrious white contemporary, Walter Johnson. Like the no-hitter against the Giants, no box score has yet been found to confirm it, and no living man can swear to seeing the game. Yet both games remain firmly a part of the legends of black baseball. One eye-witness who claimed he saw the Johnson game was Jim Keenan, the white owner of the New York Lincoln Giants when Williams pitched for them in his heyday before World War I. Keenan told the Pittsburgh *Courier* in 1927 that the game took place in New York "about ten years" earlier. He called it "the greatest pitching duel I ever saw." As a youngster in San Diego, Ted Williams heard the story from an old man named Frank Moran, who said he had seen the game in Connecticut, either Hartford or New Haven. Years later, Ted said, he met Johnson in person and asked him, "Was there ever such an incident?" Said Ted: "He nodded his head. He nodded his head."

As far as is known, only one man alive saw both Joe Williams and Johnson in their primes. Robert Berman, a semipro catcher around New York, often played against Joe Williams and in 1918 joined the Washington Senators briefly as a teammate of Johnson. "Joe Williams had the physique of Walter Johnson." Berman said. "Tall, beautifully built, long arms. Very, very fast. Weighed about 205; Walter only weighed about 197–198."

Which was faster? "There was no comparison," Berman said. "I think Johnson was faster than Williams. But what made Williams appear fast was the fact he had other pitches too. Walter didn't start throwing a curve until the middle '20s. Everybody knew what he was throwing. Joe had a combination of pitches—a curve, a change-up, and a fast ball." But, Berman maintained, Williams was faster than either Paige or Cannonball Dick Redding. "It gripes me when the papers claim that Satchel Paige was the fastest black pitcher that ever lived," he said. "Smokey Joe Williams, to my mind, was the fastest. I saw him personally strike out 18 men—18 or 19, I'm not sure—of the

New York Giants ball club. I'm certain that the Giants didn't like that, to be humbled by a black pitcher."

Satchel and Williams—among the two greatest pitchers in black history—pitched against each other twice, according to Paige. "I pitched against him in Pittsburgh and Philadelphia," Satchel said. "It's a funny thing: When I got in the big league they wanted to know did I see crowds like I saw in Cleveland, and I told 'em 'Yes,' because in fact when I played against Smokey Joe, like Forbes Field, we used to pack that park. I beat him 2–1 the first game; he beat me 3–2 the second. We ended up one–one. (One published account says Joe won two out of three.) Smokey Joe could throw harder than all of them."

And remember: Williams was almost twice as old as Satchel at the time.

As late as the 1930s, when Williams was well over 40 years old, Dizzy Dean would describe his ball as "an agitatin' fast ball, a real live fast ball," though Diz still regarded Satch as the greatest of all.

And, added Arthur W. Hardy, who played beside Williams in Chicago in 1910, "He was much faster down in Texas when he was younger."

Just how fast Joe Williams was down on the Texas plains we will never know; that's lost in the mists of prehistory. What we do know is that he was born in the town of Seguin, east of San Antonio. His father was black, his mother a full-blooded Indian—"a big handsome woman," recalls Judy Johnson, who stopped in Seguin with Williams and the rest of the Homestead Grays one spring and found Mrs. Williams living in a lumber camp.

The traditional date given for Joe's birth is 1874. He once told the Chicago *Defender* he was born in 1876. But both dates are hard to credit, since he was still pitching big time baseball in the early 1930s, when he would have been almost 60 years old. He was indeed advertised at the time as being well over 50, and his age became as much a part of his legend as it would later for Paige.

How old was he really? Back in those days small Texas towns didn't register black babies' births. Records in the Seguin Baptist church reveal that a Joe Williams was baptized there in 1885. His widow meanwhile produced a marriage license saying he was born April 1, 1886, presumably the correct date.

What a loss that no man left alive has seen the young Joe Williams popping his fast balls by those Texas batters. It must have been a sight. The only clues we have to those early years are a newspaper interview Joe gave in 1950 and a story he told his teammate, Jake Stephens. "Someone gave me a baseball at an early age, and it was my companion for a long time," Joe reminisced at the age of 74. "I carried it in my pocket and slept with it under my pillow. I always wanted to pitch."

Stephens reported:

He said when he was about 18 years old a boy hit him and knocked
him unconscious. He said, "It must have been a minute or two later when
I came to. Out in Texas you can see a long distance, and this boy was
about five miles away by then. I grabbed hold of a rock and I throwed
and hit him in the head, and he has never been right since, and that's
why I never throw at nobody." A big lie. He never hit the boy when he
was five miles away. That don't make sense. Nobody can throw a rock
four or five miles.

Joe pitched around San Antonio in 1905 and compiled a record
of 28–4. In Austin in 1906 he was 15–9. He returned to the San

Joe Williams.

Antonio Broncos in 1907 as a pitcher-outfielder, winning 20 and losing eight. He was 20–2 in 1908, then split the 1909 season between San Antonio and Birmingham, Alabama; his win-loss record was reportedly 32–8, and his ball had "the speed of a pebble in a storm." He spent the winter in Los Angeles, pitching for the Trillbys.

In the spring of 1910 Joe was 24, "a big brown-skinned fellow," about 6'4" or 6'5", when Rube Foster brought his Leland Giants through San Antonio and got his first look at the big pitcher. "Man, that boy could throw a ball!" whistled Hardy, who was hurling for the Lelands. "He was a big tall fellow, and when he came off that mound, he came *off* it! That ball looked like a pea!"

The Lelands were the best black club in the country, with sluggers like Pete Hill, Home Run Johnson, and Andrew "Jap" Payne. Williams had them flailing the air looking for his fast ball and beat them, 3–0.

"Slow down a little there," Foster joked.

The big pitcher blinked. "Do you really want me to throw hard?" he asked innocently. "If I really throw hard, they won't see it at all."

That was enough for Foster. "What's your name, boy?" he demanded.

"Just call me Cyclone," the pitcher shrugged.

And so, when the Lelands went north, Cyclone Joe went with them.

Two years later, 1912, Joe jumped to the New York Lincoln Giants, which succeeded the Lelands as the nation's number one black team, with John Henry Lloyd, Spotswood Poles, and Louis Santop, the hardest hitter of his day, black or white. Besides Cyclone Joe, they had Cannonball Dick Redding, who ranks almost alongside Williams in the list of the all-time black pitching stars.

"They'd lose about one game out of 20, those two—Cyclone Joe and Cannonball Dick," said Frank Forbes, Lincoln infielder. He continued:

> Redding was nothing but speed, but Joe—we used to call him "Yank"—Yank pitched like Satchel Paige. He was smart. Joe was a cutey, a real cutey. Joe had a lot of control, I mean like, he'd cut your throat up here with a fast ball inside and then come down on the outside corner on the knees with the next one. He'd move a guy out of the box, see? I'd tell him, "Move 'em around." He knew what I meant. You've got to be a hell of a hitter to dig in on him, especially if you take a full cut at the ball. He'd cut you down. Then you're not in there so firm. Then the next pitch he comes outside on you, you can't get to it.

Frankie Frisch, the Hall of Fame second baseman, knew Smokey Joe well. Frisch played against Williams in the early twenties, as did most of the rest of John McGraw's great New York Giants club that won four straight pennants between 1921 and 1924. "I knew tough pitchers when I hit against them," Frisch said. " I knew the guys who could get me out, and I knew the humpty-dumpties I could hit. You take a guy like Cyclone Joe Williams. When you get a guy can throw that fast ball, you don't step into it." Frisch said he wasn't afraid exactly, "but you have a little respect when you're facing guys like that."

Luckily, said Webster McDonald, Williams had perfect control. Even when Joe was well over 40 years old, everything he threw was "right in that spot.

"If he walked one man, he'd say his control was bad," laughed third baseman Judy Johnson.

Joe didn't wind up, pointed out Sam Streeter, the left-handed spitballer. "He pitched just like Don Larsen, right from the shoulder. He didn't twist or anything, he'd just come down here to his shoulder and throw."

Joe took every edge he could. "What made him tough was he would darken the ball," Judy Johnson said. "He chewed tobacco. You'd throw him a white ball and it would come back brown. But it didn't make any difference. He could throw about the hardest I ever saw."

Off the field Williams looked more like a banker than a ball player, Jake Stephens said. "He had all the traits of an Indian; he was a loner like me, very soft-spoken. You never heard him argue with the umpire about a strike or anything like that. The only thing he would do is laugh to himself."

Snapshots of Williams taken during the winter season in Palm Beach, Florida, show him posing serenely beneath the palm trees in a handsome white waiter's jacket, a stub of a cigar jutting from his mouth. "You didn't see Joe without a cigar," says Streeter. Joe smoked until the last minute before going on the field, carefully laid the butt down in his locker, and as soon as the game was over, retrieved the cigar and clapped it back into his mouth.

In the spring of 1912 he played in Havana, winning ten and losing seven; his ten victories were tops in the league, according to Jorge Figueredo.

From Cuba, Williams joined Foster's American Giants for a tour of the Pacific Coast. According to one report, Joe beat every team in the Pacific Coast League except Portland and ended with a record of 9–1, plus one tie.

Sometime in 1912 Joe apparently jumped east to the New York Lincoln Giants. The team had originated in Lincoln, Nebraska some 10 years earlier and was now playing in the little Dyckman Oval at

177th and Tremont streets in the Bronx on the grounds of the Catholic Protectory for homeless boys, where, in the words of ex-shortstop Bill Yancey, "they put Dutch Schulz and all those other bad kids."

For 20 years Joe Williams faced the best hitters in America—black, white, Cuban, semipro, and the white big leaguers. Forbes recalled,

> They didn't allow Negroes in the Majors, but hell, we were very attractive to them in October. We would practically get more games with them in October than we could play. Of course we only played them Saturdays and Sundays to get crowds. We played the Giants. The Yankees were nothing then—we used to call them the Highlanders—hell, they were no competition. We played against the Braves when they had Dick Rudolph and Bill James pitching—no, not the year they won the pennant. Yeah, we beat 'em, we beat everybody. We would win 60 percent of our ball games against the big leaguers.

An undated box score in shortstop Bill Yancey's scrapbook shows Williams beating Raymond "Hooks" Wiltse of the New York Giants, 2–0, probably in 1912.

On October 24 that year at Newark's Olympic Field Joe faced the National League champion New York Giants. The Giants were fresh from their thrilling world series against the Red Sox, in which Fred Snodgrass' famous error had set up the winning run as the Giants lost a heartbreaker four games to three. The Giants had come up against one of the hottest pitchers in big league history, Smokey Joe Wood (34–5), who whipped them three of the four games they lost. But he didn't baffle them nearly as much as did the lanky brown-skinned Williams after the series. Joe shut them out on only four hits for a 6–0 victory.

Two weeks later Williams returned to Newark for a contest against the American League Highlanders. Joe did it all over again—another 6–0 shutout on only four hits. That made three shutouts in his first three games against American and National League stars.

In 1913 the Cyclone won four and lost one against the white big leaguers. He beat Turkey Mike Donlin's all stars, 9–1, on a two-hitter with 16 strikeouts. Among his victims that day were Heinie Zimmerman (.313) of the Cubs, and Bert Daniels (.216) of the Highlanders.

Williams finally lost a game to the white big leaguers when Earl Mack's all stars, with George Chalmers (3–10) of the Phils pitching, beat him by a score of 1–0; Mack (Connie's son) threw out the Lincolns' Pop Lloyd at the plate in the ninth inning. But Williams got revenge a week later, beating Chalmers, 7–3, with 14 whiffs.

Lincoln Giants vs. Philadelphia Phils, New York, October 1913

Phils	H	R	Lincolns	H	R
CF Devore	2	0	CF Poles	3	2
SS Reid	1	0	LF Gans	0	0
1 B Becker	0	0	SS Lloyd	2	1
3B Byrne	0	1	2B Johnson	1	0
LF Paskert	2	1	RF Santop	0	0
RF Duncan	1	0	1B Grant	1	0
2B Donohue	0	0	C Wiley	2	2
C Reynolds	1	0	P Williams	1	2
P Alexander	1	0	3B Francis	2	2
	8	2		12	9

Phils   020 000 000 — 2   8 0
Lincolns 003 303 00x — 9 12 2

2B: Poles, Grant, Wiley
HR: Williams
SB: Poles 2, Lloyd 4
BB: Williams 2, Alexander 4
SO: Williams 9, Alexander 6
HP: Williams

Next he beat the great Grover Cleveland Alexander himself (22–8) by a score of 9–2.

Finally, Joe defeated the Athletics' Chief Bender (21–10) by a score of 2–1 on a brilliant three-hitter.

In his first eight games against the best of the whites, Joe had beaten them seven times and lost only once. The big leaguers need not have felt too embarrassed however—the Lincolns boasted a won-lost record for the year of 101–6. They were no pushovers.

In 1914 we got a rare glimpse of how Williams was doing against the black big leaguers he faced from May through September. The Lincolns published statistics giving Joe credit for 12 victories and two defeats. Most of his games were against semipro clubs and presumably were not included in these totals. Later the Chicago *Defender* would claim Joe had a 41–3 record that year.

That October Williams faced the sixth-place Phils and beat pitcher Rube Marshall (6–7) by a 10–4 score. Joe gave six hits to men like Sherry Magee (.314), Honus Lobert (.275), and Dode Paskert (.264). He got three hits himself off Marshall.

His next game was against the second-place New York Giants and future Hall of Famer Rube Marquard (12–22). The two men gave the customers a sparkler. It ended in a 1–1 tie, as each pitcher gave just three hits. Williams fanned 12, Marquard 14.

In the spring of 1915 Joe broke his arm below the elbow and was out for several weeks. No sooner had the arm healed than he broke his wrist and was out again.

But he was back on the pitching mound by autumn and lost to the New York Giants and big Jeff Tesreau (19–16), by a score of 4–2. Joe yielded 11 hits with six strikeouts. Tesreau whiffed 17 Lincolns, including Williams himself three times.

A week later Joe redeemed himself with a beautiful 1–0 shutout against Chalmers (8–9) and the National League champion Phils. "Joe twirled the game of his career," the Philadelphia *Bulletin* wrote. He gave up only five hits, walked three, and struck out ten of the champions. "Joe's twister had the Phillies baffled," the paper said. "Joe did a pretty bit of twirling in the fourth inning." Paskert (.244) and Bert Niehoff (.238) walked, and the bases were filled when Joe Judge (.220) singled. Williams "smiled and pitched, and the powerful right arm mowed down the next three batters."

For eight innings Williams and Chalmers dueled. In the eighth, Chalmers finally weakened, though he may be forgiven a bit—he had been married just the night before. Anyway, he walked Frank Forbes, Williams singled, and Bragg, the Lincolns' leftfielder, drove Forbes in with another hit.

Joe went into the ninth nurturing that slim lead. Niehoff, leading off, banged a single, then Judge smashed a long drive to center that hit at the base of the wall and bounced up. The scoreboard boy, sitting on the fence, caught the ball and tossed it to Lincoln center fielder Jule Thomas. The Lincolns protested vehemently, arguing that the hit should be ruled a ground rule double, and at length the umpire upheld them. Judge was ordered to stop at second and Niehoff at third. But there were still no outs. Hack Eibel, the next hitter, slapped a ground ball to third and Niehoff was out at the plate. Joe then settled down and got the next two outs easily. One report says Chalmers was so mad he tore up his glove in the dugout.

The Phils came back the following Sunday to beat big Joe, 4–2, behind Bullet Joe Bush (5–15), on loan from the Athletics. Williams gave up all four runs in a shaky first inning, then shut the door. He struck out nine and whacked a triple in his own behalf.

Smokey Joe sailed for Cuba over the winter of 1915–1916, his third season there. He found the combination of Latins and American blacks there harder to beat than the white big leaguers up north. He won three and lost three. In three years in Havana, according to Figueredo, Williams compiled a record of 22–15.

A year later, 1916, Joe faced another future Hall of Famer, Waite Hoyt, and an all-star minor league squad and defeated them easily, 5–0. Hoyt remembered both Williams and his teammate, Redding, and said they both were as fast as the modern-day Bob Gibson. He also recalled that Spotswood Poles played third base in that game and was adept at catching pop flies behind his back. The game took place at Lenox Oval in the Bronx. Hoyt remembered the police breaking up a crap game outside the park while women bombed the lawmen with flower pots from the apartment windows above.

In 1917 the Cyclone came up against Marquard (19–12) again and beat him, 5–4. Joe gave up six hits and struck out 10; Marquard yielded 14 hits and struck out three.

He beat Chief Bender (8–2 with the Phils) by a score of 11–1.

But Cyclone Joe wasn't invincible. He pitched three games that fall on loan to the Philadelphia Hilldales, winning one but getting

Joe Williams as a Lincoln Giant (c.1915). Photo courtesy Mrs. Joe Taylor.

pounded hard in the other two. He gave up four runs in relief (but didn't draw the official loss) as the big leaguers breezed, 11–5. He started the third game and was hit hard again, losing, 10–4, to Bush (11–17).

But 1917 was also the year of Joe's reputed greatest game of all, the no-hitter against the New York Giants. It may also have been the year he beat Walter Johnson, 1–0. If so, Walter was 23–16.

He followed that in 1918 with an 8–0 shutout over Marquard (8–18), then added another shutout, 2–0, against Brooklyn's Dan Griner (1–5) and a 14–1 victory over Ray Keating (2–2) of the Yankees. Seven years later the Chicago *Defender* would claim that Joe pitched a 1–1 tie against Jimmy Ring (9–5) of the Cincinnati Reds, but this has not been verified.

But the greatest game he ever pitched, Joe himself maintained, came on opening day 1919 against his old rival, Redding. The two met on Olympia Field at 136th St. and Fifth Avenue, now a housing project. "It was a no-hitter," Joe said. "I won it 1–0. Dick allowed only two singles. I pitched another no-hitter that year against a white team called the Ironsides. In my career, I had five no-hitters."

That year he also beat Hoyt, (4–6), then a Red Sox rookie. Hoyt remembered that the game was marked by some racial tensions. "Not serious," he said, "but aggravating," Finally, in October, Joe hurled two more victories over big league pitching, shutting out Keating (6–11) twice, 1–0 and 2–0.

Joe didn't face any white big leaguers in 1920. He did, however, strike out 21 Philadelphia semipros in one nine-inning game.

Meanwhile, the bright lights of Broadway were luring the taciturn Williams downtown evenings. "He was a stage-door Johnny," grinned one pretty showgirl who danced in the top Negro reviews such as "Shuffling Along" and "Running Wild." They were married in 1922. "He was very quiet," his wife Beatrice said, "didn't say much, unless you got him on baseball. Then he didn't know when to stop."

That same year Joe was promoted to manager of the Lincolns.

Players who saw him then carried vivid memories of him. Sam Streeter recalled: "Joe was the only pitcher I ever saw who could tell a man, 'They tell me you hit high balls. Well, I'm going to see if you can hit 'em. I'm going to throw you a high ball that you're looking for.' And he would throw three of them—three in a row."

Pitcher Bill Holland added: "If he caught you swinging at that ball down here at the knees, he'd raise it up to the belt, then up to the letters, pitch you outside, things like that. He didn't have much of a curve or change of pace, but he could throw that ball past the average hitter."

"He could spot-pitch you to death," said Bill Foster, who may have been the best black left-hander of all time, as Williams was the best right-hander. "He could get it high inside across your arms, then he could come outside. We always thought that we could hit Smokey, because he didn't have a curve ball. Well, he had blinding speed, he could throw hard. It looked like he wasn't throwing, just a real slow motion, but he could thread that needle."

As with Satchel Paige, the legend is that Joe Williams couldn't throw a curve ball—and didn't have to. Veteran catcher Mac Eggelston has disputed that. "That fella threw a curve ball harder than any man I've seen," he said. "It didn't take a big dip, but it would come right up there and go down." Eggelston thought Redding threw harder, but he was easier to hit: just choke up on the bat and meet the fast ball. "But Joe Williams was terrible—for *me* to hit."

Williams had what today is called a slider, said infielder George Scales, "and he could hit the corners with it. Nobody hit the ball out of the park on Big Joe Williams. He'd jam 'em."

"Joe was smarter than Redding in throwing in and out, high and low," said catcher William "Big C" Johnson. "You didn't get the same thing right behind the other. You might get the same ball, but it wasn't in the same place. He could throw that ball where he wanted it and studied his men and threw to their weakness."

In 1924 Joe jumped to the rival Brooklyn Royal Giants, owned by the colorful Nat Strong, who also owned the formidable white semi-pro club, the Brooklyn Bushwicks. Joe was 38 then, but he was still smoking them in. That's the year he struck out 25 Bushwicks in one 12-inning game, though he lost, 4–3.

In 1925 Joe moved to the Homestead Grays of Pittsburgh. In the next five years with them, he is reported to have lost only five games.

In 1926 he beat another American League all star squad before 9,000 fans at Forbes Field, Pittsburgh, letting the all stars down with six hits. One of the hits was a home run by batting champ Heinie Manush (.378), another a triple by George Burns (.358). Remember, though, Joe was 40 years old at the time.

He told people he was 50 and that he had been pitching since 1892, or 33 years! He was going after Iron Man McGinnity's record, he said. McGinnity, once a star with the New York Giants, was still pitching in the minor leagues at the age of 54. Joe was going for 55. To keep in shape, he said, he ate little meat and lots of vegetables, especially spinach.

Joe was by then, next to Rube Foster, the most famous black baseball figure in the country. He was lionized wherever he went. In Akron, Ohio, the *Defender* reported, Joe came on in relief and received an ovation like that given to Babe Ruth after a home-run swing.

"The fans in the grandstand rose and applauded and cheered vigorously," the paper said. They cheered even more vigorously when Joe struck out the first man he faced.

In 1927, at the age of 41, he faced Manush (.298), Burns (.319), and American League batting champ Harry Heilmann (.398). Williams shut the big leaguers out twice, beating Rube Walberg (16–12) and Picus Jack Quinn (15–10). Heilmann almost spoiled the second shutout with a triple but was gunned down by a fine throw to the plate.

Joe was just as rough, or rougher, on the black hitters, and he set them down with the same cheerful good humor as he did the whites. Jake Stephens, a typical banjo hitter was in an unaccustomed hot streak. "I never will forget," he laughed, "I said, 'I'm gonna change my name to 'Bullet Joe.' I was gonna hit Joe's ass out. But I looked at a third strike—I fell back when he threw me a curve ball—and when I went back to the dugout, he said, 'I'm gonna change your name from 'Bullet Joe' to 'Pullet Joe.' "

The two would be teammates later. "Joe and me were just like that," Jake said. "Joe shaved with a straight razor. It had a little white handle, and he put some red ink on the blade. Now Joe wouldn't hurt a little baby. But he'd take that razor out and show them the 'blood' on it and say, 'You want to talk to me, talk, but don't touch me.' And Joe wouldn't hurt a child. We were great buddies, me and Joe were."

Joe would never let anyone touch his right arm, said another ex-Gray, Judy Johnson. "Man, don't hit my right arm, you'll make my arm sore," he used to warn. He'd pitch every day, Johnson says. Even on his off days he'd be on the sidelines throwing. Said Johnson: "Before evey game or after every game, he would get a ball and go down to the bull pen and warm up and throw about 50 balls, and then he'd go take a shower. But the big leaguers now, they don't throw a ball for four days. How can your arm be strong if you don't use it more'n once a week? And they don't have no control, because they don't throw enough."

In 1928 Joe tossed a no-hitter against a semipro club in Akron, Ohio. That fall he beat Rube Walberg (17–12) of the Athletics, 8–4, at Sharon, Pennsylvania, and although the big leaguers raked him for ten hits, he held Jimmy Foxx (.328) to a single in four trips and stopped Heilmann (.328) cold in four times.

Joe just didn't seem to slow down. he was still throwing smoke in 1930—at the age of 44—when he got his first look at the new-fangled lights that the Kansas City Monarchs were touring the country with. The game he pitched under those bulbs was unforgettable. In 12 innings he struck out 27 Monarchs and allowed only a single hit. No doubt the candlepower was quite a bit below today's standards, because the Monarch pitcher, Chet Brewer, fanned a total of 19 Grays in the 12 innings they dueled.

Grays outfielder Vic Harris recalled the game clearly:

> Joe Williams—it was almost one in the bag when he pitched. Fine fellow. He'd spit in his glove. He chewed tobacco, you know. When he got through with the ball, you'd think it had been used two or three innings.
>
> We played the Monarchs eight games around Iowa, won seven of them. Then he went to Kansas City. Chet Brewer pitched for the Monarchs, and I called him "The Crook." He sandpapered the ball.

Brewer was one of the great hurlers in the West and would later scout Dock Ellis and many another star for the Pittsburgh Pirates. But at that time, said Judy Johnson, "he couldn't pitch in the little leagues if he didn't doctor the ball. He could make it go four ways—up, down, in, or out."

The Grays all screamed in protest before the first inning was over, but the Kansas City umpire merely waved their protests away. So, according to Harris, Seymour (See) Posey, the Grays' coowner, hopped a cab to buy some sandpaper for Williams to use.

Meanwhile, Johnson had an even better idea. "Joe," he said, "the first pitch you throw the next man, I want you to hit him right in the back." Williams did. Then Johnson walked out to the umpire. "Now look, ump," he said, shaking his head gravely, "Brewer's been cutting that ball, and now Joe doesn't know where he's throwing it. See how that ball sailed in on him? If it had hit the man in the head, it would have killed him."

That gave the Monarch hitters something to think about. Facing Williams' fabled fast balls was dangerous enough when Joe had his control—digging in against him when he was wild was suicide. To reinforce the lesson, Joe began pitching sidearm, pushing the leery hitters even farther back from the plate. Now Monarch owner J. L. Wilkinson began complaining, but Harris told him firmly that if Brewer could cut the ball, Williams could too. The poor hitters couldn't touch either man. "The outfielders were standing with their hands in their pockets," smiled Johnson.

In the twelfth the Grays finally scored on a bunt, two steals, and a bloop single. Stephens saved it in the bottom of the twelfth with a beautiful catch in short left field and Williams had won, 1–0.

Against top black teams that year, Joe had a 6–1 record.

That fall the Grays challenged the Lincolns to a series, to determine the best black team in the East. In game three in Yankee Stadium, Joe faced the Lincolns' ace, Bill Holland, who was 11–1 that year. Both men gave up six hits, but two of the Lincoln's hits were triples by Pop Lloyd and Rev Cannady, and Joe lost the game, 6–2.

Four days later the two hooked up again in Philadelphia's Bigler Field. The Grays' rookie catcher Josh Gibson slugged the longest ball ever seen in that park, and Joe was the winner, 13–7.

Finally, back in Yankee Stadium, Williams and Holland met for a third time, and Holland won it, 6–2, though the Grays went on to take the series, six games to four.

Joe was still pitching in 1931, throwing a two-hitter at the St. Louis Stars, a club of fine hitters including Mule Suttles, Willie Wells, and Cool Papa Bell. Williams' boss, Cum Posey, picked him for the all star club he named at the end of each season.

And Joe was a drawing card. His age was as controversial then as Satchel Paige's would be a quarter century later; people came out to see if Smokey Joe was really as old as they said he was. "Double Duty" Radcliffe ("pitch today, catch tomorrow, and a terror at both of them") split the Grays' catching with Gibson. Radcliffe remembered:

At that time Joe Williams was supposed to be 57 years old [he was probably 45] but he was great for us. He pitched good ball right on, he was one of the best pitchers we had still. Not many teams beat him. That's all he had, a fast ball. He had a little slider—what you call a slider now—it wasn't but a mediocre curve ball. But he didn't need it. He had plenty of smoke—at that age! You wouldn't believe it, he could throw harder than the average young man.

"I never saw anybody in Joe Williams' class," said ex-sports writer Ric Roberts. "Throwing aspirin tablets at that age! Radcliffe had to put a sponge in his glove—Joe just burned his hand so he couldn't take it." Roberts remembered as a five-year-old boy in Florida being taken by his father to see Williams pitch. Now, two decades later, "he was still throwing the ball out of sight. Just changing the size of the ball! He pitched as long as Paige did. A power pitcher. He was just absolutely magnificent!"

Vic Harris remembered another duel, one of Williams' last against the big leaguers. It came in 1932 against the great Lefty Grove (25–10). "We'd have beaten Grove," Harris said, "but Smokey Joe hit the ball and (A's second baseman) Joe Boley went half-way out to center field, back of second base, the winning run going over the plate, and threw Joe out going to first. The score was 7–6 or something like that. We got runs off of Grove."

That same year Joe Williams ambled out to face the big leaguers' bats one last time. But the Smoke was gone then, the Cyclone tamed, and Williams was battered for a 20–8 defeat.

Even after 1932 Joe could still pitch an inning or two. Cleveland historian Icabod Flewellen recalls one of Williams' sallies. "He must have been retired about six years," Flewellen says. "Out in Fairmount, West Virginia, Grandtown had about the best team in the state. They had taken some retired players and put them together. Smokey Joe appeared in the last inning of this game. He threw ten balls and struck out the side. One of the greatest ovations I ever saw given anybody."

At last Joe hung up his glove and went into retirement as a bartender in Harlem. His wife suspected that he was hired more for his public relations talents than his drink mixing ability; for years he was a magnet for customers, who dropped by to talk baseball and stayed for several drinks.

A big first baseman from North Carolina, Buck Leonard, stopped by Joe's bar in 1934, and Joe got him a tryout with the Homestead Grays.

Joe Williams (right) talking with Lincoln Giants teammates Brodie Francis (left) and Doc Wiley.

Joe always was a soft touch for people in need, the *Amsterdam News* wrote. "He gave away a good deal of what he made."

In 1950 Williams was given a day in his honor at the Polo Grounds. "My heart is weak now," Joe, 74, told a reporter. "I've got to ride elevators. No more bouncing up stairs."

Jackie Robinson, Roy Campanella, Larry Doby, Luke Easter, Sam Jethroe, and other black youngsters were big names in the white majors then. "But there were many Negro players just as good as them," Joe said. "They just never had a chance to prove their greatness." No, he said, he wasn't bitter that he had not had the chance. "The important thing is that the long fight is over," he said. "I praise the Lord I've lived to see the day."

Joe's heart finally gave out soon after that. "He'd been ailling for years," his widow said. "Just didn't give up. He was a fighter."

Cum Posey, who as owner of the Grays watched the great ones come and go from 1910 to 1945, always maintained that only Walter Johnson, and maybe Lefty Grove, could match Joe Williams' fast ball in his prime. Cubs catcher Gabby Hartnett called him "as fast as any pitcher I've seen." Veteran white sports writer Bozeman Bulger, John McGraw's "ghost," compared Joe to Christy Mathewson.

But none of them had seen the Cyclone as a youngster in Texas, say, about 1905. He must have *really* been fast then!

CYCLONE JOE
by
John F. Condon

All baseball players listen! I'll tell you what I know
Of that great Negro pitcher that's known as Cyclone Joe.
He faces batters one and all, he hears the umpire's shout:
"Just take that bat, take him away, that makes three strikes,
    you're out."
Record strike outs have been made, as sure as you're alive,
But Cyclone Joe has distanced them with his great 25.
When Joe just gets a-going, the sphere just seems to fly.
No batter gets a safe one, the champions are his pie.
He journeyed on to Brooklyn in 1924,
He startled all the Bushwicks, who thought his work was
    o'er.
He bowled these star performers; the ball just seemed to
    dive.
Of 27 batters, he fanned just 25.
When future baseball writers give honor men a crown.
The palm will go to Cyclone Joe,

He'll wear the laurel crown.
When kiddies hug the wintry fire and northern breezes
  blow,
They'll sound his praise with one accord,
They'll cheer for Cyclone Joe.

Smokey Joe Williams vs. White Big Leaguers

Year	Team	Rank	Score	W-L	H	SO	BB	Pitcher	(W-L)
1912	NY Giants	(1)	2-0	W	—	—	—	Wiltse	(9-6)
	NY Giants	(1)	6-0	W	4	9	0	Drucke	(0-0)
	NY Yankees	—	6-0	W	4	—	—	Chalmers	(3-4)
1913	All Stars	—	0-1	L	6	13	3	Chalmers	(3-10)
	All Stars	—	7-3	W	10	14	0	Chalmers	
	Phillies	—	9-2	W	8	9	2	Alexander	(22-8)
	US Leaguers	—	2-1	W	3	—	—	Bender	(21-10)
1914	Phillies	(2)	10-4	W	6	—	—	Marshall	(6-7)
	NY Giants	—	1-1*		4	12	—	Marquard	(12-22)
1915	NY Giants	(8)	2-4	L	11	6	—	Tesreau	(19-16)
	Phillies	(1)	1-0	W	5	10	—	Chalmers	(8-9)
	Phillies	(1)	2-4	L	—	—	—	Bush	(5-15)
	Buffalo (Fed. Lg)	—	3-0	W	7	9	0	Unknown	—
1917	NY Giants	(1)	0-1*	L	0	20	—	Unknown	—
	All Stars		5-4*	W	6	10	4	Marquard	(19-12)
	All Stars		4-10	L	12	—	—	Bush	(11-17)
	All Stars		5-11ᵃ		4	—	—	Unknown	—
	All Stars		11-1	W	—	—	—	Bender	(8-2)
	All Stars		1-0	W	—	—	—	Johnson	(23-16)
1918	All Stars		8-0	W	7	6	1	Marquard	(9-18)
	All Stars		2-0	W	2	8	2	Grines	(1-5)
	All Stars		14-1	W	—	13	—	Keating	(2-2)
1919	All Stars		unknown	W	—	—	—	Hoyt	(4-6)
	All Stars		1-0	W	—	—	—	Keating	(7-11)
	All Stars		2-0	W	—	—	—	Keating	
1926	All Stars		6-5	W	6	—	—	Unknown	—
1927	All Stars		5-0	W	3	—	—	Walberg	(16-12)
	All Stars		3-0	W	—	—	—	Quinn	(15-10)
1928	All Stars		8-4	W	10	3	1	Walberg	(17-12)
1932	All Stars		8-20	L	19	8	—	Frankhouse	(4-6)
	All Stars		6-7	L	—	—	—	Grove	(25-10)

* 10 innings.
ᵃ Relief, not charged with loss.

6

Dick Redding:
The Cannonball

Dick Redding was like Walter Johnson. Nothing but speed.
That's the reason they called him Cannonball. He just blew
that ball by you. I've seen Redding knock a bat out of a man's
hand.

Frank Forbes
Lincoln Giants, 1914

For three fabulous seasons on the old Lincoln Giants of the Bronx, 1912–1914, Cannonball Dick Redding teamed with Smokey Joe Williams in one of the best one-two pitching punches ever seen in America.

Many old-timers—pitcher-outfielder Jesse Hubbard is one—insist that "Redding and Williams were better pitchers than Satchel Paige. Now Satchel didn't throw as hard as Dick Redding. You should have seen *him* turn the ball loose!"

Hubbard isn't the only one who thought so. Cum Posey, owner of the Homestead Grays, ranked Williams and Redding one-two on his all-time all-black team. Satchel came in third.

James "Yank" Deas, who caught both Williams and Redding in their primes, called Redding the better of the two, although he conceded, "I don't know which was faster."

"Redding was," said outfielder Clint Thomas flatly. "When Lou Gehrig was going to Columbia, the Yankees paid Redding to get out there and pitch batting practice to him every day before he went to the Yankees."

Dick was so good that his fellow Georgian, Ty Cobb, reportedly refused to hit against him in batting practice. No wonder. Legend has it that Dick once struck out Babe Ruth three times on nine pitches. Said Deas: "Ruth told him if he was a white man how far he'd go in baseball."

Casey Stengel played against the Cannonball in Bushwick Park, Brooklyn, and, according to Deas, told Dick, "If you had a ball club in the big leagues, you wouldn't lose any games at all."

Redding reportedly racked up a total of 12 no-hitters in his long career. Though many of them undoubtedly came against semipro opposition, that's still a tough mark to beat.

Like Williams and Paige, Redding relied on his burning fast ball. He delivered it with a frightening windup, during which he turned his back on the batter before firing the ball plateward. Neither Redding nor Paige developed a curve until late in their careers. And both—mercifully, for the hitters' sakes—had very good control.

Said pitcher Sam Streeter: "Redding was another of those hardball throwers, but he'd turn his back on the hitters. When a man turns his back, the batter's going to give a little when he comes around."

Redding was a big, fun-loving Georgian who stood 6 feet 4, with hands so large he could hide a baseball in one of them. "They looked like shovels," laughed Judy Johnson. "He would turn your cap around sometime if you dug in on him. He would throw one at your head, and you would let him have the plate!"

Imagine how fast Redding must have been as a gangling 20-year-old in Georgia in 1911, pitching batting practice against John McGraw's National League champion New York Giants. McGraw's eyes popped. "If they could have taken colored in the big leagues," said Hubbard, "John McGraw would have taken Dick Redding."

McGraw brought Dick out of the South, Hubbard said, and the youngster hooked up with the Philadelphia Giants under black baseball pioneer Sol White. Dick jumped to the New York Lincolns later that year and is credited with 17 straight wins in his rookie season. (Some 28 years later the New York *Amsterdam News* would write that it was 29 straight.) Five of them were reputedly no-hitters.

Four of his victories were over Rube Foster's Chicago Leland Giants. One came against the Cuban great, José Mendez. Redding finally got beat when he hooked up against Joe Williams. They locked in a 0–0 duel through seven innings until Dick finally gave up two runs in the eighth to lose 2–0.

In January 1912 Dick sailed to Cuba, where he found the opposition much stiffer. He won four and lost eight, Jorge Figueredo reported.

The following year, 1913, when Joe Williams joined the Lincolns from Chicago, Redding really hit his stride. One report credited him with a 43–12 record, including a perfect game against the Jersey City Skeeters of the Eastern (now International) League. In another contest he went six innings and struck out 15 of the 18 men he faced. The *Amsterdam News* said he also beat the New York Giants, plus the Boston Braves, though these games have not been confirmed.

That was also the year Dick struck out 24 men of the United States League, a quasi-major league, to set what the white New York *Press* called undoubtedly the record for semipro ball. The big league record at that time was 19, set by Charlie Sweeney in the 1880s. "Redding's speed was terrific," the *Press* wrote. The dark day didn't hurt his effectiveness either, it said. Only three men got hits off Dick that afternoon, and all of them had two strikes on them when they connected. Incidentally, the losing pitcher was Al Schacht, who would later pitch for the Washington Senators.

The Lincoln Giants of that era were surely one of the finest clubs in black history, with shortstop and manager John Henry Lloyd, center fielder Spotswood Poles (who boasted a .639 batting average against white big league pitching), catcher Louis Santop, plus Redding, and Williams. It would have been interesting to see how the Lincolns could have done against the Athletics or Giants, the two white champions of 1913.

In Cuba that winter Redding was 7–2 to lead the league in victory percentage. Williams, playing on the same club, was 9–5. Together, they brought their team, Fe, to the championship.

In 1914 the Lincolns published Reddings' record as 12–3, probably counting home games only.

The next year Redding, Santop, and Poles jumped to the rival Lincoln Stars. There he ran up a record of 20 straight victories against all comers, black and white. Number 17 came against a white all-star club led by ex-Cincinnati catcher Larry McLean. Number 19 was against ex-Tiger pitcher George Mullin, and Number 20 was at

Dick Redding (seated, third from right) with the 1912 New York Lincoln Giants. Also shown are Pop Lloyd (rear, center), Spotswood Poles (rear, far right), Louis Santop, and Joe Williams (front, second and third from left).

the expense of Andy Coakley, formerly of the Athletics. Turkey Mike Donlin, an ex-Giant, played for Coakley and couldn't get a hit in four times up.

In the black world series that fall against the Chicago American Giants—Rube Foster, Pop Lloyd, and company—Redding was superb. He won three games, one a shut out, as the two teams tied at five games apiece. He also hit .315.

Redding moved to the Brooklyn Royal Giants in 1916. The next year he went west, to the Indianapolis ABCs and then to the Chicago American Giants. Against the powerful All Nations team he just missed a no-hitter, giving up his first hit in the ninth. In October he faced Dick Rudolph (13–13) of the Boston Braves and a team of International Leaguers, who beat him, 7–4.

Redding spent 1918 in the Army in France. He returned to Brooklyn in 1919 and moved to the Bacharachs that summer. But he never regained his prewar greatness. "He faded fast," said Sykes, "but he was just as good as Williams when he was good." Unfortunately, most of the statistical data we have on Dick come from 1919 and after. His record against top black teams that year was only 1–2. One of the losses was a two-hitter against Joe Williams, who had to throw a no-hitter to beat him.

Dick could still rise to the occasion against white big leaguers, however. In September he faced Carl Mays (21–13), the Red Sox' submarine baller, who the following year would kill Ray Chapman with a pitch. The two dueled for 14 innings before Mays won it, 2–1. In October the Cannonball went up against big Jeff Tesreau (14–4) of the New York Giants, who had his own semipro team, the Tesreau Bears. Redding took a 1–0 lead into the ninth but gave up two runs in the final inning to lose, 2–1. But he and fireballer Frank Wickware gained revenge, combining to beat Tesreau, 6–3, in 14 innings.

The following July—1920—the Bs challenged the Lincolns in the first black game ever played in Ebbetts field. Redding took the mound before 16,000 fans against his old teammate and rival, Joe Williams. The Cannonball was in trouble only once, when Clarence "Fats" Jenkins (a great basketball player in the off-season) lined a triple to center with no one out. Williams got so excited he leaped up from the bench and ran to the third base coaches' box to help bring the run home. But Dick bore down to get the next three men, the last one on a called strike. Redding whipped Williams 5–0, and the Bs went on to claim the colored championship of the East.

They then faced Foster's American Giants for the national championship and split four games. A fifth game was never completed because of a disturbance by "an irate female fan," the Chicago *Defender* said. That fall the Bs took on Babe Ruth's all stars at Shibe Park,

Philadelphia, with Carl Mays (26–11) pitching for the Ruths. The Babe, who had just hit 54 homers that season, hit another in the seventh inning, but Redding won, 9–4.

Dick returned to Cuba that winter, compiling a 3–7 record.

In 1921 his pitching record was 7–9 in 17 games against teams from Foster's Negro National League. He deserved a better record, however, since he allowed only 40 runs in 122 innings, or 2.97 per nine innings. (That's total run average; earned runs are not available.)

At the end of the 1921 season the Bs took on Rube Foster's American Giants in an informal black world series, and Redding locked in battle against Chicago's great left-hander, Dave Brown. Dick hurled six no-hit innings, then weakened and lost, 3–1. He tried to avenge himself in a second contest but lost again, 6–3.

In October, however, he reportedly had better success against an American League all-star team, beating Jack Scott (15–13) of the Braves, 2–1.

In 1922 the Bs barnstormed against the NNL again, but Dick was hit hard and finished with only a 1–9 record. However that's also the year he reputedly struck out Babe Ruth three times.

That winter Redding went to Cuba for his fifth season there. He found it tough to win on the island; his lifetime record was 18–23.

In 1923 Redding moved back to the Brooklyn Royal Giants as manager. He would stay with them for the next 16 years.

"The poor man was illiterate," Sykes said. "He couldn't read or write. I don't know how he made out his line-up card."

Catcher William "Big C" Johnson also felt Redding had intellectual shortcomings. "From the educational standpoint he wasn't there. I don't think he really had the ability to manage the clubs."

Ted Page, however, recalled him as "a real fine manager." He wasn't as smart as Lloyd or Oscar Charleston perhaps, but Page, an excellent base runner, always was grateful that Redding let him run on his own.

The Royals, owned by the white booking agent, Nat Strong, were one of the weak teams in the new Eastern Colored League. They had a few good players, primarily Charlie "Chino" Smith, who may have been the best black hitter who ever lived. They also had Jesse Hubbard, a good hitting pitcher, and "Country" Brown, a third baseman and crowd-pleasing comedian. But they couldn't match the talent of the other clubs in the league and usually finished last.

As a manager, Redding pitched less and less. He had a 3–0 mark in 1923, had no decisions in 1924, and was 1–1 in 1925.

Dick continued to play Babe Ruth in October. Royals second baseman Dick Seay recalled:

One game we played was in Red Bank, New Jersey. I was a kid then, my first year up, in 1925. Ruth (.290, 25 homers) and Lou Gehrig (.295, 20) were on a local team. Ninth inning. We had them by one run. A man got on, and Ruth was up. They said, "Walk Ruth," but Redding didn't listen. He threw one to Ruth, tried to get it by him and Ruth hit it into the next county, I think.

In 1926 Redding's league record was 0–2. He could still throw hard, however, at the age of 35. Rookie Laymon Yokely, one of the league's top fast-ballers, got his first look at the legendary Redding that year. "Redding was throwing hard then, and he was going out!" Yokely marveled. "They said, 'He's going out, it won't be long before he's gone.' I looked at him and said, 'Going out? Hard as that man throws?' Yeah, he could throw harder than I was, and I was just coming in!"

The Cannonball and the Babe faced each other again in October, when Ruth (.372, 47) brought a semipro team to Asbury Park, New Jersey. Fans stood in right field behind a rope fence, as the Babe smashed a dozen balls over the wall in batting practice.

The kids were yelling for another homer as Babe advanced to bat in the first inning. The Cannonball fired, Babe took it, and the umpire hollered "Strike." Babe, according to the local paper, waved his hand, like Casey at the Bat, as if to say, "Yep, it was in there." The next one was too, and the Babe took a cut. He got a piece of it and sent an easy roller back to Redding, who tossed him out.

In the fourth Ruth took two wide ones, fouled the next two, then watched a third strike streak across the plate.

On his third try, Babe finally connected. He drove one over the right-field wall, though it was ruled a ground-rule double because of the standees in the outfield. Babe even stole third but couldn't score.

Redding was leading, 3–1, in the ninth when Ruth came up for his last at bat. Again the Babe drove the ball deep over the fence for another two-bagger, but again he died on base, and the Royals went home winners.

Traditionalists maintain that the whites were not playing their best against the blacks in their frequent postseason exhibitions, and that therefore the impressive margin of black victories doesn't mean anything. Actually, the opposite was sometimes the case.

In 1927, the year Ruth hit 60 homers, Ruth and Redding met again, on October 11, in Trenton, New Jersey. Ruth, Gehrig (.373,47), and a semipro team faced Redding and the Royals. Trenton promoter George Glasco recalled that he took the Cannonball aside before the game. "Now look," he said, "you know why all these people are here.

You know what they came to see. They're out here to see Ruth hit home runs, right?"

"Right."

"Now, when the Babe comes to bat, no funny business."

"Got ya," Redding winked. "Right down the pike."

That afternoon Gehrig doubled, walked, singled, and popped to short. Ruth flied out, popped to second, and smashed three tremendous home runs over the right-field wall. The fans went home happy, and both Ruth and Redding went home richer.

Redding pitched less and less frequently, but he still could get up for a big game on occasion. In 1930 Claude "Lefty" Williams of the Homestead Grays was the hottest pitcher in black baseball. He won 29 games and lost only one—to Dick Redding, who broke his perfect record after 19 straight wins.

Everyone loved Dick Redding, whose good nature was as famous as his fast ball. "He'd raise that leg up and grin at you," said Robert Berman, the old-time semipro pitcher. "He had freckles, if I recall. He had a terrific amiable disposition.

Pictures show Redding with a broad smile and twinkling eyes, because if there was one thing Dick Redding could do better than throw a baseball, it was make people laugh. "He took everything good natured," said Page. "He didn't have a care in the world so far as I could see, yet he never had much money or anything like that. He could do the funniest things."

"He was a nice fellow, easy-going," agreed Walter "Buck" Leonard, who knew him in the 1930s. "He never argued, never cursed, never smoked as I recall; I never saw him take a drink."

"Dick Redding was just like a big kid," said outfielder Gene Benson, who played for him as a rookie with the Royals in 1933. "As a manager, I don't think he was that great. But everybody liked him. So they played for him."

Redding had a host of superstitions. Shortstop Frank Forbes remembered: "Redding wore the same sweatshirt to pitch for five days in a row. At the end of the five days that sweatshirt could stand up by itself. They made him wash it, and next day he got knocked out of the box in the first inning. Claimed he'd lost all his strength."

If he lost a game, chuckled Judy Johnson, he'd buy a new glove, "as if the glove had anything to do with it."

One winter in Cuba, Redding was lounging in his hotel room when he heard sounds of lovers on the other side of the thin partition. The wall didn't reach all the way to the ceiling, so Dick motioned to the other fellows, who pulled some chairs up for a peek. There they were, standing on tiptoes peering over the top, when they lost their balance and came crashing down, wall and all, on top of the startled couple. The story is still a favorite whenever old-timers get together.

Page remembered one game against Ruth's All Stars. The Ruths had the winning run on third when the batter hit a grounder to third. Redding, on the mound, faced first base for the expected put-out but forgot to duck low enough. The third baseman's throw hit him square on the head and caromed into right field, while the winning run skipped across the plate. "I can still see Dick bent over and the ball hitting him and bouncing into the outfield," Page said with a smile.

Little Jake Stephens loved the big, lumbering Redding. "I used to call him Beady, he used to call me Speed," Jake said. "When you talked to Beady, in ten minutes your shoulder was sore. He'd poke you to death with his finger."

Dick Redding (right) with Joe Williams.

Like all pitchers, Redding liked to brag about his hitting. "Dick wasn't much of a hitter," Jake grinned.

I never will forget the day someone got two strikes on him, then threw him an off-speed pitch up around his eyes. He got a triple. You ought to have seen Beady leg it. An ordinary guy would have gotten a home run. But they wouldn't throw him out, they wanted to tire him out. He jogged in there with a triple. "Greaaaat *God,* Speed!"—Beady was emphatic—"Greaaat *God,* Speed! You see me cut that dirt? You see me burnin' those bases up?" And I said, "Beady, you were burnin' those bases up. You were *burnin'* them up! "

On the road trips the Royals squeezed into two Pierce Arrow cars. Page remembered one night driving through the Catskill Mountains on the Rip Van Winkle Trail when one of the tires blew out. Redding, Page, and some others turned the other car around and drove 15–20 miles through the night to buy a spare. On the return trip, Redding held the spare against the running board while Page drove and the others slept. Back at the first car, Page stopped. "Ok, Dick," he said, "Give me the tire." Redding's head had fallen forward. "Huh? What?" he mumbled, waking from a sound sleep. The tire was gone. Grumbling, the men piled back into the car and made another long round-trip to buy a second tire. "Now I get a laugh out of it," said Page, "but it was no joke then."

Dick Redding remained with the Royals, spreading good humor, until 1938. He died shortly after that. The circumstances aren't clear. "I know he died in a mental hospital," said Page, "down in Long Island—Central Islip, I think. Nobody's ever told me really why, how, what happened to him."

The mystery may never be solved, but the memory of the big, grinning, good-natured black pitcher remains. "He was one of the finest men you ever saw," said Stephens. "God, he didn't enjoy money, he just enjoyed life. He was just a clean-cut, clean-living man. There'll never be another Dick Redding."

7

Louis Santop:
The Big Bertha

*Now this Santop—you haven't got a man in baseball today
like him. Tex hit a ball 999 miles. We were playing—I never
will forget—he hit a ball off Doc Scanlan down in Elizabethport, New Jersey, in 1912, and it went over the fence,
and it was 500-some feet away. They put a sign on the fence
where he hit it. To hit a ball like that then—balls they hit
today are a joke; you get these boys 150–160 pounds, hit the
ball out, forget it—that's a golf ball.*

Frank Forbes
N.Y. Lincoln Giants

A big, gruff-voiced, light-skinned Texan, Louis Loftin Santop was
the first of the great black sluggers, the head of a dynasty that
would stretch through John Beckwith, Turkey Stearnes, Mule Suttles,
Josh Gibson, Willie Mays, and right down to Hank Aaron himself.

Santop, who started hitting Texas-size blasts before most of the
others were ever born, was the only one who played most of his career
in the old dead-ball era. Perhaps no man in the country, black or
white, smashed the old softballs quite so far so often. No wonder they
nicknamed him "Big Bertha" after the monstrous German siege gun
of World War I. They say "Top" could even call his shots *a la* Babe
Ruth.

In fact, the two top sluggers of their day, Ruth and Santop, faced
each other, *mano a mano,* in Shibe Park, Philadelphia, October 12,
1920, when Ruth led a semipro team against Santop's club, the Hilldales. In four at bats the Babe walked, hit an easy fly, and struck out
twice; Santop smashed a double and two singles in four at bats against
the Yankees' Carl Mays (26–11) and Slim Harriss (9–14) of the As, as
Hilldale won, 5–0.

Columnist Red Smith called the big Texan "one of the greatest
hitters, black or white, of all time."

"They make a great deal of Josh Gibson," said Waite Hoyt, the ex-
Yankee pitcher. "I think Santop was as good a catcher, if not better."

"Even when he struck out, he scared the hell out of you," one
pitcher said.

"Santop hit the ball farther than anybody," said expitcher Jesse Hubbard. "Farther than anybody—Beckwith, Mule Suttles, Josh, anybody." Hubbard remembered the famous Santop home run in Elizabethport and still called it, more than 60 years later, the longest home run he'd ever seen. "We were playing on a race track, a fair ground," Hubbard said. "Most others, they hit home runs like I did, just over the fence. Santop hit them way over."

All the pitchers seem to remember the big left-handed swinger with a wince. Bill Holland of the New York Lincoln Giants testified to "some terrific long balls" Santop sent sailing over the center-field fence at Dexter Park, Brooklyn.

The Newark park had a sign 440 feet away offering a suit of clothes to anyone who could hit it. 'Top hit it three times one day, and they took it down.

Remarked Hilldale outfielder Chaney White: "We'd get in a big park and we'd say, 'Fences pretty far away here, Top,' He'd say, 'I reckon I'll draw 'em in some.' And like as not he would, he'd 'draw one in' before the game was done."

"Santop was big, chunky," recalled pitcher Webster McDonald. "Didn't like a low pitched ball. But a curve ball breaking away out there—it was gone!"

Santop towered over most other players of his day. He stood about six-foot four or five, weighed over 240 pounds, and swung a big shillelagh as if it were a toothpick. "Other men couldn't even drag his bat," chuckled McDonald. He threw right-handed, and, like Josh Gibson, spent most of his time on defense as a catcher.

The big "Top" was born January 17, 1890, in Tyler, Texas, between Dallas and Shreveport. By 1909 he was catching for the Fort Worth Wonders at the same time Cyclone Joe Williams was pitching for rival San Antonio. The two must have faced each other often and certainly at the annual tournament in Oklahoma City.

'Top was a tough kid. Columnist Red Smith reported that he caught one double header with a broken thumb. The bandaged digit and splint were sticking out of the catcher's mitt, but he got four hits that day. His triple won the first game, and his homer the second.

The following year Santop was up north with Sol White's Philadelphia Giants, where he teamed with another rookie, Dick Redding, to form the famous "kid battery." In 1911 they moved to the New York Lincoln Giants and teamed with 'Top's erstwhile Lone Star rival, Joe Williams, in one of the greatest batteries of all time. No team in the nation, except perhaps the New York Giants with pitchers Christy Mathewson and Rube Marquard and catcher Chief Meyers, could match them.

People who knew Santop called him "loveable" or "likeable,"

though Joe Williams' widow, Mrs. Eunice Taylor, remembered him as "kind of a little fiery, but if you didn't rub his fur the wrong way, he was a lovely person."

"He was a wonderful guy," smiled outfielder Clint Thomas. "He did so many crazy things, you had to laugh at him. He bought a Cadillac, went to take his driver's test. The people had eight or nine garbage cans on the boulevard. He knocked over all those cans, cost him a whole lot of money. He never did learn how to drive. Had to get rid of the Cadillac. Saved his money."

Statistics were published for three seasons with the Lincolns, probably including mostly white semipro opposition. They show Santop hitting .470 in 1911, .422 in 1912, and .455 in 1914. His home-run total was given for 1914, and it is surprisingly low, only two in 191 at bats. His stolen base total was even more surprising—18; Santop wasn't known as a greyhound.

That 1914 club was one of the best of all time, black or white. Besides Santop, Williams, and Redding, it boasted John Henry Lloyd, manager and shortstop, and Spotswood Poles, center field. Lloyd is already in the Hall of Fame. The others were of equal caliber.

In 1915 'Top left the Lincs to go West and join Rube Foster's Leland Giants. Two years later he was back East with the Brooklyn Royal Giants.

In October 1917 he joined Ed Bolden's amateur Hilldale club for three games against a barnstorming white squad that included Bullet Joe Bush (11–17) and Chief Bender (8–2) on the mound. Santop clipped Bush for four hits and Bender for two, as Hilldale won two of the three games.

Santop was among the first professionals to join the Hilldales, which Bolden would soon fashion into one of the powerhouses of black baseball. 'Top had hardly reported, however, when he had to leave to join the navy, missing parts of 1918 and 1919 as a result.

After the war, Santop joined the Brooklyn Royal Giants. Royals pitcher Frank "Doc" Sykes did not regard him as a great receiver or field general. But as a hitter, of course, Sykes was glad to have him on the team. "He always took the first strike," Doc said. Later, when they were opponents, Sykes put his "free" strike over the plate, then threw the second pitch "as slow as I could make it." 'Top took a mighty swing and hit it into the air to shortstop, cussing mightily: "Goddam it." "I can still hear him," Sykes laughed.

Santop returned to the Hilldales in 1920, one of the first professionals on the team. A great spitballer, Phil Cockrell, was the pitching ace. Second base was Bunny Downs, who 30 years later would manage a kid named Hank Aaron at Indianapolis. In 12 games Santop hit .311

against other top black teams, mostly in Foster's new Negro National
League.

That fall Hilldale played five games against Casey Stengel's all
stars, winning two and losing three. They lost to three Phils pitchers—
Specs Meadows (16–14), Bill Hubbell (9–10), and Dave Keefe (6–7)—
by scores of 4–3, 5–2, and 2–1. 'Top got a hit in each game. They beat
the Stengels twice; one was the 5–0 game when 'Top outslugged Ruth.
The other victory was 6–2 over Scott Perry (11–25) of the Athletics.
'Top got a single and almost got a homer but was robbed by a great
catch in center field.

'Top "was the greatest star and the best drawing card we ever
had," Bolden used to say, and backed up his words by paying his big
catcher a princely salary—$450 a month. Santop earned it by playing
almost every game the Hilldales played, which meant about 180 or
more a season. He was always advertised wherever Hilldale went, and
the fans would have been mutinous if 'Top didn't appear.

Santop was the star, and he claimed the star's prerogatives. "He
was a man, that Santop," chuckled Jake Stephens, a rookie shortstop
with the Hilldales in 1920. "He had a big bat case. At that time he
carried two bats. He was very popular, so he says to me, 'Heh, boy'—
he called me boy—'take my bag.' I said, 'I'm not about to.' He says,
'You ain't gonna be on this ball club but just so long.'"

*Louis Santop (second from left) with the 1917 Brooklyn Royal Giants. Also pictured is
Frank "Doc" Sykes (far left).*

It was merely friendly bantering (Jake stayed on the Hilldales longer than Santop would). In fact, big 'Top wouldn't let anyone mess with one of his Hilldale boys. In 1921 Rube Foster, a master of psychological warfare, brought his western champions, the American Giants, east to play Hilldale for the black championship of the country. Rube strode into the Hilldale clubhouse at Shibe Park before the first game and accosted young third baseman Judy Johnson: "Well, well, well, who's the new boy? We're gonna bunt on you today, we're gonna drive you crazy," and on and on.

It was the signal for Santop to step in. "You go on now, Rube," he growled in his gruff, bass voice, "leave the kid alone."

Rube's race horses did run Johnson and Santop crazy that first game. But the Philadelphians evened the series in the second game. In the third, Santop smashed a triple to help win it, 15–5, and in the fourth game drilled a double as Hilldale won again and claimed the black championship of the world.

Johnson remembered another game, this one against Big Jeff Tesreau, formerly of the New York Giants, who had left the major leagues seeking bigger money as a semipro with his own club, the Tesreau Bears. "We were playing in New York one Sunday," Judy recalled. "Tesreau was from Tyler, Texas, too. 'Top came to bat and Jeff threw at him. Santop hollered out to him: 'Heh, Jeff, you throwin' at your hometown boy.' Jeff just said, 'All niggers look alike to me.'"

Johnson told Donn Rogosin *(Invisible Men)* of another game in the Pennsylvania coal country involving Santop and the hometown umpire, who also happened to be the local sheriff. The ump was calling all the pitches against the Hilldales. 'Top called time and went to the mound. "Throw a hard one," he said, "and I'll let it go by and hit him." The ball was a perfect strike—in the umpire's groin. The ump doubled up in breathless agony, while the Hilldales raced to their cars. "They chased us six miles down the road," Judy said. "I was really scared."

Whitey Gruhler, Atlantic City sports editor, has another Santop story, this one about the big guy's hitting:

A lot of hotel workers, when they finished serving lunch, scooted out to the ball park. Very enthusiastic fans. A little colored lady was in the grandstand right behind him, maybe 35 feet behind the catcher. He was in the on deck circle, swinging three bats. This little lady hollered out, "Heh, Santop, what you gonna do? Bring me some wood [that is, strike out]?" Santop shook his head and pointed to the right-field fence, like Babe Ruth is supposed to have done. "I'll bet you a buck," the lady called. He went over to the dugout, got a buck from someone, went to the fence, and stuck it through the chicken wire. Damn if he didn't hit it over the fence. As he crossed home plate, he went over to the grandstand to collect his two dollars.

Hilldale pitcher Holsey "Scrip" Lee said Santop could hit the ball farther than Josh Gibson, though this may be hyperbole. Lee also insisted that 'Top could throw the ball out of any park, as well as hit it out. Judy Johnson and outfielder Chaney White nodded agreement. On the third strike, 'Top would throw to the center fielder from a squat, Red Smith wrote. "Shucks," that's nothing," said White. "If 'Top's feelin' real lively, he'd rare up and throw that ball plumb over the fence in center field."

In 1923 Bolden formed the Eastern Colored League as a rival to Foster's loop. The Hilldales, naturally, won the first pennant, as Santop batted .333.

Bolden raided the West of its stars. The biggest catch of all, in 1924, was Oscar Charleston, perhaps the finest black player who ever lived. Charleston was used to being top banana, and he had a reputation for being a scrapper. Inevitably, a rivalry flared up between the two superstars, Charleston and Santop. "Only one time Charley got out of line," grinned Stephens. "It was when he first came here from Indianapolis. Santop was our catcher. A big man, too. Santop hugged him, broke three of his ribs. He was a man, that Santop."

Santop hit .376 in 1924 and again the Hilldales finished first and thus gained the honor of playing the famous Kansas City Monarchs in the first modern black world series between the top teams of the two black leagues. In nine games Santop would bat .333, but instead of capping his career with glory at the age of 34, a few devastating seconds would transform him into a goat, the Merkle and Snodgrass of blackball history, in a bitter end to a great career.

Hilldale jumped off to an early lead, three games to one, before Kansas City tied it, three games all, plus one tie. That brought the clubs down to the eighth game in Chicago on October 19, with the African Prince of Dahomey looking on. Hilldale pitcher Rube Currie, a Kansas City native, was mastering his former Monarch teammates handily and went into the ninth winning, 2–0. Then trouble started. Currie gave up a run and had the bases loaded, as the weak-hitting Monarch catcher Frank Duncan came to bat. Currie threw, Duncan swung, and popped a towering foul a few feet behind home plate. Santop whipped off his mask, craned his neck upwards, tapped his glove, and waited. The ball hit the glove, glanced off, and bounced to the ground for an error. Duncan stepped back into the box and lashed Currie's next pitch toward third base, where Biz Mackey was guarding the line. The ball, a sure out, squirted through Mackey's legs for two bases, and two runners raced home. The Monarchs won the game 3–2 and went on to take the series five games to four.

Manager Frank Warfield "called him all kinds of so-and-so," said Hilldale outfielder Clint Thomas. "Santop cried. I said, 'Santop, pick him up and throw him out the door; throw him in the street.'"

The error virtually killed Santop's career. Though only 35, he played only 12 league games in 1925, mostly as a pinch-hitter; he hit .250, as Mackey moved behind the plate and handled most of the catching.

'Top appeared in 12 games in 1926, hitting .290. When he was released in July, the Hilldales were in last place.

Santop managed his own semipro team, the Santop Broncos. He became a Republican committee man and also tended bar at the Postal Card restaurant in Philadelphia. In the 1930s pitcher Schoolboy Johnny Taylor remembered visiting the bar to see 'Top, "with a little cigar in his mouth, joking with the guys."

His home was filled with religious and baseball mementoes. "He had a nice apartment," Clint Thomas said, "he entertained a lot of people. He was well known in New York and Brooklyn too."

"He was well thought of," Bill Holland said. "He owned property right behind the Ebbetts Hotel. He had the best collection of clippings and ball players' pictures and records. He had an office just full of them. I used to go by there and say. 'Well, I want to look at myself.' He had a wonderful collection." (The collection was willed to ex-shortstop Bill Yancey, who in turn contributed it to Cooperstown.) The prize of the collection was a gilded bat that stood in the corner of Santop's parlor with a notation that the last time Santop used it he hit a single, double, triple, and three home runs.

Eventually 'Top developed arthritis so bad that he couldn't roll his own cigarettes any more, Thomas said.

Santop died in Philadelphia's Naval Hospital January 6, 1942. He was 51 years old.

Catcher Macajah Eggelston of Baltimore remembered squatting down behind the big man in Philadelphia one day when Santop was near the end of his career. The bases were full and the Hilldales were losing by two runs. "Well," Santop announced in his deep-chested voice, "I'm gonna go to Texas now. I'm gonna let you all go home." Eggelston called for everything he could think of to fool the big slugger. "Finally," smiled Egg, "the pitcher got one right in, and Santop hit it out of the ball park, over the trees outside the fence. That's right. He 'went to Texas' on that one all right!"

Louis Santop

Year	Team	G	AB	H	2B	3B	HR	BA	SB
1912	Cuba	5	14	1	0	1	0	.071	—
1915	New York	4	16	4	0	1	0	.250	0
1919	Brooklyn	3	13	4	—	—	—	.308	—
1920	Cuba	—	19	7	3	1	0	.368	0
1922	Philadelphia	1	1	1	1	0	0	1.000	0
1923	Philadelphia	10	43	10	—	—	—	.333	—
1924	Philadelphia	48	174	59	7	4	5	.376	2
1925	Philadelphia	12	16	4	1	0	0	.250	0
1926	Philadelphia	12	31	9	1	0	0	.290	—
Totals		95	327	99	13	7	5	.303	2

Note: Against semipro opponents, he hit .470 in 1911, .422 in 1912, and .455 in 1914, according to published but unverified accounts.

Louis Santop vs. White Major Leaguers

Year	AB*	H	2B	3B	HR	Pitcher	(W-L)
1913	(4)	1	0	0	0	Chalmers	(3-10)
	(4)	2	0	0	0	Chalmers (McRubie)[a]	
	(4)	0	0	0	0	Alexander	(22-8)
1915	(4)	1	—	—	—	Bender	(4-16)
	2	0	0	0	0	Perritt	(12-18)
	4	1	—	—	—	Ragan	(16-12)
1917	(4)	1	—	—	—	Bush	(11-17)
	(4)	1	—	—	—	Bush	
	(4)	2	—	—	—	Bush	
	(4)	2	—	—	—	Bender	(8-2)
1920	(4)	1	—	—	—	B. Hubbell	(9-10)
	(4)	3	1	—	—	Harriss (9-14), Mays (26-11)	
	(4)	1	—	—	—	Harriss, Keefe (6-7), Naylor (10-23)	
	(4)	1	—	—	—	Perry	
	(4)	1	—	—	—	Meadows	(16-14)
Totals 15 games	58	18	1	0	0	Average: .316	

*At Bats in parentheses are estimated.
[a] Not a major league pitcher.

8

Oscar Charleston:
Was Cobb "The White Charleston"?

*When anybody asks me who was the greatest ball player, I
don't have to stop to think. I can name him right off. His
name is Oscar Charleston. Roberto Clemente was one of the
best friends I ever had, and he was one of our great ball
players. But the greatest ball player I've ever seen in my life
was Oscar Charleston. I'd rate Oscar Charleston over Joe
DiMaggio, over Willie Mays. The only thing that Willie
Mays could do better than Oscar Charleston was throw. And
Charleston had an offense as well as a defense. He could hit
the ball out of the ball park, in the air, or on the line. He
could drag the ball down first base. And he could run. I saw
the all-time team they announced in 1969, DiMaggio and
Mays and for those of us who remember Oscar Charleston,
I'd say he belongs in the same bracket.*

Ted Page, outfielder,
Pittsburgh Crawfords

When old-time black stars talk about the finest center fielders of all
time, they remember watching the legendary Tris Speaker, the
graceful DiMaggio, the exuberant Mays. But almost all end up insist-
ing that the best of all was a round-faced, barrel-chested Hercules
with smoldering leonine eyes by the name of Oscar Charleston.

"Willie Mays was a good outfielder, so was DiMaggio," shrugged
ex-Kansas City second baseman Newt Allen, "but this man Charleston
had, I don't know, something special about him."

Oscar Charleston played the game with the same savage, slashing
drive as Ty Cobb. At bat, they both ripped the ball to all fields; on the
bases, they were panther-fast and played for blood. But, unlike Cobb,
Charleston often swung for the fences, and, like Babe Ruth, reached
them. And in the field he ran circles around the more famous Georgian.

Small wonder, then, when some writers dubbed Charleston "the
black Ty Cobb," more knowledgeable writers scoffed. Cobb, they said,
should be called "the white Oscar Charleston."

Fast enough to stand behind second base and outrun the longest
line drive, powerful enough to loosen a ball's cover with one hand,

fearless enough to snatch the hood off a Ku Klux Klansman, Oscar Charleston may—just may—have been the best ball player, black or white, the game has ever produced. Of all the evils of baseball's long segregation policy, one of the worst was denying the vast majority of fans the chance to see Oscar Charleston for themselves.

It was Charleston's eyes that most people remembered, with a chill. "He had cold gray eyes, with a tint of blue," said Ted Page, who played under him on the Pittsburgh Crawfords of the 1930s:

> Vicious eyes. Steel-gray, like a cat. Greenish-gray. And they were steel. You could just look right through there and you could see cold-bloodedness. If you looked behind Charleston's eyes, you could see several things, like he was looking for something. What, I don't know. He had a lot of devilment, you could see. A devilish-type of guy. He was always grinning, always playing pranks, always jolly. But deep back inside you could see he was a cold-blooded son of a gun. You would say, "I sure would hate to tangle with this guy."

Charleston hit .318 against white major leaguers, .353 against Negro league and Cuban pitchers. His .361 in Cuba is the highest by anyone there, topping Cristobal Torriente by ten points. In all, he went over .400 five times.

The young Ted Williams, who always had his ear cocked for a good story about hitting, recalled hearing this tale about Charleston facing the great Walter Johnson: "Mr. Johnson," Ted quoted Charleston, "I've done heard about your fast ball, and I'm gonna hit it out of here." Charleston struck out the first two times, then on the third try pulled the ball over the fence to win the game, 1–0, for Smokey Joe Williams, who was a good fast-baller himself.

"Charleston could hit that ball a mile," Dizzy Dean said. "He didn't have a weakness. When he came up, we just threw and hoped like hell he wouldn't get a hold of one and send it out of the park."

In October 1922 white big leaguers got a taste of the many ways Charleston could beat them, when his club, the St. Louis Giants, challenged the Detroit Tigers to a three-game series. Unfortunately, Ty Cobb was not with the Tigers. Perhaps his ego was still sore from being outplayed by Pop Lloyd in Cuba 12 years earlier. Anyway, Cobb did not accompany the team to St. Louis, and we are thus denied the thrill of observing these two great matadors, Cobb and Charleston, face to face.

But, even without Cobb, the Tigers had a good club, with Bobby Veach, Lu Blue, Fred Haney, Roy Moore, Topper Rigney, and Larry Woodall—all .300 hitters—and on the mound in the first game, Howard Ehmke (17–17).

It was a beautiful game. Charleston drove in the first run with a single, as the Stars took a 4–0 lead. But the Tigers rallied for four runs in the eighth to tie it. They would have scored more, but Charleston raced into deep center field to snare Moore's long drive for the third out.

In the bottom of the eighth, the Stars' second baseman, Frank Warfield, hit and stole second. Charleston drilled a grounder to Rigney at short and beat it out for a hit, sending Warfield to third. A moment later Oscar put his head down and charged toward second. When the catcher, Woodall, fired the ball across the infield, Warfield broke for home on a double steal with the winning run.

The next day Bert Cole (1–6) was on the mound for the Tigers and, in spite of a homer by Charleston, was leading, 7–4, going into the eighth. Charleston led off that inning with a double and began dancing off the bag in the direction of third. Again Woodall fired the ball to second, but this time his throw went into center field, and before Haney could recover it, Charleston had sprinted all the way home. It so unnerved Cole that the Stars scored six more runs to win, 11–7.

Lefty Roy Moore (0–3) pitched the third game for Detroit and won, 10–3. But Charleston was just as pesky as before. When second baseman George Cutshaw threw Charleston's ground ball into the stands, Oscar ended up on second. Again he dared the Tigers to get him, and when Moore whirled and fired to second, the ball went into center again. Charleston skipped to third and scored a moment later on a grounder. When the Tigers finally boarded their Pullman that night, they were glad to see the last of Oscar Charleston.

Throughout his long career, 1915–1936, there were three things Oscar Charleston excelled at on the baseball field: hitting, fielding, and fighting. He loved all three, and it's a toss-up which he was best at.

"Oscar Charleston was one of the great hitters," Page said.

> Average-wise, if I was going to pay $100,000 for a ball player, I think maybe I would take Charleston over Josh Gibson. Josh was a terrific hitter—for distance. But I think Charleston could have out-hit Josh over a season in average. Because Charleston could bunt and drag the ball. And he could hit the ball out of the ball park, make no mistake about it. He was a left-handed hitter, and not just over the right field wall, over the opposite wall too. But he could also push the ball down third base or down first base. And he was fast. There is not much defense for a man who can hit the ball hard and can bunt and push the ball too. And this was Charleston.

"He hit so hard, he'd knock gloves off you," said Newt Allen. "He was a stronger hitter than Josh Gibson. Sure."

It's a pity Oscar Charleston didn't face the top white pitchers day in and day out, as well as the top blacks. But if he didn't face all the best pitchers in the country, it's just as true that his white contemporaries, Cobb, George Sisler, Rogers Hornsby, and Harry Heilmann, were fattening their own .400 averages against some white hurlers who would have been riding the bench if black men like Joe Williams, Cannonball Dick Redding, Bullet Joe Rogan, and others had been allowed in the so-called major leagues.

If possible, Charleston was even better in the field than at bat. He played one of the shallowest center fields ever seen. Pitcher Bill Drake, who played with Charleston in St. Louis, used to kid him: "What, are you going to take the throw from the catcher?" Only Tris Speaker played as close. Yet no one remembers seeing any batter drive a ball over Charleston's head. He turned with the crack of the bat, literally out-raced the ball, whirled at the last second, and put it away.

Willie Mays played a shallow center field too, but, said Cool Papa Bell, Mays couldn't get back in time for some of those hard drives. Sports writers applauded Willie for holding the batter to a triple, but, Bell implied, if Charleston had been out there, those triples would have been outs.

Charleston had a weak arm. That's one reason, perhaps, why he played so shallow. But he got the ball away so fast that runners didn't take extra bases on him.

On easy high flies, Charleston would do a little "showboatin'." He might stroll leisurely after the ball, arriving just in the nick of time, to the delight of the fans. Sometimes he might turn a somersault before making the catch. Or, sports writer Ric Roberts said, he would pirouette under it like a dancer, flicking out his glove at the last second to capture it on his hip or behind his back. (Of course, he did this only in semipro games, Roberts added; in a serious league game, Oscar was strictly business.)

Whether at bat, in the field, or on the bases, Charleston played with savage determination.

"He wasn't afraid of anything," said Bell. "One time on a train trip, Charleston and the other guys were kind of cuttin' up and acting noisy, and Jim Londos, the rassler, told them to shut up. Charleston went over and stood over him and said, 'If you don't shut up, I'll throw you right out the window.' We said, 'You know who you're talkin' to? That's Jim Londos, the rassler. He'll throw *you* out the window!' Charleston didn't care; he wasn't afraid of anybody."

"He was brute strength looking," whistled Page. "We used to say he was strong enough to go bear huntin' with a switch, didn't need a gun."

Charleston was tough. Traveling by train through Florida about

1935, Cool Papa Bell told historian Jim Bankes, a Ku Klux Klansman in a white hood walked into the car and "evidently got pretty mouthy." Charleston ripped his hood off, and the Klansman retired without a fight. "Charleston was an imposing figure, as you know," writes Bankes.

Charleston brought a Ruthian zest to both baseball and life. He always had a bevy of women around him, remembered Webster McDonald. "He was a big handsome guy; he loved women. He was just a rascal."

Young Oscar learned to fight on the streets of Indianapolis, where he was born in 1896, one year after Babe Ruth. His father, Tom Charleston, had been a jockey and later did construction work. While the teenage Ruth was learning to defend himself in a Baltimore reform school, Oscar Charleston was getting his training on the streets. In fact, a brother went on to become a prize fighter.

One neighborhood kid, Bill Holland, who would go on to become a top pitcher in the black leagues, remembered Charleston's early games in the city's parks. The East Side played the West Side. "If the West boys come over on the East Side, and if they beat us, they'd have to run. All the girls would be there. The West Side boys used to try to get some of our girls, and we'd run 'em back."

At the age of 15 Charleston ran away to join the army and served with the all-black 24th infantry regiment in the Philippines. He ran on the regimental track team and played on the baseball team. Professional soldiering was a hard life in those days, and Charleston came out of the army in 1915 "tough as a wolf," in the words of exinfielder George Scales.

Charleston returned to Indianapolis and signed to play with the ABCs under the great C. I. Taylor at a salary of $50 a month. (Babe Ruth, recently released from reform school, was in his first full year as a pitcher with the Boston Red Sox.)

Sponsored by the American Brewing Company, the ABCs were one of the finest clubs in blackball history. Taylor ranks among the top black managers. His brother, Ben, is considered by some old-timers as the best black first baseman ever, the man who taught Buck Leonard how to play. Second baseman Elwood "Bingo" DeMoss is regarded by many as the best of all black second basemen. In the outfield next to Charleston, was Jimmy Lyons—Ty Cobb's brother reportedly called him a better player than Ty himself!

But "Charleston was the greatest of all players," said scholarly Dave Malarcher, who first saw Charleston on the ABCs of 1916. "He was all muscle and bone, no fat, no stomach, perfect broad shoulders, fine strong legs, strong muscular arms, and powerful hands and fingers. He was fast and he was strong."

That autumn the 19-year-old rookie Charleston for the first time faced a white big league pitcher. He was George "Hooks" Dauss (23–13) of the Tigers, and he was playing the ABCs in Indianapolis with an all-star squad under Donie Bush, the ex-Tiger shortstop. Detroit's Bobby Veach starred in left field. The game was played Sunday, October 10, in the old Federal league park, where the ABCs played their home games. The kid may have been overawed by the sight of his first big leaguers. Dauss set him down four times without a hit.

On the next two Sundays, however, young Charleston seems to have gotten over his stage fright. Ewell "Reb" Russell of the White Sox (11–10) pitched both games, and Charleston lined out a single and double in five at bats, as the ABCs split the two games.

Already Charleston was ready to punch anyone who crossed him. In the final game, the Charleston temper erupted. Bush, on first with a single, broke for second, and DeMoss took the throw in a close play. Umpire Jimmy Scanlon signaled safe, and Holland, watching from the grandstand roof, recalled what happened next:

"Bingo started an argument, and the umpire shoved him. Charleston was coming in from center field, turned around and hit that umpire and knocked him out on the mound."

Fans, both black and white, charged out of the stands, and the police just managed to avert a riot. DeMoss and Charleston were both arrested and hustled into the paddy wagon. That night they quietly left town with the team for the winter season in Cuba, leaving their bail behind. It would not be the last time Oscar Charleston would leave a ball park in a near shambles.

Pitcher Juanelo Mirabal recalled that "unless you bother him, Charleston was a gentleman. But if you do something he don't like, he's going to let you know. He didn't get too violent, he was a very quiet person. But he did try to beat you any way he could. Just like Ty Cobb, rip your pants or your legs, just to beat you out of a game. To me, I don't know which one was best. Both of them were great."

Ted Page elaborated:

> Oscar Charleston loved to play baseball. There was nothing he liked to do better, unless it was fight. He didn't smoke, he didn't drink, but he enjoyed a good fight—with the opposition. Not with his teammates. Now if I was on the opposing team and an argument came up, which they always do, I would always say, "Well, if I've go to get into this fight, I'm going to try to make sure I don't get close to Oscar Charleston." Because he would slug me just like that, if I was on the opposing team. Now Josh Gibson never went looking for fights. Charleston would look for them. Charleston wasn't temperamental—he was *mean*.

Shortstop Bobby Williams of Chicago disagreed.

No, not necessarily. I don't say Charleston was temperamental. He was full of fun. But he didn't take anything. You step on his foot, why he was probably liable to hit you in a minute. Oh yeah, he was quick to fight. But he didn't pick any fights. He was always jolly and kidding, not harsh kidding, you know. He was just fun to be around. But on the field he was all business.

Malarcher agreed that Charleston was a kindly man who defended anyone he thought was being mistreated: "He was hard on bullies."

Tales of Charleston's strength are legends. Once, while Charleston was driving a carload of ball players over a narrow country road in Texas, the car went out of control and rolled over. The players were thrown clear, Page said. Charleston was found in a ditch nearby, dazed but still tightly clutching the steering wheel, which he had literally wrenched off the car as it crashed.

Catcher Larry Brown said Charleston could twist the ball in his two hands until the cover was pulled loose from the core, then pull the horsehide off. Pitcher Chet Brewer loved to pitch with Oscar on first, "rubbing up" the ball; the loosened cover made it dance and flutter like a knuckler.

Charleston had hands "like elephant hides," said Schoolboy Johnny Taylor, who pitched for the New York Cubans. "He used to kid me, take his hand and rub it on my face. Like a piece of Brillo. And he'd laugh. He was a big jolly guy."

On the bases infielders learned to hop out of the way of Charleston's spikes. "See this scar on my hand?" asked little Newt Allen:

> Oscar Charleston jumped at me at third base, cut my glove off my hand—as big a fellow as he was: he weighed 200-something. I had him out, but he hit me, he jumped high, knocked my glove and the ball.
> The catcher would catch the devil when Charleston's scoring, because he would jump on you up at your chest, knock you down. Or one of the infielders, he'd run over him. He didn't care what you did to him, because he'd get his revenge some way.

As an outfielder, Charleston played with panache. Everyone has his favorite tale of one of Charleston's miracle catches. Malarcher was a rookie right fielder in 1916. "And that's when I found out about Oscar Charleston. He could play all the outfield. I just caught foul balls. I stayed on the lines. People thought I was running over there to get the balls. I wasn't. Charleston would play all the outfield. Malarcher further recalled:

One of the greatest catches I ever saw in my whole history in the outfield was by Charleston. We were playing the Cuban Stars in Kokomo. They had a man on first, a man on second, the game close, and the hitter hit this ball to deep center field, way back, way over Charleston's head. He turned and just ran like he was going to catch a train or something. He just flew back there, because it was straight back over his head. He ran so fast that he just overran it. As he turned, it was falling back behind him, and he caught it down here just before it hit the ground. It was marvelous. Marvelous.

Floyd "Jelly" Gardner, an excellent ball hawk himself, whistled at the memory of one Charleston catch. Oscar slapped down on the ball on a dead run. "Those things happen once in a lifetime," Gardner said.

As a hitter Charleston was equally intimidating. "Pitchers used to throw at him," said Webster McDonald. "The more they threw at him, the harder he hit the ball."

McDonald tried to get him out on soft stuff—"you couldn't get any hard stuff by him." While Charleston kept nervously waggling his bat, McDonald kept slowing the ball up, slowing it up. Mac nibbled at the corners with a slow curve, hoping to get Charleston arguing with the ump. When Oscar turned around to jaw, Mac would quick-pitch a strike over. "But of course," he shrugged, "if it's a close ball game, then you've got to walk him."

Big Bill Drake of the Kansas City Monarchs threw Charleston high curve balls "right on his chest. If you got it there, you could take care of him. And if you didn't, shame on you."

Charleston was a left-handed hitter, but, Newt Allen said, he didn't care whether the pitcher was left-handed or not. "Left-handers were afraid of *him*. If a left-hand pitcher threw him a curve ball, he would punch it over the third baseman's head."

Bill Foster, one of the best left-handers in black baseball annals, nodded:

I just didn't feel like left-handers ought to hit me; I was awful surprised when left-handers hit me. But Charlie could do that. He would wait for a curve ball, because he knew a left-hander was going to throw that curve ball. So I wouldn't throw him a curve ball, or if I threw him one, it would be bad. All Charleston got from me mostly—to hit on— were fast balls. Because he waited for curve balls, and he could hit them a mile. To tell you the truth, he was just a tremendously good hitter.

In the autumn of 1916 Taylor challenged Foster and the famous Chicago American Giants to a three-game series for the championship of black baseball. Charleston's booming triple won the third and final game to give the ABCs the flag.

A few days later he was back facing the white big leaguers at Indianapolis. This time he jumped on the Boston Braves' little lefty, Art Nehf (7–5), for two hits in three tries as the ABCs won, 1–0.

The next autumn he got three hits in six at bats against Cincinnati's Hod Eller (10–5) and the Braves' Jesse Barnes (13–21). That also may have been the year he hit the home run against Walter Johnson; if so, Walter was 23–16.

In 1919 Charleston moved to Rube Foster's Chicago American Giants, where he was united with a manager who preached the Charleston style of aggressive playing. Charleston became proficient at laying down the hit-and-run bunt, Charles Whitehead reported. With Bingo DeMoss on first, Charleston dropped the ball down the third base line. When the third baseman came in, DeMoss charged round second and kept going into third. When the infield tried to catch DeMoss, Charleston kept racing around first and into second. Another time, with DeMoss on third and Charleston on second, both runners were moving, as the hitter tapped back to the mound. A wild throw to home eluded the catcher, and both Bingo and Oscar scored.

In 1920, however, the first year of Rube's new Negro National League, Foster reluctantly sent his star back to the ABCs to provide more balance to the league. Charleston hit .366.

That fall Oscar again bedeviled the whites in a three-game series against the St. Louis Cardinals at the Cards' home grounds, Sportsmen's Park. Although their batting champ, Texan Rogers Hornsby, refused to play, the rest of the Cards were on the field, including .300-hitters Jacques Fournier, Milt Stock, and Jack Smith. Sporstmen's Park, incidentally, remained segregated for the series, with black fans sitting in the right-field pavilion.

In the first inning of the first game, Oscar gave them something to cheer when he pumped a home run into the pavilion off the Cards' George Lyons (2–1) to lead the Giants to a 5–4 victory in ten innings. The next day the Cards' Jesse Haines (13–20) handcuffed Charleston and the rest of the Giants, winning 5–0. Charleston didn't stay around for the third game, won by the Cards, 6–0.

In Cuba that winter, Charleston led the league with a .471 average.

Playing for the St. Louis Giants in 1921, Charleston had perhaps the finest season of his life. In one game he swatted three home runs against the American Giants and spent five minutes gathering up the money that was rained down on him by fans in the bleachers and grandstands. By season's end he was batting .434, second to his teammate Charlie Blackwell's .448. But, playing a 60-game schedule, Charleston was tops in doubles (12), home runs (15), and stolen bases (34).

That October the Giants renewed their rivalry with the Cards. The Cardinals won the opener, 5–4, in 11 innings. The Giants evened it with a 6–2 win over Haines (18–12), helped by Charleston's home run. But the Cards won the last three games to take the series.

From St. Louis Charleston traveled to Indianapolis to help his old mates, the ABCs, against a touring big-league squad. He went 2-for-4 against Brooklyn pitcher Jess Petty (0–0). Petty was leading, 3–2, in the ninth when Charleston drove one over the center fielder's head to spark a six-run rally and win the game, 8–3.

Moving to Cuba in the winter of 1922–23, Charleston led the league with an average of .446 against top black and white pitchers from the United States and from Cuba.

The next winter Charleston went back to Cuba to play for Santa Clara. It's been hailed as the greatest club in Cuban history and even compared to the 1927 Yankees, often called the best club in U.S. white history. Charleston was flanked in the outfield by Alejandro Oms and Pablo "Champion" Mesa. The trio may have been the greatest outfield ever assembled, rivaling, perhaps surpassing, the great Red Sox trio of

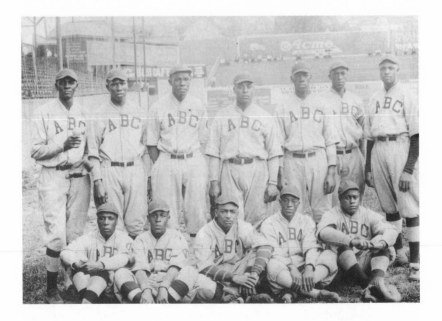

Oscar Charleston (back, center) with the Indianapolis ABCs in 1921.

St. Louis, Oct. 4, 1920

Cards	AB	H		Giants	AB	H
RF Schultz	5	0		1B J. Lyons	5	1
1B Fournier	5	2		SS Hewitt	4	2
3B Stock	5	2		CF Charleston	3	2
2B Janvrin	5	1		RF Blackwell	5	0
CF McHenry	5	0		LF Dudley	4	2
SS Lavan	5	1		C Kennard	4	1
RF Dilhoefer	5	3		2B Day	4	0
C Clemons	4	2		3B Holt	2	1
P G. Lyons	4	1		3B Wallace	1	0
	43	12		3B Mackey	0	0
				P Drake	2	0
				P Finner	2	0
					36	9

```
Cards    000 013 000 0— 4 12 5
Giants   130 000 000 1— 5  9 3
```

2B: Clemons
3B: Lavan
HR: Charleston

Tris Speaker, Duffy Lewis, and Harry Hooper. The infield of Eddie Douglass, Frank Warfield, Dobie Moore, and Oliver Marcelle was likewise one of the best of all-time, black or white.

Charleston hit .377 with 31 stolen bases, breaking the Cuban record, 28, set by Cristobal Torriente seven years earlier. It would stand for more than 20 years until it in turn was broken by Sam Jethroe with 32.

All the players called him "Charlie," and nine-year-old Pedro Cardona took up the cry in one game: "Come on, Charlie!" Said Cardona, later a successful Havana lawyer, "I remembered he looked at me, gave me a big smile with his white teeth."

To keep fans and players apart, most Latin parks had chicken wire strung from roof to grandstand, from first base to third. Still, fans often burst through the wire. There was always a black moriah police van parked along the sidelines ready for trouble. With Charleston in the game, there often was.

Cardona told of one play in a big game against Havana. The crowd was overflowing the stands, when Charleston slid into third on a close play "and almost took the trousers off the third baseman, Manolo Cueto." Cueto's brother, a soldier, happened to be in the crowd behind third, Cardona said, and ran to his brother's side and the two of them started swinging at Charleston until the umpires separated them.

Webster McDonald's version is that Charleston hit a long single and tried to stretch it to a double. Oscar and the ball arrived about the same time, "and this little shortstop took the throw. Charleston knocked him from here over to there. The little Cuban jumped up and swung at Charleston. Charleston banged him. The second baseman ran into him. Charleston banged *him*. He whipped three guys out there by himself. Grabbed one and swung him around and knocked the others down."

Ted Page said a group of soldiers leaped over the railing into the fray. Charleston's back was turned—he was probably busy pummeling some enemy—when he caught sight of a shadow bearing down on him from behind. "When the shadow got close enough," said Page, "Charleston swung around and laid him out with that left hand. There were a dozen or more soldiers, and he stretched them all over the park, just laying them out. And he had a great grin on his face, like a kid opening his Christmas present. He was enjoying it!"

At last the police subdued Charleston and tried to wrestle him into a van. Charleston dug his heels in. "I'm not going to ride in that thing," he panted. "He hit me first!"

The owner of the club, Linares, pleaded with him. "I'll pay the fine and get you out of jail, just to get you away from here, to keep you out of trouble."

McDonald continued:

> So Lenares rode down to the station with Charleston, paid his fine, changed his clothes, and took him to the hotel. We said, "Don't go back there tomorrow. Forget about playing that ball game tomorrow." Charleston said. "What did I do, I can't play ball tomorrow?" Lenares said, "Don't. I'm coming to take you for a ride." Charleston said, "I'm not going for a ride, I'm going to play ball."
> The next day he was the first one to put on a uniform. We said, "Charleston, don't go back out there, for goodness sake. If you go out there to play, we're not going to play." But he walked out of that clubhouse to the ball park. They wouldn't let him play, but he was out there. He wasn't afraid. We called him "Mulo"—stubborn—and Lenares said, "Aw, what am I going to do with him?"

Cardona, however, defended Charleston. "I don't think he had a temper," he insisted. "He would have had to have ice water in his blood not to fight back."

Catcher Larry Brown recalled another game in Cuba when Charleston raced to the fence for a long fly. As he reached into the bleachers, a fan pulled the ball from his glove. Charleston reached in, picked the fan out of the seats with one hand, and "beat the hell out of him." Some other fans jumped out of the stands, swinging their

machetes. By this time an army officer came out of the stands, took a
medal off his uniform, and pinned it on Charleston's chest. "You're a
brave man," he said.

Kansas City pitcher Chet Brewer said that in another game in
Cuba, Charleston was digging for home in a close play when catcher
Julio Rojo ran out to cut the throw off and try to make a play on the
base. "Rojo, why didn't you tag him?" Brewer asked.

"I wanted to play tomorrow," Rojo answered honestly.

"Charleston would have taken him into the dugout," Brewer says.

Back in the United States in 1923 Charleston's average fell off to
.310. That year for the first time he tried his hand at pitching, and
compiled a 2–1 record.

Brown, a rookie catcher with the ABCs, remembered how
Charleston came to his defense when the older players tried to intimi-
date Brown in the clubhouse. Charleston curtly told them, "Don't
mess with the kid."

"Charleston was a nice-dispositioned guy," Brown said gratefully.

> He'd do anything to help you. He was a good team man, but he
> didn't take any stuff. Well, he did like to fight if you messed with him.
> That son of a bitch—man, he looked like King Kong. I've seen him get
> under a shower one time. I think the pitcher made a bad pitch to some
> guy, and both of them were lathering up under there and started
> fighting right there. Man, you talk about suds and soap and everything
> else flying! I said, "Shoot, man, I'm getting out of here," and just walked
> out of the clubhouse without a stitch on me."

That October Oscar joined the Detroit Stars for a three-game
series against the St. Louis Browns. The Browns had three .300
hitters for the series, and lefty Dauntless Dave Danforth (16–14) on
the mound. But the addition of Charleston gave the Detroit Stars a
murderers' row to make any pitcher quake. Charleston hit clean-up,
with Norman "Turkey" Stearnes ahead of him, and John Beckwith
right behind him; both rank with Josh Gibson among the hardest
hitters in the history of black baseball.

In the first game, the Browns took a 6–1 lead into the sixth. Then
the Stars really burst. Stearnes doubled in two runs, Charleston singled in Stearnes, and Beckwith's home run over the center-field fence
tied the score. Ed Wesley's second homer, in the ninth, beat the
Browns, 7–6.

Elam Vangilder (16–17) started the second game for the Browns,
but the result was the same. Charleston got three hits and three runs,
and the Stars won it, 7–6, with another ninth-inning homer, this one
by pitcher Bill Force. Finally, in the third game, Ray Kolp (5–12) gave

the big leaguers a victory, 11–8, though Charleston drilled a single and home run.

After the game Charleston was on his way to Chicago to join the American Giants and bedevil his old foes, the Detroit Tigers, again. The Tigers were even stronger than the year before. They finished second in the American League and boasted the league batting champ, Harry Heilmann (.403), in addition to Heinie Manush (.334). On the mound in the first game were Bert Cole (13–5) and Dauss (21–13).

The American Giants started off fast. Bingo DeMoss singled, Beckwith (also on loan) doubled him home, and Charleston's double made it two runs. Oscar also stole third, just for good measure, but died there. Detroit rallied, however, and went into the eighth with a 5–4 lead. In that inning, Charleston walked, worked his way around to third, and scored the tying run on Bobby Williams' fly to Manush. That's how the game ended, 5–5.

The next day the Tigers' Herman Pillette (14–19) finally stopped Charleston; Oscar couldn't get a hit in four trips, and the American Leaguers won, 7–1.

In 1924 Oscar Charleston became the biggest prize in the most savage baseball war to hit the Negro leagues. Ed Bolden, the owner of the Philadelphia Hilldales, went after the top stars of Foster's loop— Pop Lloyd, Raleigh "Biz" Mackey, George "Tank" Carr, Beckwith, and, of course, the king of them all, Oscar Charleston. It's not known how much money Bolden waved, but with the depressed salaries that most black teams were paying, it didn't have to be much.

At any rate, Charleston made the jump, to the Harrisburg Giants as manager. Owned by "Colonel" Strothers, a local businessman, the Harrisburg club also featured rookie outfielder Herbert "Rap" Dixon, and center-fielder Clarence "Fats" Jenkins, who is now a member of the basketball Hall of Fame. "It was the best outfield I ever played with," said catcher William "Big C" Johnson. "Dixon was fast, maybe the best arm of the three, but all were accurate, all three of them. I caught more men trying to come home after fly balls the two years I was in Harrisburg than in all my other years put together."

Johnson said Charleston even played a left-handed second base every now and then. "He could go get those ground balls the same as any other second baseman."

Charleston hit .391 with eight homers in 54 games.

After a bad winter in Cuba (.261), Oscar rebounded in 1925 with another Charlestonian season. He hit .418 and slugged 16 home runs to lead in both departments. He was also tops with 23 doubles.

That fall Charleston was in the Bronx playing a squad of major and minor leaguers that included Charlie Dressen and the young Lou

Gehrig. Pitching was Rube Zellers of the Jersey City Giants. Charleston's club, the Lincoln Giants, went into the ninth with a 2–1 lead, thanks to Oscar's home run and his game-saving catch in the seventh. A ninth-inning error let Gehrig score the tying run. In the 11th another error with the bases loaded opened the gate for four more runs. In the home half of the inning Charleston lined out a double and scored, but it was a futile cause; the Lincolns lost, 6–5. Charleston, however, ended up with four hits in six at bats for the afternoon. Gehrig went 1-for-2.

Later that fall Charleston went 4-for-5 against ex-big-leaguer Socks Siebold, including a triple high off the left-field fence with two men on.

Hitting was down throughout the league in 1926, and Charleston's average was only .275, although his eight homers were second best in the league.

But he was still sensational in the field. Ted Page recalled a catch against Chaney White in the old park on an island in Harrisburg: "Charleston just outran the ball," Page said. "The ball got up over his head, and he just reached up like this with his meat hand—his bare hand. He was darn near to the center-field wall when he caught that darn ball."

Charlie stole hits from blacks and whites alike. At Bloomsburg, Pennsylvania, that October Charleston raced way back in the wide open fairgrounds to haul down a fly and help beat Lefty Grove (13–13) by a score of 3–0.

In another game, he whacked Grove for a homer as the Philadelphia Hilldales beat the Athletics, 6–1. It was a battle of great left-handers: Grove fell to Hilldale's Jesse "Nip" Winters, who has vied with Foster for the title of the best black lefty of all time.

Against the old spit-baller, Jack Picus Quinn (10–11), Charleston laced two singles, as Hilldale beat Heinie Manush, Jimmy Dykes, Bing Miller, and company, 4–1. Spit-ballers didn't trouble Charleston; he'd looked at enough of them in the black leagues.

That same year Charleston played behind Joe Williams against another all-star club that included Manush, Goose Goslin, and George Burns. He was in their hair all day. In the second inning he was safe on Jimmy Dykes' error and rode home on a long triple by Beckwith. In the fourth he lined a single to center to drive in a run. And in the eighth, with the score tied, 5–5, and Dolly Gray on first, Charleston dropped a sacrifice bunt down the first-base line (how many stars today would do that?), and a moment later Gray scored the winning run on an error.

That winter, as usual, Charleston played in Cuba, where he hit .403. Dolph Luque (13–16), the Cincinnati Reds' right-hander, managed one of the teams, and the black curve-ball specialist Arthur "Rats" Henderson recalled the final game of the season, with John McGraw and baseball commissioner Kenesaw Mountain Landis both in the stands. "At the end of the season we'd split up into whites versus coloreds for a game. Well, I pitched against Luque, and we were tied, 0–0, until the seventh, when Oscar Charleston got hold of a fast ball. It went over the infield like a bullet about as high as your head and just kept on rising on a line over the center-field fence. I beat Luque, 1–0."

In 1927 Charleston was a holdout, and Strothers called Beckwith from Baltimore to manage the club. That brought Oscar back into the fold. Beckwith was one of the all-time great power hitters of blackball history. His arrival gave Harrisburg almost as awesome a one-two home-run punch as the Yankees' had in Babe Ruth and Lou Gehrig that same year. Beckwith, many old-timers insist, could hit them harder than any man alive, including Ruth or Josh Gibson. But he was weak on outside pitches. Not Charleston, however, "You couldn't fool Charleston," said Jake Stephens. "You'd walk him and pitch to Beckwith." The rivalry was a tonic to both men. Beckwith hit .361 with nine home runs. Charleston hit .335 with 12 homers, best in the league. He was also tops in doubles with 18.

Oscar also led the Cuban league in home runs that winter, while hitting .368. His 11 stolen bases were tops in the league.

The following summer, 1928, Charleston moved to Hilldale as manager and hit .360. In October, against Philadelphia A's hurler Ed Rommel (13–5), Oscar collected two hits, one of them a double, although Rommel won the game, 8–5.

In 1929, Charleston punched Hilldale owner Ed Bolden in the nose over some disagreement. Bolden fired him. But a month later, Oscar was back in the lineup. No explanation was ever offered, though perhaps Charleston's .339 batting average is as good as any.

In 1930 the Great Depression descended, almost destroying black baseball. The leagues broke up, and only individual clubs struggled on. The best of them was the maverick Homestead Grays. Owned by Cumberland "Cum" Posey, they had refused to join Bolder's league, preferring to barnstorm as independents. As the other teams folded, Posey picked up the best black players in the country. Cyclone Joe Williams, the black-Indian half breed, was the pitching ace; many authorities consider him the best black pitcher of all time, better even than Satchel Paige. Judy Johnson was on third, and George Scales at second. Steady Vic Harris and Bill Evans patrolled the outfield. And midway through the season a young goliath named Josh Gibson joined the club as catcher.

Into this star-studded lineup stepped Charleston, the greatest of them all. Charleston's fabled speed in the outfield had begun to lose its zip, and he moved to first base, but his bat was as dangerous as ever. He hit .333.

The Grays were the kings of the East that year and in September challenged the New York Lincoln Giants to a world series. Charleston hit only .181; he may have been injured, since he had missed at least three games. The Grays won, six games to four, and proclaimed themselves the best black club in the land.

Charleston turned next to his old foes, the white big leaguers. In Baltimore's spacious Westport stadium, he sprinted to the deepest corner of right-center field to pull down a drive by Max Bishop of the world champion Athletics, then whirled and held the runner on second, to help beat Jimmy Foxx's All Stars, 2–1.

He traveled to Chicago for two games against an all-star club that included Charlie Gehringer, Harry Heilmann, Lefty O'Doul, and pitcher Earl Whitehill (17–13) of Detroit. Oscar went 1-for-3 against Whitehill in a 6–1 victory. Facing Earl again a week later, Charleston doubled in one run to help force the game into extra innings. In the tenth he came up with the bases loaded and drove out a single, his third hit of the night, to win it, 6–5.

Yankee pitcher Waite Hoyt recalled meeting Whitehill and New York Giant first baseman Bill Terry sometime after that. "They had just played a black team and were talking about Charleston," Hoyt said. "He got about six hits in a double header [it was actually only four]. They said he was one of the finest looking hitters they'd ever seen."

In 1931 the Grays boasted an ever more powerful club. Ted Page added speed to the outfield. Barrel-chested Jud Wilson, one of the great hitters of black baseball, replaced Johnson at third. Ted "Double Duty" Radcliffe bolstered both the pitching and catching corps. Altogether, the Grays claimed to have won 134 games and lost ten for the year, playing mostly white semipros. In 17 games against other black clubs, Charleston hit .333 with six homers, or one every 11 at bats. Josh Gibson also hit six home runs while batting .296.

In 1932 a new figure walked into the Pittsburgh baseball scene: Gus Greenlee, genial tavern owner, numbers king, and sportsman, who already owned an impressive stable of fighters, including future world light-heavyweight champ John Henry Lewis. Gus wanted a ball club too. He literally bought Posey's club right out from under him: Gibson, Wilson, Page, Radcliffe, and shortstop Jake Stephens. To these he added speed demon Cool Papa Bell, plus the one and only Satchel Paige. To manage this Hall-of-Fame crew, Greenlee hired the greatest star of them all, Charleston.

In all, it may have been the best black team in history—Monte Irvin and many others believe it was. It boasted as many as seven present or potential Hall of Famers—Paige, Gibson, Bell, Johnson, Wilson, Posey, and, of course, Charleston himself.

Charleston held his thoroughbreds on a tight rein. Ted Page, who loved to run, objected that Charleston wouldn't let him run on his own. "But he was a smart manager," Page admitted. "All great ball players don't make good managers, but Charleston made the right moves. You're guessing, of course, maybe you're lucky. But he made good moves in shifting his players around."

Charleston's stardom hadn't gone to his head, either. While Satchel Paige was a bit stand-offish with the press, Ted Page remembered that Charleston was more like Gibson. "He would talk with you anywhere, with anybody, it didn't matter, and almost under any conditions."

Perhaps managing affected Charleston's hitting. He finished the season with .271, though his five home runs were only one below Josh Gibson's six.

That fall Charleston led the Crawfords against Casey Stengel's all stars, who included Hack Wilson, Woody English, Johnny Frederick, and others. For pitchers Casey brought Larry French (18–16) and Bill Swift (14–10) of the Pirates, Roy "Tarzan" Parmelee (0–3) of the Giants, and Fred Frankhouse (4–6) of the Braves. In seven games, Charleston's Craws won five, including Satchel Paige's 15-strikeout beauty at 10–2. Oscar scored three times himself that day. In another contest, he smacked two homers against Parmelee and Frankhouse, though the Stengels crushed the Craws, 20–8.

"I had a good curve ball," Frankhouse said. "I struck Charleston out throwing a lot of curves. Then I threw him a fast ball and he took it. I grinned at him: 'Heh, you were guessing on that.' He said, 'Yeah, I was.'"

The two smiled at each other. After the game they struck up a friendship. "Charleston had a good disposition," Frankhouse said. "I had heard so much about him. We got to talking, he wanted to know some things about baseball and asked me if I would go along with him from Pittsburgh to Altoona, with some of his boys. He wanted to talk big league baseball. We got a little friendly driving in the car. They were itching for information from white ball players."

"Do you think the colored people will ever get in baseball?" Charleston asked.

"I don't know any reason you shouldn't," Frankhouse said. "I wouldn't be surprised the day will come up when you'll be there.

"I pitched pretty hard, I can tell you that," Frankhouse recently recalled. "Big leaguers had more polish (than the blacks), but they didn't have any more stuff."

The ride, however, was a hair-raising experience for Frankhouse, as Charleston careened around the mountain curves with wheels spinning wildly. "I wouldn't go back with him," he said. He told Charleston: "You scared the devil out of me going down those hills wide open."

For two years, 1932–1933, the Craws often played twilight games in Forbes Field after the Pirates' game in the afternoon. Often the white big leaguers would hang around the park to watch. Babe Herman of the Dodgers remembered Charleston. "He could run like an antelope," Babe said. "Hit the ball a mile. But he wasn't at that time a really consistent hitter."

Wally Berger of the Braves also admitted that, "I wanted to see Charleston hit." "He belted one a mile"—a 450-foot homer over the center-field fence. "I don't think anyone had hit it over, Ruth or anyone. He did." (Actually, Josh Gibson had done it as an 18-year-old in the black World Series of 1930. But it wouldn't be done again until Mickey Mantle did it in the World Series of 1960. Dick Stuart also reportedly reached the same spot.)

Buck Leonard, the so-called black Lou Gehrig, got his first look at Charleston in 1933 and still calls him the best left-handed hitter he ever saw. Leonard recalled prodigious Charleston homers in Forbes Field and in old Greenlee Field, plus another in Paterson, New Jersey, that, Leonard said, "they're still talking about."

Leonard remembered another night in 1933 when Charleston, by then a fat 37 years old, barreled into Homestead Gray's catcher Tex Burnett in Pittsburgh. "Charleston just undressed him, just cut his shin guards off, his uniform, everything. Burnett was out for about a month." The Grays thought that was going too far. "Burnett was just trying to make a living, the same as you are," they protested. But to Charleston the issue was simple: Burnett had tried to block the plate. What else did he expect?

Charleston hit .376 with nine home runs in 1933; Gibson hit .385 with six homers, and the Craws made it to the play-offs in Greenlee's new Negro National League. They lost to the American Giants.

Not one to hold a grudge, Cum Posey at the end of the year named Charleston to his all-star team, considered the authoritative selection.

In 1934 Greenlee conceived an East-West, or all-star game, that was played in Chicago's Comiskey Park a few days after the white majors played their first all-star game in the same park. Charleston was easily voted to the East team with 43,000 votes, more than any other man on either team. He was also given the honor of managing the East. Although he didn't get a hit, Oscar starred afield and scored twice as the Easterners lost to the West, 11–7.

Charleston made Posey's all-star team again in 1934 with a .289 average.

In October the Craws went barnstorming in Forbes Field against Dizzy Dean, who had just won 29 games to lead the Cardinals to the world championship. Although Diz was backed by mostly a semipro lineup, he did have big leaguers Moose Solters, Mike Garbark, George Susce, and brother Paul.

Susce had never caught Dean before, but he did know Charleston from previous semipro games. The bases were loaded and Susce was trying to decide whether to give the great Dean any tips. Susce recalled: "I says I'd rather see him call me a busher than see Charleston hit one off him." So he finally went to the mound. "I said, 'Heh, Diz, I don't know if you know these guys.' Diz put his arm around my shoulder, said, 'George, go back there.' He struck Charleston out on three fastballs. Shows how great Dizzy was."

The Craws won the game, 4–3. But the highlight was the riot that ensued when Vic Harris of the Craws hit umpire Ahearn on the head, then pulled his face mask and snapped it. Both clubs waded into the melée, manager Charleston leading the way. It was like old times again. Gibson got Susce in a hammerlock and had to be pulled off him.

In 1935 Charleston hit .288 with only one home run. But he led the Craws into the play-offs against the New York Cubans. The Cubans took the first two games. In the third game Gibson tripled against the wall for one run, Bell tripled in another, and manager Charleston clinched it with a home run over the center-field fence, one of the longest hit in New York's Dyckman Oval that season, as the Craws won, 3–0, and stayed alive in the series.

The Cuban's great pitcher, Martin Dihigo, won the fourth game,

Oscar Charleston (far left) and the 1935 Pittsburgh Crawfords.

however, giving them a lead of three games to one. If the Crawfords wanted to take the flag, they would have to sweep the final three games.

They did win the fifth game in Pittsburgh, pulling to within one of the Cubans.

But in Philadelphia's Shibe Park for the sixth game, they faltered. Losing, 6–3, in the ninth and all but out of it, they put two men on, and manager Charleston himself walked up and lashed a pitch over the wall to tie it. A hit, a walk, and an error loaded the bases, and Judy Johnson hit a 3–2 pitch on the ground just out of reach of Cuban first baseman Showboat Thomas, and the Crawfords had won it, 7–6. The series was all tied up.

Under the stands, the Cubans' business manager, Frank Forbes, was already counting out the winner's share of the receipts when he heard the screaming up above and learned that the Craws had won. He almost threw the money across the room in disgust.

For the seventh game, Cuban manager Dihigo sent lefty Luis Tiant, father of the latter-day Boston Red Sox star, to stop the Crawfords. Tiant struggled through seven innings holding onto a 7–5 lead. In the eighth, Gibson's homer over the center-field fence made it 7–6. Charleston immediately smacked another over the wall to tie it, 7–7. A few moments later Bell singled Sammy Bankhead home with the winning run, and the Crawfords were champs in one of the great comebacks in black world series History.

Charleston had grown stout and slow in 1936, at the age of 40, and his average dropped to .211 in 12 games. The Craws won half of the split season, but this time there would be no play-off. Instead, they traveled to Denver for the annual national semipro tournament, which they won handily, splitting $5,000 in prize money, a big payday for the depression. After the tourney they barnstormed back East with a big-league all-star squad. Aging Rogers Hornsby was in the lineup. So were Johnny Mize, Harlond Clift, Big Jim Weaver, and a 17-year-old farmboy phenom named Bob Feller.

The blacks won the first game, in Denver, 6–3. Charleston got two hits in five at bats against Jim Winford (11–10) and Mike Ryba (5–1) of the Cardinals, but he complained to little Jimmy Crutchfield, the Craws' left fielder, that it just wasn't much fun any more hitting with the bases empty.

In the next game, against Jim Weaver (14–8) in Des Moines, Cool Papa Bell opened with a walk, stole second, stole third, and scored on Charleston's smart single. In the third inning, second baseman Sammy T. Hughes reached on an error and Charleston waddled to the plate again. "This is what I've been waiting for," he winked to

Crutchfield, then lined a drive against the fence and puffed into second. In the seventh, singles by Bell, Hughes, Charleston, and Wild Bill Wright brought in three more runs, as the Craws won again, 5–2. The game was enlivened by what one newspaper called "a brief but lively fight" involving—naturally—Charleston. A hundred fans poured onto the field to help out before police finally broke it up.

A month later Charleston and Hornsby were facing each other again, this time in far-away Mexico City. Hornsby had a truly all star club: Foxx, Manush, Doc Cramer, Pinky Higgins, Boob McNair, and on the pitching staff Earl Whitehill (14–11), Vern Kennedy (21–9), and Jack Knott (9–17).

The Craws had just arrived in the rarified altitude, expecting to rest a few days and then play some Mexican clubs. Instead, they were hustled to the park to play the major leaguers. "Major leaguers!" exclaimed Bell. "We didn't know *they* were here!" Losing, 4–2, in the ninth, the Craws put on one of their typical rallies. Sam Bankhead (Dodger Dan's older brother) tripled, and catcher "Spoony" Palm pinch-hit a homer. With two outs, Judy Johnson singled, Gibson walked, Charleston singled in Johnson to put the Craws ahead, and Crutchfield scored Gibson to make it 6–4.

The big leaguers sent the top of their batting order up in the last of the ninth. McNair and Cramer went out, and the game was just about over when Manush hit an infield bouncer that was bobbled for an error. Muscular Jimmy Foxx was next up, and with the count 3–2 drove a home run over the wall to tie the game. (At dinner after the game Foxx would confide to Bell that "that was a strike, the third ball the umpire called.")

The two clubs battled for two more scoreless innings. In the bottom of the 11th the All Stars loaded the bases with one out and the mighty Foxx up next. Jimmy ripped a grounder to third, and Johnson fired it home for a force out. Hornsby drove another ball to the infield for a force out at second, and the umpire promptly called the game. "The sun's still in the sky and they call the game!" Bell protested. But it went into the records as a 6–6 tie.

The Mexico series marked the end of the great Pittsburgh Crawfords. The following spring the Dominican dictator, Rafael Trujillo, opened suitcases full of dollar bills and waved them in front of the Craws. When Charleston caught the Dominican agent trying to hand a wad of bills to one player, he grabbed the man by the throat and told him to take his money and give it to the whites. But it did no good. Paige, Gibson, Bell, and Bankhead all followed the lure of big dollars.

Charleston drifted to Toledo as manager of the Toledo

Crawfords, then took over as pilot of the Philadelphia Stars.

"I thought Charleston was a good manager," said Stars outfielder Gene Benson emphatically.

> He was a little gruff, but he didn't mean nothin. A manager has to know how to get his players to play. You have to have the good will of the ball players. If you have this, they'll play for you. But if you don't know how to get 'em goin', you're not gonna make a good manager. We had some guys, sometimes they did some harsh things, but the result is what you go by. If a manager makes a better ball player out of you, then his job was well done. That's the way I look at it. Charleston was that type of manager.
>
> A manager's biggest job is with his pitchers. I remember one time we had a fella, Chester Buchanan, a pitcher. But he didn't have too much heart. If you got a couple of hits off him, he would kind of give up.

After one rocky inning, Charleston called the players to a huddle in the dugout. Buchanan apparently thought the skipper would send in a relief pitcher. Instead, Oscar told Benson, "The next time anybody hits the ball over your head, let it go. Don't run after it, let him get a home run." Then he told Buchanan, "You gonna pitch this game. You gonna get no help, so you might as well make up your mind that you gonna pitch it."

Benson said, "You know, Charleston made a better pitcher out of him. He became a better pitcher after that. Gave him some heart."

"But Charleston was a stickler for time," Benson continued.

> If he said, "We're gonna leave tomorrow at 12 o'clock," don't you come one minute after 12. Because if he saw you walk down the street and it was after the leavin' time, you know what he'd do? He'd pull off and leave you and laugh at you! But the result of this is, you don't come late any more.
>
> And the fellows, after they found that out, why they loved him! 'Cause he wasn't a bad guy to play for. He never complained if you missed a ball, because he knew this was all part of baseball, to make an error or whatever. He didn't rip you up about those things. But anything that you knew that you were supposed to do, then you had to do it! Like being on time. And you had to be able to catch the signals. And he saw to it that you did it. Or you didn't play. If you got that kind of manager, you'll straighten up. I think Charleston was a terrific manager myself. He was the best manager I ever had.

Stars catcher Bill "Ready" Cash recalled:

> He would tell us, "I don't care how good you are; you can be the best player in the world. But if you're not a team man, I don't want you."

Charlie was a good disciplinarian. He said, "I don't know how many of you go out and dissipate at night—I'll go with you, because I don't have to play the next day—but if you get out there and can't cut the mustard, I don't want you."

I've seen him leave two ball players. He'd say, "Synchronize your watches by mine, because we're leaving such and such a time." Charlie'd say, "Let's go." I've seen two ball players running behind the bus. He really meant it.

When he was manager he was about 50 years old, and he would dare any left-hander—give him two strikes and dare him to throw anything he wanted to throw, and he'd never get it by him for the third strike.

During World War II Charleston worked at the Philadelphia quartermaster depot and played for the team there while also manag-

Army Cooper (left) and Oscar Charleston (right) as managers of the 1938 East-West game at Comiskey Park.

ing the Stars. A young GI named Oliver Compton pitched for the depot team, managed by Charleston. At first Compton didn't comprehend who Charleston was until his father asked incredulously, "Do you know who you're playing for?"

Charleston played first as well as managed. "Even then he could hit that ball," Compton said. "He'd hit it out by the car barns in the outfield, and it rolled a city block. And he could bunt, put a back spin on it, the third baseman would throw wild across the diamond and he'd end up on second. He was fast, even for his age, still playing ball for the fun of it."

Compton and Charleston had the same initials. "Well," Charleston would tell his pitcher, "the old C-boys did it tonight."

But "he had a temper, he could get mad," Compton said. "One game he called the umpire 'Hitler.' They threw him out of the ball game of course."

Charleston had two uniforms in his trunk, Compton recalled, one for the Philadelphia Stars, the other for the Brooklyn Brown Bombers, Branch Rickey's team that played in Ebbets Field and that Rickey used as a cover to scout Jackie Robinson and other black prospects.

It was Charleston who urged Rickey to sign a good-looking catcher by the name of Roy Campanella. So it was Campanella, not Charleston, who would make it to the white major leagues and eventually become the second black elected to the Hall of Fame.

That marked the death of the Negro leagues. Charleston moved back to Indianapolis to manage the Indianapolis Clowns, a pale version of the once mighty black teams of the past, although later they did send a kid named Hank Aaron to the big time.

Charleston was always ready to coach youngsters. Sam Jethroe, who would go to the Boston Braves, says Charleston taught him how to stay in the box against side-armers: "Draw that line; you can't go back on a side-armer like Ewell Blackwell. Charleston taught me that."

In 1954 Charleston was living in Philadelphia, as unknown and neglected by a new generation of fans as he had been ignored by the white world for almost four decades. In October he suffered a heart attack and tumbled down a flight of stairs. His death, like his life, went virtually unreported in the white press, which remained, to the end, almost thoroughly ignorant of the man who may have been the greatest baseball player of all time.

How good was Oscar Charleston?

John McGraw reportedly thought he was the best player ever. So did George Moriarity, ex-Detroit Tiger third baseman and umpire. And Grantland Rice, the sports writer, enthusiastically concurred. Black historian Ric Roberts, said that Rice in a column entitled "No

Greater Ball Player," wrote flatly: "It's impossible for anybody to be a better ball player than Oscar Charleston."

McGraw just shook his head and sighed: "If only I could calcimine him."

OSCAR CHARLESTON
by
David J. Malarcher

Sleep, Charlie! thou, the great, the strong!
　Within the depths of mud and mire!
While high above the diamond throng
　Thy sterling statue in retire
Proclaims the splendor of thy game,
　Thy paramount, unequaled fame!

Thou were the best who roamed the field!
　Thy stalwart fingers never failed
The batters' erring fate to seal,
　The pitchers' powers wrought too frail!
Oh! would thy skill could live always
　To stir the sportsman happy praise!

Sleep, Charlie! I, who knew thee well,
　Do here declare to Earth and time
In Heaven's language, thus to tell,
　In poignant poetry divine,
The glory of thy destiny
　Thus this undying rhyme to thee!

Sleep, Charlie! now in holy dust!
　(As mighty Cobb and Petway rest)
Bearing the praise of all of us,
　The diamond's greatest and the less
Here honor we on thee bestow,
　That ages will thy greatness know.

Oscar Charleston

Year	Team	G	EABᵇ	H	2B	3B	HR	BA	SB	(W-L)
1919	Chicago	4	17	4	—	—	—	.222	—	
1920	Indianapolis	45	142	52	7	4	6	.366		
	Cuba	—	39	16	2	0	0	.471*	2	
1921	St. Louis	60	212	92	14	11*	15*	.434	34*	
1922	Indianapolis	65	264	93	17	7	15	.366	21	
	Cuba	—	92	41	9	3	1	.446*	—	
1923	Indianapolis	60	213	66	12	7	8	.310	13	(2-1)
	Cuba	—	236	89	9	5	3	.377	31*	
1924	Harrisburg	54	207	81	16	5	8	.391	3	
	Cuba	—	153	40	10	4	4	.261	—	
1925	Harrisburg	—	237	99	15*	4	16*	.418*	—	
	Cuba	5	19	8	—	—	—	.421	—	
1926	Harrisburg	52	153	42	8	1	8	.275	—	
	Cuba	—	144	58	—	—	—	.403	—	
1927	Harrisburg	69	244	84	18*	5	12*	.335	4	
	Cuba	—	125	46	—	—	—	.368	11*	
1928	Philadelphia	50	197	71	8	2	7	.360	9	
	Cuba	—	24	6	—	—	—	.250	—	
1929	Philadelphia	22	82	27	1	1	1	.339	2	
1930	Grays	17	69	23	2	4*	6	.333	0	
1931	Grays	27	101	40	11	2	1	.396	0	
1932	Pittsburgh	32	129	35	6	2	5	.271	2	
1933	Pittsburgh	37	117	44	9	4	9	.376	3	
1934	Pittsburgh	34	127	42	6	2	5	.333	1	
1935	Pittsburgh	33	118	34	3	0	1	.288	1	
1936	Pittsburgh	12	38	8	2	0	2	.211	0	
1937	Pittsburgh	3	10	1	0	0	0	.100	0	
Totals			3479	1228	183	70	136	.353	144	

Post-Season

1930	Playoff	7	27	5	0	0	1	.181	0	
1935	Playoff	1ᵃ	2	1	0	0	2	.500	—	
Totals		8	29	6	0	0	3	.207	0	
East-West		3	10	0	0	0	0	.000	0	

* Led league.
ᵃ Incomplete.
ᵇ Estimated At Bats.

Oscar Charleston vs. White Big Leaguers

Year	AB	H	2B	3B	HR	Pitcher	(W-L)
1915	4	0	0	0	0	George Dauss, Detroit	(23-13)
	4	2	1	0	0	Reb Russell, White Sox	(11-10)
	1	0	0	0	0	Reb Russell, White Sox	
1916	3	2	0	0	0	Art Nehf, Braves	(7-5)
1917	(4)*	2	0	0	0	Jess Barnes, Braves	(13-21)
	2	1	0	0	0	Hod Eller, Reds	(10-5)
	(4)	—	—	—	1	Walter Johnson, Washington	(23-16)
1920	3	2	0	0	1	George Lyons, Cards	(2-1)
	4	0	0	0	0	Jess Haines, Cards	(13-20)
1921	6	1	0	0	0	(Dixie Walker), Bill Pertica, Cards	(14-10)
	4	2	1	0	1	Jess Haines, Cards	(18-12)
	4	0	0	0	0	Lou North, Cards	(4-4)
	5	2	—	—	—	Bill Pertica, Cards	(14-10)
	4	2	0	0	1	Jesse Petty, Dodgers	(0-0)
1922	4	2	0	0	0	Howard Ehmke, Tigers	(17-17)
	5	3	1	0	1	Bert Cole, Tigers	(7-4)
1923	3	1	0	0	0	Dave Danforth, Browns	(16-14)
	(4)	3	—	—	—	Elam Vangilder, Browns	(16-17)
	(4)	2	0	0	1	Ray Kolp, Browns	(5-12)
	2	1	1	0	0	Bert Cole	(13-5)
						George Dauss, Tigers	(21-13)
	4	0	0	0	0	Howard Pillette, Detroit	(14-19)
1923-4	4	1	0	0	0	Oscar Fuhr, Red Sox	(3-6)
1924-5	4	0	0	0	0	John Cooney, Braves	(8-9)
	3	1	0	0	0	John Cooney	
1926	(4)	1	0	0	1	Lefty Grove, Athletics	(13-13)
	(4)	2	0	0	0	Jack Quinn, Athletics	(10-11)
1926-7	(4)	—	—	—	1	Dolph Luque, Reds	(13-16)
	4	1	0	0	0	Dolph Luque	
	4	2	0	0	0	Dolph Luque	
	4	1	0	0	0	Dolph Luque, Reds	(13-12)
	4	0	0	0	0	Dolph Luque, Reds	
1928	(4)	1	0	0	0	Joe Bush, Athletics	(2-1)
	(4)	0	0	0	0	Johnny Ogden, Browns	(15-16)
	(4)	2	1	0	0	Ed Rommel, Athletics	(13-5)
	(4)	1	0	0	0	Lefty Grove, Athletics	(24-8)
1930	3	1	0	0	0	Earl Whitehill, Tigers	(17-13)
	(4)	3	1	0	0	Earl Whitehill	
	2	1	0	0	0	Snipe Hansen, Phils	(0-7)
	3	1	0	1	0	George Earnshaw, Athletics	(21-7)
	3	1	1	0	0	Bobby Burke, Senators	(8-3)
	3	1	1	1	1	Jim Weaver, Cubs	
	4	1	0	0	0	Fred Frankhouse, Braves	(8-8)
1932	5	1	0	0	0	Frankhouse; Bill Swift, Pirates	(14-10)
	3	1	0	0	0	Frankhouse, Swift	
	5	2	1	0	0	Swift; Larry French, Pirates	(15-13)

continued on next page

Oscar Charleston vs. White Big Leaguers (continued)

	(4)	—	—	—	2	Frankhouse; Parmelee, Dodgers	
	(4)	1	0	0	0	Roy Parmelee	(0-3)
1934	1	0	0	0	0	Dizzy Dean, Cardinals	(29-7)
1936	1	0	0	0	0	Jim Weaver, Pirates	(14-6)
	5	2	1	0	0	Weaver; Mike Ryba, Cardinals	(13-2)
	5	2	0	0	0	Ryba, Jim Winford, Cardinals	(11-10)
	5	2	0	0	0	Earl Whitehill, Senators	(14-11)
						Vern Kennedy, White Sox	(21-9)
	4	0	0	0	0	Kennedy; Jack Knott, Browns	(9-17)
	4	0	0	0	0	Ted Lyons	(10-13)

Total 53 games	195	62	10	2	11	Average .318	

* At bats in parentheses are estimated.

9

Cristobal Torriente:
The Cuban Strongboy

I was down in Havana in 1920 with Babe Ruth and about 12 of the New York Giants. That's over 50 years ago, but I can still recall Torriente. He was a tremendous guy. Big left-handed hitter, played the outfield. I think I was playing third base at that time, and he hit a ground ball by me, and you know, that's one of those things—look in the glove, it might be there. But it wasn't in my glove. It dug a hole about a foot deep on its way to left field. And I'm glad I wasn't in front of it! He was a power hitter. He could hit a ball! Pretty good? In those days Torriente was a hell of a ball player. Christ, I'd like to whitewash him and bring him up.

Frankie Frisch

In the early 1920s Cristobal Torriente, the hefty Cuban, was Rube Foster's power hitter on the great Chicago American Giants. Speedsters like Jelly Gardner, Jimmy Lyons, Dave Malarcher, or Bingo DeMoss would bedevil the opposition with their bunting and running. "Then," said pitcher Bill Foster, "here comes Torriente, and he would hit the runs in.

"A big strong fellow, with a good disposition. We'd say, 'Torriente, you gonna get 'em?' He'd say, 'Me get 'em!' And he would too. He could get wood on that ball."

Torriente wore bracelets on his wrist, recalled Jay Wiggins, a youthful Chicago fan at the time. "When he'd shake those bracelets, look for the ball up against the fence; that's where he was going to hit it."

The experts agree. Cristobal Torriente was one of the three best Negro league outfielders of all time—Cum Posey said he was the best.

In picking Torriente on their all-time all-black team in 1952, the editors of the Pittsburgh *Courier* called him "a prodigious hitter, a rifle-armed thrower, and a tower of strength on the defense." He had "deceptive speed and the ability to cover worlds of territory, from the right-field foul line to deep right center. He was one of the best bad-ball hitters in baseball and could hit equally well to all fields."

Torriente was a steady .300-hitter. His high was .402 as a youth in Cuba in 1915–1916. His lifetime .352 there is third highest ever, behind Jud Wilson and Oscar Charleston, reported historian Jorge Figueredo. Torriente hit .339 in the U.S. Negro leagues (including Cuba) and .311 against U.S. big leaguers.

And when Torriente got a ball in the air, it sailed for distance. "I've seen a lot of home runs," Jelly Gardner said, "but I think Torriente hit the longest one I ever saw. The American Giants had a fence there over 400 feet, and the ball went out of there on a line. The fence was about 20 feet tall. It didn't just get out, it went *way* out. Center field, dead center."

Torriente was built like Muhammad Ali, said Webster McDonald. "A beautiful pair of shoulders."

He wasn't a big man, added old-time fan Pedro Cardona, "but he had a wonderful big swing." He was built like Babe Ruth, Cardona said, with a strong upper torso and thin legs. Torri liked to play with a red handkerchief around his neck, standing for the Havana Reds.

Torriente stood deep in the batters' box, like Roberto Clemente, said old-time pitcher Frank Sykes, a teammate of the great Smokey Joe Williams. But Torri hit Joe "just like he was his cousin."

Besides being a heavy hitter, Torriente was almost as fast as the other "race horses" who were the American Giants' trademark. He took bunting practice right along with them, and though he usually was given the "hit" sign in games, if the score was onesided, he'd look at Foster and ask, "Jock, me bunt, no?" He also played a pretty good second base or third base (left-handed!) and could pitch and win a game on occasion.

Torriente even played third base on occasion (left-handed!) and he was a good pitcher in a pinch. His lifetime pitching record in the Negro league was 15–5.

No wonder the New York Giants were scouting him. Since he was a relatively light-colored Cuban ("Indian color," said Kansas City pitcher Chet Brewer; the same complexion as Babe Ruth, said Cardona), he might have passed and gone on to stardom in the big leagues, but his hair gave him away.

Torriente was born in Cuba in 1895. At the age of 17 he joined the army and was assigned to the artillery because he was husky enough to hoist the heavy artillery pieces onto the mules. The artillery team played all the teams in Havana, according to Rogelio Crespo, and in 1913 promoter Tinti Molina signed Torriente to play in the United States with the Cuban Stars against the best black and semipro teams. That winter Torriente joined the famous Havana Reds and hit .301.

The next winter the youth joined the great Almendares Blues and raised his average to .337. The Blues' stadium was a huge park, and Crespo said he never saw a ball hit out of it. Torriente hit only two home runs that winter, presumably on the road, but they were enough to lead the league.

The following winter he hit a league-leading .387 and was also tops in triples.

In 1915–1916 Torriente, now 20, raised hits average to .402 and led the league in triples, home runs, and stolen bases.

"The first time I saw him was in 1916," said Dave Malarcher, a young outfielder with C. I. Taylor's Indianapolis ABCs. "The Cubans came over that summer, and he was hitting them against the fences. He was powerful—big, strong, and a fine fellow to get along with."

Perhaps Torriente remained in the United States for a few years,

Cristobal Torriente as a Chicago American Giant.

because he did not play in the Cuban league again until 1919. In 1917 he signed to play with J. L. Wilkinson's All Nations club.

The following year he signed up with Foster's American Giants. That fall he faced Yankee spitballer Picus Jack Quinn (5–1) and former New York Giant Jim Middleton. Unimpressed, Torri slugged three hits against them.

In 1919 Oscar Charleston himself joined the American Giants, but he couldn't budge Torriente from center field. Charleston played left, and Jimmy Lyons, one of the great greyhounds of baseball, played right. They gave the American Giants one of the finest out-fields of all time.

Back in Havana that winter, Torriente played for Almendares against a touring squad of Pittsburgh Pirates, who finished third in the National League that year. In his first game, against Leon Cadore (14–12), on loan from the Dodgers, Torriente came up in the ninth still hitless, then smashed what one Havana paper called "a phenomenal home run" to center field. Hal Carlson (8–10) held him hitless in the second game. But he went 1-for-3 against Jeff Pfeffer (17–13) in his third contest. Still, Almendares had lost all three games. In the fourth game, against Elmer Ponder (0–5), Torriente collected two hits in four at bats, knocked in one run, and scored the other, as Almendares triumphed, 2–1.

The Pirates were followed to Havana by an All-American squad led by Quinn. Torriente clipped Quinn (15–14) and Mule Watson (0–1) for a double in four times up to help Almendares' Adolfo Luque win the opener, 3–2. Two days later Quinn got revenge by a score of 1–0, as Torriente went 1-for-3. Torri went hitless in the third game, another 1–0 thriller won by Quinn. In the fourth game, however, the Cuban muscle-man exploded with a two-run homer to tie the game, and Almendares won it in the ninth, 6–4. Then in the final game, against Watson, Torri cracked another homer plus a single in a 16–5 rout. In 11 games that winter, the Cuban strongboy had slugged the big leaguers at a .359 clip.

In the regular season, after the Americans had left, Torri hit the Cuban hurlers for a .360 mark and led the league in doubles, triples, homers, stolen bases, and batting. (He hit only one home run in 25 games, but it was good enough to top the league.)

In 1920 Torriente was with the American Giants to inaugurate the new Negro National League. He hit .396 and just missed the batting crown by three points.

That fall, 1920, John McGraw's New York Giants arrived in Havana, along with the new home-run phenom, Babe Ruth, who received the unheard of total of $1,000 a game from Cuban promoter

Abel Linares. Young Frankie Frisch was along with the rest of the Giants.

In the first game, against the Havana Reds, Ruth got a single and triple. In his next game, however, he struck out three straight times against Jose Acosta, the little knuckle-baller who was 5–4 for the Washington Senators that summer; the Reds won the game, 7–1, Figueredo said.

In game-three Ruth faced Almendares—and Torriente—for the first time. McGraw put his first baseman, George "High Pockets" Kelly, in to pitch against the Cubans' Isidro Fabre. In the first inning Ruth walked and scored a run. In the second, Torriente clouted a home run over the left-center-field fence.

In the third Ruth hit a ground ball and was safe on an error. In the bottom of the inning Torriente again cleared the left-center-field wall.

In the fifth, according to Figueredo, Ruth grounded out weakly, then decided to pitch himself against the pesky Torriente, as Kelly moved to first base. Ruth, of course, had been a star pitcher with the Red Sox in 1917–1919, setting a World Series record for consecutive shutout innings which still stands. Apparently unimpressed, Torriente drilled a hard shot toward left, which Frisch said later "almost took my leg off!" and Torriente slid into second with a two-run double. The crowd went wild, and, Figueredo wrote, "the Bambino frowned incredulously." Ruth ended the inning by fanning the next three men. Shaken, he left the mound, never to pitch seriously again.

In the sixth Ruth walked. An inning later Kelly, back on the mound, finally got Torriente on a grounder to the box. But in the eighth, with a man on base, Torriente smashed his third home run over the wall, giving him three homers and six runs batted in for the day.

The Los Angeles *Times,* in reporting the game, referred to Torriente as "the Babe Ruth of Cuba." This wasn't entirely apt, however, since Torriente had hit three home runs, while Ruth hadn't gotten a hit all day. In fact, on the entire tour, Ruth got only two homers.

When I asked Kelly about Torriente 60 years later, High Pockets volunteered that he was "the best hitter down there." But he did not mention—and I was too tactful to mention—the three home runs the big fellow had smacked off him. Since Torri had led the Cuban league with one and two home runs in a full season, three in one game was quite a feat!

Torriente continued hot against Giant pitchers Pol Perritt (0–0), Jesse Barnes (20–15), and Rosy Ryan (0–1). He got one single in two at bats in a 15-inning, 7–7, tie. He slapped a triple and single off Perritt

Game of November 4, 1920—Havana, Cuba

New York Giants		AB	R	H	Almendares		AB	R	H
LF	George Burns	4	0	1	3B	Bartolo Portuondo	2	4	1
SS	Dave Bancroft	4	1	2	1B	Armando Marsans	4	1	2
CF	Ross Youngs	5	0	1	RF	Bernardo Baro	1	0	0
1B/P	Babe Ruth	3	1	0	LF	Merito Acosta	5	1	2
3B	Frank Frisch	4	1	2	CF	Cristobal Torriente	5	3	4
P/1B	George Kelly	5	0	0	SS	Papo Gonzalez	4	0	1
2B	Larry Doyle	4	1	0	2B	Paito Herrera	4	1	1
C	Earl Smith	4	0	1	C	Eufemio Abreu	4	0	0
RF	Frank Snyder	4	0	1	P	Isidro Fabre	4	1	1
		37	4	8			33	11	12

New York   300 010 000— 4 8 2
Almendares 041 021 21x—11 12 2

Home Runs: Torriente 3.   Two-Base Hits: Torriente. Sacrifice Hits: Baro 2. Stolen Bases: Bancroft, Frisch. Hit-by-Pitch: Frisch (by Fabre), Portuondo (by Kelly).   Strike Outs: Kelly 6, Fabre 2.   Walks: Kelly 4, Fabre 4. Passed Ball: Smith. (Courtesy of Jorge Figueredo)

in a 6–5 victory. And in his last two games against Perritt, he lined out four more hits in eight at bats.

The Giant pitchers must have heaved a sigh as they embarked for home.

Next the touring Bacharach Giants, a big-league black team from Atlantic City, felt the sting of Torriente's bat. He slugged three triples in one game against them.

The Cuban pitchers did much better. Over the winter they held Torriente to a .296 average, four triples, and one home run in 27 games.

In the summer of 1921 Torriente was back in Chicago, where he hit .332. He also pitched five games and won four of them.

"He hit right- or left-handed pitching." Jelly Gardner whistled. "I've seen him hit balls so close to fellows that they would just have to reach out for them—one or two feet from them—and they still couldn't touch them, he'd hit them so hard."

Torriente once hit a line drive at Kansas City second baseman Newt Allen and almost broke his foot.

Chicago shortstop Bobby Williams remembered a Torriente home run in Kansas City. "There was a clock about 17 feet above the center-field fence, and Torriente hit one so terrifically, it hit the clock and the hands just started going around and around. He got a double on it."

Pitchers learned not to throw at him. "You get him wild and scared," Webster McDonald warned. "The more you throw at him, the harder he hits them."

Torriente's English was colorful at times. The U.S. income tax laws upset him, and when his pay check was thinner than anticipated, he'd say in disgust, "The ducks (deductions) got it. Me going back to Cuba this winter. Don't want the ducks to get my money."

"He liked to clown," McDonald said. "Torriente, Jelly Gardner, and Jimmy Brown, a catcher—they were the playboys on the club, always at the nightclubs. Rube used to take their money away from them, suspend them, when they had a bad day."

But Torriente didn't have many bad days. That fall he won the Negro world series for the American Giants against Cannonball Dick Redding of the Bacharachs. In the third and final game, with the series tied one game each, Torri took the mound himself for the first three innings, then slugged one of the longest home runs ever seen in Dyckman Oval in the Bronx, to win it, 6–3. That same year his homer in Philadelphia's Shibe Park helped give Chicago a 5–2 win over Hilldale, another top club in the East.

In 1922 Torriente hit .350 for the American Giants and .350 that

Cristobal Torriente (seated, far left) with the 1921 Chicago American Giants. Also pictured are Bobby Williams (seated, second from left) and Jelly Gardner (seated, second from right).

winter for Havana. He led the Cuban league in steals for the third time, runs for a record-breaking fourth time, and homers for the fifth time, Figueredo says.

Back in the United States in 1923, Torriente led the league with a .389 average. He followed it with .356 in Cuba that winter. His 1924 marks were .331 summer and .380 winter.

His average fell off to .241 in Chicago in 1925. It's not clear why, although it may be that the nightlife was beginning to affect his playing. Though he bounced back with a .344 mark in Cuba that winter, Foster traded the big guy to Kansas City.

Torriente responded with a .339 average for his new club in 1926. Then he bedeviled Chicago in the play-off that fall. In the opening game, against Bill Foster, Torriente slugged two doubles, good for two runs and a 4–3 victory. In the second game his sacrifice fly knocked in the winning run. He went 0-for-3 against Webster McDonald in game three, which Kansas City also won, 5–0. It looked like a rout. But, though Torri kept hitting—he hit .407 for the series—Chicago swept the last four games and the play-off.

Torriente's average tailed off to .294 that winter.

Kansas City dealt him to the Detroit Stars for 1927, and Torri rewarded his new owners with a .320 mark; he also was 2–1 as a pitcher. He raised those figures to .336 and 7–3 in 1928.

But the drinking was getting to him. "Instead of going back to Cuba to manage, he stayed in Chicago and made his own booze," Crespo said. "The winter was cold, and he drank, drank, drank. His face swelled up from the booze. At spring training he couldn't stand up in the batters' box without falling. He was in such bad condition, no team wanted him."

Crespo took his friend to Spring Valley, Illinois to play with Gilkerson's Union Giants, a step down from the Negro National League. From there Torriente drifted to New York. He resurfaced in 1934 for one game with the Cleveland Cubs.

In 1935 pitcher Rodolfo Fernandez ran into Torriente in Chicago. Some time later the great Martin Dihigo found him living there in poor circumstances and brought him to New York. He died there about 1938, Fernandez said. He had no money; "the only friend he had was liquor."

Crespo said they draped a Cuban flag over his coffin, and a politician arranged to return the body to Havana.

Torriente left the memory of a younger, healthier man, probably the greatest batter Cuba has ever produced. Surely the choice lies between Torriente and Martin Dihigo, who came up a little after him. "If you give me Torriente or Dihigo in right field," said at least one observer, Cardona, "I'd say Torriente."

"He was a powerful man," nodded Malarcher. "C. I. Taylor [owner of the ABCs] said if he was standing on the street and saw Torriente go by, he would say, 'There goes a ball club!'

"And he was too."

Cristobal Torriente

Year	Team	G	AB	H	2B	3B	HR	BA	SB	(W-L)
1913	Cuba	58	206	62	6	5	3	.301	19	
1914	Cuba	34	124	48*	5	5*	0	.337	19	
1915	Cuba	2	8	4	0	2	0	.500	0	
1916	Cuba	39	139	56*	5	6*	2*	.402	28*	
1919	Chicago	4	16	4	—	—	—	.250		
	Cuba	25	100	36	5*	5*	1*	.360*	10*	
1920	Chicago	25	93	37	7	3	1	.396	2	
	Cuba	27	98	29	3	4*	1*	.296	3	
1921	Chicago	64	199	66	5	10	7	.337	18	(4-1)
	Cuba	5	20	7	0	1*	0	.350	0	
1922	Chicago	—	120	42	1	2	3	.350	3	
	Cuba	46	174	61*	9	6	4*	.351	15*	
1923	Chicago	58	216	84	15	3	5	.389*	6	(2-0)
	Cuba	—	239	85	9	1	2	.356	12	
1924	Chicago	68	239	79	21*	4	7	.331	9	
	Cuba	46	163	62	13*	2	4	.380	6	
1925	Chicago	—	278	67	7	6	6	.241	2	
	Cuba	32	122	43	7	4	1	.344	0	
1926	Kansas City	70	254	86	17	5	4	.339	5	
1927	Cuba	6	17	5	0	0	0	.294	0	
	Detroit	84	297	95	18	2	4	.320	6	(2-1)
1928	Detroit	37	107	36	5	3	2	.336	3	(7-3)
1934	Cleveland	1	4	1	0	0	0	.250		
Totals			3233	1095	158	79	57	.339	166	(15-5)
Post-Season										
1921	World Series	4	16	4	0	1	0	.250	—	(0-1)
1926	Play-off	8	32	11	2	0	0	.344	0	
Totals		12	48	15	2	1	0	.313	0	(0-1)

* Led league.

Cristobal Torriente vs. White Big Leaguers

Year	AB	H	2B	3B	HR	Pitcher	(W-L)
1918	(4)*	3	1	0	0	Quinn (5-1), (Middleton)a	
1919	3	1	0	0	1	Cadore	(14-12)
	4	1	0	0	0	Ponder	
	2	2	—	—	—	Unknown	
	3	1	0	0	0	Pfeffer	(17-13)
	4	0	0	0	0	Carlson	(8-10)
	3	2	1	0	0	Ponder	(0-5)
	4	2	0	0	0	Ponder	
	4	1	1	0	0	Quinn (15-14), Watson (0-1)	
	3	1	—	—	—	Quinn	
	3	0	0	0	0	Quinn	
	4	2	0	0	1	Geary (0-3), Watson	
	5	2	0	0	1	Watson	
1920	2	0	0	0	0	Ryan, Perritt, Barnes	
	1	0	0	0	0	J. Barnes	(20-15)
	4	0	0	0	0	Ryan	(0-1)
	4	2	0	1	0	Perritt	(0-0)
	4	1	0	0	0	Perritt	
	4	3	—	—	—	Perritt	
1923	3	1	0	0	0	Pillette	(14-14)
	2	0	0	0	0	Dauss	(21-13)
1923-24	4	1	0	0	0	Luque	(27-8)
	3	0	0	0	0	Luque	
	4	0	0	0	0	Luque	
	3	1	1	0	0	Luque	
	3	0	0	0	0	Dibut	(3-0)
	2	1	0	0	0	Dibut	
	1	0	0	0	0	Dibut	
Total 28 games	90	28	4	1	3	Average: .311	

*At bats in parentheses are estimated.
a Not a major league pitcher.

10

Dick Lundy:
King Richard

If you could speak another language, you'd be my second base combination.

Connie Mack
to Dick Lundy
and Bunny Downs

Pop Lloyd, Dick Lundy, Dobie Moore, Willie Wells—the Negro leagues produced at least four top-notch shortstops. Many authorities who saw all four insist that Lundy was the king of them all.

"Lundy was the greatest at shortstop," said Napoleon "Chance" Cummings, who had seen Pop Lloyd since boyhood days in Florida.

> Yeah, field and bat. Lloyd wouldn't have a chance. Lundy could go behind second base and get a ball and throw you out, go behind third and do the same thing. There's nobody in the big leagues could beat Lundy playing shortstop. Nobody. Hans Wagner? Yeah, I've seen him play. And Joe Cronin, I didn't think he was such a heck of a shortstop because he had to do this—go down on one knee when he fielded a ball. I've seen shortstops come and go, but Dick Lundy was my favorite.

It's a view shared by many others, including catcher Yank Deas and outfielder Ted Page. Jake Stephens, a great fielding shortstop himself, also called Lundy the best. "Lundy had great range. He could shoot you out from left field."

Satchel Paige, who did not see Lloyd but did see Willie Wells, liked Wells at bat but Lundy in the field. "It looked like he knowed where you were going to hit the ball," Paige said. "He was just like Lou Boudreau."

For years Lundy played beside Oliver Marcelle, considered by many the slickest fielding third baseman in black history. In Cuba one winter, said Judy Johnson, then playing second base, one hard hit grounder went through Marcelle's legs. Lundy dashed behind third, back-handed it, and leaped to make a force play at second, only to

135

find Johnson several feet from the bag with his mouth agape—Judy just couldn't believe that Lundy had gotten to the ball. John McGraw, who saw Dick play in Havana, shook his head. "It a shame you're a black boy," he said. "You could name your own price."

"Dick Lundy did everything with swing," said pitcher Webster McDonald. "He was a big man for a shortstop, but he was graceful."

"Lundy was very graceful, a nice rhythm to him," said sports writer Henry "Whitey" Gruhler, who covered the Bacharachs for the Atlantic City *Press*. "He was somewhat like Lloyd. They were both long-armed guys. They covered a lot of ground. Lundy looked slow, but he was moving fast." (He was faster than Lloyd, said Bob Berman, an old-time semipro catcher who often played against the black teams.)

For two brief years, 1923 and 1924, Lloyd and Lundy played side-by-side on the Bacharach Giants of Atlantic City. Lloyd, ten years older than Dick, gladly moved himself to second to let the younger man handle the more demanding shortstop.

After Lloyd left the Bacharachs, Lundy replaced him as manager and accomplished something that Lloyd was never able to do—he led the team to the Eastern Colored League pennants in 1926 and 1927.

Originally a right-hander, Lundy learned to switch-hit. His specialty was wicked line drives, and pitchers found they couldn't throw a fast ball by him. Lundy's lifetime average was .327 against Negro League pitching, .221 against white big leaguers.

Dick Lundy was born July 10, 1899, in Jacksonville, Florida, near Lloyd's hometown of Palatka. He went to school with Willis Crump, McKinley "Bunny" Downs, Shang Johnson, and Chance Cummings. "Lundy was out of this world," Crump said. "A big fine boy. One of his hands was as big as two of yours." Though younger than most of the others, Lundy earned a place on their team, the Jacksonville Giants, in 1915. That was the year Atlantic City mayor Harry Bacharach went through Jacksonville, saw the Giants play, and signed the whole team to play in Atlantic City as the Bacharach Giants. In the words of sports writer Ric Roberts, "He told them to put down their suitcases forever and come north with him."

Lundy played both third and short, but he was so fast that he was shifted to short permanently. He played one year with the Bs, then jumped to the Philadelphia Hilldales in 1917. That fall the 18-year-old Lundy got his first look at white big-league pitching. Bullet Joe Bush of the Athletics shut him out the first two games before Dick finally solved him for two hits in game three.

Lundy returned to the B's in 1921, hitting .484 in 17 games.

When the Eastern Colored League was born in 1923, the Bacharachs joined up. Dick hit an even .300, then sailed to Cuba, where he hit .308.

Lundy played to win. Judy Johnson played on the rival Hilldales in the United States, but the two were teammates and roommates in Cuba. However, friendship was forgotten when they got back home in the spring. On one play, Johnson says, he took the throw in plenty of time to tag Dick. Instead, Lundy ripped Judy's arm with his spikes. "Heh, Lundy," Johnson protested, "I'm your roommate."

"We're playing baseball now," Lundy growled. "Get out of the way."

The usually mild-mannered Johnson said he tried to spike only

Dick Lundy.

two men in his life. "One was Lundy. I said, 'OK, I'm gonna try to get that so-and-so.' We used to have a little handbag, and there was always a file in the bag." After preparing his spikes appropriately, Johnson lit out for second on a steal. "Lundy ran over to cover. I was waiting for him to come down to tag me—I was going to cut him in half. But when I let out to hit him, he hit me up side the head with the ball. I was going through the air, and he just popped me right side of the head. He just *blinded* me."

In 1924 Pop Lloyd joined the Bs as manager and second baseman. It was one of the great infields of all time, with Chance Cummings (named for Frank Chance) at first base and Oliver Marcelle at third. Dick raised his average to .360, with 13 home runs in 131 at bats, his all-time high.

In 1926 Lundy replaced Lloyd as manager. He hit .329 and led the Bs from fourth place to their first pennant. If there had been a vote for most valuable player that year, Dick Lundy would surely have won it.

The World Series against the Chicago American Giants went ten games, and Lundy delivered several key hits. In the opener, he lined out two singles in three at bats against Chicago's great lefty, Bill Foster, to help gain a 3–3 tie. In the fourth game his triple with the bases loaded, also against Foster, helped the Bs earn another tie, 4–4. And in the fourth game Dick drilled two singles and a double, the two-bagger igniting a six-run rally in a 7–5 Bacharach victory.

All in all Lundy hit .306 in the series.

Cummings, however, blamed Lundy for the Bs eventual defeat. Dick was a proud man, a sharp dresser who liked to smoke big cigars. So was Cummings, and a jealousy sprang up between them. In the sixth game, with the Bs ahead two games to one (plus the two ties), the jealousy burst into the open. Curve baller Rats Henderson was on the mound for the Bacharachs in the ninth inning with the score tied, 4–4. Chicago manager Dave Malarcher was on third with two out and catcher Johnny Hines up. Cummings urged Lundy to walk Hines. Lundy refused. Whereupon Hines smacked a sharp single over the infield to win the game, tie the series, and give the Chicagoans the momentum for final victory. "Lundy was bull-headed at times," Cummings muttered.

In 1927 Lundy hit .306 and once again brought the Bs home first in the East.

The World Series was another thriller against Chicago. The American Giants won the first four games, and the Bs were all but dead. They would have to sweep the last five games to win the best-of-nine series. They did win the fifth game, and Dick's two singles helped gain a sixth game tie, 1–1. The Bs added two more victories to tie the series four games apiece, but then Foster closed the door and won the final game, 1–0.

Unfortunately, the Bacharachs were not doing well at the box office—their park, a former greyhound track on South Carolina Avenue, was padlocked by the sheriff before one game because they owed back rent. In fact, the whole league was hurting financially, and in 1928 the Eastern Colored League was no more. The teams continued to play, however, and Lundy hit .410, second best among the Eastern clubs—Lloyd topped him with a sensational .564.

That autumn Lundy joined the Baltimore Black Sox for the traditional barnstorming series against white big leaguers. He ripped the Philadelphia A's Ed Rommel (13–5) for two hits in one game, then

Dick Lundy.

clipped the great Lefty Grove (24–8) for two more in another for a 9–3 win.

In the spring of 1929 Lundy and Marcelle joined the Black Sox in the new Negro American League and anchored what just may have been the finest infield in the history of American baseball, black or white. Flashy Frank Warfield played second, and burly Jud Wilson, though no great glove man, hit a long ball at first base. Lundy hit .296, as the Sox swept to the pennant.

There was no World Series that year. But in two post-season games, Dick collected 3-for-8 against Rommel (who was 12–2) and St. Louis' Johnny Ogden (4–8).

In 1930 the league broke up again, a victim of the depression, but the Black Sox struggled on as an independent club. Dick hit .407 against other top black teams that summer and .357 against touring big leaguers that fall. In one game against Roy Sherid (12–13) of the Yankees, Dick found the bases loaded and the score tied, 5–5, in the ninth; he smashed a triple to win it, 8–5.

Lundy's average slipped to .255 in 1931, though Cum Posey of the Grays picked him on his authoritative black all-star team that year.

Dick made Posey's team again in 1932. That autumn he played his final two games against white big leaguers, clipping Buck "Bobo" Newsom for four hits in nine at bats. He hit the only home run he ever hit against the whites in one of the games. It helped win the game for the blacks, 9–8.

Lundy moved to Philadelphia in 1933 to manage the new club, the Stars, which owner Ed Bolden was forming to replace the Hilldales. After a year Dick moved on to manage the new Newark team, where he would help to develop youngsters such as Hall of Famers Ray Dandridge and Monte Irvin. That year Lundy was himself elected to the first black East-West, or all star, game, by vote of the fans. He also served as manager of the East.

Lundy remained at Newark until 1940 when his leg went bad and he had to retire. He returned to Jacksonville, working at the railroad station as a redcap. His old friends used to make it a point to stop and chat with him on their way to and from Cuba each winter. Later his eyesight failed, and he turned to shining shoes.

Cummings saw him one day and got a shine. "When he got through, I gave him a nickel note"—five dollars.

In 1965 death came to the man who many consider the king of shortstops.

Dick Lundy

Year	Team	G	EAB[a]	H	2B	3B	HR	BA	SB
1917	Bacharachs	2	6	0	0	0	0	.000	—
1919	Philadelphia	10	37	13	—	—	—	.351	—
1920	Atlantic City	2	8	0	0	0	0	.000	0
	Cuba	—	8	3	0	0	0	.375	—
1921	Atlantic City	17	62	30	3	4	2	.484	3
1922	Atlantic City	3	14	5	1	0	1	.357	0
1923	Atlantic City	14	54	16	—	—	—	.300	—
	Cuba	—	143	44	3	2	0	.308	0
1924	Atlantic City	33	131	39	9	3	13*	.360	7
	Cuba	—	139	49	11	2	3	.353	11*
1925	Atlantic City	51	191	55	8	2	3	.289	0
	Cuba	—	71	23	1	0	0	.324	—
1926	Atlantic City	62	225	74	13	2	2	.329	—
	Cuba	—	127	52	—	—	—	.410	—
1927	Atlantic City	95	408	125	9	4	11	.306	7
	Cuba	—	137	44	9	2	2	.321	1
1928	Atlantic City	48	173	71	5	3	5	.410	4
1929	Baltimore	54	206	61	10	0	4	.296	4
	Cuba	—	195	65	7	3	1	.333	—
1930	Baltimore	20	75	29	1	0	2	.407	0
	Cuba	—	56	19*	0	1	0	.339	3
1931	Baltimore	37	137	35	2	0	2	.255	0
1932	Baltimore	4	15	4	0	0	0	.267	1
1933	Philadelphia	12	39	6	0	0	0	.154	0
1934	Newark	8	29	8	2	1	0	.276	0
1935	Cubans-Newark	24	84	26	3	0	1	.310	0
Totals			2757	899	99	29	54	.321	40

			Post-Season						
1926	World Series	10	36	11	2	1	0	.306	4
1927	World Series	9	36	9	1	0	0	.250	0
Totals		19	72	20	3	1	0	.278	4
East-West		2	7	0	0	0	0	.000	0

[a] Estimated At Bats.
* Led league.

Dick Lundy vs. White Big Leaguers

Year	AB	H	2B	3B	HR	SB	Pitcher	(W-L)
1917	4	0	0	0	0	—	Bush	(11-17)
	4	0	0	0	0	0	Bush	
	4	2	—	—	—	—	Bush	
1919	5	1	0	0	0	—	Sharkey	(20-11)
	(4)*	0	0	0	0	—	Pennock	(16-8)
1928	(4)	2	0	0	0	—	Rommel	(13-5)
	4	2	0	0	0	0	Grove	(24-8)
	(4)	0	0	0	0	—	Ogden	(15-16)
1929	4	1	0	0	0	—	Ogden	(4-8)
	4	2	0	0	0	—	Rommel	(12-2)
1930	4	1	0	0	0	0	Rommel	(9-4)
	4	1	0	1	0	1	Rommel	
	4	1	0	1	0	0	Sherid	(12-13)
	4	0	0	0	0	0	Frankhouse	(9-9)
	3	0	0	0	0	0	Frankhouse	
1931	4	1	0	0	0	0	Burke	(8-3)
	2	1	1	0	0	0	Weaver	
	1	0	0	0	0	0	Frankhouse	(8-8)
1932	5	3	0	0	1	0	Newsom	(0-0)
	4	1	0	0	0	0	Newsom	
	4	0	0	0	0	0	Frankhouse	(4-6)
	3	0	0	0	0	0	Frankhouse	
	3	0	0	0	0	0	Frankhouse	
Total 23 games	86	19	1	2	1	1	Avg. .221	

* At bats in parentheses are estimated.

11

Oliver Marcelle:
The Ghost of New Orleans

*Oliver Marcelle could do everything! A fielding gem who
could go to his right or left with equal facility, could come up
with breath-taking plays on bunts. . . . He was a ball player's
ball player and the idol of fandom.*

Pittsburgh *Courier,*
naming Marcelle the
best black third baseman
of all time

Who was the greatest black third baseman of them all? The
Cooperstown Hall of Fame committee voted for Judy Johnson
and Ray Dandridge. But many an old-timer agrees with the *Courier's*
1952 poll of experts that the best of all was the handsome, graceful
Creole, Oliver "Ghost" Marcelle.

"They used to argue who was better, Marcelle or me," Johnson
said. "I could always out-hit him, and I could run faster. But he was
wonderful, made all the plays look easy." And, Judy admitted candidly: "I went to Cuba five times and never played third base. I always
played second base, and Marcelle played third."

Pitcher Holsey "Scrip" Lee played with Johnson on the 1924–1925
champion Hilldales and with Marcelle on the 1929 champion Baltimore Black Sox. Marcelle was the best, he said. "He made some of
the greatest stops you've ever seen." Lee considered himself a good
fielding pitcher, but Marcelle hollered him away from any ball on the
third-base side of the mound.

Another pitcher, Sam Streeter, agreed. "I think Marcelle got
more hard hit balls on the line than Judy," he said. At bat, Johnson
pulled the ball; Marcelle sprayed it to all fields. "And Marcelle was a
little more scrappy player. That was the biggest thing. A little more
lively player, all the time talking and boosting everything up."

Marcelle was faster than Johnson, nodded Dave Malarcher, who
himself was one of the top third basemen in the black leagues. And
Marcelle "always had a lot of fight, a lot of daring. That was one of his
failings, of course. He had a temper. I think that always handicaps a
man. Marcelle would squabble and argue all the time."

"Yes, he had a temper," admitted pitcher Juanelo Mirabal, "but

143

he was a terrific player in my book." To Mirabal, Marcelle was the best player who ever lived, "big league or whatever."

Marcelle once even picked a fight with Oscar Charleston. "I think Charleston was riding him from the bench," said Whitey Gruhler of the Atlantic City *Press*. Marcelle picked up a bat and smote Charleston over the head with it—a feat of courage that no other man ever dared attempt. "He was a spirited player," Gruhler said with an admiring shake of his head—"one of the game's most torrid hot-heads."

Marcelle could hit too. "A good hit-and-run man," said John "Buck" O'Neil, who later coached the Chicago Cubs. Marcelle stood deep in the box, then quickly stepped to the front of the plate.

Marcelle had a distinction shared by no other man, black or white. He held down third base on not one but three of the greatest infields ever put together—the Santa Clara Cuban champs of 1923–1924, the Bacharachs of 1925–1928, and the Baltimore Black Sox of 1929. They may have been the three finest infields of any time, of any race, of any league.

On Santa Clara, Marcelle played beside Kansas City shortstop Dobie Moore. On the latter two teams he joined graceful Dick Lundy. It is doubtful if any other two men, even Brooks Robinson and Mark Belanger of the Orioles, covered the left side of the infield as tightly as those two, unless it was Dandridge and Willie Wells of the Newark Eagles and Vera Cruz a decade later.

Santa Clara had Eddie Douglass on first and Frank Warfield on second. The Bacharachs boasted little Bunny Downs at second (he would later manage the young Hank Aaron on the Indianapolis Clowns) and slick fielding Chance Cummings at first. The Black Sox were perhaps the strongest of all, with Warfield on second and hard-hitting Jud Wilson on first.

Only two white infields of that era rivaled these three quartets— Connie Mack's "$100,000 infield" of Stuffy McGinnis, Eddie Collins, Jack Barry, and Home Run Baker; and the fabled Chicago Cubs' 1910 combination of Tinker-to-Evers-to-Chance, plus Harry Steinfelt at third. The two white groups are part of the tradition of the game. The almost unknown black aggregations may well have been just as good—or even better.

Marcelle was a handsome guy, said second baseman Dick Seay— "a Creole, nice brown skin, dressed neat."

"He was a dandy!" said O'Neil. "A little man. Pretty hair. Great hands. Quick."

Born in Thibedeaux, Louisiana, June 24, 1897 (his death certificate says 1890, probably erroneously), he began playing on one of New Orleans' city teams, Giovanni's, in 1913. He was a great third baseman even then at the age of 16, said Malarcher, who played for a rival club.

In 1915 Marcelle was with the New Orleans Black Eagles, and Ric Roberts, a boy in Gainesville, Florida, at the time, recalled Oliver's backhand stabs down the third baseline and "that pistol arm." But, Roberts sighed, "he was nasty."

By 1918 Marcelle had attracted the attention of the Brooklyn Royal Giants, one of the top black clubs of the era. He traveled north with them and played beside the legendary shortstop, John Henry Lloyd.

In 1921 Marcelle moved to the Bacharach Giants, where he teamed with Lundy. There was no league, but he hit .303 in 28 games against Rube Foster's Negro National League teams. That October he faced his first white big leaguers, getting three hits in two games against Hank Thormahlen (7–3) of the Red Sox and Freddie Heimach (1–0) of the As.

In 1922 Marcelle boosted his average to .379.

He jumped to the New York Lincoln Giants in 1923 and hit .390.

That winter he joined Santa Clara, where he faced top black and white pitchers, including Dolph Luque, Freddie Fitzsimmons, Jakie May, Jess Petty, and others. He did particularly well against Luque, the major leagues' winningest pitcher at 27–8. Marcelle stroked him for six hits in 12 at bats, including two triples. Marcelle was in a tight race for the batting title against outfielder Alejandro Oms. The race went down to the final game, when Marcelle forged ahead to win with .371 and collect a $500 prize. (The league played a special season after the first. Marcelle averaged .346 in both halves.)

In New York the following summer, 1924, Marcelle hit .310 and captained the Lincolns on the field. Marcelle "is in a class by himself when it comes to tipping in on slow bunts," the Philadelphia *Tribune* wrote.

"I call him crazy," muttered outfielder O.K. "Buddy" Burbage. "He'd walk in on anybody. He'd even walk in on Mike Schmidt."

"He had a lot of guts," agreed Lincoln Giants pitcher Bill Holland. "Just pure nerve. I've seen Marcelle be in, looking for a bunt, the guy would hit it down the line, and he'd dive and catch the ball, get up and throw the man out. That takes heart."

All was not well, however. Booker T. Washington's paper, the New York *Age*, wrote that the flashy third baseman was "a victim of almost uncontrollable temper," as he let both the fans and the umpires get his goat. The paper blamed the Lincolns' poor showing on Marcelle and second baseman George Scales, another temperamental star.

That winter Marcelle hit .310 in Cuba. He fattened his average against Luque with five hits in eight at bats.

The following summer, 1925, Marcelle was abruptly traded to the Bacharachs. It was a great move by the Bs. With Lundy at short and

Marcelle on third, they had an air-tight left side of the infield and two strong .300-hitters. Marcelle's batting average fell to .289, but his deportment improved. "He was the nicest fellow you'd want to meet," said Bacharach pitcher Jesse "Mountain" Hubbard—"on the field and off."

In 1926 Marcelle hit .303 and Lundy .329, as the Bacharachs won the pennant.

The World Series against the Chicago American Giants was a wild seesaw affair. It opened with a tie game, then Chicago won, but the Bs came back with a no-hitter by Claude "Red" Grier, as Marcelle made a fine play in the ninth to help preserve the gem.

The Atlantic City *Press* was ecstatic. "Marcelle, Lundy, and Garcia (the second baseman) pulled off some of the most phenomenal fielding that we have seen through these long years," it wrote. Some of the plays "bordered on the impossible." The two clubs moved into the tenth game all tied up—four wins apiece, plus one tie.

In the finale, Chicago's great lefty, Big Bill Foster, was locked in a duel with the Bs Hubert Lockhart. Marcelle collected three hits and stole a base, but still the clubs went into the ninth tied, 0–0, when Chicago pushed across one run for the victory.

The 1929 Baltimore Black Sox. Front (left to right) are Rap Dixon, unknown, Dick Lundy, Frank Warfield, Jud Wilson, unknown, Laymon Yokely, and, rear (left to right), Eggie Clark, Pud Flournoy, Scrip Lee, Oliver Marcelle, Jesse Hubbard, Red Ryan, and two unidentified players.

Marcelle had done his best, however. He had hit .333 and driven in six runs, to tie with Lundy as the top run-producer on the team.

The next year, 1927, Marcelle hit .324 as the Bacharachs won the pennant again and met the American Giants for the championship once more. Again it was Chicago, as Marcelle was held to a .235 average.

It had not been a good series at the gate, and the Bacharachs were in financial trouble throughout 1928. The league broke up and finally the Bs folded too. Marcelle's average was .259.

In 1929, Marcelle and Lundy moved to the Baltimore Black Sox in the new Negro American League, teaming with Warfield and Wilson in another great infield combination. Lundy fell off to .269 at bat. Wilson wasn't much of a fielder, but he was one of the greatest hitters ever produced by the Negro leagues. It was a temperamental foursome. Wilson, on first, was a two-fisted scrapper. And Warfield, the manager and second baseman, was at least as flammable as Marcelle. But the Black Sox easily won the pennant.

Warfield and Marcelle sailed to Cuba for the winter. They were shooting craps one night, outfielder Clint Thomas said, and Warfield was winning. "Marcelle asked him to loan him five dollars. Warfield told him he wasn't going to loan him anything. They got in an argument. Marcelle smashed Warfield in the mouth. Warfield grabbed him, bit his nose off."

The blemish on Marcelle's once handsome face must have affected his play. The next summer he was with the Brooklyn Royal Giants but got into only four games. It was the end of his Negro league career.

In 1932 he managed Wilmington, a farm club of the Hilldales. "He wore a patch on his nose," said pitcher Bill "Sleepy" Crawford. But the old fire was still there. "He would fight in a minute. I wouldn't say he was a great manager, but he hated to lose."

In 1933 Marcelle and veteran shortstop Orville Riggins moved to Miami to play on the Miami Giants. Although Marcelle was on the way out, Buck O'Neil said, he still had great hands. The Giants barnstormed out to Kansas, living the desperate hand-to-mouth life of itinerant ballplayers in the depression. When the team got an offer to play in the Denver semipro tourney, they snapped it up. While O'Neil and the younger guys rode the rails in freight trains to get there, Marcelle went in style—jammed in with several men in the team car.

Denver was Marcelle's last hurrah. "I'm going to hang it up, right here," he announced. "He'd had enough," O'Neil said. Marcelle remained in Denver, living in obscurity as a laborer, while his son, Everett, played briefly for the Chicago American Giants and Newark Eagles. On June 12, 1949, the Ghost was dead at the age of 51.

Oliver Marcelle

Year	Team	G	EAB*	H	2B	3B	HR	BA	SB
1919	Brooklyn	4	17	4	—	—	—	.222	
1920	Atlantic City	2	8	0	0	0	0	.000	
1921	Atlantic City	28	109	33	3	1	0	.303	5
1922	Atlantic City	26	95	36	5	1	0	.379	2
1923	New York	—	41	16	—	—	—	.390	
	Cuba	—	283	98	5	5	3	.346	
1924	New York-Atlantic City	36	142	44	12	2	1	.310	7
	Cuba	—	126	39	5	3	0	.310	
1925	Atlantic City	52	190	55	5	2	4	.289	0
	Cuba	12	80	23	3	1	0	.288	—
1926	Atlantic City	59	208	63	9	0	2	.303	
	Cuba	—	78	26	—	—	—	.333	—
1927	Atlantic City	97	352	115	7	1	2	.324	5
	Cuba	—	128	41	—	—	—	.320	—
1928	Atlantic City	—	148	38	2	1	2	.259	0
1929	Baltimore	58	208	56	4	2	0	.269	7
1930	Brooklyn	4	17	7	—	—	—	.412	—
Totals			2230	692	60	19	14	.310	26

	Post-Season								
1926	World Series	0	36	12	1	0	0	.333	2
1927	World Series	9	34	8	1	0	0	.235	0
		19	70	20	2	0	0	.286	2

*Estimated At Bats.

Oliver Marcelle vs. White Big Leaguers

Year	AB	H	2B	3B	HR	Pitcher	(W-L)
1918	(4)*	0	0	0	0	Thormahlen	(7-3)
1921	(4)	3	—	—	—	Heimach	(1-0)
	4	3	0	1	0	Luque	(27-8)
	4	2	0	1	0	Luque	
	4	1	0	0	0	Luque	
	4	1	0	0	0	Luque, (Cooper),[a] Ryan	(16-5)
1924-25	4	1	0	0	0	Cooney	(3-5)
	2	0	0	0	0	Cooney	
	4	3	—	—	0	Luque	(10-15)
	4	2	0	1	0	Luque	
	4	1	0	0	0	Luque, (Cooper),[a] Ryan	(8-6)
1926-27	4	1	0	1	0	Luque	(13-16)
	4	1	0	1	0	Luque	
1927	4	1	—	—	—	Rommel	(11-3)
1928	4	1	0	0	0	Ogden	(15-16)
	4	0	0	0	0	Rommel	(13-5)
	5	2	0	0	0	Ehmke, (Haas)[a]	(9-8)
Totals 17 games	99	23	0	5	0	Average: .232	

*At bats in parentheses are estimated.
[a] Not major league pitchers.

12

Judy Johnson:
The Man Named Judy

Judy Johnson was the smartest third baseman I ever came across. A scientific ball player, did everything with grace and poise. Played a heady game of baseball, none of this just slugging the ball, a man on first base, and he just dies there because you didn't hit the ball up against the wall. Judy would steal your signals. He should have been in the major leagues 15 or 20 years as a coach. They talk about Negro manager. I always thought that Judy should have made a perfect major league manager.

Ted Page, outfielder
Pittsburgh Crawfords

William "Judy" Johnson was one of the slickest fielding third basemen in the history of black baseball—or any other baseball. Old-timers who saw him cavort with the old Philadelphia Hilldales or Pittsburgh Crawfords of the 1920s and 1930s inevitably link his name with that of Brooks Robinson. Not, however, little Jake Stephens, Johnson's shortstop-playing side kick. "Robinson," snorts Jake, "couldn't carry Judy's glove."

Connie Mack, the sweet-natured owner of the Philadelphia As, watched Judy dance around the bag at Shibe Park and sighed. If Johnson were only white, he said, "he could write his own price."

The old Negro leagues produced many great third basemen: Jud Wilson, Marcelle, Ray Dandridge. But many authorities consider Johnson the finest of all, and he was the first of the four to be enshrined in Cooperstown.

Dandridge may have been flashier, but Johnson "was like a rock," said ex-outfielder Jimmy Crutchfield, "a steadying influence on the club. Had a great brain, could anticipate a play, knew what his opponents were going to do."

"He had intelligence and finesse," said Willie Wells, one of the game's best short stops.

And Judy was an excellent sign-stealer, added Ted Page. "He and Josh Gibson—boy, they trapped more men off third base! Judy'd put a little whistle on to Josh, who was catching, and I'd say, 'Oh-oh, they got something cooking.' "

In Cincinnati in the early 1930s, Leo Durocher's club of white big league all stars was playing the Crawfords. Leo reached third base and began dancing off the bag down the line to rattle the pitcher.

Lippy was a show-off. They called time and said to him, "Don't talk to Judy." Lippy kept dancing up and down the line, showing off. I went over to Leroy Matlock, the pitcher, said, "You dumb son of a bitch, that guy's gonna steal the cover right off you"—loud, so Leo could hear it. I go back to third, tell Leo, "That's the dumbest pitcher we got on the ball club!"*

Then Judy gave Josh "the whistle."

Durocher started in toward home, and I moved up with him. Then I backed up, put my foot about two feet in front of the base. Josh had the best snap, wouldn't move to throw, just snapped the ball. I caught it. Here comes Durocher sliding in, sprawling all over the base line. Umpire says, "You're out!"

Leo leaped to his feet, ready to fight: "What, me out?"

"Heh, Lip," Judy chuckled, "get off my foot."

Leo had made a perfect hook slide into Judy's ankle, hadn't come anywhere near the bag. He stomped off the field, still cussing.

Some 20 years later Johnson and his wife were leaving Milwaukee's County Stadium where their son-in-law, Bill Bruton, had just finished playing a World Series game against the New York Yankees. In the crowd they jostled against none other than Leo Durocher. "Durocher," Judy said, "do you remember playing a barnstorming game in Cincinnati back in 1934 or so?"

Durocher stepped back and blinked. "Yes," he said, "I remember you, Judy, damn your soul. That's the day you tricked me!"

Johnson was born October 26, 1899, in Snow Hill on Maryland's eastern shore, not far from the birthplace of another famous third baseman, Frank "Home Run" Baker. He remembered frosty mornings in Snow Hill, when he and his sister slept in a loft they reached by climbing a ladder and awoke to the smell of country breakfast cooking.

Of course the children did chores. They don't now. I think it's a shame. It helps them be better citizens. We had our work to do, and I thank God for it.

---

*Quotations set off in italic type are extracts from interviews conducted by the author with the subject of the chapter.

Judy's father, a sailor, moved to Wilmington when Judy was ten.

> *My dad liked sports. He was an athletic director of the Negro Settlement House. Our backyard had everything you'd find in a gym. I could do a lot of things you see in a circus now.*
>
> *My daddy wanted me to be a prize fighter. My sister was my sparring partner. She boxed me all over the place; she said, "Defend yourself!" How'm I gonna defend myself against a girl? Where could I hit her?*
>
> *I wanted to play baseball; it was my first love. I lived on the West Side on Delmar Place right in back of the park they dedicated to me, Judy Johnson Park. I could come right out of my backyard and into the park. That's where I started playing baseball. Mostly it was a pasture. A gentleman lived a few blocks away, had cows and horses that grazed there. We would clean it off. When we came home from school, we'd play ball there; we'd play until dark.*

He remembered his first uniform vividly. His mother sewed a big "D" on the shirt.

> *I was strutting around at five A.M.—didn't play until two. She washed it and washed it until the D was as blue as the rest of the uniform.*
>
> *My first glove was my father's. He used to have a baseball team called the*

Members of the Pittsburgh Crawfords (from left) are Oscar Charleston, Rap Dixon, Josh Gibson, Judy Johnson, and Jud Wilson.

Royal Blues; they played only on Saturdays. I could hardly hold the glove on my hands, there was so much dry rot. I kept it until it just about fell apart. Finally he bought me a glove; it looked like a (little) dress glove alongside the ones they use now.

The first baseball shoes I had, I bought spikes and had a shoemaker put them on a pair of shoes of mine. Metal spikes. I thought I was a big leaguer then—few boys had baseball shoes. But I forgot to take the heel off first, and he nailed the spikes to the heel. I had to walk tipped forward.

They had a league in Wilmington—Newark, Harrisburg, six or seven teams. I used to keep score. My teacher let me out of school five minutes early so I could go and get my ten cents a game. I would spend a nickel of that for a fishcake sandwich.

When I got a pretty good size, I joined an organized team called Rosedale. We played several teams around town. Some white clubs and three or four Negro teams. Every Saturday we'd play.

We also played ball at Second and Adams, Eden Park. We'd walk out here to Marshallton from Wilmington, to Newcastle, Rockford Tower. We were dedicated. Kids wouldn't go around their block today without a car. You'd always have a good crowd. Pass the hat around to get a couple balls for the next game.

After the game Judy always managed to hang around the team captain's house to talk baseball—and steal glances at the captain's sister, Anita. Somehow he and Anita ended up sitting on the bench in front of the house, until her father coughed. Said Judy: "That meant, 'Get!' She'd walk me to the corner, I'd give her a 'hit-and-run' kiss." The two were married for more than 60 years until Anita's death in 1986. "Next to my wife," he said, "I loved baseball best."

I thought I was pretty good. I figured I was the best around. I wanted to move up. Now Chester had a pretty good ball park, just above the team I was on in Wilmington. They'd pay me a couple dollars and trolley fare—there weren't any buses then. They were my first professional club.

Johnson got his first big break when World War I called many of the stars of the top black teams into service.

I must have impressed the manager of the Philadelphia Hilldales club, because he asked me to play with them on Thursdays and Saturdays at their field in Darby. Sundays they'd go to Atlantic City as the Bacharach Giants. Same club, just different suits on. Like the Globetrotters. I got five dollars a day.

After the war Judy was farmed out to the Madison Stars of Philadelphia, sort of a minor league training ground for the Hilldales, who were developing into the top black club in the East. Pitcher Webster McDonald was another youngster who served his apprenticeship on the Stars, along with Judy. With only 11 men on the team, they played the small towns in Pennsylvania and New Jersey, and if they missed the last ferry back from Camden, McDonald recalled, they sat up all night in the ferry slip, waiting for the first boat back in the morning.

The oldest man on the club was a character by the name of "Greasy" Swigot. Johnson explained: "He never bought a pair of baseball shoes in his life. If you threw away a pair of old shoes, he'd wear 'em! He wore size 10½, but if they were a size six, he'd cut the toes away and play in them like that. But he could hit that ball!"

It was abut that time, incidentally, that Johnson picked up his unusual nickname. It was passed on to him by veteran outfielder Robert "Judy" Gans, whom Johnson apparently resembled. Just where Gans got the monicker from is unknown.

By 1920 Hilldale owner Ed Bolden was ready to bring young Johnson up and to pay the Madison Stars the munificent sum of $100.

The Hilldales had begun some eight years earlier as a neighborhood amateur club in Darby, a suburb south of Philadelphia. The taciturn postal official, Ed Bolden, took them over and began attracting professional players. By 1918 he had signed Phil Cockrell, an excellent spitballer who would gain a name as the conqueror of several big-league clubs. Little McKinley "Bunny" Downs was at second—some 30 years later he would managing the Indianapolis Clowns and send a kid named Hank Aaron to the major leagues. A local boy, Otto Briggs, was in the outfield. The jewel of the team was hulking Texan, Louis Santop, who could hit the old dead balls out of sight. Johnson, at 21, was the baby of the ball club.

The Hilldales built up a rabid fan following.

We had our own park in Darby, and our crowds got so large we had to enlarge the park. Not just for Negroes, for white fans too. The Athletics and the Phillies were down then, and people were getting season tickets to see us. You couldn't buy a box seat. Once or twice we came to Wilmington to play. This was on Harlan's Field at Market Street bridge. Golly, the fans almost tore the stands down coming to see the game.

On the Hilldales Judy understudied Bill "Brodie" Francis, a little fireplug of a man. "He was close to the ground," Johnson said, "could get ground balls easily, and hit pitches at his eyes." Francis, a veteran of Rube Foster's great Chicago teams, was from Wilmington also and took a liking to Judy. He taught the kid how to brace his foot and make the throw to first and other tricks of the craft. Eventually, "I took his job away from him," Judy said, "but he turned out to be the manager, so he got the best of the deal."

Judy remembered first baseman Bill Pettus, who took the stuffing out of his mitt and filled it with chicken feathers. "Every time he caught the ball, poof, all the feathers would fly out. Like plucking a chicken."

Ball players then, as now, were superstitious. They kept their bats in careful order, Judy recalled, unless they were losing. Then they'd mix them up to change the luck. Judy once innocently brought a bag of peanuts onto the bench, a taboo, as any veteran would have known. "They ground the bag underfoot—crunch, crunch, crunch. I almost cried."

Rookies were at the bottom of the pecking order. "Here, Slacky, take my bats," Santop ordered when the team passed through New York. While the older guys grabbed a subway to Harlem for a little fun, they made Judy get off at 42nd Street and showed him how to follow the lights to Grand Central Station to catch a train back to Philadelphia, laden with Santop's uniform roll, Santop's bat bag, and his own roll and bag. "I looked like a porter. I had to hire a taxi to carry those bats. But you had to. You had to do it."

The next year they signed me to play every day. The manager said, "You work hard this winter, come back in the spring, and we'll sign you on as a regular." I worked hard all winter. I would get anybody to hit me a ball, have a catch. In 1921 I started right out.

Johnson took over the third base job, ousting Francis, and writers began comparing him to the great Marcelle. The rivalry would follow both men throughout their careers.

Johnson had the respect of the players around the league, both on and off the field. "Marcelle was sort of a lush," said Stephens, "but Judy was a perfect gentleman."

"He was a great ball player and gentleman," nodded Monarch second baseman Newt Allen. "He was a gentleman all through those baseball years when baseball was just as rough as could be. He was the type of fellow that didn't try to hurt anyone. He just went along and played the game. You have respect for a man like that. And in all those years, he never was hurt, because the ball players respected him as a ball player. Never argued with you about anything. Very seldom he argued about a strike or a play on the bases."

Judy hit .214 in his rookie season.

I was no great hitter, but I would try almost anything to get on base. Our philosophy was, if you didn't get on base, you couldn't score. I'll give you an example: Me being a right-handed batter, I would have the left sleeve a little baggier than my right, and then I'd lean and just let the ball tick my sleeve, or I'd puff up my shirt in the front and let the ball tick me there. How many ball players today would do that?

The Hilldales and Bacharachs were the cream of the still unorganized black clubs in the East in 1921, and the great Rube Foster, whose American Giants were the best in the West, came to play them both, to settle just who was best in the land. Foster arrived with his "race horses"—Gardner, DeMoss, Lyons, Malarcher, Torriente, Bobby Williams. Against the Bacharachs, he boasted that his boys were going to lay the ball down to third base to see just how good the vaunted Marcelle really was. Sooner or later, Rube knew, Marcelle would bobble it. Sure enough, the scheme seemed to work, and Chicago beat the Bs two games to one.

Moving to Philadelphia's Shibe Park to meet the Hilldales, Foster tried the same tactics on young Judy. Whether Foster succeeded in "psyching" Judy or not is not clear, but Judy hit only .188 in the four games. The Giants did run wild in the first game, stealing six bases and winning, 5–2. Hilldale evened it, as Cockrell won the second game, 4–3. In the third game Judy slugged a triple and home run to help rout the Fostermen, 15–5. Then Cockrell won the fourth game, 7–1, to send the Rube packing for home.

In 1923 Hilldale owner Ed Bolden formed the Eastern Colored League, raiding Foster's Negro National League of many of its stars. To the Hilldales Bolden brought Raleigh "Biz" Mackey, regarded, even ahead of Josh Gibson, as the top catcher in black baseball annals. He split the catching with Santop. George "Tank" Carr, a solid batsman, came from the Kansas City Monarchs to hold down first base. Frank Warfield was plucked from Indianapolis to play second.

At shortstop was the peerless and popular John Henry "Pop" Lloyd, who also managed the club.

Otto Briggs, Clint Thomas from Detroit, and George Johnson patrolled the outfield, and Cockrell, lefty Nip Winters, and forkballing Red Ryan led the pitching staff. They gave the Hilldales the strongest crew in the East.

Judy's contribution was a modest .237 but he played a strong, steady game at third.

> We had more trouble with violence playing in the Negro leagues than playing with white boys. My leg's got all cut up. They would take files and sharpen their spikes.
> Mother, she never wanted to see me play. The only time she saw me play, we were playing Philadelphia, this boy was stealing third. I'd always put my foot down and block them. This guy came up high as I went down to tag him, and he ripped my face to my teeth. I got cut open for five stitches. She fainted in the stands. So she never watched me play again.

Judy wore shin guards, as did Lloyd and other black infielders.

John Lloyd, he was the best shortstop ever, along with Honus Wagner, according to Mr. Mack. He taught me more baseball than I learned all 15 or 16 years I played. He showed you how to protect yourself. Back then you had to watch how they came into base. Were they gonna hook slide or come straight in? Sometimes I'd decoy guys. I'd act as if the ball wasn't coming and then tag 'em when they came in standing up. They'd call you a lot of bad names.

Cool Papa Bell, if he hit it behind the outfielder, I'd make him run in back of me, take that extra step.

That was our game—run, steal, make them make mistakes. Well, most Negroes can run—I guess you've noticed that.

Baseball is like everything else: You got to study every angle to win.

Judy also gave the Hilldale pitchers a little extra help. The pitcher would turn and wave his outfielders this way and that, and while everyone in the park was watching this Academy Award performance, Judy was rubbing up the ball with sand paper. "There I am," he laughed, "going scrape, scrape, scrape."

In one playoff against the Bacharachs, a Hilldale rookie had the Bs handcuffed, and though they kept demanding to see the ball, they never could find any proof. Players used to leave their gloves on the field between innings back then. Whitey Gruhler of the Atlantic City *Press* said Bacharach center fielder Chaney White picked up Judy's glove and found a hole cut in the pocket; a piece of emery paper fell out.

Hilldale won the pennant in 1923, but Foster was so incensed over the raids against his loop that he wouldn't hear of a world series. So the Hilldales went looking for other foes—the white major leaguers. In nine games they won seven and lost two, splitting their two games with the Philadelphia As.

Johnson journeyed to Cuba that winter, along with many other stars of the stateside big leagues, both black and white. Dolph Luque, who had just won 27 games in the National League, was down there. So were Jesse Petty of the Brooklyn organization and Fred Fitzsimmons, soon to go up with the New York Giants, plus most of the pitching stars of the two Negro leagues. Against this stellar pitching, Johnson raised his average to .345.

I was a contact hitter. Though I'm only 5-11 and never weighed more than 155 pounds in my life, I used a 40-ounce bat; it was a log, but all I would do is try and meet the ball. I was trying to hit behind the runner, drag the ball. I never tried to hit home runs, I tried to move the ball around.

"Hitting is like driving a nail," he said. "If you take a big swing you either hit your thumb or bend the nail. But if you take two or

three short strokes, the nail goes down straight and true." Judy hit
.287 lifetime.

Judy hit .327 in the summer of 1924, as the Hilldales repeated as
champs.

This time Foster agreed to bury the hatchet and gave his blessing
to a world series, the first modern championship in black history. The
Hilldales would face the Kansas City Monarchs, the kings of the
western league. They were a hard-hitting club. Dobie Moore, who
ranks with Lloyd and a handful of others as one of the best black
shortstops of all time, sparkled with little Newt Allen on the dou-
bleplay. Bullet Joe Rogan led the pitching staff and hit clean-up. Oscar
"Heavy" Johnson and George "Never" Sweatt were in the outfield.
Fiery Frank Duncan caught. The pitching staff was bolstered by Bill
Drake, the bean-ball specialist, and by ancient Jose Mendez.

It was a magnificent series, going ten games, including a tie,
before a decision (they had agreed to a best-five-out-of-nine series).

Rogan and Kansas City won the first game, 6–2. Hilldale came
back in the second game, as Nip Winters shut out the Monarchs, 11–0.
In the third game, Rogan battled for 13 innings before darkness
ended the game. Hilldale took the lead in the series the next day when
Hilldale's Reuben "Rube" Currie, a Kansas City native who had just
defected from the Monarchs, faced the curses of his old mates and
beat them, 4–3.

The teams moved next to Kansas City, where the series resumed
after a five-day delay, each club sending its ace into the game after a
long rest. Rogan went up against Winters. In the fourth inning,
Johnson's single helped set up one run. In the ninth Judy stepped to
bat again with the score tied, 2–2, and two men on. He smote Rogan's
first pitch over the center fielder's head and raced around the bases on
an inside-the-park homer that put the game on ice and gave Hilldale a
two-game lead.

The Monarchs won the sixth game, and the two aces, Rogan and
Winters, met again in the seventh game and dueled for 12 innings
before Rogan won, 4–3. The series was all tied up, three games apiece,
plus the tie.

The turning point came in game eight, one of the classic games in
blackball annals. Rookie shortstop Jake Stephens had a bad case of
jitters, so Johnson moved to short. Biz Mackey, a great catcher, had to
play third. And Santop, a hard hitter but a weak receiver, caught. The
Hilldales went into the ninth with a 2–1 lead against Rogan. The
Monarchs rallied in the ninth, putting two men on with two out and
the weak-hitting Duncan at the plate. Frank lofted a pop foul, which
Santop circled under. Johnson remembers the big catcher tapping his
mitt confidently as he waited for the easy out that would end the

game. The ball hit the heel of his glove and twisted out again. Given a new life, Duncan stepped in again against his old boyhood playmate, Currie, and hit a hard ground ball to third. It shot between Mackey's legs into left field while Johnson, the non-pareil regular third baseman, watched in helpless horror and both runners scored to give the Monarchs the victory.

Then Mendez beat young Scrip Lee in the finale.

Nip Winters came back the next day to win his third game of the series.

It was a heart-breaking series. But Johnson had done his best, hitting .364 to lead both teams. His 16 hits included six doubles, a triple, and a home run.

The following year, 1925, Johnson hit .364. The Hilldales won their third straight flag and grimly entrained for Kansas City and a chance for revenge against the Monarchs.

It started as another tense series. Hilldale had to go 12 innings to win the first game, 5–2, though Judy didn't get any hits against Bill Drake. Johnson got two hits in game two, but Kansas City won it, 5–3. Mendez took the mound for the third game, and the two rivals battled to a 1–1 tie after nine innings. Judy opened the tenth with a sharp single to center, his third hit of the day, and a moment later scored on a two-base hit to win it. His run broke the Monarchs' back. The Hilldales took the next two games and the championship, as Johnson ended up with an even .300 average.

That winter Johnson joined the many other black stars who were finding Palm Beach, Florida, a lucrative wintering spot. Two rival hotels, the Breakers and the Poinciana, hired the best black professionals to wait on tables and entertain guests on the baseball diamond. The rivalry between the two hotels was intense, but it was the money-making that lured many of the players down there. The pay and tips were excellent. Beyond that there were floating crap games and, for the really adventuresome, rum-running from nearby Cuba to the Prohibitionist but thirsty mainland. Many a man could "hustle" himself a nice bit of cash in just a few months, as much as he could make in a whole year of playing ball back north.

Judy didn't participate in these off-the-field enterprises, but he observed them—the rum was sometimes stacked against the wall of the dormitories, right up to the ceilings. He remembered being awakened one night when several white men burst into the dorm, shining flashlights in his eyes and demanding to know where his "brother" was. They apparently meant outfielder George Johnson and assumed that Judy was related. Judy shrugged that he didn't know, and the men, presumably underworld figures in search of their cut, eventually went off. It was a close call. Some others were not so lucky.

Pitcher Bill "Rube" Chambers, a fine left-hander, was found one morning propped up in a boxcar dead. Whether he had crossed up a business associate or had broken one of the racial taboos is not clear. His death has never been solved.

Back north in 1926 Judy's average was .302, and the Hilldales finally lost the pennant to the Bacharachs and Marcelle. There were compensations, however, for it meant that the Hilldales were free to barnstorm against the white big leaguers again—and make a lot more money doing it. They won three out of four games against the all stars—batting champ Heinie Manush, Jimmy Dykes, Ernie Padgett and others.

Two of the victories came against Lefty Grove, the American League earned-run leader, by 6–1 and 3–0. The only loss was 1–0, when the wind blew Mackey's throw into center field, allowing Padgett to score.

Johnson sailed back to Cuba for the winter season of 1926–1927, hitting .372. The following winter his average was .329. Up north, meanwhile, Johnson slumped to .228 in 1927 and .231 in 1928.

But in 1929 he had the best year of his life, swatting .416, sixth best in the league (there were no less than four .400 hitters). In 1929, he was chosen MVP by sports writer Rollo Wilson, who wrote:

> If you've ever seen him play and have marked his pep and ability, you know why I chose him over all the rest. If colored athletes were as earnest generally as this boy, there would be a vast improvement in the game, the box offices would pick up, and everyone would prosper.

In 1930 the league folded under the impact of the depression, and Johnson jumped to the independent Homestead Grays, which had remained out of the league but may actually have been the best black club in the East, if not in the country. The infield was made up of Oscar Charleston; George Scales, one of the best right-handed hitters in black history; salty Jake Stephens, and Johnson. In the outfield were Vic Harris, a fiery base-runner, and rifle-armed Bill "Happy" Evans, one of the all-time top utility men. Pitching were big Joe Williams; Lefty Williams, who won 26 straight games that year; little Oscar Owens; and scrappy George Britt. The catching was shared by Britt and Buck Ewing until one muggy night in Pittsburgh, when the Kansas City Monarchs brought their new-fangled light poles to town for the first night game ever seen in Forbes Field. Ewing had his hand split by a foul tip, and Judy, who was captain that night, called time. Vic Harris hopped in a cab, dashed to a neighborhood playground, and returned with a big, grinning, raw-boned 19-year-old sandlotter named Josh Gibson.

Gibson could hit right off the bat. But he couldn't catch. Pitchers scornfully called him "boxer," and the whole team winced when Josh whipped off his mask and began dazedly searching for a pop foul. Johnson, who had spent more than a decade studying the ballistics of a wildly spinning foul ball, patiently took the kid under his wing and drilled him hour after hour until he became pretty fair defensive receiver.

Only 16 games have been found against other black clubs in 1930. Judy's average in them was .275.

That fall Cum Posey, the Grays' owner, challenged Pop Lloyd's Lincoln Giants for the mythical championship of black baseball. The Grays won, six games to four, and claimed the flag. Johnson hit .286.

Johnson moved back to Hilldale in 1931. The depression had really hit now. To make ends meet, salaries were waived and players divided whatever was left after expenses.

In those days a player played anywhere he could make a buck. In 1932 Judy jumped to the Pittsburgh Crawfords, the Grays' bitter crosstown rivals owned by numbers king Gus Greenlee. Some authorities call that the finest black team ever put together.

Johnson recalled those days:

The white ball players at that time were always glad to play against our Negro ball players, because there weren't salaries like there are today. They made almost as much money playing us after the World Series was over as they would make almost the whole season. I played against every big leaguer, from Babe Ruth on down. On Sundays we'd go up to New York and play the Bushwicks, a white team in Brooklyn, and they had some major leaguers on that club. It got so for a while we'd play the Bushwicks on the first and last Sunday of every month. We were drawing more people with the Bushwicks than the Dodgers in Ebbetts Field sometimes.

In the spring we'd leave Pittsburgh and travel all the way to Hot Springs, Arkansas, without stopping. We had nine men in two cars, and they had built sort of a box where the uniforms were kept. Once we got on the road, we'd never stop until we got where we were going, except to rest and, of course, to buy food— cheese, baloney, sardines, or anything that was filling. Of course, they didn't have Gino's and all those places. Hot-dog stands, we weren't even allowed to stop there to eat. If we stopped for food, we'd have to send one man around to the back door and take the orders for hot dogs, and we'd eat the hot dogs, and cheese, and sardines, and so forth.

We used to get $1.50 a day eating money. My wife was a teacher then, and she would always send me some money, but, of course, I couldn't let the other fellows know, because they would all try to borrow it from me. I don't know how we managed to stay married so long with me being away from home as much as I was.

We stayed at Negro hotels, and if they were crowded, we'd go to individual houses. People would offer to take two or three players.

After ten days training in Hot Springs, we moved on to New Orleans. We'd play a double header there, then start back north, playing every day until we got to Pittsburgh. Season started right then on into September. In the fall we'd play winter ball up until New Year's almost.

We didn't have many lay-offs. Sometimes we would play three games a day—that was common. When we'd play a double header, we'd think it was a holiday. We played in Chicago one Sunday, a double header. We put all our clothes and things on top of the bus. We left Chicago six o'clock Sunday night and rode to Philly without stopping. We got in Philly Tuesday morning and played a double header that afternoon. No interstates either. We played after two nights without rest. You see the travel we put up with?

We used to play two games every Thursday, two on Saturday, and three on Sunday. After we played that double header and had to go for that third game at night, boy, you heard some bad words! We'd fuss like a bunch of chickens. But when we put those uniforms on and got in the ball park, we'd forget the games we'd just played. As soon as we hit the field, it was all forgotten.

In those days as soon as I hit the front door my wife could tell if we'd won or lost. I'd play the game over again all night. If we'd lost by one run, I'd sit down and go over the game—now, what could I have done to help win? If I got two base hits, I'd say they were wasted because nobody was on base. I didn't worry too much about hitting, as long as we were winning. If I went 0-for-4 and we won, I wouldn't worry.

Do you think ball players would do that now? They wouldn't do it! We enjoyed playing more than the boys do now. We had to! It was better than being a janitor. But it was fun.

Johnson said he didn't think of what he was missing.

Not until I was inducted into the Hall of Fame. Then I would think of times past. Look at the money I lost, the high life, the things I could have bought for my wife. My life could have been better.

I don't go to ball games much. I get so disgusted looking at the players. The first and the 15th, payday, I think are more interesting to them than the game. You can go to a ball game in Philadelphia, and by the time you get to the exit, you see some of the ball players coming out. They've been in and showered and out so quick, they never think whether they won or lost or not. You could come past our clubhouse the night after we lost a ball game and you might think we were fighting in there. I could tell you from the first batter up every play until the last ball was thrown.

And some of the ball players now in the big leagues, they sit up there and they talk about everything but the ball game. They're not interested in it at all. And it's a shame, because the money they're making now—I would play in my bare feet, bare hands, and a bathing suit! I wouldn't deprive anybody from making as much as he can, but they're paying just too much money. Until they stop that, we won't get back to that good baseball.

On their rare days off, Johnson and the Crawfords went to watch the white major league games to see what they could learn.

We never had to pay to go to see the As or the Yankees. The only park we had to pay was St. Louis, and they put us in the Jim Crow section in back of some chicken wire. Other than that, every big league park knew us.

Mr. Mack [As owner] told me, "Judy, it's a shame you're a Negro." I never asked him why, but I knew what he meant. I knew I was at my highest level; regardless of how well I played, I'd never go up.

Later Johnson did ask why. "If you want to know the truth, Judy," Mack replied, "there are just too many of you to go in."

In spite of their troubles, the blacks were genuine heroes to their community. Henry Wiggins of Chicago remembered going to a game, his glove hanging from his belt. "The great Judy Johnson said, 'Kid, come on, let's take your glove off, play catch.' One of the greatest thrills of my life! I told my dad I played catch with Judy Johnson!"

In 1934 Johnson hit .243, and the Craws met Dizzy Dean, World Series hero and 29-game winner, and whipped him three times, though admittedly Dizzy wasn't backed by an all-star cast.

In 1935, he found himself in another world series, this one between the Crawfords and the New York Cubans. He was in a long slump when he came to bat in the ninth inning of the sixth game, the Craws one game behind, the score tied, 6–6, and the bases loaded. He drove a 3–2 pitch on the ground past first base, too hot for even the great Showboat Thomas to handle, and the Craws had tied the series three games each. The following day Gibson and Crawford manager Oscar Charleston slugged homers to wrap the series up.

In the autumn of 1936 Judy accompanied the Crawfords to Mexico, where they met the big-league all stars featuring Rogers Hornsby, Jimmy Foxx, Boob McNair, Roger Cramer, Earl Whitehill, and many more. The two clubs battled to a 6–6 tie after 11 innings of the first game, when the all stars filled the bases with one out and the dangerous Foxx up. Jimmy drilled a grass cutter to third, Johnson speared it and rifled it home for a force out at the plate. The next man went out, and the game ended all tied up. It would be Johnson's final game.

After Jackie Robinson broke the color line in the big leagues, Judy was hired by the Athletics as a scout.

I could have gotten Hank Aaron for them for $3,500 when he was playing with the Indianapolis Clowns. I got my boss out of bed and told him I had a good prospect and he wouldn't cost too much, and he cussed me out for waking him up at one o'clock in the morning. He said, "Thirty-five hundred! That's too much money." Too much for a man like that! I could have gotten Larry Doby and Minnie Minoso too, and the As would still be playing in Philadelphia, because that would be all the outfield they'd have needed.

From the As Judy switched to the Phillies and helped sign Richie Allen.

He lived in Wampum, Pennsylvania, about 60 or 70 miles out of Pittsburgh. The Pirates had him at their park I don't know how many times, but they wouldn't give a nickle to Babe Ruth if they could get him for nothing, so I told our general manager, "That's the best looking prospect I've ever seen, please don't lose him," and he went out there and signed him.

But I wish you could have seen the players back when I was starting out. I guess I'm a loner now. There's very few of us left now, very few and far between.

I love to teach baseball. I'd rather do it than anything. I coached a sandlot team in Wilmington, my home. It's like putting a seed in the ground, you like to watch it develop. As long as they're ball players, they're my kids. I love 'em all.

Until his retirement in 1974, Johnson went to Florida with the Phils every spring.

Mr. Carpenter, the Phillies' owner, liked me, because I can help the Negro boys, also the white boys. If a kid does something wrong, I've got to go through the motions and show him the right way. You can't just holler at him, you've got to show him how the ball is handled, and that's what my boss liked about me. I played a lot of baseball, and I always tried to learn. I tell the kids, "Baseball is like school; you get promoted if you learn."

At least one authority, Ted Page, believed the majors squandered one of their most valuable resources in not employing Johnson years ago as a manager or at least a coach. "He had the ability to see the qualities, the faults, of ball players and have the correction for them," Page said and then continued:

I can tell you, "Man, you're popping the ball up." Heck, you know that better than anybody else. But why are you popping the ball up? Now Willie Stargell and I are good friends, but a few years ago Stargell was popping the ball up. He was turning his head. I don't think he even saw the ball. Judy could see things like that. I bet Judy could have helped Stargell out of his slump. Some have it and some don't. Judy should have been in the major leagues 15 or 20 years as a coach. He was a scout, but he would have done the major leagues a lot more good as somebody who could help develop ball players.

Judy Johnson

Year	Team	G	EAB*	H	2B	3B	HR	BA	SB
1921	Philadelphia	21	84	18	2	2	2	.214	1
1923	Philadelphia	18	76	18	—	—	—	.237	—
	Cuba	—	58	19	—	—	—	.345	—
1924	Philadelphia	68	272	85	9	3	4	.327	3
	Florida	3	12	6	0	0	0	.500	—
1925	Philadelphia	44	184	67	6	6	5	.364	0
	Cuba	6	24	6	—	—	—	.250	—
1926	Philadelphia	67	268	81	14	3	2	.302	—
	Cuba	—	145	54	—	—	—	.372	—
1927	Philadelphia	66	259	59	4	3	1	.228	2
	Cuba	—	134	44	—	—	3	.329	—
1928	Philadelphia	50	199	46	3	3	1	.231	0
	Cuba	—	88	30	7	1	0	.341	1
1929	Philadelphia	23	89	37	4	0	1	.416	1
1930	Phila Grays	16	69	19	0	1	0	.275	0
	Cuba	—	50	12	1	7	0	.240	1
1931	Philadelphia	49	176	50	4	3	0	.284	2
1932	Phil.-Pittsburgh	17	57	14	0	1	1	.246	1
1933	Pittsburgh	32	109	26	8	0	0	.239	0
1934	Pittsburgh	—	144	35	8	3	1	.243	1
1935	Pittsburgh	45	167	43	8	4	2	.257	2
1936	Pittsburgh	23	81	19	1	1	0	.235	1
Totals			2745	788	79	41	23	.287	16

Post-Season

Year	Team	G	EAB*	H	2B	3B	HR	BA	SB
1921	World Series	4	16	2	0	1	0	.188	0
1924	World Series	0	44	16	6	1	1	.364	0
1925	World Series	6	24	6	1	0	0	.250	1
1930	Play-Off	9	42	12	1	1	0	.286	0
1933	Play-Off	1	5	3	0	0	0	.600	—
1935	Play-Off	3	10	2	—	—	—	.200	—
Totals		33	141	41	8	3	1	.291	1
East-West		2	2	1	0	0	0	.500	0

*Estimated At Bats.

Judy Johnson vs. White Big Leaguers

Year	AB	H	2B	3B	HR	Pitcher	(W-L)
1926	(4)*	1	1	0	0	Quinn	(10-11)
	(4)	0	0	0	0	Grove	(13-13)
	4	2	0	0	0	Heimach	(3-9)
1927-28	4	2	0	1	0	Luque	(13-12)
	4	1	0	0	0	Luque	
1928	3	0	0	0	0	Bush	(2-1)
1931	3	0	0	0	0	Earnshaw	(21-7)
	(4)	1	0	0	0	Heimach	(9-7)
	(4)	0	0	0	0	Heimach	
	(4)	2	0	0	0	Heimach (Huggins)	
1932	(4)	1	0	0	0	Parmelee	(0-3)
	4	0	0	0	0	Swift	(14-10)
						Frankhouse	(4-6)
	4	3	0	0	0	Swift, French	
	3	0	0	0	0	Swift	
1934	1	0	0	0	0	Dean	(29-7)
	4	1	0	0	0	Dean, P. Dean	(19-7)
						Kline, (Cullop)	(7-2)
1935	4	2	0	0	0	Dean, Ryba,	
						Winford (28-11), (1-1)	(0-0)
1936	6	2	0	0	0	Whitehill	(14-11
						Kennedy	(21-9)
	4	2	0	0	0	Winford, Ryba	(11-10)
	4	0	0	0	0	Knott, Kennedy	(9-17)
Total 20 games	76	20	1	1	0	Average: .263	

* At bats in parentheses are estimated.

13

Joe Rogan:
Bullet Joe

Yeah, I pitched against Bullet Joe. Rogans was one of the world's greatest pitchers. I never did see him in his prime, if you want me to tell you the truth. I came up from Birmingham to Kansas City. He beat me 1–0 in the 11th inning. Yeah. He was the onliest pitcher I ever knew, I ever heard of in my life, was pitching and hitting in the clean-up place. He was a chunky little guy, but he could throw hard. He could throw hard as Smokey Joe Williams—yeah. Oh yes, he was a number-one pitcher, wasn't any maybe so.

Satchel Paige

Everyone who saw both Satchel Paige and Joe Rogan agrees: Little Bullet Joe was even better than Satchel, the man who succeeded him as the ace of the Kansas City Monarchs staff.

Newt "Colt" Allen, who, man and boy, played second base behind both stars in their primes, insisted that Rogan was the greatest pitcher he ever saw. "Rogan was better than Satchel because Rogan was smarter," Allen said. "Satchel was just a stuff pitcher; he had the stuff, but Rogan had the brains. I give Rogan the edge, because he knew how to pitch."

Judy Johnson nodded: "Satchel was fast. But Rogan was smart."

"Old Rogan," chuckled Dizzy Dean, "he was a showboat boy, a Pepper Martin ball player. He was one of those cute guys, never wanted to give you a ball to hit. Should be in the Hall of Fame."

Monarch pitcher Chet Brewer, later a scout for the Pirates, played with both Rogan and Paige and saw Walter Johnson, Grover Alexander, Bob Feller, and Sandy Koufax. "Rogan was the best pitcher I ever saw in my life," he said flatly and added:

Smokey Joe Williams was next in my book. Both were better pitchers than Satchel, but Satchel got all the publicity. Rogan could throw a curve ball faster than most pitchers could throw a fast ball. And he was the inventor of the palm ball. He had such a terrific fast ball, then he'd palm the ball and just walk it up there. Hitters were well off stride. I saw him one winter just make Al Simmons crawl trying to hit that ball.

Casey Stengel said Rogan was one of the best, if not the best, pitcher that ever pitched. He's told me that. I said, "Casey, I know it."

167

Brooklyn Dodger outfielder Babe Herman played against Rogan in California in the 1920s and in Canada in the 1930s, when Rogan was well over 40 years old and pushing 50. Herman said:

> He was the best colored pitcher I hit against, had one of the best curve balls I ever saw and a good, live fast ball. I always said he was much better than Satchel Paige. Satchel was real fast, but he had a lousy curve, and his fast ball was pretty straight. Rogan's fast ball was just *alive!* Did you ever see Luque play? I think Rogan must have learned his curve ball from him. Broke straight down. He could field his position good, and he used to hit a few over the fence in that small park they played in in Los Angeles.
> They ought to put some of those guys in the Hall of Fame. I told Casey Stengel, "The guys they put in the Hall of Fame are a joke. Rogan's the guy ought to go in." Casey recommended it to the commissioner, but it never took.

Frank Duncan, who caught Paige, Rogan, Joe Williams, and Dean in their heydays, rated Satchel and Rogan a toss-up as pitchers:

> I'd say Rogan and Satchel threw the fastest balls I ever saw, but Rogan also had a great curve with a three-foot drop on it. Bullet had a little more steam on the ball than Paige, and he had a better breaking curve ball. The batters thought it was a fast ball heading for them and they'd jump back from the plate, and all of a sudden, it would break sharply for a strike. I've never seen a pitcher like him, and I've caught some of the best.

Jocko Conlan, the Hall of Fame umpire, said he saw Rogan beat Red Faber of the White Sox. He had "an easy delivery," Conlan said, "and fast—much faster than Paige."

There could hardly have been a greater contrast between two men. Satchel was long and languid, Rogan short and explosive; Paige was comic and droll, Rogan moody and withdrawn; Paige's "be ball" actually buzzed as it flashed across home plate, Rogan threw an assortment of fast balls, curves, change-ups, and spitters; Paige made his windmill windup famous, Rogan was the first of the no-windup pitchers who delivered straight from the shoulder; Paige was an automatic out at bat, Rogan hit clean-up on black baseballs' most powerful murderers' row.

Perhaps no one in baseball history, except Babe Ruth and Martin Dihigo, could match Joe Rogan for all-round versatility at the bat and in the box. Yet Rogan was much smaller than either of them. Allen said he stood no taller than 5'5" and weighed about 155.

John "Buck" O'Neil of the Monarchs and later a coach for the

Chicago Cubs, said Rogan had thin legs, tremendous wrists, and a smooth swing. "You saw Ernie Banks hit in his prime—that was Rogan."

Duncan summed up:

> If you had to choose between Rogan and Paige, you'd pick Rogan, because he could hit. The pitching, you'd as soon have Satchel as Rogan, understand? But Rogan's *hitting* was so terrific. Get my point? Rogan was one of the best low-ball hitters I ever saw, and one of the best curve-ball hitters. Rogan taught Bob and Irish Meusel [of the New York Yankees and Giants] how to hit curve balls. They'd go out to the Coast in the winter time and play against him.

Bullet Joe stood deep in the batter's box, much like Roberto Clemente of a later generation and strode into the ball. "And he'd use a heavy bat," said ex-Monarch outfielder Willard Brown, who would play big-league ball with the St. Louis Browns. "He's the one started me to hitting with a heavy bat."

Buck O'Neil said Rogan "advocated getting the barrel of that bat out in front. And don't stand too close to that plate, because they'd jam you with the ball. He taught me footwork, hit off the balls of your feet, didn't want you to get on your heels."

Holland winced at the memory of one brush with Rogan's bat. "I had a 1–0 lead in the ninth, there was a man on and I had two strikes on Rogan. I just knew I was going to get this game, until one pitch I broke him a drop ball, and he lifted it up and hit it into the left field stand—home run—and beat me, 2–1."

Joe's Negro league average was .341. In 16 games against white big leaguers, from Lee Meadows in 1920 to Bob Feller in 1937, he hit .389.

No one knows how great the Bullet had been at his peak years in his twenties. He was already 30, toiling in obscurity for an army team under a boiling Arizona sun in 1919, when he was discovered by a former Kansas City dental student named Charles D. ("KC") Stengel, then an outfielder with the Pittsburgh Pirates barnstorming through the Southwest. Casey recalled:

> I first saw Rogan down below Albuquerque. We were down near the Mexican border, and the army brought these buglers and made all the soldiers line up and march across the ball field like this and pick up pebbles and rocks so we could play.
> We had a big guy pitched for St. Paul in the American Association who cheated. So before the game I went out behind home plate and announced:
> [Stentorian voice]: "Ladies and gentlemen"—but there were no ladies there—"ladies and gentlemen, we're now going to have a young

man that pitches this game today that throws that new, mysterious ball known as the *Tequilla Pitch!* It's taken from the tequilla plant." And Jesus, he was spitting all over the ball and everything else, you know, and cheating. So we won the game.

But Casey was impressed with the stocky black doughboy with the jug handle curve. "You know how Rogan pitched, don't you?" Stengel asked. "He pitched like this: without a windup. If you lean in, see, he pitches close; if you step back, you know what he'd come with? Outside."

When Casey got back home to Kansas City that winter, he looked up J. L. Wilkinson, a white man who was forming a new club called the Monarchs, and told him about Rogan and half a dozen other black soldier stars. Bullet Joe's pro career was launched at the age of 30.

Rogan—his real name was Wilbur Rogan—was born in Oklahoma City in 1889 (some records say 1893) and grew up in Kansas City, Kansas, where he started out as a catcher with Fred Palace's Colts in 1908. Three years later, according to Kansas City historian Phil Dixon, Rogan was with the Kansas City Giants, along with Bill Pettus, who also boxed as a heavyweight when he wasn't playing ball. (Pettus went on to the black big leagues as a first baseman.) The Giants won 54 straight games, Dixon said. Stengel was playing with the semipro Kansas City Benstons and may have played Rogan and the Colts some ten years before their traditional first meeting in Arizona.

In the autumn of 1911 Rogan joined the army and the following year was in the Phillippines and apparently captained the all-black 26th Infantry regimental baseball team there. Possibly he and the great Oscar Charleston served together.

Bert Cholston, who soldiered in the same company and later became an umpire in the Negro National League, would write that Rogan inspired confidence in his players because he knew the game thoroughly and gave encouragement to his men. He was open-minded, analytical, and courageous, Cholston said.

Cholston recalled one scrap Rogan got into with an exboxer named Bristoe, who had once been a sparring partner for the great heavyweight, Sam Langford. They went out behind the barracks to settle things, "and the fight lasted fully 45 minutes. Neither one gave an inch of ground. Rogan finally landed a terrific right hook to the stomach. It was ten minutes before his opponent recovered consciousness."

At some time in the army—perhaps then, perhaps later—Rogan picked up his scar, an ugly line across his cheek. Was it a memento of some unremembered fracas? Bullet Joe's catcher, William "Big C" Johnson, disagreed. The scar was the result of an operation, not a fight, Johnson said. Rogan had an abcessed tooth pulled, complications developed, "and they had to operate three times before they got the jaw straight."

By 1915 Rogan was serving in the machine gun company of the 25th Infantry, another black unit, in Schofield Barracks, Honolulu. He teamed up with three other buck privates—shortstop Dobie Moore, outfielder Oscar "Heavy" Johnson, and first baseman Lemuel Hawkins—to give the 25th a reputation on the diamond.

C. Johnson regarded Rogan as the best player he ever saw. "Charleston was everything—but Rogan was more," he said. "Rogan could do everything, everywhere. When I first met him, he was a catcher, he and Heavy Johnson. Whenever they needed a pitcher, Rogan would go on in there."

The army had some good teams in the Islands. Lefty Jim York, who would later join the Athletics, pitched for the First Infantry in Honolulu.

Years later the Kansas City *Star* would say that Rogan won 52 games in one year in the army, including 25 strikeouts in one game.

"Rogan looked like a soldier," Johnson said—"his deportment, his carriage." When he went to Honolulu on leave, he "put his Sunday clothes on—he was dressed."

By contrast, Moore was "a fair soldier," and Heavy Johnson was the typical army sad sack, in the guardhouse as often as he was out. But Heavy could hit and was given time off to play. He often won games with timely hits, and before he could be locked up again, his colonel had sent word to let him stay out. "He'd always hit himself out of jail." Johnson laughed. "I don't think he ever worked out a whole sentence."

On the diamond, Rogan had a good fast ball "and an exceptional curve ball," Johnson said. "He could throw a curve ball with the count three balls just as soon as a fast ball. He was almost sure he was going to throw it over the plate."

Joe Taylor, a crack rider and member of the army's bareback exhibition team (who later married Smokey Joe Williams' widow), also soldiered in the 25th and played with Rogan. "Rogan was very gentlemanfied," he said,

easy going, a jolly good fellow. In those days there was a syndicate in the army. If you didn't click in with that syndicate, you didn't get nowhere. His greatest pitch was his fast ball. They called him Bullet even then. You were also allowed to throw the spit ball in those days. Rogan used to chew slippery elm, and that made the saliva slippery. We had another outstanding pitcher named Linden, about five-feet-four tall, a very cunning pitcher. He had some of the greatest curves I have ever seen. He and Rogan were the mainstays of the 25th pitching staff.

Bill Holland, a top pitcher himself in the Negro leagues, said a lot of all-star teams stopped in Hawaii to play. "They say any time Rogan was pitching, all the army officers would bring a sackful of money to bet. You couldn't beat him."

In February 1917 the Portland Beavers of the Pacific Coast league arrived in Honolulu to train. With past or future big leaguers like Charlie Hollocher and Babe Pinelli, they scheduled a game against the 25th Infantry and Rogan. The Bullet whipped them, 3–0, on a two-hitter, with 13 strike outs. He walked three. At bat, he drilled a double in three times up.

Rogan left the service briefly in the fall of 1917 to pitch for the Los Angeles White Sox, a black team, in the California winter league, then returned to the army, to the old Indian-fighting outpost of Fort Huachuca on the sun-parched Mexican border. Besides Rogan, who both pitched and caught, the post's all-black baseball team boasted shortstop Dobie Moore, Bob Fagin at second, Hurley McNair and "Heavy" Johnson in the outfield, Hawkins at first, and lefty Andy Cooper pitching. It must have been one of the strongest nonprofessional clubs in the country. Rogan may have reached the pinnacle of his abilities out there in the Southwest, far from the big cities and the newspapers that would have insured his fame.

After Stengel touted them to Wilkinson, Rogan and his army buddies bought their way out of the service and reported to the Monarchs in mid-season in 1920.

Joe Rue, who later umpired in the white majors, got his start working in the Negro National League of 1920. He told author Larry Gerlach that, next to Bob Feller and Walter Johnson, Bullet Rogan was the fastest pitcher he ever saw, and his fellow Monarch, Rube Currie, had "as good a curve as Tommy Bridges."

Rue added:

> There were great players in that league, who, had they not been denied on account of their color, would have been major league stars. The Monarchs had a wonderful ball club. . . . [They] played barnstorming major leaguers each year—Casey Stengel, George Sisler, Zach Wheat, Hal Chase, those kinds of players—and beat them. Boy, I mean they'd *beat* them. There were ball players in that league. They were terrific. If Branch Rickey had been there, he would have gotten a handful.

Fifteen-year-old Chet Brewer shinnied up a tree outside the Kansas City park to get a look at the team's new pitching star. "He was raw-boned and tough as nails," Brewer remembered. "Rogan had that running fast ball. And he was the master of the palm ball. The same big delivery, and the ball just walked up to the plate. That pitch, right behind that fast fall, was something!"

Rogan also threw a fork ball, spit ball, and a "master" curve ball, Newt Allen said. His side-arm curve jumped in on the batter like an emery ball.

(Rogan had three curves, said outfielder Crush Holloway: a slider, a regular curve, and a jug handle that looked like an "L.")

"I'd never seen a straight drop before," Monarch first baseman George Giles whistled. "Rogan's looked like it was falling off the table." "Every pitch had a reason and a spot," said Giles, whose grandson played shortstop for the Mets. "He pitched from the side. Never did wind up. He'd watch the batter, and if the batter was swinging his bat too much getting ready, if Rogan caught him with his bat out front, he never did get a chance to get it back. Bullet was that quick."

And he perfected the no-windup delivery 40 years before Stengel taught it to Don Larsen and Bob Turley of the Yankees. "He'd just throw from the shoulder, and it was gone!" Allen whistled. "He threw hard!"

"Yeah," sighed pitcher-outfielder Jesse Hubbard, "Rogan was the smartest pitcher you'd want to see. He'd throw you three straight changes of pace, and throw you strikes, then turn around and throw you three drop balls, you couldn't see them, and fast balls right here at the knees all day long."

Rogan mixed this farago up, keeping the hitter off stride, then fooled him with the pitch he'd been waiting for all along. By this time "the hitter just stood there and looked at it in surprise," said Allen. "Six out of ten times he wouldn't even swing."

Satchel was easier to catch, Duncan said. "He could throw it in a quart cup." But Rogan was all over the plate—high, low, inside, outside. "He'd walk five-six men, but he didn't give up many runs."

Rogan was just keeping the hitters off balance. He "could thread a needle with that fast ball or curve" when he wanted to, insisted Bill Foster, Rogan's long-time rival on the Chicago American Giants.

Joe used to inspect players' bats before the game, then taunt them: "That bat's no good. No sir, today old Bullet Joe's pitching, and no bat's gonna help you."

"On the 3-and-2 he'd tell you he was going to throw a curve," Duncan said. "Oscar Charleston was one of the greatest ball players ever lived; they rated him better than Tris Speaker. He and Rogan were in the Army together. Rogan would tell me, 'Get down behind him, Frank, he ain't gonna hit nothin'."

Chicago shortstop Bobby Williams noted that Rogan could field too: "He was another infielder when he was pitching."

Stengel recalled another game, so far unconfirmed: "We had 11,000 people in the bandbox, we filled the park and went 11 innings, and we won the game on a home run by Bob Meusel. I think the umpire missed the pitch before it, or he'd have been struck out."

Statistics for 1920 are incomplete, particularly for home games, which were rarely reported that year in either Kansas City's black or white press. But for 17 road games that have been found so far, Rogan hit .269. His pitching record was 5–1. He started six games and completed all six.

He hit better against white big leaguers, however. In November Rogan and most of the other new Monarchs journeyed to Los Angeles for the winter league, which also drew several stars of the white major leagues. In his first game, Bullet faced Pittsburgh's Lee "Specs" Meadows (0–0), who was backed by a lineup that included Stengel and both Meusels. Irish hit .319 with the Phils and Bob .309 as a rookie with the Yankees. Together they came up eight times against the Bullet and failed to get a hit. Rogan himself punched two singles against Meadows and won the game, 6–4.

Six days later he smashed a home run and double off Speed Martin (4–15) of the Cubs to help his club win again, 6–3. The next day he lost, 4–0, to Walter "The Great" Mails, who had a perfect 7–0 mark with Cleveland that year, plus a 1–0 victory in the World Series against Brooklyn.

In 1921 in the Negro league Rogan won 14 and lost 7. He started 20 games, completed every one of them, and gave up an average of only 2.72 runs per game in the free-hitting Negro National League (earned runs aren't available). He also raised his batting average to .263 and stole 13 bases in 45 games.

That fall the Monarchs challenged the hometown Kansas City Blues of the American Association. The Blues finished third that year and boasted a team batting average of no less than .315. They had Bunny Brief, the Association's home run champ with 42 homers and 191 runs batted in, plus the league's leading batter, Artie Butler, and Gus Bono, a 25-game winning pitcher. The Monarchs won the first game, 7–5. Rogan pitched the second contest, striking out Brief three times and holding Butler hitless, only to lose, 3–2, when Duncan's error let in two runs in the seventh.

The next year, 1922, the Bullet raised his average to .326 and slugged 13 home runs in 47 games, only two homers behind the league leader, Oscar Charleston, who played 18 more games. Many Kansas City home games went unrecorded; if they are ever found, Bullet Joe might turn out to have been the real home-run leader that year. Hit pitching record was 7–5, and for the third year in a row he completed every game he started, 12.

That fall Rogan gained his revenge on the Blues. Again the Blues had Brief (40 homers), plus Glenn Wright, who would go on to star at shortstop for the Pittsburgh Pirates. But they were no match for the Monarchs, who won five of the six games played. Rogan won his game 7–6; he also went 2-for-4 at bat and for good measure added a stolen base.

Monarch pitcher Bill "Plunk" Drake won his game, 6–2. Drake recalled:

> That was just a wonderful feeling for the Blues to play the Monarchs. It was just something exciting, and the crowds were wonderful. And when we played the Blue or those teams, we got a lot of recognition from the fellows. We talked with those boys. They'd come right over and chat with you and tell you what a good ball player you were. I've had lots of white ball players say to me, "It's a shame you're black," meaning if I was white, I'd be playing up there too.

Rogan was the pride of Kansas City, his picture prominently displayed on movie screens to advertise the game.

Off the field, though, he had a reputation for being arrogant and hard to get along with. Newt Allen disagreed. "Rogan was a good fellow if he knew you well," Allen said,

> but he didn't associate with too many people, only his real friends. He was the kind of guy, if he liked you, he would talk baseball with you, but if he didn't like you, he wouldn't. He never was a fellow to talk about how good he was or anything of that sort. We've gone to bars and if there was some fellow he didn't take to, why, he wouldn't talk any baseball. It

The U.S. Army's 25th Infantry team (c.1922). Front (left to right) are Dobie Moore, Joe Rogan, Lemuel Hawkins, unknown, Oscar Johnson, and, rear (left to right), four unidentified players, Andy Cooper, Hurley McNair, and an unidentified player. Photo courtesy John Coates.

wasn't that he was arrogant. A lot of people said he was that way because
he was such a star, but when you knew him, you would understand him.

In 1923 Rogan hit a rousing .435 in 20 games—his slugging
average was a Ruthian .768. His pitching record was a disappointing
10–7, and for the first time in his professional career he was knocked
out of the box; he started 16 games but completed only 15 of them.
However, his statistics are deceiving, for he gave up only 99 hits in 134
innings, meaning that opponents batted a low .167 against him. (The
white major league record is .168, by Luis Tiant in 1968.) In August
Rogan and Jose Mendez combined to throw a no-hitter, Mendez going
the first five innings and Bullet Joe the last four.

Two months later Joe faced big Jim Bagby (3–2) of the Pirates,
who was backed up by Zach Wheat (.375) with Brooklyn, Cotton
Tierney (.312) of the Phils, and Pat Collins (.177) of the Browns. Joe
beat them, 7–6.

The 1924 season was the finest in Rogan's life. He played in 50
games as pitcher, outfielder, and second baseman, hit .411, second
only to Moore's (.470), and led all pitchers in victories with a 15–5
record, as the Monarchs won their first pennant.

Rogan held a jinx over the American Giants; they never could
seem to beat him in Chicago on a Sunday. The jinx held in September,
when the Monarchs came to Chicago for a crucial four-game series.
The Giants won three of the games, but Rogan won the fourth—on a
Sunday—by a score of 9–5 (he also got two hits), and the Monarchs
held onto their lead and won the pennant.

If there had been a vote for Most Valuable Player that year,
Rogan would surely have been the unanimous choice.

It was a fortuitous year to win because the Eastern Colored
League has been formed the year before, and by 1924 the two leagues
had agreed to meet in the first black world series. So it was the
Monarchs versus the Hilldales of Philadelphia in the first game in
Shibe Park. To Bullet Rogan naturally went the honor of pitching the
opening game against Phil Cockrell, Hilldale's spitball ace with an 11–
2 record.

"Rogan was tough," muttered Hilldale shortstop Jake Stephens.
"He had a good hard one and just enough meanness in him to keep
you honest up there at home plate. If you dig in, you make him wild."
Rogan won the game, 6–2, and clipped Cockrell for two hits.

Hilldale won the second game, and when the series shifted to
Baltimore, the two clubs battled into the 11th inning tied, 5–5. In the
top of the inning, Newt Allen's double and Rogan's single put the
Monarchs ahead, but Hilldale tied it again just before darkness descended, and the final score was 6–6.

There was a five-day hiatus before the two clubs met for the first game in Kansas City in old Muehlebach Park, which was also home to the Blues and later the Athletics.

Rogan took the mound against Hilldale's ace left-hander, Jesse "Nip" Winters (26–4), perhaps the best lefty in black history, and carried a 2–1 lead into the eighth. Two infield errors (one of them his own) and a hit filled the bases with no outs, but the Bullet bore down and got the next two outs on force plays at the plate, then fanned Winters, a good hitter (.333), to end the threat.

In the ninth Rogan hit Otto Briggs (.243) and got Frank Warfield (.251) on a pop-up. Then luck turned against him. Biz Mackey (.363), later Roy Campanella's tutor, singled to center field, and outfielder Carroll "Dink" Mothell let the ball get by him, putting runners on second and third and ending the chance of a double play. Catcher Joe Lewis (.254) hit a ground ball and was safe when first baseman Hawkins missed touching the bag, and one run scored. Then Judy Johnson (.327) stepped up and smote one over Mothell's head for a homer to win the game.

That put the Monarchs down, three games to one, but they fought back to take the next one. In the first inning, Rogan, playing center field, drilled a hit against Cockrell to start a three-run rally. Although he made two bad plays in the outfield, letting two runs in, the Monarchs won, 6–5.

In the next game, facing Winters again, Rogan walked in the eighth and scored on Heavy Johnson's single to tie the score, 3–3, and send the game into extra innings. Finally in the 12th, George Sweatt of Kansas City smashed a long triple, and Rogan's infield hit to shortstop Judy Johnson scored the winning run. The Monarchs had tied the series, three games all.

Kansas City named Rogan to pitch the tie-breaking eighth game. They really wanted this one, because the Hilldale hurler was Rube Currie (2–5), a Kansas City native who had jumped the Monarchs to go East in the baseball war of 1923. He had already beaten his old mates once in the series and had played so long in Rogan's shadow that he wanted to crush his old rival. And Currie was in command, with a 2–0 shutout going into the ninth. Then, with one out, Rogan himself beat out a hit to third, moved to second on a ground out, took third on Moore's infield hit, and scored on McNair's single. After Heavy Johnson was hit by a pitch to load the bases, Duncan hit a high foul to the screen, which Hilldale catcher Louis Santop dropped for one of the classic muffs of black baseball history. Duncan promptly whacked the next pitch through third baseman Biz Mackey's legs for two runs and victory.

Hilldale won the next game to tie it again, four games to four, but the Monarch's 40-year-old manager, Jose Mendez, won the final game, 5–0, on a five-run rally in the ninth.

Rogan came out of the historic series a hero. He had pitched four games, won two, lost one, and tied one, and had played the other six games in center field. In every game, whether he pitched or played outfield, he hit in the third slot and batted .325, second best on the Monarchs.

That winter, 1924–1925, Rogan went to Cuba, where he was 9–4. His batting average is not available. He pitched the championship game for Almendares, managed by the Cincinnati Reds' great pitcher, Adolfo Luque. Rogan was winning, 2–1, in the ninth, Brewer said, with the bases loaded and "a great Cuban hitter named Alejandro Oms up. Everybody in Cuba knew Oms could hit the curve ball." So Biz Mackey, probably the greatest catcher in blackball history, wagged one finger for a fast ball. Rogan shook him off. Mackey called time and went out to the mound.

"Bullet," he said, "you know this man can hit a curve ball."

"He can't hit mine," Rogan replied.

"You have to be crazy," Mackey muttered.

"You do the catching," Rogan said, "I'll do the pitching."

Mackey squatted back down behind the plate and flashed the sign for a fast ball again. Again Rogan shook him off. This time Mackey trotted over to Luque in the dugout. "This man out there must be crazy," he said. "He wants to throw a curve ball."

"Well," Luque shrugged, "it's his money, just like it's ours, and he's doing the pitching. I guess we'll have to go along with it."

Said Brewer: "Rogan threw Oms a drop ball, an overhand breaking ball. Oms left the ground. His cap came off, swinging at it. Rogan threw him two more and walked away. Oh, he could throw that ball!"

In the summer of 1925 Joe batted .368 and had another excellent year on the pitching mound, with a 14–2 mark, again topping the league in victories. He gave up only 2.11 total runs per game. Back in that error-prone era, unearned runs often made up to half of all runs, so Rogan's ERA, if it could be known, might well have been down around 1.25. With only 113 hits in 145 innings, enemy batters hit a mere .206 against him, estimated—a very low figure for the lively ball era. With Joe leading the way, the Monarchs won the second half pennant and met the St. Louis Stars—Cool Papa Bell, Willie Wells, Mule Suttles, etc.—in the play-off.

Rogan won the first game, 8–6. Then, with the Monarchs trailing three games to two, he pitched the sixth game. Though he collected three hits, he went into the ninth still losing, when the Monarchs put two men on, with Moore at bat and Rogan on deck. St. Louis manager

Candy Jim Taylor ordered a walk to Moore, then, said Wells, "Rogan came up and got his fourth straight hit and beat us, 5–4."

Playing center field the next game, Rogan made a brilliant over-the-head catch to try to save the game, though the Monarchs lost, 2–1.

He pitched and won the third game, 5–4.

Bullet went back to the mound in the finale and played in Chicago amid a snow flurry. He collected one hit in two at bats and won with a shutout, 4–0. In all, he had won three games, all complete games, and batted an even .500 to lead the Monarchs to victory.

"He beat us out of the championship," Wells said. "You know, on the way back to St. Louis, I really cried. Rogan could pitch, he could hit, he could run. Satchel Paige was more like a kid, he was just playful. But Bullet Rogan was something else!"

Rogan was all set for a rematch with the Hilldales in the World Series when bad luck struck. He was romping on the floor with his infant son when the boy ran a needle into the Bullet's knee. It took an operation to remove it. Rogan rode the bench throughout the series, and the Monarchs lost, five games to one, though several contests went extra innings.

That winter Rogan played in the California winter league and pitched his club of Negro leaguers to the pennant with a 4–3 victory in the final game over Charlie Root, who won 23 games in the Pacific Coast League and was on his way up to the Cubs. Rogan gave up a home run in the second inning and walked the bases full in the fourth but pitched out of the jam. Then, with two men on, he drove a double off the center-field fence to take the lead. Rap Dixon singled him in, and Rogan went on to win.

In 1926 Jose Mendez stepped down as manager of the Monarchs, and Rogan was named to succeed him. Mothell didn't like the decision. "Rogan wanted to run the ball club like they did it in the army," he said. "He liked to give orders too much, even before he was managing. He used to bawl players out for different things. I could take it, but we had ball players, when he'd get on them, they'd go into a shell, resented it, and didn't give him their best. But Rogan was a good man, even though he and I didn't get along so well off the ball field."

"Rogan wasn't the best manager," Brewer agreed, "because he was such a great ball player himself. He couldn't teach pitchers much, because he'd say, 'All you have to do is go out and throw the man what I threw.'" Brewer recalled one game when the Monarchs' Henry McHenry was pitching against Mule Suttles, who, old-timers say, could hit as hard as Josh Gibson. "But he couldn't hit Rogan's curve—very few people could. Rogan told McHenry to throw Mule a curve ball, and Mule hit it 500 feet." When McHenry came back to the dugout, Rogan said, "I thought I told you to throw him a curve ball."

"I did."

"Well," Rogan said drily, "you didn't have nothin' on it then."

"It was so easy for him," Brewer said. "he thought it should be easy for you. He didn't know how great he was."

"He was pretty strict," George Giles recalled. "Maybe he didn't like a youngster like me coming in, taking Lemuel Hawkins' place at first base. He wouldn't let me drink any water at the water fountain. All the guys could drink, but it looked like he rode me. The next year Mr. Wilkinson told me he was going to let Hawkins go. I told Rogan, 'I'm going to drink water this year.' He said he was just kidding me, wanted to see how much guts I had, see could I stay with the team."

However, Willie Powell, a rookie with the rival American Giants, remembered Rogan fondly. Just before his first game with the Giants, Powell asked Rogan how to throw the screwball. Bullet Joe gladly showed him, much to the anger of Frank Duncan, Newt Allen, and other Monarch batters. Rogan brushed their protests off. "I'll help any man I can," he told Powell. "If he tries to help himself, I'll help him; but if he doesn't try to help himself, forget it."

Rogan was a gentleman," Powell said. "He was the best pitcher I ever saw, except Dave Brown of the Giants. Later I played on the same ball club with Satchel Paige. I'd take Rogan over Satchel."

In May the club's top hitter, Dobie Moore, was shot in the leg, and it thus fell on Rogan's shoulders to carry the team alone. The strain didn't seem to bother him. He hit .314, with a 12–4 record on the mound. The Monarchs won the first half but, without Moore, stumbled in the second half, which was won by their old rivals, the American Giants. Once again the two foes met in the play-off.

Bullet Joe came in in relief to win the first game 4–3 against Chicago's rookie ace, Big Bill Foster.

The next day Rogan also won in relief, 6–5; he yielded three hits and no runs over the last four innings. In the sixth, with the score tied, two outs, and a man on third, Rogan hit a ground ball and beat it out. Chicago catcher Jim Brown "raised the devil," the Chicago *Defender* wrote, but Rogan got the hit, as well as the winning RBI.

Brewer shut Chicago out in the third game. The Monarchs lost the fourth game to their old teammate, Currie, now with Chicago. But Rogan started the fifth game against Foster and whipped him again, 11–5. The Monarchs led the best-of-nine series four games to one.

Then Chicago made its move. Currie shut out Brewer on a two-hitter. In game seven, Chicago led, 2–1, after eight innings, when Hurley McNair reached second on a two-base error. Rogan then knocked the ball over Sandy Thompson's head in center field for two bases. McNair stopped at third. Hawkins' double drove both runners in to put the Monarchs ahead, 3–2. However, in the bottom of the ninth, two walks and an infield single loaded the bases. Hawkins' error let in one run, and a passed ball let in another, as the American Giants won.

The play-offs thus came down to the final double-header, and the two aces, Rogan and Foster, would face each other in the first game. It was a classic, which Foster won by a score of 1–0 to tie the series.

Rogan retired to the clubhouse between games, while the rookie, Brewer, with a 12–1 won-lost record, warmed up to pitch the finale. Chet was confident of victory. It was getting dark, he said, "and no way did they want to see me coming in."

When the Bullet walked back onto the field, he was surprised to see Foster warming up for Chicago. "You gonna pitch?" he demanded, incredulous.

"Yeah, I'm gonna pitch," Big Bill replied.

"Well, I'm coming back too," Rogan replied, grabbing the ball out of Brewer's hand.

It was the worst managerial decision of his career. Possibly he had cooled off too much between games; in the first inning he was banged for five runs. Then he settled down, but it was too late. The final score was 5–0 and Chicago was champ. The outcome was bitter, but it had been a great series for the Little Giant, who ended up hitting .583.

Over the winter of 1926–1927 he returned to the Coast and reportedly won 17 games out of 21 starts. In two games against Cubs rookie Charlie Root (18–17), Rogan got four hits in five at bats, including a double and a home run.

A fine pool shark as well as pitcher, Rogan invested in a pool hall at 18th and Grove in Kansas City. The Kansas City *Call* reported that the establishment was newly decorated, with a soda fountain, candy case, and a ticker tape with the latest scores of all the games, white and black. No liquor was allowed, as well as "no singing, whistling, dancing, boisterous noise, or gambling." In fact, it was a place "where ladies can visit during the day on weekdays."

Rogan had another fine year in 1927, with a 15–6 win-loss mark and a .337 batting average, although the Monarchs, without Dobie Moore, finished second.

In 1928 Bullet Joe picked up his average to .354, with a 9–2 pitching record and a total run average of just 2.84.

In 1929 he hit .344 and stole 23 bases in 73 games—at the age of 39! He virtually gave up pitching. But he had one masterpiece left in his arm.

October 31, 1929, San Francisco

All Stars	AB	H	R		Royal Giants	AB	H	R
2B Morehart	3	0	0		2B Mothell	4	1	1
2B Pick	1	1	1		SS Allen	4	1	0
SS Haney	4	2	0		CF Holloway	3	2	2
CF Simmons	5	0	0		1B Mackey	5	2	1
RF Jolley	4	1	0		RF Livingstone	3	1	1
1B P Foxx	3	3	1		C Young	5	1	0
LF R Meusel	4	1	0		3B Joseph	3	2	2
CF Wingo	4	0	0		LF Taylor	4	2	1
C McMullen	3	1	1		P Rogan	3	2	2
P A Campbell	0	0	0			34	14	10
P Gould	1	0	0					
P Edleman	2	1	0					
PH Cotter	1	0	0					
	35	10	3					

HR: Mackey, Pick, Joseph
3B: Holloway
2B: Foxx 2, Rogan
SB: Rogan, Holloway, Taylor
SO: Rogan 8, Foxx, Gould
W: Rogan 2, Campbell 3, Gould
LP: Campbell

In October he traveled to California for the winter season. Young Wally Berger, later an outfielder for the Braves, saw Joe pitch in San Jose. "He really could fire," Berger said.

That was the year the Bullet gave Al Simmons fits. "I'm not surprised," Berger said. Rogan opened with a homer against Hollis Thurston, former Dodger, to help win the first game, 12–8. He got a single and double off Washington's Archie Campbell (0–0) to win the second game, 6–5.

Then Bullet Joe took the rubber for the third game against Simmons (.365), Jimmy Foxx (.354), Bob Meusel (.261), and Fred Haney (.115). Rogan beat them, 10–3, scattering ten hits, with eight strikeouts. He got two hits himself, one a double, and stole a base. That gave him five hits for 12 at bats for the three games. Foxx hit him hard, with a single and two doubles for a perfect day. But poor Simmons couldn't touch him. He went 0-for-5 with three strikeouts.

Bullet Joe pitched that game on October 31. Only two days earlier, the stock market had crashed, and though no one suspected it yet, the depression had begun. It killed the Negro leagues, and the once proud Monarchs were reduced to barnstorming and passing the hat.

In August 1930 Rogan was hitting .311 when he was struck down by an ailment that was not identified, was hospitalized in very serious condition, and was out for the rest of the season.

But he returned to the club as manager, pinch-hitter, and some-time pitcher.

The Monarchs dropped out of the league for a few years, prefer-ring to barnstorm with their new lights, criss-crossing the prairies from Texas to Canada.

Rogan faced his share of racism, and not only in the South. "We were playing in Neosha, Kansas," Brewer said, "when some kids called out, 'Look at the niggers, look at the niggers.' "

Rogan called one of the boys over. "Come here, son, I want to talk to you."

"Yes sir."

"Where did you learn to say niggers? Did your father and mother teach you?"

"No sir."

"Well, did your teachers teach you?"

"No."

"What do they teach you to call us?"

"They teach us to call you colored people. But I call you niggers because it's easier."

"When I first saw Rogan," said Bill Cornelius, a rookie pitcher in 1933, "he wasn't able to pitch a full nine-inning ball game any more; age had caught up with him. But for four or five innings he could show you as much as any pitcher." Joe could still hit too. That year he came in fourth in the vote of the fans for an outfield berth in the East-West, or all-star, game.

That fall Rogan faced Dizzy Dean (20–18) and Lou Garland, who was on his way up to the White Sox. Bullet walked and scored on a double steal. In the ninth, with the Monarchs losing, 4–3, he came to bat with men on first and third, missed two strikes, then dropped a single over the infield to score both runners and win the game.

In the fall of 1934 Rogan faced Dean's All Stars for two games. That was the year Diz led the Cardinals to the world championship with a 29–7 in the regular season and three more victories in the World Series. (Dean is usually credited with 30 victories, but one of the victories was actually a Save, according to G. L. Fleming in *The Dizziest Season*.) Joe got one hit in four tries against Diz and brother Paul (19–11) and drove in a run.

In 1935 Dizzy's record was 28–12. Again he and Paul (19–12) faced Rogan, who went 1-for-3, as Diz beat the Monarchs 1–0.

Then the Monarchs embarked for the Orient and a tour of China, the Philippines, Japan, and Hawaii. They marveled at the teeming junks in Hong Kong, were impressed with the caliber of ball in Japan, and were tempted by an offer from Dole Pineapple to play semipro ball in Hawaii.

Instead, however, they returned to the United States. In the fall of 1936 Rogan faced the Phils' Joe Bowman (9–20) and young Mort Cooper, then still a minor leaguer. Joe got one hit in three at bats against them.

In 1937, at the age of 48, Joe stepped in to bat for the last time against white big leaguers. His opponents: Mace Brown (10–11), Lon Warneke (18–11), and a teenage rookie phenom named Bob Feller (9–7). The trio gave up only four hits, three of them by Rogan. He even stole a base.

Those would be his last three hits against white big leaguers, to their immense relief. He left with a .341 average against them. But remember, the earliest box score recorded is in 1920, when the Bullet was already 31 years old. What might he have hit in the decade before that?

Rogan coached Monarch youngsters like Willard Brown and Buck O'Neil. He still had that smooth swing of his youth, O'Neil said.

> He could hit that ball. And even then his arm was pretty good. A good curve ball. He could just about tie you up. He would talk hour upon hour about hitting. He taught me quite a bit. He was the type of guy stood a long way from the plate. Not too close, because they'd jam you. It really worked for me; my arms were kind of long anyway. And he taught me footwork, hit off the balls of your feet. He wouldn't only tell you, he did a pretty good job of demonstrating it. He was very smooth, swung that bat good. He would stand in the box and announce, "This one's going over third." And, he'd hit it there—pfft. "This one over shortstop"—pfft.

Rogan managed the Monarchs and pitched occasionally until about 1938, when Chicago's Nat Rogers drilled a hit through the box that almost broke his fingers.

The Bullet took to umpiring and often called balls and strikes on the Monarch's new ace, Satchel Paige. That's where he was when Monarch rookie Othello Renfroe joined the team in 1945.

"Oh ho, they used to tell some stories about that guy!" Renfroe said. "What they say about him was unbelievable, how hard he could throw. He wasn't a big guy, but he was as hard as a rock. You could just look at the guy throwing the ball around at 50-some-years-old and see how agile he must have been."

After Rogan left baseball he worked for the post office, living quietly with his wife on their farm by a lake outside of town. He died there in 1964.

News of Rogan's death stirred memories going back 40 years for Paul W. Fisher of the Pittsburg, Kansas, *Times:*

Go a hundred or so miles in any direction from Kansas City and stop in any of one of 200 or more towns south as far as Texas, west of the Rockies, north well into Montana, and east to the Mississippi. Ask a thousand or so men and women if they were living in that particular town in, say, 1927, or 1929, or 1933, when Bullet Joe Rogan and the Kansas City Monarchs came to play. And if they had, there will be a sudden animation and an astonishing number of them will volunteer, "I'll never forget how Bullet Joe. . . ." or "I can see him now. . . ."

And sometimes dozing on the square of a Girard or a Neosho, a Sulphur Springs or an Afton, a rickety old man will struggle to his feet, face his cronies, plant his right foot on an imaginary mound, cup his hands at his waist, and illustrate Bullet Joe's distinctive windup. No one laughs.

The mimic may be 75 too, as the mortal Rogan was at death, and the mimic's old bones may pop and groan with his artistry. But no one laughs. They are all looking back into the hot sunlight of 40 years ago, seeing Rogan exactly as he was to them then, as he is to them now, gravely pleased that their minds can summon into motion at will that gifted, supple man they so esteemed.

Yet what the people of the plains gave to Rogan and the Monarchs was far more than esteem. It was an instant, warm, and enduring affection. They were superb athletes but they had a far higher quality. They were superb men. They were young and full of laughter. They were erect, gracious, and unafraid.

"We went into every town with two ideas," Frank Duncan, the able catcher and manager, said yesterday. "We would give the people our very best and we wanted to be their friends. I never heard an unkind word and we found an awful lot of nice people. They once said Picher, Okla., was a tough, rowdy town where we'd find trouble. We went in as men expecting the best and we got the best. I got pretty badly hurt there but the Picher people took care of me like I was one of their own family. . . ."

Consider one of those great and wonderful days. It is a warm, yellow September Sunday in the late 1920s, barely noon, ordinarily a time when there is little motion in Pittsburg, Kansas. Today the town is in ferment. Broadway, the main street, streams with traffic, all bound north to the fairgrounds. The Fords and Essexes, the Chevies and Darts, the Buicks and Hupmobiles growl along, bumper to bumper, many bearing Missouri, Oklahoma, or Arkansas tags.

The pedestrian traffic swings along the walk thickly. Some fathers carrying picnic baskets in one hand, support young sons on the opposite shoulder. Strangely, there are no bicycles.

Then, abruptly at Fourth Street, the traffic breaks. A moment passes. Into the vacuum an army of boys and girls come sweeping and planing on their bikes, the vanguard for the Monarch bus carrying the team. The players had dressed a block down the street at the Y with its showers and lockers, essential for all the fried chicken, hams, picalilli, cakes, pies, and other edibles the townsmen will present through the day to the Monarchs.

At the fairgrounds, scores of little boys and girls stand shyly on the plot of grass where the bus unloads. Each of the 16 Monarchs picks his thralls. Each goes marching off toward the field with this little girl carrying his sunglasses, this small Negro boy with his baseball shoes, these blond brothers with his two bats, this barefoot Italian lad with his glove. Frank Duncan resembles a Pied Piper, since it requires a small battalion to carry his vast array of catching equipment. Rogan, the old soldier of the 25th Infantry, who usually marches with quick steps, comes last, accommodating his steps slowly to two tough little Irish kids, who are choked with their good fortune, each holding one of Rogan's hands just like little old sissies.

Pittsburgh has finished its hitting drill and the Monarchs now go to the cage. Big Chet Brewer is the Monarchs' batting practice pitcher today; the Monarch bats go spat, spat, spat, the drives fly on a line to every corner of the park. The stands are already packed. Hundreds of

Joe Rogan examining old clippings. Photo courtesy Black Archives of Mid-America.

onlookers are moving along the ropes stretched to distant reaches of the outfield along the foul lines. Why, 6 or 7,000 fans are here if you count the kids and that toddler who somehow has decided that if Bullet Joe is going to sit on the bench, he's going to sit on Joe's lap.

At last, Bullet Joe marches to the mound. Absolute silence. He idly throws four soft tosses to Duncan, then nods, and the first batter steps to the plate.

It's so quiet you think you can hear the crowd breathing. Every eye is strained on the mighty Rogan. He is a trim, square-shouldered, deep-chested man, with slim legs and hips. He brings his hands softly to his belt buckle, his hips begin to pivot slowly right, the hands come slowly and softly toward his face and then—

His right arm has swept back quicker than the eye, whipped around and over and at slightly less than a three-quarters motion. In the yellow afternoon a mote of white light flies from his black hand. The fortunate among the thousands caught its split-second speed; even at the far reaches of the roped outfield, they heard its crash into Duncan's big glove. WHAP!

A kindly soldierly man has thrown a sunbeam. A great, friendly appreciative roar. A sight a man will remember to his dying day.

Bullet Joe Rogan

Year	G	AB	H	2B	3B	HR	BA	SB	SA
1920	17	67	18	4	3	0	.269	5	.418
1921	45	137	36	7	2	3	.263	13	.409
1922	47	172	56	6	5	13	.326	8	.703
1923	20	69	30	3	1	6	.435	4	.768
1924	50	146	60	11	7	5	.411	0	.685
1925	57	157	58	12	8	3	.368	6	.605
1926	46	118	37	6	3	2	.314	3	.466
1927	49	101	34	3	2	2	.337	1	.465
1928	59	189	67	14	4	5	.354	5	.550
1929	73	262	90	17	8	6	.344	23*	.538
1930	28	103	32	5	0	1	.311	5	.388
Totals	491	1521	518	88	43	46	.341	74	.546
Post-Season									
1924 World Series	10	40	13	1	0	0	.325	3	.350
1925 Play-Offs	5	14	7	0	0	0	.500	1	.500
1926 Play-Offs	6	12	7	1	0	0	.580	0	.667
	21	66	27	2	0	0	.410	4	.439

* Led League.

Bullet Joe Rogan
Pitching

Year	G	GS	CG	IP	H	R	SO	BB	(W-L)	TRA[a]	PA[c]
1920	8	6	6	56	45	27	32	20	(5-1)	4.34	.221
1921	21	20	20	172	120	52	68	46	(14-7)	2.72	.196
1922	15	12	12	114	98	50	56	19	(7-5)	.394	.232
1923	17	16	15	143	99	49	61	31	(10-7)	3.0	.167
1924	22	21	16	163	138	77	62	37	(15*-5)	4.25	.220
Cuba	—	—	—	—	—	—	—	—	(9-4)	—	—
1925	21	15	14	145	113	34	60	30	(14*-2)	2.11	206
1926	19	11	9	105	87	48	46	21	(12-4)	4.11	.216
1927	29	16	15	152	121	48	89	30	(15-6)	2.84	.210
1928	15	10	8	94	108	40	46	14	(9-2)	3.82	.277
1929	1	—	0	3	2	0	3	0	(0-0)	0.00	.182
Totals	167	126	114	1138	926	425	520	246	(109-43)	3.34	.215

Post-Season

Year	G	GS	CG	IP	H	R	SO	BB	(W-L)	TRA[a]	PA[c]
1924 World Series	4	3	3	28	27	9	33	35	(2-1)	2.89[b]	.252
1925 Play-Off	—	—	—	—	—	—	—	—	(3-1)		
1926 Play-Off	3	1	1	22	14	14	6	7	(3-2)	5.73	.182
	7	4	4	50	41	23	39	42	(8-4)	4.14	.224

* Led league.
[a] Total Run Average (Earned Runs not available).
[b] ERA, 1.89 compiled by Merl Kleinknecht.
[c] Pitching Average (At Bats/Hits given up).

Bullet Joe Rogan vs. White Major Leaguers

Year	AB	H	2B	3B	HR	Pitcher	(W-L)
1920	4	0	0	0	0	Mails	(7-0)
	3	2	1	0	1	Martin	(4-15)
	(4)	2	—	—	—	Meadows	(0-0)
1924	3	2	0	0	0	Ludolph	(0-0)
1926	2	2	1	0	0	Root	(18-17)
	3	2	0	0	1	Root	
1929	3	2	1	0	0	Campbell (0-1), Gould, (Edelman),* (Foxx)	
1933	4	1	1	0	0	J. Dean (Garland)*	(20-18)
1934	1	0	0	0	0	J. Dean	(29-7)
	2	1	0	0	0	J. Dean	
	2	0	0	0	0	J. Dean, P. Dean	(19-11)
1935	4	0	0	0	0	J. Dean	(28-12)
						P. Dean	(19-12)
						Ryba	(1-1)
	3	1	0	0	0	J. Dean, P. Dean, Ryba, (Cooper)*	
	4	0	0	0	0	Bowman	(7-10)
						Rowe	(19-13)
						Bridges	(21-10)
1936	3	1	0	0	0	Bowman (Cooper)*	(9-20)
1937	4	3	0	0	0	Feller	(9-7)
						Warneke	(18-11)
						Brown	(10-11)
Totals 16 games	49	19	4	0	2	Average: .389	

*Not major league pitchers.

14

Dobie Moore:
The Black Cat

Has anybody ever told you about Dobie Moore? Well, I'll tell you something about him. That Moore was one of the best shortstops that will ever live! That fella could stand up to the plate and hit right-handed, he could hit line drives out there just as far as you want to see.

Casey Stengel

Casey Stengel should know what he was talking about. He discovered Dobie Moore, along with Bullet Joe Rogan and other black stars, playing with the 25th Infantry team in Fort Huachuca, Arizona, in 1919.

If an untimely accident hadn't abruptly ended Moore's career seven years later, there are some who say he might have become the finest black shortstop of all time. Others say he already was.

We don't have the box score of Moore's game against Stengel's stars. But a year later, in November 1920, Dobie traveled to Los Angeles for the winter league season. In his first game, against Lee Meadows (16–14) of the Phils, Dobie drilled two doubles. The first, a line drive over second, scored Rogan. The second came ahead of catcher Jaybird Ray's triple, as Moore's club won, 6–4.

A week later Moore smacked a home run against Chicago's Elwood "Speed" Martin (4–15). Then he lashed a single and triple off Walter "The Great" Mails (7–0), the Cleveland Indians' World Series hero.

Moore "was the best hitting shortstop I ever saw," said George Sweatt. Richard Wilkinson, son of the Monarchs' owner, considered him "just as good as Jackie Robinson." Chet Brewer called him the best black shortstop ever. Dodger outfielder Babe Herman said the best black *player* ever. Herman and other whites who played against him in California referred to him as "The Black Cat."

Like Roberto Clemente and Yogi Berra, Dobie Moore was a bad-ball hitter. "There were no bad pitches for him," said Newt Allen. All the Monarchs learned to hit bad balls, Allen said, because when they barnstormed the prairie towns, the hometown umpires would call

191

All Stars vs. LA White Sox
Los Angeles, November 21, 1920

All Stars	AB	H	R		LA White Sox	AB	H	R
CF Pirrone	3	1	0		LF McNair	4	1	1
3B Boeckel	4	0	0		3B Carr	4	1	1
LF I Meusel	4	1	0		1B Hawkins	4	1	1
1B B Meusel	3	1	0		CF Rogan	4	0	0
RF Eddington	4	1	1		SS Moore	4	2	1
SS Elliott	4	2	1		RF Kyle	3	1	0
2B Rawlings	4	0	0		C Ray	3	1	0
C Thomas	4	1	0		2B Fagin	3	0	0
P Mails	4	0	0		P Curry	3	0	0
	34	7	2			32	7	4

All Stars   000 000 200 2 7 3
White Sox   100 003 00x 4 7 0

E:	Boeckel, Elliott, Rawlings
2B:	Carr
3B:	Moore
SB:	Carr, B Meusel
SO:	Mails 4, Curry 5
Umpire:	Reardon, Shore

practically everything a strike. "Moore used a long bat, and he'd swing overhand, bat down on the high pitches," Allen said. "I'd let them go, but he'd knock them two blocks. And a ball below his knees and outside was just right for him. The only way to get him out was to throw the ball right down the middle. Don't pitch outside or inside."

Said Frank Duncan: "I've seen them throw a curve ball to him, break in the ground, bounce up, and he hit it all up side the fence."

Willie Powell of the American Giants pitched Moore tight, "right up in his arms. Don't get it out there where he could get the big end of his bat on it. He'd walk over and hit it."

Moore's lifetime average in the Negro leagues was .360, with a high of .470 in 1924, when he led the league in hitting and tied for the lead in home runs.

In five games against white big league pitching, he hit .250.

All in all, Chet Brewer considered Moore "about the greatest shortstop I ever saw. He could come up and hit the ball out of the park. That, to my mind, made him the best of the shortstops. Willie Wells was as great a fielder, but he didn't have the strong arm or the power Moore had. Moore was the best I saw, all around."

In the field "he had an exceptionally strong arm," said Brewer. "Newt Joseph at third base would dive for a ball he just couldn't get to.

Moore, way on the edge of the grass, would scoop that ball up and throw strikes from deep shortstop."

What of Moore and Allen as a double-play combination? "Wonderful," said Duncan. "Couldn't ask for anything better. When you see Newt Allen and Moore, you could take Charlie Gehringer, Frankie Frisch, and any of that bunch. Brother, you're talking about a combination!"

Allen shrugged modestly. "In the World Series against Philadelphia in 1924, we made six double plays in one game," he said. "Two of them came in the eighth and ninth innings. The last one ended the ball game with what would have been the winning run crossing the plate."

Moore—round-faced, chubby, and cherubic—hardly looked the part as a great shortstop. But he had big hands, Allen said, as big as Honus Wagner's; he could grab the ball out of the air barehanded, palm down.

Moore didn't "sweep" the ball with his glove, Big C Johnson said. He just plucked it on the hop, palm down, and threw the runner out.

"Dobie may not have been as agile as some of them," Sweatt said, "but he had a rifle arm and made good plays. His thinking wasn't too good at times. It was that liquor, see? But as far as fielding his position, and throwing and hitting, you couldn't beat him."

Moore and Rogan had an uncanny pick-off play. Even Duncan didn't know how they did it, but when Rogan whirled to throw, Moore was just arriving at the bag. He was already between the runner and the base, and nothing, not even razor-sharp spikes, could move him. Runners soon learned they had better stay closer to second than they did to first.

"He'd drive you nutty picking men off," Babe Herman said. One of Herman's teammates scoffed at Moore's reputation. "He'll never catch *me* off," he declared. Smiled Herman: "He hadn't said that more than 30 seconds, he was out. Took two steps off and Moore touched him. I don't know where he got the ball from."

Dobie Moore—his real name was Walter—was born in Georgia, probably about 1893. He liked to brag about his home state. His favorite song, according to Sweatt, was "Georgia on My Mind." Moore was illiterate, added Sweatt, a schoolteacher in the off-season, "but of course most of the players were illiterate at that time. They couldn't help that."

In 1911 Moore was serving in the all-black 25th Infantry regiment in the Pacific, teaming with Rogan on perhaps the finest service team in the country.

"He was a sensation even then," remembered Joe Taylor, an

outfielder (who years later would marry the widow of Smokey Joe Williams). "He was a great hitter, base runner, and a sensational shortstop. I don't ever recall seeing Moore make an error. I never saw Honus Wagner play, but I don't think Wagner could have been any better than Moore."

Dobie was a "likeable kind of fellow," Taylor continued.

> Not much of a mixer; he kept to himself. Moore was a neat soldier, he was what we called in those days an "orderly bucker." See, each company had a day to go on guard duty. One man is usually picked as orderly for the commanding officer. Usually there are two or three jokers out of each company that always buck for orderly. Instead of doing guard duty, all they do is go to headquarters and report to the commanding officer and run errands. Then when the others come off guard, they get a 24-hour pass too.

In 1915 Moore left Jefferson Barracks, St. Louis, on orders to Hawaii. He stopped in San Francisco, where the world's fair was going on, and met "Big C" Johnson, another doughboy on his way to Honolulu. They would soldier together, in the same company, for the next four years. "He was a fair soldier," Johnson said. "There were better soldiers, but he got along all right, wasn't in trouble."

The 25th Infantry team, the "Wreckers," was one of the best nonprofessional clubs in the country.

From Hawaii, Moore, Rogan, and Hawkins transferred to Fort

The 1922 Kansas City Monarchs. Pictured (left to right) are George Sweatt, Bill Drake, Carroll Mothell, McColl, Frank Duncan, Hawkins, C. Bell, Dobie Moore, W. Bell, Jose Mendez, Joe Rogan, Newt Allen, unknown, Heavy Johnson, and Newt Joseph.

Huachuca on the Mexican border. Private Moore was assigned to the cavalry, and a score card of July 1919 lists him as competing in an all-army track meet in the running broad jump and the 440-yard relay.

That fall Casey Stengel found him on the baseball diamond and sent him, Rogan, and the others on to fame with the Kansas City Monarchs. Moore was probably 27 years old.

Researchers have uncovered 19 games in which Moore appeared in 1920, the first year of the Negro National League. He hit .276.

White big-league pitchers wouldn't have believed it, however. That was the year Dobie slugged Meadows, Mails, and Martin for a .500 average.

The next year, 1921, Moore raised his Negro league average to .264. Again, however, many of his home games are not included. Presumably he hit better at home than on the road; if the missing games are ever found, his batting average should go up.

Dobie wasn't popular with all the Monarchs. "Some fellows on the team didn't care too much for him," said Carroll Mothell. "He was out-spoken. If you were doing something he didn't like, he'd tell you about it. If you resented it, he didn't stop at that, he'd keep on telling you your faults. The way he talked to you, a person might resent it."

In 1922 and 1923 Dobie slugged the black pitchers for .367 and .358 though many home games are still unknown. That fall the Kansas City Blues of the American Association felt the sting of Moore's bat, as the Monarchs beat the Blues five games out of six. In one game Dobie started out with a home run over the right field fence (a bad pitch?). In the fifth inning he caught an inside pitch on his head and was knocked cold, though he got up and stayed in the game. Then in the ninth he singled and scored on Heavy Johnson's homer, as the Monarchs won, 7–6.

In Cuba in the winter of 1923–1924, Moore joined the Santa Clara club, regarded by experts as the greatest team in the history of Cuban baseball. The great Oscar Charleston and Bernardo Baro were in the outfield. Moore teamed with third baseman Oliver Marcelle, second baseman Frank Warfield, and first baseman Eddie Douglass in one of the best infields ever assembled in any league, black or white.

Dick Lundy—"King Richard"—of the Bacharach Giants was considered the class of black shortstops. Lundy and Moore never played on the same field in the United States. Only in Cuba could fans compare them side by side. Moore was the better of the two, said old-time Cuban fan Pedro Cardona. "If I had the choice, I'd pick Moore."

Moore hit .380 that winter, compared to .308 for Lundy, against some of the game's best black pitchers, as well as top whites. Dolph Luque of the Reds, the white majors' biggest winner that year at 27–8, held Dobie to two hits in 16 at bats. But against future and past big leaguers—Freddie Fitzsimmons, Jesse Petty, Jakie May, and Buck Ross—Moore hit .404 (19-for-47).

Back home in 1924 Moore erupted with a sensational year at bat, hitting .470, with eight home runs in 59 games, to tie for the league lead with teammate Newt Joseph, though Muehlebach Field was not an easy park for right-handed sluggers. The Chicago *Defender* called him "the greatest Negro shortstop of all time."

Dobie's army pals, Rogan and Johnson, hit .411 and .423, and the Monarchs won their second pennant in a row and met the Philadelphia Hilldales in the World Series. Moore was in the middle of all the key action.

"I never will forget it," said Hilldale third baseman Judy Johnson. "I was getting ready to steal, and Moore just blocked me. When I went to make my slide, he had his backside right in me. I couldn't get into the base. He blocked me off and just put his foot in my stomach. And that was the end of me. He just outsmarted me."

"Moore was mean, and he was strong," said Hilldale shortstop Jake Stephens. And Dobie had another little trick, Jake added: "He'd grab the belt of a runner rounding second. That half-stride the runner lost was often the difference between safe and out at third base or home.

In the fifth game, with the bases loaded and none out, Moore fielded a sizzling grounder by George Johnson and nipped a run at the plate. In the ninth, however, he bobbled Joe Lewis' grounder, setting the stage for Judy Johnson's home run that beat Rogan and the Monarchs and gave the Hilldales a three-to-one lead in the series, plus one tie.

The next day Moore atoned for that with a nice catch of George Johnson's foul, taking it over his shoulder with his back to the plate. Then in the eighth Moore singled to right, his third hit of the day, and raced home with the winning run on Sweatt's triple, as the Kansas City crowd went crazy.

In game seven, Moore came up in the fourth inning with Newt Joseph on base and lined another single to right against Hilldale ace Nip Winters (26–4). Joseph took third on the hit. On the next pitch Moore dashed for second, drawing catcher Joe Lewis' throw, while Joseph sped home on the classic double steal. Moore himself scored a moment later on Bill Drake's single to tie the game. The Monarchs went on to win it in the 12th, and the series was all tied up.

In the eighth game Moore's bad-hop single in the eighth helped load the bases for Duncan's game-winning hit that put the Monarchs ahead at last, four games to three (plus a tie), in the best-five-out-of-nine series.

Hilldale won the ninth game to tie up the series again.

The tenth and final game went down to the last of the eighth tied, 0–0, as the Monarchs' Jose Mendez and Philadelphia's Scrip Lee hurled almost perfect ball. Moore, first man up in the home eighth, smacked a 3–2 pitch to center to touch off a five-run rally. Then in the ninth he raced into short left to snatch a Texas-league pop up for the final out that gave the Monarchs the black world championship.

In 1925 Moore's average dropped off to .326 though he led the league in doubles. He also helped to lead the Monarchs to a play-off win over their arch-rivals, the American Giants. In the opening game he knocked in the first run with a triple and scored himself on a ground ball. In the eighth inning, with the score tied, 6–6, Moore drove a two-run homer over the fence to win the game, 8–6.

The Monarchs would face Hilldale again in the World Series, but just before the series opened, they received the news that Rogan suffered a freak accident and would be out for the series. Moore did his best to take up the slack. In the opening game he drilled three hits—a single, double, and triple—and stole a base against ex-Monarch Rube Currie, who had defected to the Hilldales. In all, he led both teams at bat in the series with a .364 mark, though Philadelphia won in five games, all of them close and many in extra innings.

Moore began the 1926 season with some of the hottest hitting of his life. By May 23 he was hitting .381 after the first 18 games. "The Monarchs really had something going," Brewer said. "We had won about eight or nine out of the first ten games. When we went off the road and came back home, they gave a big party for all the Monarchs and their wives. Everyone was there but Moore. He was out with that woman."

Moore, who was married, had started out for the party but went instead to a woman's house on 17th Street. He told police later that he knocked on the door, and when she replied that she was in bed, he left through an alley. Her version is that she came to the door and he hit her three times in the face and head before she could push the door closed. As he passed her alley window, she said, he threw something at her. At any rate, she grabbed a gun and emptied it at him. (Moore later insisted that if he had hit her three times, she could never have gotten the gun.) He was rushed to a hospital, where doctors told him his leg was fractured in six places. "The bullet went down under that big bone," Brewer said, "and they never did get it out. Today they probably could have saved him, but those doctors didn't know much about that."

Moore's playing career was over. Without him, the Monarchs lost the pennant for the first time in four years. The black Kansas City *Call* newspaper appealed for a fund to help the crippled star, pointing out that he had little saved for emergencies. A local businessman was the first to respond with a contribution of five dollars. Moore drifted to Detroit, Brewer said, and nothing is known about him after that. He disappeared completely from baseball history.

Richard Wilkinson, son of the Monarchs' owner, shook his head sadly. "Moore was at his prime," he said. "Dad always said he would have been one of the great ones."

John McGraw of the Giants reportedly shared that view. In the all too familiar words heard by many a black star in those days, McGraw reportedly assured him, "You'd be worth $50,000—if only you were white."

Dobie Moore vs. White Big Leaguers

Year	AB	H	2B	3B	HR	Pitcher	(W-L)
1920	(4)	2	2	0	0	Meadows	(16-14)
	—	—	—	—	1	Martin	(4-15)
	4	2	0	1	0	Mails	(7-0)
1923-24	4	1	0	0	0	Luque	(27-8)
	4	1	1	0	0	Luque	
	4	0	0	0	0	Luque	
	4	0	0	0	0	Luque, (Cooper, Ryan)*	
Total 8 games	24	6	3	1	1	Average: .250	

*Not major league pitchers.

Dobie Moore

Year	Team	G	AB	H	2B	3B	HR	BA	SB
1920	Kansas City	19	76	21	3	0	2	.276	2
1921	Kansas City	36	125	33	7	4	6	.264	4
1922	Kansas City	45	180	66	13	2	5	.367	2
1923	Kansas City	35	131	46	7	6	6	.358	2
	Cuba	—	184	71	9	6	1	.380	—
1924	Kansas City	59	234	110	20	5	8*	.470*	1
	Cuba	—	97	29	—	—	—	.299	—
1925	Kansas City	65	267	87	18	8	6	.326	9
1926	Kansas City	18	63	24	3	3	0	.381	2
Totals		—	1357	487	80	34	34	.359	22

Post-Season

Year	Team	G	AB	H	2B	3B	HR	BA	SB
1924	World Series	10	40	12	0	0	0	.300	0
1925	World Series	5	20	4	0	2	1	.200	—
1925	World Series	6	22	8	3	1	0	.364	1
		21	82	24	3	3	1	.290	1

15

Jud Wilson:
Boojum

*Jud Wilson was the only ball player on the Grays used to hit
Satchel Paige regular. More than Josh or Buck Leonard.
Now he wouldn't hit them a long ways. He'd punch them
around, he very seldom would pull the ball. He didn't care
who was pitching, he didn't care if anybody said they were
going to do something to him. He'd say, "You're not gonna do
nothin'." He had one of those real low voices, carried a long
ways. He wasn't a real good fielder now, but he'd knock the
ball down and throw you out. He had plenty of guts, plenty.
He was one of those old-time ball players, wasn't nothing
modern about him. Wasn't fast, didn't have a real good arm,
but he just believed in winning.*

Wilmer Fields,
Homestead Grays

The black leagues produced some excellent hitters—Josh Gibson,
Chino Smith, Oscar Charleston, Turkey Stearnes, Buck Leonard,
Cool Papa Bell, Mule Suttles, and many, many more. But when old-
timers get together to argue who was the best of all, a surprising
number ignore these legendary sluggers. To them, the greatest of all
was a squat, fog-horn-voiced left-hander, Judson "Boojum" Wilson.

Satchel Paige, who pitched against Ted Williams, Stan Musial, and
Joe DiMaggio, once named Wilson and Chino Smith as the two toughest hitters he faced. Satchel knew his hitters. Smith hit .375 lifetime
and Wilson .370.

Wilson was over 30 when he got his first look at the skinny fast-
baller from Birmingham. "Paige just tried to blur that ball by you,"
Wilson recalled years later. "I timed his blinding stuff and just raked
him for a base hit." Eventually Satch added a curve and experience to
his high hard one, but, said Jud, "it still didn't make any difference to
me."

Josh Gibson considered Jud the best of them all. "Boojum was a
better hitter than Josh," nodded Double Duty Radcliffe, who played
with both men on the Washington Homestead Grays. "He didn't hit as
many home runs, but he hit so many doubles and singles."

That's why they called him "Boojum"—from the sound of his line drives rattling off the fences. In Cuba he was known as *Jorocon*—"the Bull."

His lifetime average, .370, has been topped by only two men— Josh Gibson with .379 and Chino Smith with .375, though Gibson's figures are inflated by his stats in Mexico, Puerto Rico, and the Dominican Republic (Josh hit .328 in the Negro League), and Smith died early before his stats began to decline with advancing age. Wilson's .372 in Cuba is the highest ever compiled there.

In all, Jud hit over .400 five times in the United States and Cuba. Even at the age of 42 in Puerto Rico, he hit .404. A couple of younger fellows destined to go on to the Brooklyn Dodgers—Luis Olmo and Roy Campanella—hit only .319 and .267, respectively. If Campanella was great—he received a Hall of Fame berth and three MVP awards— how great might Wilson have been?

He faced the best of the whites—Lefty Grove, Dizzy Dean, and many others—and in 23 games he hit .330. It was an even .400 until age caught up with him.

"They all looked the same to me," Jud shrugged.

He hit lefties just as easily as right-handers. Outfielder Ted Page said Jud hit Lefty Grove "like Grove came off the sandlots." In Baltimore in 1928 Wilson lined two singles and a double to help beat Lefty, 9–3. The following winter in California exmanager Vic Harris said Jud and Lefty faced each other again in a night game. The box score hasn't been located yet, but Harris said Jud watched two fast balls whizz past ("Invariably he looked at two pitches," said Washington sports writer Ric Roberts, "I don't care what they were") then lashed the next one through Lefty's legs into center field. Grove threw his glove down, grumbled that the lights were bothering him, and stalked off the field.

Jud was as famous for his fighting as for his hitting. He hated umpires. "The minute he saw an umpire, he became a maniac," said Jake Stephens, his best friend and the instigator of some of Wilson's greatest fights. Even a loaded pistol in an umpire's hand didn't deter Wilson, who would give chase waving his baseball bat.

Rival ball players also gave Jud a wide berth. "He'd kill you," said outfielder Clint Thomas. "He was *dangerous!* He was like a goddam gorilla. He was never out, the pitcher never throwed a strike. All ball players were scared of him."

Page recalled stopping at a rooming house in Zanesville, Ohio. The landlady filled the tub with hot water, and the whole team, about 14 men, stood in line to use that one tubful—everyone, that is, except Wilson. "He was first," smiled Page, "and I was second, because I was his roommate. Nobody fooled around with Jud Wilson."

Actually, several players insist, Jud was a sweet-natured guy. "He was good-hearted," said Judy Johnson. "He'd do anything in the world for you."

Ben Taylor, Jud's manager at Baltimore, insisted that Wilson was one of the easiest men on the team to handle. "Wilson was a kind-hearted individual," Page agreed. "Would give you the shirt off his back. The writers made him into a villain."

Jud Wilson looked like a baseball version of "The Angel," the grotesque French wrestler of the 1940s. The old players say he had shoulders like King Kong, tapering down to a small waist. "He could wear my belt," said Judy Johnson, "but he couldn't put on my coat; he was too big for it. He was built like Hercules."

Jud Wilson at bat.

"He was built like a gorilla," says George Giles. "He didn't know his own strength. He could hit a ball around his knees farther than you ever want to see."

"From the knees down he had little legs," said Page, "but from there up, he was big! He was pigeon-toed and a little bowlegged. Babe Ruth was too, but Ruth was fat. Wilson was strong enough to go bear-huntin' with a switch."

Johnson whistled: "I think he could hit a ball with his fists and knock it out of the park. He could tear you apart, he was so strong."

A white semipro catcher in Trenton named Barlow once made some racial remark within Wilson's hearing. "Wilson let Barlow have it. The cops and everyone ran out there, three or four cops pinned Jud's hands in back of him, and Barlow hit Wilson right between the eyes. Wilson didn't even flinch. His arms went up and down like a bird trying to get off the ground: 'Turn me loose, I'll tear him limb from limb!'"

Even Chino Smith, another famous scrapper, gave Wilson a wide berth. Jake Stephens recalled:

I never will forget, one day we were playing down in New Jersey, Smith came sliding into third, slid into Wilson. Wilson picked him up, said, "I'll break every bone in your body," threw him maybe 15–20 feet away, said, "You better go about your business, boy." That's how mean Wilson was.

You know what Wilson did to me one time? We were roommates, and we had played the all-star game out in Chicago. I came in about one or two o'clock in the morning half juiced up. I said, "Get up! Tonight's the night." He grumbled, "God damn it, pipe down." I said, "Get up, get up!"

So he got mad, he grabbed a hold of my leg and held me out the window 16 stories above the street. He said, "You goddam midget." I said, "Oh please, Willie, don't drop me." Those people looked like flies down there on the sidewalk. Then I started kicking. I said, "Turn me loose," and I was kicking his arm with my free leg. So he shifted hands on me, just like that—from one hand to the other, 16 floors above the street. And I'm trying to shake loose.

When they told me about it the next day and I saw that man's arm all scuffed up where I was kicking him, I couldn't believe it. For two days I couldn't walk. I just couldn't walk, I got so scared. I'd try to walk, and my legs would buckle.

There were only a few people who could control Jud's temper. Stephens was one. Kindly Webster McDonald, his manager at Philadelphia, was another. A third was Judy Johnson's father. "My father could almost make him cry," Johnson said. "He'd say, 'Willie'—that got him—'Willie, you shouldn't do that.' One time in Philadelphia Jud knocked the umpire out. He said, 'Mr. Johnson, I didn't hit him, I just slapped him a little.' "

The only other person who could tame Jud was a little soft-spoken woman named Betty Wilson, his wife. He had courted her in rural Virginia, crossing a backwoods stream on a log to reach her home.

"Jud Wilson was all man," she said. "He was all man. He was a man of few words, but when he said those words, he meant them. If someone started arguing with him, he'd push them away and just say, 'Go on . . . go on.' If you didn't go away, he'd slap the heck out of you. I'd say, 'Jud, that's not right.' He'd be standing there with his fists clenched, and I'd say, 'Now come on, come with me,' and he'd just follow me off the field."

Wilson was born in Remington, Virginia, February 28, 1899. He served in the army in 1918, then played sandlot ball around Washington, D.C. until shortstop Scrappy Brown of the Baltimore Black Sox saw him in 1922 and took him off to Baltimore for a tryout. Jud stayed with the Sox for about two weeks, then jumped the club, explaining that he "got tired" of Baltimore. He came home to Washington's Foggy Bottom, then a black ghetto but now, like Georgetown, a posh white neighborhood. Brown pursued him and coaxed him back, only to have him jump again. Finally, on the third trip, Wilson stayed.

Jud played second base mostly. With his skinny legs and barrel chest, "he didn't look like a ball player," said the old Baltimore spitballer, Frank "Doc" Sykes. "I said to myself, 'This guy's over-rated.' Biggest mistake of my life." Jud hit .471 in 36 games against the still unorganized Eastern clubs and began making believers out of everyone.

The next year, the Eastern Colored League was born, and Jud became its first batting champ with a .464 average.

Wilson hit line drives mostly, said Cool Papa Bell. "He could hit that ball just as hard as anybody, but it would go on the ground or loop over the infield. He hit those line drives that would curve or bend down."

And Jud didn't pull the ball. His power was to the opposite field, which in Baltimore's Westport Park, his home park, was the long field. He couldn't pull the ball over the nearby rightfield stands but could slice one over leftfield farther than the right-handed sluggers could. Pitcher Holsey "Scrip" Lee, his teammate on the great Baltimore Black Sox of 1929, said Wilson hit the longest home run Lee had ever seen, and he saw the greatest, including Babe Ruth and Jimmy Foxx.

Kansas City Monarch catcher Frank Duncan (Jackie Robinson's first manager) once saw Wilson throw his bat at a change of pace and hit it into the seats.

Wilson crowded the plate and wouldn't back off. He'd let the ball hit him on the arm or anywhere to get on base.

One day in Baltimore, Stephens remembered, pitcher Jim Wilson, who could throw "hard's a skunk can bump a stump," dusted Boojum off with a fast ball to the head. The ball bounced into the screen behind the plate. "It would have killed anyone else," Jake marveled. "It would have killed them."

Jud played third base the same way. He didn't catch ground balls, he blocked them with his chest. The hottest grounders bounced off it, he picked the ball up and got his man at first.

Judy Johnson shook his head. "I often wonder why Wilson didn't put the glove on his chest," he said. "He got hit more up there than he did in his glove."

"He just smothered the ball," said Ted Page. "And he had a slingshot for a right arm."

"He could throw lightning out," Stephens agreed.

At game's end the other players would crowd around him in awe, inspecting the bruises on his torso and the knots on his arm where he'd been hit.

Actually Wilson was an effective fielder. A decade later he gave Ray Dandridge some key advice on playing third. Ray, then a young-ster with Newark, was waiting on ground balls and just missing the runners at first base. "Kid," Wilson told him, "always charge the ball." Dandridge tried it and discovered that "Boojum was right." Ray went on to become the Brooks Robinson of the black leagues.

In 1924 Wilson teamed with big John Beckwith, as moody as Wilson and one of the most powerful men, black or white, ever to swing a bat. The two gave Baltimore a formidable murderers' row. Jud hit .394 in 36 games; Beckwith topped him with .452, though he played 14 less games.

In October 1924 Jud got his first taste of white big-league pitch-ing, when Black Sox owner George Rossiter, a white restaurant owner, invited some of the Philadelphia As and other big leaguers to Bal-timore for a Sunday double header against his Black Sox. Ed Rommel (18–15) and Fred Heimach (14–12) of the As pitched the first game, and Jud spanked them for two singles in four at bats, though the As won, 4–2. In the second game Jud slashed a single and double in three at bats against Bob Hasty (1–3), as the Black Sox triumphed, 8–7.

The white pitchers were ruefully learning what the black hurlers already knew. "Boojum could hit lightning if you threw it to him," chuckled Stephens. "If you held him to two doubles and maybe a single, you had a good day."

In 1925 Jud hit .397, highest in the league, though Oscar Charleston, .392, had 100 more at bats. Beckwith hit .378. And both Jud and Beck could punch an umpire as quickly as they could swat a pitch. They both got into a memorable fight with an ump that summer. Wilson was arrested; Beckwith left town for a few days.

That winter Jud sailed to Cuba and topped all hitters there with a .430 mark. He was also tops in home runs and stolen bases. "He was strong as a tank," said Pedro Cardona, who was then a boy in Havana. "He looked like he was going to eat the world." But, Cardona insisted, Jud was really an easygoing player. "I don't ever remember a problem with him in Cuba."

Back in Baltimore in 1926 Jud hit .358. Beckwith, who had moved to Harrisburg, hit .322, according to statistics compiled by Paul Doherty and this author.

Jud raised that to a league-leading .412 in 1927 (official statistics credit him with .495, but research has corrected this to .412).

Returning to Havana that winter, Wilson hit .424 to lead the league. He was also first in triples, with seven in 118 at bats, or equal to 30 or 35 in a 162-game schedule.

Jud hit .375 in Baltimore in 1928. That autumn Rossiter brought the As stars back to Baltimore to face his Black Sox again. Jud smashed a double and a single in one game against Rommel (13–5). Then, facing the peerless Lefty Grove, the major league leader in wins (24–8) and strike outs, Boojum drilled three hits in five at bats as the Black Sox beat the great one, 9–3.

The league reformed in 1929, and this was the year that Rossiter put it all together. He brought a skinny kid named Satchel Paige from Birmingham to join Laymon Yokely, who many say could throw just as fast as Satch. Jesse Hubbard, Scrip Lee, and Pud Flournoy added finesse to the staff. Rap Dixon, a fine hitter with a strong arm, played right field.

But the pride of the team was its infield. It may have been the best black infield ever put together—perhaps the best of any color anywhere. Wilson played first base. Manager Frank Warfield, an adroit and underrated glove man, played second. Dick Lundy came from Atlantic City to play short. And Oliver Marcelle played third. Except for Jud, it was a brilliant defensive four-some. Jud's contribution was at bat. He hit .346, with a league-leading 20 stolen bases, and the Black Sox won the flag.

Floyd "Jelly" Gardner of the Homestead Grays, an excellent base runner, had a close brush with Wilson's temper.

> I remember one game we beat 'em over in Baltimore. A close game, I was on first, a man singled to right, and Jud Wilson at third had the base blocked. He reached for the ball, I kicked it right out of his hand and scored the winning run. He didn't chase the ball, he chased *me!* He wanted to fight, but he couldn't beat me. I was pretty good with the dukes then myself.

Baltimore Black Sox vs. Major League All Stars,
Baltimore, Oct. 14, 1928

All Stars		AB	H	R	Baltimore		AB	H	R
2B	Bishop	4	0	0	LF	Holloway	4	0	1
1B	Neun	4	0	0	RF	Dixon	4	3	3
CF	Porter	2	0	1	3B	Wilson	5	3	1
LF	Moore	4	1	1	1B-CF	Carter	2	1	1
SS	Thomas	4	0	0	C	Mackey	4	0	0
3B	Mooers	3	2	1	SS	Lundy	4	2	0
RF	G. Maisel	4	2	0	1B	Taylor	1	0	0
C	Davis	1	0	0	2B	Warfield	5	2	3
P	Grove	3	0	0	P	Farrell	2	0	0
C	Artigiani	1	0	0	CF	Washington	4	0	0
PH	F. Maisel	1	1	0			34	11	9
		31	6	3					

```
All Stars    000 200 001— 3   6 5
Baltimore    002 124 00x— 9  11 2
```

2B: Dixon, Moore, Warfield, Wilson
HR: Dixon
SB: Dixon 2, Warfield 2, Holloway
SO: Farrell 7, Grove 10
W: Farrell 3, Grove 7

That fall Jud faced the whites again. His old "cousin," Ed Rommel, was back, sporting a 12–2 mark with the world champions, but Jud raked him for his usual 2-for-4, as Yokely won the game, 8–3. A week later Johnny Ogden (15–16 with the St. Louis Browns) didn't have any better luck. Jud faced him four times and drove out a double and home run, as Yokely won again, this time 5–2. Jud's .500 batting average against the big leaguers was still intact.

The series was to be the high point of the twenties. That month the stock market crashed, wiping out the leagues in 1930 and driving the black players to a hand-to-mouth existence. Jud's average for the year was .371.

Jud made some badly needed pocket money playing the whites again in October. Roy Sherid, 12–13 for the Yankees, was rocked for a double and two singles in four at bats, as the blacks won, 8–5.

In 1931 Jud jumped to the Grays, which just might have been the greatest black team ever assembled. Defending black champions of 1930, they boasted, besides Wilson, Hall of Famers Oscar Charleston and Josh Gibson, pitchers Smokey Joe Williams and Lefty Charles Williams, plus Vic Harris, George Britt, Ted Page, George Scales, Double Duty Radcliffe, and many others. A fifth Hall of Famer, Judy Johnson had to leave to make room for Jud. It was a club of great talent as well as high tempers. Charleston, Britt, and Scales were all free-swinging fighters. Wilson was probably the toughest of all.

One day Page and Scales tangled in a fight under the shower. "Buff naked, both of us were," Page chuckled. Britt broke them up and ordered them to sit down. Still bleeding, they went back under the shower and soon started throwing punches again. Scales produced a knife. This time Wilson joined the peacekeeping forces. Britt slammed Scales one way, Boojum grabbed Page by the arm and slammed him out of the shower, into the locker room, down on the floor. "Sit down!" he ordered. "You behave!" Said Page laconically: "We did just that."

On the field the Grays vented their aggressions on the other teams. Jud hit .362 against black teams, and the Grays won 186 and lost only 17 against top black clubs and white semipros.

They played their home games at Forbes Field, home of the Pittsburgh Pirates. "Ball parks didn't mean much to Josh and Boojum," George Giles said. "Wilson could pick 'em up off his ankles and hit 'em out of the ball park." Giles said Hack Wilson and the Chicago Cubs used to stick around the ball park after a Cubs-Pirates game to watch the Crawfords' twilight game that followed "just to see Josh and Boojum hit."

The next year, 1932, practically the whole club jumped across town to the Pittsburg Crawfords being formed by racketeer Gus Greenlee. Jud jumped with them. If anything, the Craws were even more powerful than the Grays had been, for Greenlee had enticed Satchel Paige and Cool Papa Bell to join them. Jud hit .370, good enough to move Hall of Fame third baseman Judy Johnson off the team.

The Craws were so cocky that they challenged Casey Stengel and his All Stars to seven games that fall. The Craws won five of them. Jud's contribution: eight hits in 22 at bats for a .364 average, including two line-drive home runs against Fred Frankhouse (4–6 with the Braves).

Vic Harris remembered another exhibition game against Babe Didrikson, the 1932 Olympic champ and all-round woman athlete. Babe often pitched on male teams to draw a crowd. "We told Wilson to take it easy on her," Harris said—they didn't want to injure her or destroy her publicity appeal either. "She don't have no business out there," Wilson growled and swatted a line drive within inches of her ear.

"I took him out of the game," Harris said. "If he had hit her, he'd have killed her. He used to like to win. Don't tell him to strike out on purpose."

In 1933 Jud jumped again, this time to Philadelphia and the new team being put together by owner Ed Bolden and manager Webster McDonald. Patiently, McDonald began assembling a fine pitching staff, led by Stuart "Slim" Jones, a left-handed Satchel Paige. To catch, he lured Raleigh "Biz" Mackey. Wilson played first base alongside a snappy double-play combination of Dick Seay at second and Stephens at short.

Jake was Wilson's best friend and a chief partner in his mischief. He recalled:

> One time we were playing in Baltimore and I hadn't hit a home run all year. I hit a line drive to right field, the right fielder charged in and at the last moment saw he couldn't get it. He slipped, the ball went over his head, and I circled the bases. Home run. The third baseman called for the ball and the umpire called me out for not touching second and third base. So me and Boojum charged him. I said, "When that so-and-so turns his back, I'm gonna bust him in the mouth." I was behind Boojum, see, and I hit the umpire in the mouth under Boojum's arm. He turned around to Boojum: "He hit me!" So the cops came charging out on the field. They charged Wilson see?
>
> I never will forget, they put Boojum in the patrol wagon, the black moriah, and they started to work him over. The inside of the patrol wagon started shaking. One cop run out, here comes another copper out, and here comes the third copper out. And there was Boojum standing in the back end, and they had hit him with a blackjack across the eye.
>
> So they took him to jail, and when Boojum got out, he says, "I'm gonna kill that little fella"—he was gonna kill me. "This time I'm gonna kill him. He's got me in trouble for the last time." He had tears in his eye. "I got to kill him. I got to kill him this time!"
>
> McDonald says, "Jake, you go home to York. I'll let you know when to come back." About three days time Mac sent a telegram, said, "Jake, everything's OK." So I went back. Boojum says, "You little midget"—he called me a midget—"you do something like that again, I'm gonna kill you."

"He was one of the finest men you ever met, but he was always getting into fights," Stephens said. Jake once left Wilson at a pawn shop to buy a suitcase, an argument apparently started, and someone slugged Jud with a blackjack. When Stephens got back to the team's rooming house that night, he found Jud bandaged up "like a hindoo."

Stephen added: "There was never a meaner, nastier man than Boojum when he put his uniform on, but you couldn't find a nicer man when he took it off. And here's something funny: He loved me. I could do anything with him. I was his roommate. On road trips he'd say, 'I'll take the midget.'"

The soft-spoken McDonald just sighed:

I said, "Willie, keep things going smooth. No fighting." He said all right. Seventh inning. I hear, "Get the po-lice. . . . Hit him in the head with a bat!" What's going on here? There's Jud, one man's head under his arm, another under that arm—he was strong as an ox. I flew there, went up behind him to break his grip. He threw me off, then picked me up off the ground with one hand. He'd bang you in the jaw in a minute. He'd hit you and then ask questions later. He was a warrior.

But I didn't want that. I didn't want somebody who would fight but somebody who would talk in the right sense and advocate the rights of all the players on the club.

People didn't understand how I handled him as well as I did. I made him captain to calm him, to curb him—gave him responsibility. It helped, and he appreciated it. When I resigned, I made him manager, but he only stayed a year.

"Turkey" Stearnes played with Wilson briefly in Philadelphia. "They said he was a mean guy," Stearnes said; "the same thing they said about Charlie [Oscar Charleston] and Beckwith. But I played with him a whole season, and I didn't have any trouble with him. I don't think anybody did. One thing about him, he liked to win. That's where a lot of people take the fellow wrong."

Perhaps the two toughest physiques to play the game were Wilson and Oscar Charleston. In Cleveland one day, they collided head-on, as Charleston tried to beat Wilson in a close play at first base. "Both got knocked out right there on the field," pitcher Bob Harvey said. In a couple of minutes Jud came to. "You feel all right, Boojum?" the players asked. "I'm OK," Jud said. They both went on to finish the double header. Back at the hotel, they each fainted in the lobby and were unconscious for six hours, Harvey said. For the next two games they didn't know what they were doing. "They had just been playing off their courage."

Jud hit .354 in 1933 and that fall faced Jack Russell, 12–6 for the American League champion Senators. He lined out a single and double in four ties.

His .355 topped all hitters in 1934. In the East-West game that August, Wilson was in the middle of one of the great plays of blackball history. Satchel Paige of the East was locked in a 0–0 duel with Bill Foster of the West. In the eight, Cool Papa Bell reached second and Wilson was up. "Jud was dangerous," Foster said."He was just plain dangerous! If you got that ball away from him, curve ball or fastball, you were pitching in his alley. He'd hit it a couple of miles. That's how strong he was." Foster concentrated on keeping the ball inside. Jud hit a bloop grounder toward Willie Wells at short, as Bell got a good jump and rounded third. Bell scored before Wells could whip the ball home, and the East were winners, 1–0.

The Stars won the second-half title and met the Chicago American Giants in the play-off. Unfortunately, the black papers, suffering from depression-inspired economy moves, gave sketchy coverage to the games. It's a pity, for the series was a thriller, going seven games. We have just one box score and few other written details. Much of what we know is reconstructed from the memories of the men who took part. Chicago pitcher Bill Cornelius ruefully remembered his introduction to Wilson:

> Willie Wells, our shortstop, told me, "Don't throw Jud no curve ball." I asked why, and he said, "He's a curve ball hitter." We were playing in Philly, and I had a seven- or eight-run lead, and I threw him a curve ball. There was, I guess, a six-story apartment house across the street over there. The guy hit the ball on top of that. Wells told me, "That's why I didn't want you to throw him that with men on base."

Chicago had taken an early lead, three games to one, when Jud Wilson was embroiled in one of his famous fights with an umpire. He was promptly ordered off the field. Storming around menacingly, Wilson refused, and the umpire caved in. The game resumed. Chicago manager Dave Malarcher saw red. "Jiminy Christmas!" the mild-mannered Malarcher swore. "He knocked the man down! What's he have to do to get put out of the game?" Malarcher lodged a protest— he wanted the big Wilson bat out of the series.

That night Bolden and McDonald hustled over to the league commissioner and pleaded to have Wilson reinstated. With Jud back in the lineup, the Stars won the fifth game, then swept the final double header to win the title.

The white champions that year were the Gashouse Gang, the St. Louis Cards, led by 29-game-winner Dizzy Dean. The Dizzy One traveled to Philadelphia after the World Series to get a look at Jud Wilson first-hand. Jud punched a single in his only at bat. It gave him a lifetime average of .412 against white pitching up to that point.

Wilson hit .331 in 1935, though the Stars faded in the standings. That fall, in two games against Dean, he managed only one hit in seven at bats. His slump continued in Cuba that winter, when he hit only .263.

In 1937 the Stars' bus overturned, and Wilson broke several ribs.

In 1939 Wilson hit .261, and that October the White Sox' Pete Appleton (5–10) and Washington's Bud Thomas (7–1) held him to one hit in four at bats.

Wilson's old owner, Cum Posey of the Grays, still eyed him enviously, and in 1940 the 41-year-old Wilson made the switch to the Grays. The team had just won three straight pennants. With Jud in the lineup they would win six more, for a total of nine in a row, a record equalled by no other professional team in any sport.

Jud joined a Murderers' Row—Josh Gibson, Buck Leonard, and

Cool Papa Bell, all three of whom are in the Hall of Fame. When Wilson is added, as he surely should be, it will make four Grays in the pantheon, a rare honor for any team.

Boojum still hit as savagely as a youngster; his batting average (unconfirmed) was .351. He beat Satchel Paige in one game with a ringing single in the ninth inning before 30,000 persons in Washington. It was also Jud's hit that clinched the pennant for the Grays, driving in two runs with two men out, as the fans swarmed onto the field and carried him off on their shoulders.

Jud's average was still a dangerous (though unconfirmed) .340 in 1941, when he was 42 years old. In Puerto Rico that winter he hit .404.

In the 1942 World Series he was reduced to pinch-hitting but was still a threat. He got two hits in four trips, including a screaming triple against Paige and the Monarchs, while the Grays' big guns, Gibson and Leonard, went out meekly.

Jud continued his vendetta against umpires without letup. One of his favorite targets was an arbiter named Gabby Kemp. Jud dumped a bucket of water on him and was fined $15 for it.

Buck Leonard recalled:

> I remember one time in Bushwick Park in Brooklyn, he was called out at the plate and he turned around to the umpire with his bat, the umpire ran out to second base with Wilson right behind him with the bat. We caught up with him around shortstop.
>
> Another time we were playing in Philadelphia, and Kemp was umpiring and called him out on strikes. It was the last out of the game, and Wilson ran Kemp all across the infield and into the clubhouse in right field. We understood that Kemp had a pistol in the clubhouse, but Wilson was standing outside the door with his bat, and wouldn't let Kemp out. We had to get him away, because he still had a bat. And Kemp had a pistol in his hand!
>
> Another time he was called out in Baltimore by a fellow name of Moe Harris. After the game was over we came up to Pennsylvania Avenue in Baltimore, where we were staying, and we saw Moe Harris. He had a room upstairs in the hotel. Wilson was hanging around the stairs, and when the umpire finished changing his clothes, Wilson was standing at the bottom of the steps. Moe Harris says, "The ball game is over and I call them as I see them. Heh, fellas, come here and get Wilson, will you?"
>
> That's the kind of player he was. He played to win.

Grays pitcher Wilmer "Red" Fields marveled at the Wilsonian temper. He once saw Jud clap a water bucket over a man's head, then beat on the bucket.

The Grays' Sam Bankhead, older brother of Dodger pitcher Dan Bankhead, insisted that Boojum was "a good-natured person," though he conceded:

He didn't take no crap. I remember one time he got called out on strikes. He raised hell, he threw his bat, then he came on over to the dugout, over to the cooler to take a drink of water. Out on the field the umpire yelled "Strike!" on the next batter. Somebody on the bench said, "Did you see that pitch?" Now Jud didn't see anything, but he ran over to the umpire, said, "You blind so-and-so, how could you call that a strike?" We said, "Come on back here, Wilson." He ain't seen nothing, 'cause he was drinking water at the time!

Philadelphia's catcher Bill "Ready" Cash said he once saw Boojum "snap the umpire out of his coat. He was strong as a mule."

But Jud could also laugh at himself. Newark first baseman Lenny Pearson recalled an altercation between Wilson and Newark catcher Charlie Parks. Wilson charged Parks, who cried out, "I know darn well you can find someone bigger than me to pick on." Wilson stopped dead in his tracks and laughed with everyone else.

In 1943 Wilson raised his average to .349 and was called in to pinch-hit against Hilton Smith and the Monarchs one day with 26,000 fans on hand, two out in the ninth, a man on second, and the Grays down, 2–1. Jud looked at two beautiful curve balls, then drove a double to left-center to tie the score.

The next year, in Baltimore, with the Grays behind 4–2, and two men on base, the Baltimore manager ordered Josh Gibson walked intentionally to get to "the old man." That's where he made his mistake. The "old man" walloped a triple to win the game 5–4.

In 1946, at the age of 47, Jud faced a white big-league hurler for the final time. Johnny (Double No-Hit) Vander Meer of Cincinnati shut him out in four tries in beating the Grays, 1–0, and Jud ended up with a final career average against the whites of .360.

As he grew older, Wilson had increasingly become the victim of epileptic fits. Mrs. Wilson said they were the result of an automobile accident. Stephens and Grays manager Vic Harris blamed them on the many beatings he took over the years. At any rate, the fits gradually grew more frequent. Buck Leonard remembered one game in Washington's Griffith Stadium, Jud was playing third, and one of the players suddenly said, "Oh, wait a minute, look at Boojum." He was down on the ground, his finger tracing little circles in the dirt. Another time, on the ferry to Chester, Pennsylvania, Jud suddenly began taking off his clothes. He had to be restrained.

At last Boojum retired from the game. He worked for several years on a road crew building Washington's Whitehurst Freeway. He was reportedly a great favorite with the foreman and the other men.

But Jud's mind grew more erratic, and he had to be committed. When his old friend Judy Johnson came to visit him, Jud didn't recognize him. "Who you, boy?" he kept muttering until Judy mentioned the name of Jake Stephens. Jud's eyes showed a glimmer of recognition. "He thought the world of Stephens," Johnson said quietly.

In 1963 Jud Wilson died.

"A very sincere man," summed up Stephens. "But when he put that uniform on, he played for keeps. He was a little like me, he hated umpires."

Cool Papa Bell nodded. "Wilson was one of our great players," he said, "but he was mean. Ball players are like that a whole lot. As soon as they walk on that ball field, they want to win. Sometimes they can't hardly get along with their teammates. Well, he was that type of guy. Good fellow, but he's just got so much heart and soul in this ball game."

Laymon Yokely, a teammate from Baltimore days, agreed. "He hated to lose," Yokely said. "He wasn't afraid of anything, a tough ball player. I'd like to have nine men on a team like Jud Wilson."

Jud Wilson

Year	Team	G	EAB[a]	H	2B	3B	HR	BA	SB
1922	Baltimore	36	119	56	9	3	6	.471	—
1923	Baltimore	25	98	33	—	—	—	.464*	—
1924	Baltimore	36	142	56	4	1	1	.394	2
1925	Baltimore	36	136	54	7	1	4	.397	1
	Cuba	—	149	64	3	3	3*	.430*	10*
1926	Baltimore	47	165	59	13	2	4	.358	—
	Cuba	—	54	18	4	1	2	.333	—
1927	Baltimore	63	245	100	21	6	9	.412*	8
	Cuba	—	118	50	6	7*	4	.424*	3
1928	Baltimore	27	109	41	14	0	2	.375	5
	Cuba	—	151	60	6	7	4	.397	3
1929	Baltimore	58	214	74	9	1	9	.346	20*
	Cuba	—	160	58	10	4	5	.363	—
1930	Baltimore	38	148	55	12*	2	2	.371	—
1931	Grays	25	94	34	8	3	2	.362	0
1932	Grays, Pit	13	46	17	4	0	0	.370	1
1933	Philadelphia	13	48	17	2	0	1	.354	0
1934	Philadelphia	27	102	42	1	1	1	.412*	1
1935	Philadelphia	25	97	30	7	1	2	.309	0
	Cuba	—	137	36	9	5	0	.263	—
1936	Philadelphia	24	91	29	1	0	4	.380*	1
1937	Philadelphia	—							
1938	Philadelphia	14	47	15	1	0	1	.319	—
1944	Puerto Rico	—	52	21	—	—	—	.404	—
1945	Grays	21	52	15	2	0	0	.288	0
Totals			2772	1034	153	48	66	.373	55

Post-Season

Year	Team	G	EAB[a]	H	2B	3B	HR	BA	SB
1934	Play-Offs	1	3	1	0	0	0	.333	
1944	World Series	4	17	5	0	0	0	.294	
1945	World Series	2	4	0	0	0	0	.000	
East-West		3	11	5	0	0	0	.455	0

*Led League.
[a] Estimated At Bats.

Jud Wilson vs. White Big Leaguers

Year	AB	H	2B	3B	HR	Pitcher	(W-L)
1924	4	2	0	0	0	Rommel	(18-15)
						Heimach	(14-12)
	3	2	1	0	0	Hasty	(1-3)
	4	0	0	0	0	Dibut (Grier)*	(3-0)
1927-28	4	1	0	0	0	Luque	(13-12)
	3	0	0	0	0	Luque	
1928	(4)	2	1	0	0	Rommel	(13-5)
	5	3	1	0	0	Grove	(24-8)
1929	4	2	1	0	1	Ogden	(4-8)
	4	2	1	0	0	Rommel	(12-2)
1930	4	3	1	0	0	Sherid	(12-13)
	4	0	0	0	0	Fitzsimmons	(3-4)
						Grove	(28-5)
	3	0	0	0	0	Burke	(3-4)
1932	(4)	1	0	0	0	Parmelee	(0-1)
	5	2	—	—	—	Frankhouse, Swift	
	3	1	1	0	0	Swift	(14-10)
	3	1	0	0	1	Frankhouse	(4-6)
	3	2	0	0	1	Frankhouse	
	4	1	1	0	0	Swift, French	(18-6)
1933	4	2	1	0	0	Russel	(12-6)
1934	1	1	0	0	0	Dean	(29-7)
1935	5	1	0	0	0	Dean	(28-12)
						Swift, Winford	(0-0)
	2	0	0	0	0	Swift	(15-8)
	3	1	—	—	—	Vance	(3-2)
1939	4	1	—	—	—	Appleton	(5-10)
						Thomas	(7-1)
1946	4	0	0	0	0	Vander Meer	(10-12)
Totals	86	31	9	0	3	Average: .360	

* Not major leagues.

16

Biz Mackey:
Artist in a Face Mask

In my opinion, Biz Mackey was the master of defense of all catchers. When I was a kid in Philadelphia I saw both Mackey and Mickey Cochrane in their primes, but for real catching skills, I didn't think Cochrane was the master of defense that Mackey was. When I went under his direction at Baltimore, I was 15 years old. I gathered quite a bit from Mackey, watching how he did things, how he blocked low pitches, how he shifted his feet for an outside pitch, how he threw with a short, quick, accurate throw without drawing back. I got all this from Mackey at a young age.

Roy Campanella

Black baseball produced at least a half dozen superb catchers: Bruce Petway, the little man with the rifle arm, who cut down Ty Cobb in three steal attempts in Cuba in 1910 . . . Louis Santop, the "Big Bertha" . . . Larry Brown and Frank Duncan, excellent defensive receivers. . . Josh Gibson, the best known black hitter of his day. . . and the last of the line, Roy Campanella, the first to be enshrined in the Hall of Fame.

But when black veterans get together to debate an all-time, all-black, all-star team, the choice for catcher is none of these. For all-round ability, the vote is overwhelmingly for a jolly, roly-poly Texan named Raleigh "Biz" Mackey. (The more famous Gibson would be the designated hitter or play left field.) Even Josh's owner, Cum Posey, picked Mackey over Gibson as his all-time black catcher.

Mackey's fellow Texan, pitcher Jesse "Mountain" Hubbard, went even further. "Mackey," he declared, "was the greatest *player* I ever saw. He was the greatest shortstop, the greatest catcher, a great hitter. Any position you put him in, he'd be champ if he could stay there for a month or two."

"Of all the catchers, I'd pick Biz Mackey as smartest of all of them," said expitcher Webster McDonald. "He was an artist behind the plate, he was the master."

One can even get a lively debate from black old-timers over whether Mackey was the best catcher of all time, black or white. His closest rival was his Philadelphia contemporary, Mickey Cochrane of the As. One person who saw them both, Campanella, enthusiastically picked Mackey as the better: "Cochrane got a lot of his superiority by being a good hitter, but I still liked Mackey better defensively. For real catching skills, I didn't think Cochrane really was the master of defense that Mackey was."

Actually, Mackey was a fine hitter as well as a master receiver. He hit .319 lifetime in the black majors, .326 in 14 games against white big leaguers.

Campanella himself may be the finest monument to Mackey's contribution to baseball. Biz was his mentor. "You saw Campanella catch, you saw Mackey," the old-timers nod.

There may never have been a greater handler of pitchers than Mackey, black or white.

In the winter of 1943, Kansas City Monarch pitcher Hilton Smith was trying to come back after two years with a sore arm. Mackey went behind the plate to handle him for one game, and the result was miraculous.

Smith recalled:

> ,Oooh, my goodness, I didn't know he was such a catcher! I think I struck out 15 of those guys. That guy was a marvelous catcher! I had pitched to Frank Duncan, who I thought was a good catcher, I pitched to Joe Greene, Leon Ruffin, who used to be with Newark, Larry Brown— I've pitched to some great catchers, but my goodness, that Mackey was to my idea the best one I pitched to. The way he handled you, the way he just got you built up, believing in yourself. He was marvelous! He caught me that day and I just—ooh, I was just on *edge*, and it looked like all my stuff was just working. Had the hitters looking like they didn't know what to do. Mackey told me, "I don't see how in the world you *ever* lose a ball game!"

By a one-in-a-million coincidence, Mackey, the best catcher in blackball annals, was born in the same Texas town, Seguin, that also produced the best black pitcher of all time, Smokey Joe Williams. Mackey was born in 1897, Williams about ten years earlier. Biz was 12 when Joe went up to the American Giants in 1909. There is no record of how much the boy may have been influenced or helped by his illustrious fellow townsman, but it's intriguing to imagine the lanky fireballer tossing a few to the eager kid.

Mackey started his own pro career in 1918 with the San Antonio Black Aces. "He was a good pitcher too," according to Crush Holloway, who played on the same team, "and he played a little infield."

"He had that underhand curve ball and an overhand drop ball, and he could throw hard," Jesse Hubbard recalled. "Why, shoot man,

I shut him out, 1–0, in Beaumont in 1920. Up until he died he still fussed with me about that game."

The Black Aces were a pretty fast club. They had fancy fielding Bob "Highpockets" Hudspeth on first; big Henry Blackman, a good glove man and long ball hitter, on third; and Holloway, a slashing base-runner, in center. They had been organized by a white restaurant owner from Waco named Franks, but for three straight months it rained, while Franks slowly went bankrupt. He finally sold out to a man named Moore, who moved the Aces to San Antonio.

There a hero-worshipping kid named Willie Wells recalled following Mackey around, carrying his glove, for a chance to get into the park free. Wells would later go on to become one of the best shortstops of all time.

(Why do so many great black players come from Texas? In addi-

Biz Mackey.

tion to such white greats as Tris Speaker and Rogers Hornsby, the Lone Star black stars included Williams, Mackey, Wells, Hubbard, Holloway, Rube and Bill Foster, Hilton Smith, Ernie Banks, and Frank Robinson. "Well, we played in the white Texas league parks—Dallas, Fort Worth, Houston, Beaumont, Wichita Falls," Holloway said. "That's why those boys from Texas could play so good, they had good grounds. Not like out East, where they had to play on those little old lots.")

In 1920 the Black Aces broke up. Seven of the best players, including Mackey, Hudspeth, and Blackman, were sold to C. I. Taylor of the famous Indianapolis ABCs. "That was the greatest team I ever played on," said Holloway, who followed them a year later. The ABCs also boasted center fielder Oscar Charleston, first baseman Ben Taylor (C. I.'s brother), third baseman Candy Jim Taylor (another brother), second baseman Connie Day, shortstop Mortie Clark, and outfielder Namon Washington.

The ABCs played throughout Indiana, and the Muncie *Star* marveled at the play of Mackey against the Kansas City Monarchs. "The big feature of the game was the work of C. I.'s new catcher, Mackey," it wrote. "He does as clever a job of backstopping as is ever seen, and his throwing is nothing less than marvelous. Base runners have no business monkeying with his arm. To make the would-be base-stealers look worse, he waits until they are half-way to the objective and then his whip catches them several feet away. Four K.C. men came to grief in this manner, and they were caught so far off that they didn't even slide."

Another pitcher, Holsey "Scrip" Lee chuckled: "Mackey had to wait for the infielder to cover the base, then he'd cut loose, or else the center fielder would get it on one hop." ("That's right," center fielder Gene Benson agreed. "I'd have to come in and try to get the runner at third.")

"He could squat down on his honkers (haunches) and throw you out," said Holloway. The ball would pass the pitcher about belt-high and still reach second right on the dot." ("That ball would come by my mound knee-high," Lefty Bill Foster said. "Zing! It came right back by me.")

Judy Johnson added: "You wouldn't have to move your glove six inches. He could throw it right on a dime."

"His arm?" McDonald asked rhetorically. "Terrific. And he threw a light ball, the infielders could handle it. Those other guys threw the ball hard, but a heavy ball. You ever been catching when somebody threw a heavy ball, keep your hands sore? That's a heavy ball. Mackey's was just like a feather. It was a pleasure for infielders when Mackey was catching."

"You could catch him bare-handed," nodded shortstop Jake Stephens.

"And he was funny," Holloway added, "he was jolly, especially with those fast men who said they were gonna steal on him. When he'd throw them out, he'd get such a kick out of it, he'd fall down laughing."

McDonald, who pitched to Mackey later in Philadelphia, said Mackey could call for curves and still throw the runner out. Mac recalled how Mackey once threw out Cool Papa Bell. "Mac, let's get Cool," Biz said. "You've got control. Three off-pitches [pitchouts] will get him going to second." After the first two wide ones, Bell took off. Mackey threw him out. "Cool Papa jumped that high. He thought he had the jump. And he didn't figure he was going to get three off-pitch balls. I said, 'Mackey and I do that all the time.'"

Mackey would stay with C. I. for three years, playing almost every position on the team. In spite of his 240 pounds, he cavorted in the infield almost as nimbly as a lightweight. Mackey hit .306 that first year.

The next year, 1921, Biz hit .289. His 11 home runs in 63 games were second only to teammate Oscar Charleston, who hit 15, as the ABCs finished fifth in the eight-club league. That autumn Mackey got his first look at white big-league pitching, when he faced Cleveland rookie lefty Jesse Petty and slammed a triple in four at bats.

In 1922 Biz hit .352, as the Hoosiers climbed to second.

In the baseball war that broke out that winter, when the East went raiding the western clubs, Mackey, Charleston, Holloway, and Blackman all listened to the lure and headed east. Biz settled in Philadelphia on Ed Bolden's Hilldales.

The Hilldales already had a star catcher, slugging Louis Santop, so Mackey played wherever he could help the team most, including shortstop. "Mackey didn't have the range I had," said Stephens, the peppery rookie shortstop, "but he was a better shortstop than I was. He never throwed the ball no harder than he had to. A hard-hit ball come to Mackey, you know what Mackey'd do? He'd take and bounce it down on the ground, throw the man out."

Mackey liked his liquor. Stephens recalled him playing while drunk, "his eyes rolling around in his head." But it didn't seem to affect either his fielding or his hitting. "You better not run on him— he'd throw your ass out."

"I know he drank a lot," said pitcher Chet Brewer. "He'd party all night and go out to the ball park ten o'clock in the morning, take a shower, come out and catch a double header. What a man he was! After staying up all night!"

Mackey did have one other weakness, said Judy Johnson. "He

would drag his tail if he was behind and the umpire called a couple bad ones. He would kill the whole team." So, Judy said, he would call time and come in from third base and talk about girls or what they would do after the game, until Mackey forgot about the bad call and went back behind the plate.

Biz hit .364 in 1923. (Published figures say he hit a league-leading .440, but this is apparently erroneous.) He sprayed hits to all fields. "He hit low line drives from the left side. From the right side he hit with power," said pitcher Chet Brewer. McDonald added: "No right-hander would throw him a curve ball, or someone would get hurt in right field."

The Philadelphians won the pennant in Biz' first season.

In 1924 Mackey hit .363 and gradually took over more of the catching from Santop. The Hilldales won the pennant again and faced the western champion Kansas City Monarchs in the first modern black World Series.

Biz hit .360 in the series. Hilldale took a quick lead, two games to one, plus a tie. In the fifth game Philadelphia was losing, 2–1, when Mackey singled to center against the great Bullet Joe Rogan and scored on Judy Johnson's homer, as Philadelphia beat Rogan, 5–3, to take a three-one lead in the best-of-nine-game series.

In the sixth game Mackey singled to shortstop in the first and scored on Johnson's triple, though the Monarchs won the game, 6–5.

After KC won the seventh game in 12 innings to tie the series three games apiece, the Hilldales made a defensive change in game eight. Young Stephens was suffering from a severe case of nerves, so Judy Johnson, the game's best third baseman, moved to short, and Mackey, the game's top catcher went to third, while Santop went behind the plate. In the sixth inning, Warfield singled against Rogan, Mackey sacrificed him to second, and Santop singled him home to give Philadelphia a 2–1 lead.

The ninth inning would be one of the most dramatic in blackball history. With two men on and two out, the Monarchs' weak-hitting catcher, Frank Duncan, lifted a foul behind the plate. Santop went back for it, tapped his glove—and dropped the ball! Given a second chance, Duncan drilled the next pitch straight at Mackey—and through his legs for an error, as two runs raced across the plate to give Kansas City the victory and a four-to-three lead in the series.

Hilldale came back to win game nine, but the Monarchs won the series the following day with a rally in the ninth to break a 0–0 tie.

In 1925 Mackey hit .345 and at last was given the first-string catching job. He blossomed into the finest defensive catcher in Negro league history.

Biz was death on foul balls. "Never did pull his mask off," said Jim

Canada of Birmingham, "rarely missed a pop fly. He was the greatest catcher I ever saw."

Webster McDonald called it "a pleasure" to pitch to Mackey. "Santop and Gibson could probably outhit him, but I didn't call them catchers, as far as I was concerned. They used to drop too many balls. They'd take strikes away from pitchers. Mackey could help a pitcher steal a strike, the way he received the ball. He fooled the umpire sometimes if it was a little low or whatnot."

First baseman George Giles explains: "Mackey would move his body. A low ball, he'd raise his body; high ball, he'd lower it. See, you couldn't tell whether he was moving his glove or not. I've never seen another catcher do that. A big league umpire finally caught him, I think it was Beans Reardon, said, 'I caught ya!'"

Like Yogi Berra, Mackey would "tantalize" the hitters, McDonald said. ("All kinds of conversation, except the ball game," Ted Page smiled.)

Hall of Famer Buck Leonard recalled:

> He was a jovial fellow, full of fun, full of life, full of pep, always had something funny to say. You'd go up to bat, "Well," he'd say, "you're hitting .400, let's see how much you can hit today." Or he'd say, "You're standing too close to the plate." Anything to upset the batter, throw him off. "What kind of bat you using?" He'd tell the umpire: "Look at his bat there, I don't believe his bat's legal." Just anything to upset you. "How'd you all do last night? Where'd you all play last night? Aren't you tired? Don't you need no rest? Where'd you all sleep last night? I know, you all slept in the bus. You mean you rode all night last night and you all think you're going to win this ball game?" In other words, he was trying to get hitting off of your mind, get your mind on something else. Psychology, you know.

"Mackey pitched the ball game," Stephens said. "He'd call the pitches. Take Johnny Bench—he's so over-rated; on the 2–0 he calls for a fast ball. That don't make sense—the hitter knows what to look for. Mackey would call for four curve balls, different speeds, but never a fast ball."

That year Mackey and Winters formed one of the greatest batteries ever seen, black or white. Nip ran up a 26–4 record, and the Hilldales won the pennant for the third straight year.

They met the Monarchs in the series once again, but this time Philadelphia won five games to one. Biz hit .375. With Hilldale ahead three games to one, he doubled high off the Shibe Park right-field fence and scored the winning run to beat the Monarchs, 2–1. The following day they wrapped it up.

The next year, 1926, Biz hit .270, though it was not a hitters' year—the league leader, Luther Farrell, hit .359. Hilldale finished second, which meant that, instead of going to the World Series, they could barnstorm against Connie Mack's Philadelphia As, who finished third in the American League that year. The Hilldales beat the As five out of six games. We have box scores for only two of them. In one, Biz got a single and stole a base against Jack Quinn, the spitballer (10–11 on the year).

The other game pitted Winters against Lefty Grove (13–13), who had led the American League in both strikeouts and ERA. It was a battle of perhaps the two finest left-handers in the country. Winters won it, 6–1. Mackey collected one single off Lefty.

Unfortunately, Grove's catcher Mickey Cochrane did not catch Lefty that day. It would have been a historic matchup between the two best receivers in the game. Five years younger than Mackey, Cochrane was 24 and in his third year in the American League. He hit .338.

Philadelphians had the great opportunity of seeing both the two best lefties of their day, Grove and Winters, and the two best catchers, Cochrane and Mackey, almost side by side in the same city. Yet only a handful of the city's whites were aware of the rare opportunity which was theirs. How many took advantage of it?

Who was better, Cochrane or Mackey?

"I don't know who was better," drawled Winters, when I asked him almost half a century later. "But Mackey could throw harder."

"I think Cochrane outhit him," said expitcher Bill Holland of the rival New York Lincoln Giants. "But Mackey had a great arm, didn't have to stride and throw. He'd just raise up, and that ball would go down to second."

"Mackey was the greatest, smartest catcher," Stephens nodded vigorously. "In 1925, I think, Snooks Dowd of Newark was the best base-runner in the International League—set a record, I think it still stands. We played the Newark club three games, and seven times Mackey threw him out—*seven times!* He shot you out. Listen, please believe me, nobody—*nobody*—could catch as much baseball as Mackey. Mickey Cochrane couldn't carry his glove."

Though Biz often played against the As stars and Cochrane often played the blacks, no box score has yet been found to prove that the two ever played against each other. McDonald recalled one game that he says they did—he said Biz was telling Mickey all Mac's pitches, but Cochrane still couldn't get a hit. We will never know who was better, Mackey or Cochrane, and it's a great pity that the two could not play on equal terms in the same league so the debate could be settled once and for all.

In April 1927 Mackey did not report for spring training to the Hilldales. He had sailed to Japan with other blacks from the California winter leagues. SABRs Kazuo Sayama has chronicled that visit in his book, *Gentle Black Giants,* and comes to a revolutionary conclusion. Most Japanese historians credit Babe Ruth's tour of Japan in 1934 with inspiring the birth of the Japanese professional leagues in 1936. Sayama thinks the real germ of Japanese pro ball was planted by Mackey and the other blacks in 1927 and in subsequent visits.

Ruth and his All Stars—Lou Gehrig, Grove, Al Simmons, and others—treated the games as farce. Babe played outfield with a parasol, and Gehrig played first base in galoshes. Simmons laid down on the grass while Grove was pitching. The Americans thought they were being funny, but their antics were actually a slap in the face to their Japanese opponents.

On the other hand, the blacks left an entirely different impression, Sayama said. Most Japanese had never seen a black or *kokujin,* before and were relieved to find that they were not cannibals. Sayama has interviewed many of the Japanese college players who faced them. In one game, he reported, Mackey had been hit by a pitch and must have made a face, because the pitcher, overcome with embarrassment, swept off his hat and bowed in apology. In turn, Biz made a Japanese bow back, "and a happy mood prevailed."

The blacks lost only one game on their tour. With two on and one out, the black batter hit a fly to score one runner, but the other runner was doubled off first for out number three. The umpire refused to allow the run, an obviously wrong call, as even the Japanese players

Biz Mackey (second from left) in the California Winter League (c.1929). Also pictured are Jesse Hubbard (far left), John Beckwith (center), Rap Dixon, and Clint Thomas.

realized. But the blacks just shrugged it off, as if to say, "If you say so, OK."

The blacks entertained the fans after each game with their "shadow ball" routine, going through a spirited infield drill without any ball at all. Outfielder Herbert "Rap" Dixon gave a base-running exhibition, circling the bases in 14.5 seconds. He also did some long-distance throwing, putting balls over the fence, 100 meters (328 feet) away on the fly.

Mackey gave exhibitions of throwing to second from the squat position. But in the game he stood up to make the peg. The Japanese appreciated that, Sayama said, as earlier U.S. teams had tended to humiliate the host players by show-boating. "The *Kokujin* were real gentlemen," one Japanese said.

The blacks won the rest of their games, though they held the scores down, unlike Ruth's squad, which would run up one-sided victories. Sayama believed the blacks gave the Japanese confidence. Therefore, he said, it was the black tours that were the real inspiration for Japanese pro ball.

Tokyo's newest stadium in 1927 was Meiji Shrine Stadium, which is still used for the Japanese college championships. It was one of the two biggest parks in Japan in terms of playing area, and Mackey was the first man to hit a ball out of it. Playing a team of Japanese-Americans from Fresno State College, Biz hit a drive that flew over the center-field fence "like an arrow," one Japanese writer said, bounded onto the grass bleacher area, and disappeared beyond it, while the fans applauded. The drive was estimated at 127 meters (427 feet). In fact, in all, he hit three over the fence in three games, one to center, one to left, and one to right.

Mackey also played shortstop a few games. He was so popular, said Ted Page, that on subsequent visits the Japanese put it in his contract that he had to play at least one game at short, "otherwise it was no deal."

For their part, the Americans liked their hosts. "What a good country!" one exclaimed. "No racial barriers here. I'd like to come back."

Biz and the others got back to the United States midway through the season and got a slap on the wrist for abandoning their teams. Hilldale had finished next to last in the first half of the season without him. Biz hit .315 and pulled the team up to third in the second half.

That winter Mackey sought the sun in Southern California, play-ing for the Sun Oil Company, an all-black club from the Negro leagues. In one game against white big leaguers Tony Lazzeri, Bob Meusel, Babe Herman, Ping Bodie, and pitcher "Sloppy" Thurston

Washington (13–13), Biz drilled two hits in four at bats for a 2–1 victory.

Biz was back with Hilldale in 1928, and though the league broke up in the spring, he hit .330 that year against other top black clubs. That autumn he barnstormed against the As again. He got three hits off veteran Bullet Joe Bush (2–1). Grove (24–8) held him hitless, but he got two hits against Ed Rommel (13–5), as the Hilldales won two out of three.

There was no league in 1929, but Mackey's batting average in 11 games against other top black clubs was .375. That fall he was back in Los Angeles, playing white stars such as Simmons, Foxx, and Meusel. In one three-game series, he went 5-for-13, including two home runs, as his club swept all three contests.

Beginning in 1930, the depression almost destroyed black baseball. Clubs passed the hat and divided the meager receipts among the players. Mackey played with both Philadelphia and Baltimore, hitting .365 against top black opponents.

That fall Biz faced the Yankees' Roy Sherid (12–13) and got one hit in three tries in an 8–5 victory, then faced Fred Fitzsimmons (19–7) and Lefty Grove (28–5) and managed one single in three tries, as Fitzsimmons won it 6–3.

Mackey hit .351 in 1931, but no record has been found for 1932.

In 1933 Mackey joined a new Philadelphia team, the Stars, under Hilldale owner Ed Bolden and white booking agent Ed Gottlieb. That autumn Biz accepted another offer to tour the Orient, playing in Japan, China, the Philippines, and Hawaii with Bullet Joe Rogan, Frank Duncan, and Newt Allen.

In 1934 the Stars put together a championship team. Besides Mackey, they had Jud Wilson at first. Dick Seay and Jake Stephens formed the double-play combination, one of the best in the game, black or white. In the outfield, Chaney White was a slashing lead-off hitter, and Rap Dixon hit with power.

Mackey made a great pitcher out of a rookie left-hander named Slim Jones. Jones is often called the left-handed Satchel Paige, and Paige himself usually mentioned Jones first when asked to list the great pitchers he saw in the Negro leagues. Jones and Winters were among the four top left-handers in blackball history. Both pitched to Mackey.

Under Mackey, Jones ran up a 13–1 record, and the Stars won the second half pennant and met the winners of the first half, the American Giants, in a seven-game play-off. Unfortunately, there are few details of what was a thrilling series, as impoverished black newspapers turned their meager sports budgets to football coverage.

We do know that Chicago won the opener in Philadelphia, beating Jones, 3–0. The teams then moved to Chicago, where the American Giants took two out of three games. Back in Philadelphia, the Stars had to sweep the final three games. They won the first one, on Thursday night. Rain the next day forced the clubs to play a final double-header showdown, with Philadelphia needing a sweep to win.

"Slim, how you feel?" McDonald, the manager, asked.

"Mac, I'm feelin' good," Jones said, and Mackey kept begging, "Mac, pitch Slim, pitch Slim."

Jones won the first game, 2–1, to even the series at three games apiece, then came right back to start the second game too against Chicago's Bill Cornelius. With the score 0–0 in the fourth, Mackey singled and scored the game's first run. In the seventh, Jones, a good hitter, drove in the second run with a screaming double to give the Stars the championship, 2–0.

That winter Biz was back in Japan for his third and final trip.

The Stars finished poorly in 1935, but it would turn out to be a historic year: Mackey discovered a chubby 13-year-old kid who used to hang around the ball park, Roy Campanella. "Campanella looked like Mackey," said Ted Page. "He was little, round, fat, and chubby—just like Mackey."

"Campanella was a fat boy, round face and all," Stars manager Webster McDonald said. "Mackey fell in love with him."

Biz began to show the kid some of the fine points of catching. Roy remembered Mackey's fingers vividly.

> To look at his hands, you'd say, "This guy must have been a butcher," the way his fingers were curved and broken from foul tips. His fingers would turn all kinds of ways. But this guy was a master. He had so much he could teach a young catcher. And he wasn't a stingy old catcher, meaning his advice was always right on his tongue. I must have been a pretty good observer, because I gathered quite a bit from Mackey by just watching him—how he did things, block low pitches—that's one of the main things—shift his feet for an outside pitch or an inside pitch and always try to keep the ball in the center of your body.

Mackey is credited with a .300 average in 1935. That winter he returned to California and got one hit in two at bats against Lee Stine of the White Sox.

In 1936 Mackey's average dropped to .242. Midway through the summer he left Philadelphia to manage the Nashville Elite Giants, who were in the process of moving to Washington. Campanella was still in school in Philadelphia, and McDonald remembered how the boy continued to hang around the park. On Sunday mornings the Stars would go down to Baltimore after the season to play the white big-league all stars. "Mac, you gonna take me along?" Roy would ask. "I'd say, 'Yes, you can go along with me.' Sunday morning six o'clock he'd be sitting on my front steps waiting till I come out. In case somebody got a bad finger (in the game), he would be ready. I'd get him in the game somehow."

In 1938 McDonald had two veteran catchers on the roster, and Roy was still only 16 years old. "You've got two catchers, Mac," owner Ed Bolden said. "You don't need the third boy."

Mackey came to McDonald and told him, "I'd love to get that boy,"

"They won't let me have him," McDonald replied.

"Tell 'em I'll take him on," Mackey said.

Roy was still in school, so "They went to my father and mother," he recalled, "and said, 'Just let him play on weekends.'"

And so it was agreed that Roy would join Biz in Baltimore. "They would see that I got back home Sunday night to go to school Monday."

Biz Mackey.

When summer vacation began, Roy got permission to travel with the team full time.

"I was tickled to death to see Mackey get him," McDonald said. "Mackey's gonna teach him everything he knows. When Mackey gets through with him, what a combination that will be!"

"I sat beside Mackey in the dugout," Roy said. "I relied on everything he told me. I wouldn't say I was catching regular with the ball club," Campanella said, but within a week both Mackey and backup catcher Nish William got hurt, and Roy was rushed behind the plate. Mackey watched his every move. "He wouldn't let me get too far off base," Campy said. "If I was doing something wrong, he'd be the first to correct me. I appreciated it. Mackey was, oh, a tremendous catcher. And what a leader and manager he was. You never did see him get angry. He would get mad on occasion, but not too often. But you know why I liked Mackey so much? The technique that he used to impress the pitchers was tremendous—tremendous."

"He was the dean of teachers," said Monte Irvin, who would play under Mackey later in Newark. "He taught Campanella how to think like a catcher, how to set a hitter up—throw a hitter his favorite pitch at a time when he's not expecting it, and he'd just stand there and take it."

"Truthfully, Mackey never hardly worked with me about hitting," Campy said. "He stressed catching defense to me, how important a catcher meant to a team if he was a good defensive catcher—'Don't worry about swinging the bat.' Catching the spitball, giving my pitcher a low target, blocking low pitches, learning how to release my throw quick—he was the first to advise me that it's the quickness in getting the throw away. I came up under the best coaching I could have."

"Campanella had all Mackey's moves," Judy Johnson said. "If you see him up there and didn't see his face, you'd swear it was Mackey. If you saw Campanella in one game and Mackey in the other, you would say Campanella caught in both games, because he had all Mackey's moves."

"He was Mackey made over," nodded Ted Page. "He had moves and everything back there. You had to notice him."

Campy admired Mackey, of course, "although I admired Josh Gibson tremendously too. But Josh was not the handler of pitchers and the master in technique that Biz Mackey was. I think Mackey by far—by *far*—in technique and in defensive catching could do it all." Larry Brown and Frank Duncan were also outstanding catchers, Campanella conceded. "But in my opinion, Mackey had it over all of these guys. Josh to me was the cream of the crop. But Josh had it because of his big bat; Josh could hit so much." Mackey also, Roy hastily added, was a pretty good switch-hitter. Indeed, Biz' uncomfirmed average was .320 in 1939 (to Campy's .281).

The other players liked Biz too. "Biz Mackey was a dream, really a dream," said Elite second baseman Sammy T. Hughes. "You couldn't find a better guy to be around. He'd give you everything he had at all times. On the field and off. He was a prince."

And he was "a wonderful general in running the team," added Frank "Doc" Sykes, a former pitcher and at that time a dentist in Baltimore. Sykes recalled one game when Mackey came up with the score tied and men on second and third. "Come on, hit a homer, Mackey," a fan yelled.

"You don't need a home run, brother," Sykes told him. "Mackey's going to bunt." They each put $20 on it. On the 3–2 count, "I thought my $20 was gone." But Mackey laid one down, and the winning run crossed the plate. "Mackey," Sykes said, "was one of the best bunters we ever had. Had a whole lot of baseball sense."

When Mackey left in 1939 to manage Newark, the most bereft man in Baltimore was Campanella. "I wasn't exactly left on my own, but I was left without a catcher that I admired. Those three years with Mackey played an important role in my catching."

With Campanella as first-string catcher, the Elites won the pennant in 1939, beating Gibson's Homestead Grays in the play-off.

At Newark meanwhile, said pitcher Leon Day, Mackey was "always laughing, always jolly, friendly, always full of fun. But I don't see how he threw at all—his fingers were all broken on his right hand, all messed up." Still, Day said, "he was a *good* catcher, could have caught in any league. He couldn't throw too hard—not at that time—but he was still getting the ball away. He'd still throw you out going to second. And a good receiver. I liked for him to catch."

And he was still "the dean of teachers," said Irvin, who joined the Eagles as a rookie in 1941. "He was a nice man, congenial, and he told all these stories about Wickware, Rap Dixon, Chino Smith, Santop. And he could evaluate players better than anybody I've ever seen."

In 1941 Biz was selected as top catcher for the East-West game by vote of the fans, defeating Campanella by 209,000 votes to 180,000.

In 1945 Mackey, then 48 years old, was credited with a .307 average. The Eagles' owner, Mrs. Effa Manley recalled several times, "when it's real late in the game and the pitcher has stopped all our good hitters, and just one hit was all that was needed, I'd say, 'Mackey, go in there and hit that ball.' He was over 50, but I've seen him go in there, get a hit."

"He couldn't run a lick," said first baseman Lenny Pearson. "He'd get a single and sort of wobble to first base. But he was an inspiration to us guys, because he was old enough to be our father, and he made all of us get up and hustle a little bit more."

"He never had bed check," said third baseman Clarence "Half a Pint" Israel. "But if you had a bad day, Mackey would write a note on pay day the reason why you were being docked." Pint objected when Mackey tried to change his stance at the plate. "We got into some words about it—I ran my mouth a lot. Mackey was the type got along with everybody, so I felt kind of bad about it."

Mackey helped groom Irvin, Larry Doby, and Don Newcombe for the major leagues. He was "one of the most knowledgeable baseball men that I ever knew," Newcombe said. He and Mackey roomed together, Newcombe told Peter Golenbeck in *Bums*. "We got along famously. He tried to counsel me like a father about taking care of myself and not cursing so much. . . . He always used to be on me, on

Biz Mackey (right) and Chet Brewer.

the bus, in the clubhouse, on the field, and in the hotels: 'Newcombe, you gotta stop cursing so much.'"

Even after the white majors took Doby and Newcombe, Biz won the 1946 pennant with Irvin, Day, Israel, and Pearson. They also won the black World Series, beating Satchel Paige and the Monarchs in seven games.

In 1948 it was Mackey who urged the Cleveland Indians to move Doby from second base to center field, and when Larry proved to be a temperamental problem, Indian general manager Hank Greenberg went to Mackey for help in handling him.

After his boys made good in the majors, Mackey retired to Los Angeles, where he spent his last years driving a forklift truck, his immense gifts as a teacher and coach squandered by the game that had also turned its back on his talents as a player.

Mackey was still living in Los Angeles in 1959, when 90,000 people filled the Coliseum for a mammoth tribute to Campanella.

"I invited him out to the game," Roy said, "and I had him stand up, and I told them, 'This is the man that gave me all of the techniques in my catching ability, that started me out at a young age.' He was there, and he felt so proud. And then he passed away right after that."

Biz Mackey

Year	Team	G	AB	H	2B	3B	HR	BA	SB	(W-L)
1920	Indianapolis	15	49	15	3	1	1	.306	0	
1921	Indianapolis	63	211	61	8	8	11	.289	4	(0-3)
1922	Indianapolis	59	210	73	13	12	6	.352	3	
1923	Philadelphia	18	66	24	2	1	2	.364	4	
1924	Philadelphia	68	268	87	3	0	1	.363	0	
1925	Philadelphia	34	135	48	8	4	3	.356	0	
1926	Philadelphia	65	252	68	13	0	7	.270	—	
1927	Philadelphia	28	108	34	1	2	0	.315	1	
1928	Philadelphia	51	197	65	3	2	2	.330	3	
1929	Philadelphia	11	40	15	1	0	0	.375	0	
1930	Phil.-Baltimore	31	126	46	3	2	3	.365	1	
1931	Philadelphia	46	151	53	4	2	2	.351	0	
1932	Philadelphia	30	104	30	4	1	2	.288	0	
1933	Philadelphia	13	47	14	2	0	0	.298	0	
1934	Philadelphia	6	24	6	1	0	1	.250	0	
1935	Philadelphia	25	70	21	3	0	1	.300	1	
1936	Washington	16	66	16	3	1	0	.242	0	
1937	Washington	4	14	5	0	0	0	.357	0	
1938	Baltimore	17	60	19	3	0	1	.317	—	
1939	Newark	3	16	4						
1945	Newark	36	114	35	2	2	1	.307	0	
Totals		610	2377	755	80	38	44	.318	17	

	Post-Season									
1924	World Series	10	41	10	0	1	0	.241	1	
1925	World Series	6	25	9	3	1	1	.360	0	
1934	Play-Off	1*	4	0	0	0	0	.000	0	
Total		17	70	19	3	2	1	.271	1	
East-West		2	7	1	0	0	0	.143	0	

* Incomplete

Biz Mackey vs. White Big Leaguers

Year	AB	H	2B	3B	HR	Pitcher	(W-L)
1921	4	1	0	1	0	Petty	(0-0)
1926	(4)*	1	0	0	0	Quinn	(10-11)
	(4)	1	—	—	—	Grove	(13-13)
	3	0	0	0	0	Root	(18-17)
1927-28	(4)	2	1	0	0	Thurston	(13-13)
1928	(4)	2	1	0	0	Rommel	(13-5)
	(4)	3	—	—	—	Bush	(2-1)
	4	0	0	0	0	Grove	(24-8)
1929	3	1	0	0	0	Campbell	(0-1)
1930	3	1	—	—	—	Sherid	(12-13)
	3	1	—	—	—	Fitzsimmons	(19-7)
1935	4	2	—	—	—	Vance	(3-2)
1935-36	2	1	0	0	0	Stine	(0-0)
1939	3	0	0	0	0	Appleton	(5-10)
						Thomas	(7-1)
Total 14 games	49	16	2	1	0	Average: .326	

* At bats in parentheses are estimated.

17

Martin Dihigo:
El Maestro

Dihigo could do everything—pitcher, good hitter, good fielder. He was a big ol' guy, looked like Joe DiMaggio. Weighed 200, a big tall guy. That man could play outfield, and ooh, could he throw! You better not try to stretch a hit— he could throw. And pitching, he threw everything, overhand or sidearm. Good curve ball and a good fast ball—a good fast ball. Had he come along today, he'd lead the major leagues in winning. Would have hit .300 too. Tremendous power. And he was really a likeable guy, jolly. He loved baseball, he knew baseball—he loved it.

Pitcher Hilton Smith
Kansas City Monarchs

Virtually everyone who saw Martin Dihigo agrees that he was the greatest all-round ball player who ever lived, black or white. He could play every position except catcher—and some say he could do that too. White baseball has never produced anyone quite like Dihigo, whom the Mexicans called *El Maestro* and the Cubans *El Immortal*. John McGraw called him one of the greatest natural ball players living. Only two men in baseball history, Babe Ruth and Bullet Joe Rogan, could rival him as a double threat man with the bat and on the pitching mound. He was a lifetime .304 hitter, hit with power, and over his long career in the United States and the tropics won 256 games while losing 133.

Tall and graceful, he has been compared to Dave Winfield or DiMaggio. Dihigo—or Don Martin to the Latins—hit with Jolting Joe's power and covered center field with the same class and grace. "He had an arm like a cannon," said "Scrip" Lee. "Oh yeah, stronger than DiMaggio's."

He had a better arm than Roberto Clemente, said outfielder Ted Page, a close friend of Clemente. "As much as I liked Clemente, Dihigo had a better arm."

Judy Johnson compared Dihigo's arm to a jai alai player's. Johnson remembered a game in Havana, when a jai alai player, using his long basketlike *cesto,* unleashed a throw that hit the center field wall on one bounce. Using his bare arm, Dihigo hit it on the fly.

How he loved to gun down runners at the plate. "He'd fall down and just laugh," said Johnson: " 'You no run on me, boy, you no run on me.' "

Dihigo anchored perhaps the finest outfield of all time, the Cuban trio of Dihigo, Pablo Mesa, and little Alejandro Oms. They were perhaps the flashiest trio since Boston's Tris Speaker, Harry Hooper, and Duffy Lewis. Oms reputedly invented the Willie Mays basket catch—only Oms caught the ball behind him. The three Cubans probably outhit the Red Sox trio; neither Hooper nor Lewis were outstanding at bat, while Oms and Mesa led the Cuban league with averages of .409 and .385.

Dihigo's highest mark was .434 in 1930. And he hit with more power than Speaker; he won three home run crowns and in 1935 tied Josh Gibson for the championship. His lifetime total is low in proportion to his at bats because much of his career was spent in Cuba, where outfield walls were a half hour hike from home plate. But Schoolboy Johnny Taylor recalled one Dihigo home run in Cuba that cleared the fence 370 feet from home and was last seen clearing the weathervane of a house 40 feet beyond that. Both Taylor and Buck Leonard witnessed another Dihigo blast in Pittsburgh over the right-field fence at Greenlee Field. It landed on a hospital roof. Both men estimate it at 500 feet plus.

Born in 1905 in Matanzas, Cuba, about 50 miles from Havana, Dihigo broke in with the Havana Reds at the age of 17, when he hit a mere .179. The following summer the boy made his first trip to the United States with the Cuban Stars as a second baseman and short stop. That's when Page got his first look at him—"a big old skinny kid, but he had so much grace, he attracted attention." Page compared him to Marty Marion, the long-legged Cardinal shortstop of the 1940s.

Infielder Dick Seay, himself one of the best second basemen in blackball history, compared him to Dick Lundy—"so graceful, big, stylish—just a picture ball player."

"You couldn't hit the ball past him," said shortstop Bill Yancey. "His range was so great."

The kid was still weak at bat. "He was plate-shy," Yancey said. But Fay Young, sports editor of the Chicago *Defender,* was impressed. "Dihigo," he wrote, "the rookie infielder for Alex Pompez' Cuban Stars, is, in this writer's opinion, the best youngster to come off the Island since pitcher Jose Mendez. He fields like a veteran and has good speed but has not learned how to hit the curve ball."

"Dihigo could hit no curve," agreed Juanelo Mirabal. But one day in batting practice, the kid told him, "Listen, don't throw me any more fast balls. I can hit them like anything. Throw me curves." Said Mirabal: "He learned to hit them like George Scales," who was considered one of the best curve ball hitters in the Negro leagues.

Dihigo improved steadily. His average climbed to .263 in 1924, .292 in 1925, and .325 in 1926. At home in Cuba, against the best Latin pitchers, as well as top blacks from the United States and white big leaguers such as Dolph Luque, Dihigo was making equally rapid progress—.179, .300, .334. By the winter of 1926–1927, still only 21 years old, he was hitting .421, a year later .415.

Dihigo was popular with the Americans. "He learned how to talk English quicker'n anybody you've ever seen," said excatcher Frank Duncan. "Dihigo was just a big ol' kid. Got along with everybody, full of fun all the time."

Martin Dihigo.

"He was a nice kid," agreed pitcher Sam Streeter of Pittsburgh. "Most of the Cubans had something like a clique when they played against the North Americans, but Dihigo wasn't that way. He'd help you if you helped him. He was a different type of man from, say, Clemente. Clemente had an air like he's in demand or something. Dihigo wasn't like that, he didn't carry his feelings in his hand."

The big fellow had a sly sense of humor. In Cuba he introduced catcher Larry Brown, a great toper, to an exotic island drink called "Piña Fria." Larry drank all night without even getting a buzz. Later he learned that "piña fria" in Spanish means cold pineapple juice.

Dihigo was a smart ball player, the fan, Pedro Cardona said. One time, on third base, he suddenly hollered to the pitcher: "You balked! You balked!" Dihigo walked all the way to home plate loudly complaining to the umpire, touched home, and continued into the dugout before anyone thought to tag him out. The stadium was in an uproar with laughter.

Another time, Cardona recalled, Dihigo was playing center field with a man on first when the batter singled. Dihigo fielded the ball and ran into the infield to talk to the shortstop, then turned to the runner on second: "Excuse me," he said, "I have to fix the bag." "And everybody in the park knew he had the ball," Cardona laughed. But the runner politely lifted his foot while Dihigo just as politely put the ball on him.

Dihigo did not hit the white major league pitchers as well as some of the other black stars did. But in 1928 he barnstormed against the Philadelphia As and cracked two hits in five at bats against Rube Walberg (17–12).

Dihigo's managers were using his arm on the pitching mound more and more. He would win two or three games a year until 1928–1929, when he blossomed into a big winner with ten victories and four losses in the abbreviated winter season.

"I don't think he had much of a curve," Cardona said. "But he had a lot of speed and a lot of control."

In the winter of 1929 the Louisville Colonels, champions of the American Association, arrived in Cuba, starring pitcher Paul Derringer, who went on to fame with the Cincinnati Reds. Dihigo played shortstop in the first game and outfield in the second game, both won by the Cubans. "We'll get them tomorrow," the Colonels declared, according to pitcher Chet Brewer, Dihigo's teammate; "they don't have anyone left to pitch." When they saw Dihigo, an apparent utility man, warming up for game three, the Colonels chortled. They said, "Here's a fellow who's a shortstop and outfielder, going to pitch against us."

But, said Brewer, "Dihigo wound up and went into that knot and, boom! he threw that fast ball. The batter dropped his bat! He shut them out, 3–0."

The following summer in the United States, Dihigo hit .434.

He deserted both Cuba and the United States in 1932 for Venezuela, where he played for the next three seasons. He tossed a no-hitter his first year there. The next year he posted a perfect 6–0 won-lost record; his earned run average was a near zero, 0.15!

The big man returned to the United States in 1935, and Roger "Doc" Cramer, then a semipro in southern New Jersey and later a star outfielder with the Boston Red Sox, remembered picking up bats for him. Cramer would later play against Josh Gibson, Oscar Charleston, and other black stars but insisted that Dihigo was the best black player he ever saw.

Johnny Taylor, who pitched for Dihigo on the New York Cubans, said one night in New York Dihigo hit a ball three inches from the shortstop's head. Before the frightened fielder could get his hands up, the ball was bouncing off the left-center field fence. "Four inches lower and it would have killed him," Taylor said.

In 1935 Dihigo had one of the finest—and at the same time one of the most disappointing—years of his career. He batted .323, slugged nine home runs to tie Josh Gibson for the league lead, played eight positions (all but catcher), boasted a 6–2 record on the pitching mound, and managed the Cubans to the second-half championship. He might have been the Most Valuable Player of the year (his only rival was pitcher Leroy Matlock, whose 17–0 record led the Crawfords to the first-half title).

Cum Posey, owner of the Homestead Grays, picked Dihigo on his authoritative all-star team, and the fans voted him first place in their balloting for outfielders in the annual East-West All-Star game.

Dihigo opened the game for the East in center field. In the sixth he crashed into the wall pursuing Josh Gibson's 400-foot double. Dihigo crumpled to the grass as players rushed to aid him, but he shook the injury off and remained in the game. After nine innings the score was all tied up, 4-4. In the tenth the East scored four runs, but the West came back in their half of the inning, loading the bases against Luis Tiant, Sr.

Dihigo was rushed in from the outfield to put out the fire. He took a few warm-up tosses, then faced pinch-hitter Felton Snow, who quickly singled down the first baseline for two runs. Alex Radcliff's ground ball brought in another run, Turkey Stearnes singled Snow to third, and Buck Leonard's long fly scored the tying run. In the eleventh Dihigo walked Cool Papa Bell, gave an intentional pass to Gibson, then threw perhaps the most famous gopher pitch in blackball history to Mule Suttles, who drilled it high into the upper right field stands to win the game.

The Cubans won the second-half pennant that year and met the first-half winners, the Pittsburgh Crawfords—Gibson, Charleston, Bell, and company—in the play off in September. The Cubans started out strong.

Dihigo himself won the opener, 2–1, plus the fourth-game victory that gave them a three-to-one series lead. The Craws won the next one to make it three-to-two.

In the sixth game Johnny Taylor was coasting with a 5–2 lead after seven innings. "It looked like a walk-away," he said. Even Pompez, the owner, left the game to return to New York and prepare a big victory celebration. "I was already spending the winners' bonus," Taylor said. He stood up to go to the mound for the eighth, but Dihigo waved him back. "Johnny, give me the ball," he said. Taylor was mad, "but what could I do?"

Dihigo got the Craws out 1-2-3 in the eighth. In the ninth he yielded a walk and a scratch hit, with the dangerous Oscar Charleston advancing to the bat. The two toyed with each other until the count reached 3–2. Under the stands Cuban business manager Frank Forbes was confidently counting the winners' share when he heard the crowd let out a roar. Charleston had slugged a three-run homer to tie it up.

A double, an error, and a walk filled the bases with the slump-ridden Judy Johnson coming up. Judy hit a 3-2 pitch on the ground down the right-field line. The Cubans' stylish first baseman, Showboat Thomas, flagged the ball but couldn't hold it, and the Crawfords had tied the series.

Forbes was so angry, he threw the wad of bills across the locker room. "Dihigo," he muttered, "he was one of the greatest ball players of all time, but he was so cocky!"

"That broke our hearts," said Taylor. The next day the Crawfords won, 8–7, and claimed the title. Taylor never did spend that bonus. But, he insists, Dihigo "was still a great manager."

Martin hit .358 in Cuba that winter, but more important, he suddenly became a big winner on the pitching mound, with an 11-2 record.

In the United States in 1936, he led the league with .393 and tied with Gibson in home runs. On that note he said *adios* to the United States to spend the rest of his career South of the Border (except for a brief return in 1945). More and more he concentrated on pitching.

He may have reached his peak in Cuba in the winter of 1936–1937, with a 14–10 record—another new high for him—and a .323 batting average. (His first baseman, Buck Leonard, hit .304.) Dihigo's team, Marianao, went into the final three games of the season three games behind Santa Clara and swept all three, including the final double header, to force a play-off. Dihigo faced the Homestead Grays' great knuckle-baller, Ray Brown, who had won 20 and lost three, a great performance in the short Cuban season. Brown whipped Dihigo in the opener, 6–1. Silvio Garcia pitched a beautiful game for Marianao to even the series. Then, with one day's rest, Dihigo and Brown squared off against each other again. This time Dihigo shut them out for eight innings and won the game—and the championship—7–3.

Dihigo was still going strong in March 1937, when the National League champion New York Giants came to Cuba for spring training. Dihigo usually did not hit white big leaguers well (his lifetime average against them was only .246), but he got two hits in six at bats against several Giant pitchers, including Bill Melton, who would be 20–9 that year. The U.S. champs lost five out of six games, and though it was only spring training, manager Bill Terry was as unhappy as his predecessor, John McGraw, had been 26 years earlier. "This thing has long ceased to be a joke," he told New York *Times* writer John Drebinger after the fifth loss, 4–0, to Rodolfo Fernandez.

Playing for Aguila of Vera Cruz, Mexico, in 1937, Dihigo had a 4–0 pitching record, with an 0.93 ERA, as Aguila won the pennant.

The next year he did even better, as U.S. black stars such as Josh Gibson, Ray Dandridge, Willie Wells, Wild Bill Wright, Ray Brown, and others began crossing the border to Mexico in increasing numbers. Dihigo not only led the league in victories, strikeouts, and batting average, he managed his club in a tight race to the pennant against Agrario of Mexico City, starring Satchel Paige.

The two great pitchers clashed head to head on September 5, 1938. For six innings they dueled, 0–0, Dihigo going to his fast ball, and Paige, with an injured arm, relying on underhand and trick pitches. In the seventh Paige loaded the bases on a hit plus two walks, then wild pitched the game's first run home. Paige was lifted for a pinch-hitter in the eighth, but three hits off Dihigo tied the score, 1–1.

In the ninth, Ramon Bragana, with the flashing gold tooth, one of the top Latin pitchers of all time, replaced Satch on the mound. He gave up a lead-off single, then Dihigo smashed a home run over the center field wall to win it.

Three days later Aguila clinched the pennant. And two weeks after that Dihigo made history by hurling Mexico's first no-hit game ever. He ended up with an 18–2 record, an 0.90 ERA, 184 strikeouts, and a .387 batting average.

In 1939 his pitching record was 15–8; he again led the league in strike outs with 202, and batted .336, including a perfect six-for-six day, the first time it had ever been done in Mexico. For six straight years, 1937–1942, Dihigo hit over .300, and as a pitcher led the league in strike outs at least four times (records are missing for several of his years there).

In 1942 Martin hit .319, won 22 and lost seven on the mound, again led the Mexican league in strike outs and ERA—and managed his club, Torreon, to the pennant to boot!

Meanwhile in Cuba Dihigo was posting records of 8–3, 8–3, 4–8, and a splendid 8–1 in 1943–1944, though his hitting fell off to .249.

In 1945 he returned to the United States for a swan song. Although he hit only .205, the Cubans, with young Minnie Minoso on third, did reach the play-offs.

That winter, 1945–1946, Dihigo played for Dolph Luque's championship Cienfuegos team, compiling a 5–4 record. (Teammate Sal Maglie was 9–6.)

In Mexico in 1946 at the age of 41, Dihigo hit .316, while winning 11 and losing four. Back in Cuba that winter he posted a 1–3 mark. At last he hung up his toe plate and glove.

Dihigo was lionized in Havana. "He was tall, strong, distinguished," George Wehby, former editor of the Havana *Post,* said. He impressed people with his very voice and presence. People would flock to the open-air Cafe Las Avenidas in Havana to listen to Dihigo "hold court." "People would listen to him like God. The name 'Dihigo' was like saying 'Mr. Baseball.' It was like saying 'Babe Ruth.' He'd sit and give lectures about baseball, and people would sit there in awe and listen." Wehby used to hail him as *el que mas sabe*—"the one who knows the most." Dihigo smiled and waved back. "He liked that," Wehby said. "But the man was not ostentatious, he never bragged. He didn't have to brag."

"He was very quiet," agreed Willie Portuondo, later sports editor for the Voice of America. "He wasn't a prima donna. He always had a smile, a very friendly guy."

One honor escaped him, however. Dihigo wanted to manage the Havana Reds, but Mike Gonzalez had held that job for years, and as long as he lived, no one could displace him. "Dihigo didn't like to be number two," Wehby said; "he was always number one."

Dihigo dropped out of the limelight in the 1950s. He did color commentary on radio for the games, but though he knew baseball thoroughly, he was not a glib announcer. Jorge Figueredo said he "became arrogant or bitter, maybe because he thought he wasn't getting the attention he deserved."

Dihigo's radio comments became tinged with political overtones, and he became a supporter of the rebel leader, Fidel Castro. "I think he was used," said Wehby, "or they tried to use him, I'm not sure." Martin's son also became very close to the revolution, Portuondo said.

"Nobody could tell if he was a communist or not," Figueredo said, "but he had very revolutionary ideas." Later Dihigo "took a low profile. We didn't hear much of him."

But whether Dihigo admired Castro or not, the Cuban dictator, a great fan, admired Dihigo immensely. Dihigo was almost a national hero. He died there May 21, 1971.

Rene Cubas, former sports writer of Havana's *El Tiempo* and now a public relations official at Madison Square Garden, recalled congratulating Satchel Paige on Paige's induction into Cooperstown in 1971. "I'm not happy," Satch told him. "I'm not number one; Martin Dihigo is."

Finally, in 1978, Dihigo joined Satch in the Hall.

What kind of player was Dihigo? Wehby used a prize fighting analogy. Muhammed Ali was a boxer, Jack Dempsy a mauler; Joe Louis was both. Dihigo was the Joe Louis of baseball.

"He was the greatest all-round player I know," said Buck Leonard. "I say he was the best ball player of all time, black or white. He could do it all. He is my ideal ball player, makes no difference what race either. If he's not the greatest, I don't know who is. You take your Ruths, Cobbs, and DiMaggios. Give me Dihigo. I bet I would beat you almost every time."

Martin Dihigo vs. White Big Leaguers

Year	AB	H	2B	3B	HR	Pitcher	(W-L)
1924-25	3	1	0	0	0	Luque	(10-15)
	2	0	0	0	0	Luque	
	2	0	0	0	0	Luque	
1926	(4)*	0	0	0	0	Quinn	(10-11)
1926-27	4	1	0	0	0	Luque	(13-16)
1927	(4)	3	2	0	0	Walberg	(16-12)
1927-28	4	1	0	0	0	Luque	(13-12)
	4	0	0	0	0	Luque	
1928	4	1	0	0	1	Uhle	(12-17)
	(4)	0	0	0	0	Quinn	(18-7)
	5	2	0	0	0	Walberg	(17-12)
1931	(4)	1	0	0	0	Heimach	(9-7)
	(4)	1	0	0	0	Heimach, (Huggins)	
1936	4	0	0	0	0	Hilcher (Nelson)[a]	(1-2)
1937	3	1	0	0	0	Gumbert	(10-11)
						Gabler (Meketi)[a]	(4-7)
	3	1	1	0	0	Schumacher	(13-12)
						Melton	(20-9)
						Castleman	(11-6)
1946	3	2	—	—	0	Feldman	(0-2)
Total 17 games	61	15	3	0	1	Average: .246	

*At bats in parentheses are estimated.
[a] Not major league pitchers.

Martin Dihigo

Year	Team	G	EAB[a]	H	2B	3B	HR	BA	SB	(W-L)	ERA
1922	Cuba	12	28	5	—	—	—	.179	—	—	
1923	Cubans	1	48	11	—	—	—	.230	—	(1-1)	
	Cuba	—	2	0	0	0	0	.000	0	(2-3)	
1924	Cubans	32	132	31	1	3	3	.263	2	(1-1)	
	Cuba	27	50	15	5	1	2	.300	1	(2-3)	
1925	Cubans	28	96	28	3	2	1	.292	0	(4-7)	
	Cuba	9	32	11	3	0	2	.334	—	(0-0)	
1926	Cubans	40	169	55	8	0	11*	.325	8		
	Cuba	27	95	40	4	1	3	.421	12	(3-0)	
1927	Cubans	61	246	77	3	1	12*	.313	5	(1-0)	
	Cuba	33	130	54	12	3	2	.415	0	(4-2)	
1928	Grays	5	20	4	1	0	0	.200	4	(0-1)	
	Cuba	—	152	46	—	—	5	.303	2	(2-1)	
1929	Philadelphia	23	79	24	2	0	—	.304	12	(4-2)	
	Cuba	—	180	51	—	—	6	.282	2	(1-2)	
1930	Phil.-Cubans	14	60	26	1	2	5	.434	0		
1931	Philadelphia	65	245	65	2	3	0	.265	2	(1-1)	
	Cuba	—	49	16	2	0	—	.327	—		
1933	Venezuela	—	—	—	—	—	9*	—	6	(6-0)	0.15
1935	Cubans	46	161	52	11	4	—	.323	—	(6-2)	
	Cuba	47	176	63	—	—	11	.358	3	(11-2)	
1936	Cubans	28	92	36	9	1	—	.391*	10	(5-3)	
	Cuba	69	229	74	—	—	—	.323	—	(14-10)	
1937	Mexico	7	28	10	1	2	1	.357	—	(4-0)	
	Dominican Republic	25	97	34	6	2	4	.351	—		
	Cuba	52	165	50	—	—	—	.303	6	(11-5)	0.93

Year	Team							AVG		(W-L)	ERA
1938	Mexico	42	142	55	8	2	6	.387*	9	(18-2)	0.90*
	Cuba	—	145	37	—	—	—	.255	5	(14-2)	2.87
1939	Mexico	51	187	63	11	3	5	.336	5	(15-8)	3.54
	Cuba	—	79	23	—	—	—	.291	3	(6-4)	4.01
1940	Mexico	78	302	110	17	6	9	.364	9	(8-6)	2.53*
	Cuba	—	110	20	—	—	—	.182	4	(8-3)	3.10
1941	Mexico	92	329	102	25	4	12	.310	7	(9-10)	2.23
	Cuba	—	123	28	6	0	1	.228	1	(8-3)	3.14
1942	Mexico	85	279	89	12	4	8	.319	9	(22-7)	3.84
	Cuba	—	135	36	—	—	—	.267	2	(4-8)	2.83
1943	Mexico	75	238	66	14	3	7	.277	5	(16-8)	10.80
	Cuba	—	87	22	—	—	—	.253	0	(8-1)	4.37
1944	Mexico	60	189	47	10	2	4	.249	5	(12-10)	
	Cuba	—	110	20	—	—	—	.182	4	(3-3)	
1945	Cubans	17	54	11	0	0	3	.204	0	(1-2)	
	Cuba	34	71	16	3	0	0	.125	1	(5-4)	
1946	Mexico	66	177	56	9	2	3	.316	8	(11-4)	
	Cuba	15	10	1	0	0	0	.100	0	(1-3)	
1947	Mexico	20	46	9	3	1	0	.196	0	(4-2)	
Totals			5496	1660	193	50	134	.304	152	(256-136)	—
Post-Season											
Play-Offs	1935	5	19	5	—	—	—	.263	—	(1-1)	—
East-West		2	6	1	0	0	0	.167	0	(0-1)	—

*Led League.
a Estimated At Bats.

18

Norman "Turkey" Stearnes: "I Never Counted My Homers"

There's no ball player I know that hit more home runs than Turkey Stearnes. And he was one of our best all-round ball players. Everybody knows he was a great outfielder. He could field, throw, run, hit. If they don't put Turkey Stearnes in the Hall of Fame, they shouldn't put anybody in.

Cool Papa Bell

"I never counted my home runs," Turkey Stearnes said.

I hit so many, I never counted them, and I'll tell you why: If they didn't win a ball game, they didn't amount to anything. It didn't make any difference if I hit four or five over the grandstand, it didn't make any difference to me, as long as I hit them to try to win the game. That's what I wanted: to win the game. Wanted to win. As long as I was winning, I wouldn't think about it.

I remember one year, my first season with Detroit—1923—I think I hit about 50-some. But after I was up here about a year, I hit so many that that's the reason I didn't count them.

If Turkey Stearnes didn't count his home runs, SABR scholars have. From 1922 to 1936 Turkey Stearnes hit 160 known home runs in the Negro leagues, more than any other man, including the great Josh Gibson, whose verified total so far stands at 137.

Three of Josh's best seasons, 1942, '43, and '46, have not yet been counted. Unofficially, for those missing years, Gibson is credited with 30 more homers, which, if confirmed, would make a total of 167, though most of the unofficial published figures are believed to be highly inflated. Stearnes also has some missing years in his record, but they are at the end of his career. When all missing seasons are filled in, it will be interesting to see if Josh can take over first place. Even if he does, Turkey will surely remain ahead of everyone else—including Mule Suttles, 150, and Oscar Charleston, 136.

In all, Turkey led the league or tied for the lead seven times. Josh led four times.

And Stearnes, like Gibson, hit with consistency. In his best year,

1935, he led the league with .430. His lifetime average was .352 in the black leagues, .313 against white big leaguers.

Turkey didn't look like a slugger. He weighed under 170 pounds, used a short, 35", 39-ounce bat, and whipped it from one of the oddest stances ever seen. A lefty, he put his front (right) foot in the bucket and, his teammate at Chicago, Nat Rogers, recalled, "he used to twist his right heel like this and point his right toe up. He didn't swing from the end, he'd choke up on the bat." With that stance Turkey Stearnes hit some of the longest home runs seen in baseball, black or white.

"Yeah, he had a stance worse than [Gil] McDougald or [Minnie] Minoso, or Stan the Man [Musial]," Satchel Paige said. He continued:

His stance was way different than any baseball player's. Those men had stances, and it was hard to pitch to those people. Yeah, Turkey had a funny stance at the plate, but he could get around on you. I tried to pitch him on the inside, but he could hit it over the right-field fence, he could hit it over the left-field fence, or the center-field fence. So I pitched to him on the outside low, where he'd have to pick it up to hit it over the fence. Turkey Stearnes was one of the greatest hitters we ever had. He was as good as Josh. He was as good as anybody ever played ball.

Stearnes recalled his own hitting:

The longest ball I hit was—let's see, it was in St. Louis or here in Mack Park, Detroit, one. I hit a ball out here over that fence about 470 feet. But I hit one in St. Louis they called a foul ball. That was about 500 feet, that ball was. That was in the St. Louis Stars' park on Compton Avenue. There was a house set up there about 400-some feet, with the fence behind the house. That old park they had down there, they had a car barn taking up part of the ground in left field. Center field was about 550 feet, right field about 400. That ball went about 10 feet over the fence. I hit it off Ted Trent, and that was one of the finest pitchers you had in the league at that time too. We had two men on base, Trent threw a curve ball about knee-high, and I picked it up. The wind was blowing that day, and that ball curved about 30 feet. The umpire said the last time he saw it, it was in foul territory. They beat us, 1–0, that game.

I hit another ball one night playing an exhibition game in North Dakota somewhere. We were barnstorming, playing white clubs up there. There was a house sat behind the fence about 450 feet in center field. I hit it about 30-40 feet on the other side of the house. I hit that ball so far the people talked about that ball all night; they said they'd never seen anyone hit it that far before. But I never counted it, 'cause we were way ahead anyway, and it didn't win a ball game. If it wins a ball game, I'll put it down maybe, but other than that I didn't worry about the home runs I hit, they didn't mean anything. I knew the job I had to do, and I just kept trying to do that.

Yet Stearnes was not a big man.

I never did weigh over 168 pounds. Well, I have reached up to 175 my last few years in baseball. But people couldn't understand how I hit the ball so hard and far. Like this boy Yastrzemski playing for Boston. He's the type player I was. There are larger fellows on the club than he is, but they can't hit it farther. I was strong in my shoulders; that was the difference.

Only one man in Detroit history—Hank Greenberg—could equal Stearnes' mammoth blasts. When Greenberg asked Cool Papa Bell if the stories he had heard about Turkey were true, Bell assured him that they were.

At least two men picked Stearnes as their all-time Negro league center fielder, even ahead of Cool Papa Bell—Double Duty Radcliffe and Ray Sheppard.

"Everybody knows that Cool Papa Bell was the fastest man," said Radcliffe. "He was one of my favorite ball players. But Cool Papa Bell couldn't field with Turkey Stearnes. He was faster, but Turkey Stearnes was one of the best fly ball men."

Sheppard played third base on the Detroit Stars when Turkey was their biggest star. "I'm not trying to knock guys like Cool Papa Bell, but Stearnes was better. My God, he was great! If the big-league doors would have been open, Turkey Stearnes would have been a star."

When I interviewed Stearnes on the front porch of his home in Detroit in 1968, with his three grandchildren crawling on his lap, competing for attention, he was still as lean and hollow-cheeked as he had been almost a half a century before. (Incidentally, Stearnes spelled his name with two "e's," although newspapers when he was playing spelled it "Stearns.")

Turkey got his nickname because he flapped his elbows when he ran, his daughter said. But Stearnes himself said it came from a pot belly he had as a kid in Nashville, where he was born in 1901, one of five children. "I was around 15 or 16 years old when my father died." Stearnes recalled that his mother was making only seven dollars a week as a cook.

So I had to go to work to help. I just did any job that popped up, taking care of hogs and cows and anything like that. I worked at a grocery store, driving a wagon, delivering groceries. I worked at the Baptist Publishing Board, a janitor mostly, running errands.

Turkey played sandlot baseball on Saturdays and Sundays while trying to finish high school. Nat Rogers said Stearnes had been a natural right-handed hitter, "until he burned his arm when he was young, and he turned around to hit from the left side." He remembered his early baseball days:

> I hit against Cannonball Dick Redding when I was in high school, and he could throw about as hard as anybody I guess I ever saw play, until Satchel Paige come in.
> I went down to Montgomery, Alabama, to play with the Montgomery Gray Sox in 1921. John Staples had the team. I played down there all summer with them, then came back home for school. The Cuban Stars and all of the big colored teams used to come through that way. We used to play them. Redding was with the Bacharach Giants. Well, the Bacharachs had the two best pitchers up here at that time, Redding and Harold Treadwell. Treadwell was one of the finest pitchers ever was in baseball. He threw everything—underhand, side arm too. A good curve ball, good fast ball, and he had good control. Could hit too. Oh, I hit Redding—I wore them both out. And I mean they were darn good pitchers. The Bacharachs also had the greatest third baseman ever was in colored baseball— Oliver Marcelle. And one of the greatest shortstops, Dick Lundy.

The Gray Sox starred pitcher Steel Arm Dickey; the three Cunninghams, who played first base, second base, and shortstop; and Turkey, who led off because of his speed. They played in the Southern Negro League, one step below Rube Foster's Negro National, which at that time was the only major black league in the country. The Sox got into the play-offs against Nashville, and in the opening game, Turkey knocked in the tying run with a single in the ninth, then scored the winner, as Montgomery took the pennant in four straight.

> In 1922 I played in Memphis, Tennessee. All those clubs down there were affiliated with the league up here. They had eight teams, and they'd more or less barnstorm with the clubs down South, like they have exhibition games now. We'd draw 10-15,000. Memphis was a good baseball town, but Birmingham was the best in the South.
> The big league colored teams had scouts, that's how the Detroit Stars picked me up. Bruce Petway of the Stars was one of the finest catchers we had in colored baseball. He was sent down there to watch me, they had heard so much talk about me. I was pitching and playing first base. But they changed me to the outfield after I got up here, 'cause I was hitting too good. He begged me to come up here in '22, but I couldn't make it in '22. I was trying to finish high school. That was my last year. I at least wanted to finish high school, because I knew I couldn't go to college.
> I came north in 1923, March 1. I came here to Detroit. I worked at the Briggs Manufacturing Company, the same man that owned the Tigers. All our gang. He gave us a job out there and we'd play semipro. We were painting the bodies of the cars. I was putting them on the drier myself. The white boys were painting. I'd put them on the drier for them.
> In '23 I was playing professional ball with the Detroit Stars out on Mack Avenue. Tenny Blount was the owner at that time. He was the policy king. That was the biggest thing doing around here in Detroit among the colored. But he was

one of the squarest men; I never worked for anyone better. If you worked, you got paid. Nothing but the best.

The Stars had Petway, Frank Warfield, Orville Riggins, and a lot of old fellows going out of baseball at that time—Joe Hewitt, all that gang. And they had Pete Hill, he was about one of the finest hitters in colored baseball at that time.

Saturday, Sunday, Monday, Tuesday we'd play league games against Chicago, Kansas City, and them. Wednesday and Thursday we'd play exhibition games with the white kids. We used to work Canada, all those places, the little leagues they got over there. Sometimes we'd go 300 miles. Everybody thought they could beat us, until they found out.

First baseman George Giles recalled Stearnes as a dead pull hitter: "Used to hit them over the bag down that line. Half the time I'd catch it outside the line." "Mack Park had a tall fence in right field with a screen wire up there," Turkey said. "You got to hit a tall fly ball. In center field it was a long way."

Turkey hit .353 his rookie year and hit 16 home runs to tie for the league lead with teammate Ed Wesley. (Stearnes' estimate of 50 probably included semipro games.) He played in 57 league games, so his total is equivalent to about 52 homers in a present-day schedule. He also topped the league in triples, and his slugging average, .737, was the highest of his life. SABR's Dick Clark reported that Turkey even pitched a game and lost it. Thanks in large part to their sensational rookie, the Stars moved up a notch in the standings to finish second behind the Monarchs.

Turkey was "a peculiar guy," Sheppard said. "He was a loner. He didn't run with anybody or fool around or drink. You couldn't use his bat or glove. Some time he didn't want a locker near you."

"Turkey would never let anyone use his bat," Judy Johnson agreed. In batting practice, after he had hit, he'd carry it half-way to the outfield where he would shag flies. "Nobody used his bat. He was very particular about it." He even talked to it. "If he made out, he'd sit there holding it and talking." "They say I can't hit," he'd mumble. "Why can't I hit?" Or, "I hit that good, but he caught it. Next time I'll get one." Laughed Judy: "I believe sometimes he carried that bat to bed with him."

Several players commented on Turkey's habit of talking to himself in center field. But he didn't say much to his teammates. Turkey was "very, very nice," said Paul "Country Jake" Stephens, who played with him later in Philadelphia. "And very quiet. About all he would say were 'yes' and 'no'—he was a fellow never popped off."

"Turkey wasn't a good mixer," agreed second baseman Dick Seay. "After he left the ball field, that was it. You have to get out and meet the public. He wasn't that type."

But Stearnes avoided getting into the troubles that ball players traditionally get into. "You've got to take care of yourself good," he would tell Detroit *Free Press* writer Joe Falls. "Be careful what you eat, what you drink, where you go, and what you do when you go to those places."

Stearnes faced white big leaguers for the first time in the fall of 1923, when the fifth-place St. Louis Browns came to Detroit to play the Stars. The first Brownie Stearnes faced was Dauntless Dave Danforth (16-14). "Danforth used to squeeze the ball, make the cover loose," Stearnes recalled. "He had an argument with the umpire about it." Turkey struck out three times but doubled in two runs, as the Stars beat Danforth, 7–6.

He got two singles in four at bats against Elam Vangilder (16-17), as the blacks won again, also by the score of 7-6.

Finally, Ray Kolp (5–12) beat them, 11–8. "Ray Kolp told us he was going to beat us," Stearnes chuckled, "said he was going to hit his run in. And that's what he did, hit a home run." Turkey got a double and two singles in three at bats to finish the series with a .500 average (6-for-12).

Detroit Stars vs. St. Louis Browns,
Detroit, Oct. 10, 1923

Browns		H	R	Stars		H	R
SS	Gerber	1	1	LF	Watson	4	1
2B	Wambsganss	2	2	SS	Riggins	0	0
3B	Robertson	4	2	CF	Stearnes	3	2
LF	Williams	1	1	1B	Charleston	2	2
C	Severeid	2	0	3B	Beckwith	2	2
CF	Jacobson	2	1	2B	Pryor	1	0
1B	Schleiber	2	1	RF	Smith	1	1
2B	Whaley	0	1	C	Petway	1	0
P	Kolp	3	2	P	Combs	0	0
		17	11	P	Force	0	0
				P	Cooper	0	0
				PH	Wesley	0	0
						14	8

Browns   001 050 005— 11 17 0
Stars   101 400 030— 8 14 2

2B: Stearnes, Beckwith, Kolp, Robertson, Williams, Severeid, Schleiber
3B: Smith, Beckwith
HR: Charleson, Robertson, Jacobson, Kolp
SB: Schleiber
SO: Combs 1, Cooper 1, Kolp 4
W: Combs 1, Force 1
DP: St. Louis (2)

Black players didn't make a great deal of money, of course, and Stearnes was keenly aware that his salary depended on box-office receipts. John Glover, later a writer with the Detroit black *Chronicle*, recalled trying to sneak into the park as a kid. "Stearnes called time and stopped the game and personally put us kids out of the park through the same hole in the fence that he saw us sneak in."

We worked in the paint shop in the winter and played ball in the summer. All that gang, about 19 of us, with the secretary and manager and all, about 22 or 23 of us. We went to New Orleans in '24, round about March, to go to spring training. The day after we left, the Briggs plant blew up. That shows how lucky we were. As soon as we hit the street in New Orleans it was in the paper.

Stearnes continued hitting in 1924, with a .346 average and ten home runs, which were enough to lead the league again that season. Across town Ty Cobb hit .338, as the Tigers finished third.

I never played against Ty Cobb. They passed a rule that teams in the same town can't play one another. I never cared for that rule. A game's a game to me, and a man's a man to me. Cobb couldn't do enough to me to fight him, I don't care how rough you come into base.

The next summer, 1925, he raised his batting average to .364 and his home runs to 18 in 84 games (equal to about 35 in 162 games). Again he tied Wesley for the league lead. Turkey was also tops in triples, with ten, and second to Cool Papa Bell in doubles, with 20.

I used to talk to Babe Ruth, Lou Gehrig, Tony Lazzeri, Jumping Joe Dugan a lot of times. All that bunch used to be around the hotel. Babe Ruth was just like Satchel. He liked the game, he was interested in the game, quiet fellow, wouldn't brag about nothing. No, I don't think I hit more than Babe Ruth. I ain't going to lie to you like a lot of people.
We used to play them quite often. We beat the Yankees as often as they beat us. People didn't think that we had the team that we did have. Then they found out we were as good as the big leagues. It didn't make any difference to me who I was hitting against. I'd do the same against the Yankees as against anybody else. A ball game is a ball game to me, regardless of who pitches. We used to play the big leaguers often around '24, '25, until the white clubs got to fighting among themselves. Judge Landis, the commissioner, came in and told them to break it off, wouldn't let them barnstorm any more. After that they had to call themselves all stars. Oh, we made good money too, playing them. I was sorry the thing ended like it did.

Unfortunately, no confirming box scores have been found of any games, except for the Browns.

In 1926 Turkey increased his average to .375 and his homers to 20. For the first time he failed to lead the league, as Mule Suttles slugged 26. But Stearnes did lead in doubles, 24, and stolen bases, 13, the best total of his life. (These totals can be doubled for a modern 162-game schedule.)

People began saying Stearnes was even better than Oscar Charleston.

Never did take that seriously. I watched them all, but the greatest man I watched was Charleston. He was playful, a big fella like Babe Ruth. Oh yeah, Charleston and I were great friends. We'd talk about batting. We turned out to be great friends.

In the Negro league, the beanball was a common weapon.

I had pitchers I knew were throwing right at me. I knew they deliberately threw at me—I knew that. But I didn't say anything. If he threw the ball where I could hit it, I tried to hit it as well as I could as far as I could.

But most pitchers didn't throw at me, 'cause they knew it wouldn't do no good. It didn't make no difference, I didn't think about it. I just figured the pitcher was trying to get up his own nerve.

Turkey Stearnes (third from left) with friends including Newt Allen (far left) and Joe Rogan (far right).

Chet Brewer used to throw close to me. We got together on it afterwards though. He was my personal friend. I used to talk to him about it. I used to tell him, "When you throw at me, you make it harder for you." He wasn't scaring me a bit. I let him know it. I said, "You think by throwing at me, when you throw the ball across the plate, I'll be looking at it, I won't be swinging." But I said, "I get up there to hit. If the ball comes across, I'm gonna hit that ball. You don't scare me." He just laughed. We're good friends now. He's a nice kid, he didn't mean no harm by it. He's the only pitcher I don't know whether I ever hit a home run off or not. He had more nerve than the average youngster who came into the league. He wasn't scared, you didn't frighten him. He acted just like he'd been here all the time.

Big Bill Foster, one of the game's premier black left-handers, said Stearnes murdered right-handed pitching but couldn't hit lefties. Stephens and Bell disagreed. "He hit left-handers as good as he hit right-handers," Stephens insisted. "They didn't take him out for any left-handed pitcher," Bell declared.

Turkey himself maintained, "It didn't make any difference to me, left-hander or right-hander, I hit them both."

One right-hander, Willie Powell of Chicago said that he, "just loved to see him [Stearnes] come to bat, because I could handle him like nothing. I could strike him out practically any time. He was my strikeout bait. Fastballs right close to him, he'd go for them, that was just a big out. And he could not hit a curve ball up at his shoulder. But you'd have to pitch high to him. Don't throw him nothing down here by his shoe top. Throw it low, he would kill you." Once, Powell recalled, he struck Turkey out three times, then Stearnes hit a home run off him. When they became roommates on the American Giants later, Turkey would keep Willie awake, laughing and talking about it.

Right-hander Bill Holland was another top pitcher in the league back in those days.

Holland's arm got sore trying to strike me out. Wasn't anybody who threw fast could get me out. I don't see how I could miss it. A fast ball wasn't any more to me than hitting that post there.

"Turkey's weakness was so obvious," second baseman Sammy T. Hughes said: "Slow pitch. He used to hit that fast ball good. And he always looked for it. Every home run he hit was always a 'curve ball'— so he said. But it very seldom was a curve ball, because he was weak on curve balls. Every time he would come in you'd say, 'What kind of pitch was that, Turkey?' He'd say, 'Oh, that was a curve ball.'"

While the players debated how to get him out, Turkey just kept hitting. In 1927 he upped his home runs to 21, tops in the league, while hitting .339.

Turkey said he hit against Lefty Grove on the Coast about 1928, although, again, no box score has been found of the game.

No, I never hit a home run off Lefty Grove. I got hits off him, but I never got a home run. In fact, we didn't get many runs off him nohow. He beat us one Sunday, beat Satchel Paige, 1–0, and Satchel beat them the next Sunday, 1–0.

Lefty Grove and Satchel Paige are about the two hardest pitchers ever put on a glove. I've hit at a lot of people, I've hit at George Earnshaw, Red Ruffing, a lot of them, but I don't think anyone threw as hard as those two boys. I'd sit and watch them when I wasn't playing and they were in town. Grove could throw hard like that all day long.

Those two boys, they could throw hard. Satchel could throw a ball right through there. He had good control. Grove was so wild he was sent back to the minors for seven years.

Stearnes maintained that he once took a sore-armed Cool Papa Bell along to the Coast and let him play center field after the team was seven or eight runs ahead. Turkey said that winter he taught the right-handed Bell how to switch-hit.

In 1928 Turkey's average fell to .316, but he raised his home runs to 24, his all-time high, and won his fifth home run crown in six years.

The next year he sacrificed some power (16 homers in 63 games) but raised his average to .381.

In 1930 the depression struck, and Turkey went east, to the New York Lincoln Giants, in search of more money. He played 20 games there, hitting .341 with three home runs, before returning to Detroit, where he added four home runs and batted .353. For the year, he batted a combined .340.

The Stars were glad to see him back. He helped lift them from fifth in the first half to the title in the second half. That meant they would meet the St. Louis Stars—Bell, Suttles, and Willie Wells—in the play-offs. It was a fan's dream, a matchup between the two top power hitters of black baseball—Turkey Stearnes and Mule Suttles.

Turkey won it, bats down. Here is how the games went, according to SABR historian Dick Clark:

In game one, a night game in St. Louis, Mule got a single in two trips, but Turkey smashed three hits in four at bats. In the first inning his two-run home run off his nephew-in-law, Radcliffe, gave Detroit a quick lead. However, Cool Papa Bell's lead-off home run, plus an error and two infield balls quickly tied it, 2–2. Then St. Louis' ace, Ted Trent, came in and won the game, 5–4.

Double Duty was a good ball player. Catch and pitch. He used to think he could strike me out. Broke his arm trying it. He was about the only pitcher I batted against that couldn't strike me out. I guess I was prepared for him all the time.

Certain pitchers, you know, they brag, they run their mouth, you pay more attention to them.

In game two Mule got two hits in six tries; Turkey cracked five hits, including a home run and double; he even stole a base. He got Detroit off to another quick lead with an RBI single in the first. Two innings later he knocked in another run and scored a third, to put Detroit ahead, 5–0. He added a solo home run in the eighth, as Detroit won, 11–7, to tie the series up.

In the third game, another nighter in St. Louis, Stearnes faced Trent again. Suttles slugged a home run in two official at bats. Turkey got only one double in four at bats, as Trent won it, 7–2, to take the lead again.

Neither Mule nor Turkey apparently played in game four, won by Detroit to tie the series once more.

The clubs entrained for Detroit and after a three-day layoff opened game five in huge Hamtramck Stadium, where the right field foul line was 45 feet from home. "You couldn't hit it out of right field hardly," Turkey moaned. In fact, no man ever had. Suttles drilled one over the left-field fence in four at bats that day. Turkey led off the second inning with a double off Trent and scored the game's first run. In the fifth he hit another double to drive in two runs, giving Detroit a 5–3 lead and knocking Trent out of the box. Detroit scored two runs in the eighth off reliever Radcliffe to win it, 7–5. For the first time, Detroit moved into the lead, three games to two.

Game six. We have no report on how Suttles did. But Stearnes accounted for all Detroit's three runs. In the fourth he blasted a solo home run over the right-field wall, the first man ever to do it. "He hit it to right-center," Radcliffe said, "and it cleared the fence with room to spare." That drove in two runs and tied the score at 3–3, though St. Louis went on to win, 4–3.

So it all came down to the seventh game. St. Louis finally stopped Turkey—no hits in five at bats, as St. Louis won the game and pennant.

Suttles had batted .357 in four games for which we have data. His teammate, Willie Wells, hit .438. But Turkey topped them all with a .481 average, including three home runs. RBIs were not tabulated in the newspaper box scores, but Clark said Turkey knocked in at least 11 in the seven games.

In 1931, Stearnes said, the Detroit park burned down, so he went to Kansas City to play. Dick Clark has found 40 box scores of games Turkey played. He hit .350, with eight home runs, best in the league.

The next year, 1932, Stearnes was with the Chicago American

Giants, where he clashed with manager Dave Malarcher. "He'd been a slugger, hit a lot of home runs," Malarcher said. "And he was fast. I knew that." "Now that you're here," he told Turkey, "we're going to diversify your play. You have to fit into our plays. If a guy at the wrong time just happens to hit a ball to the infield, it's a double play." To use Stearnes' speed, Dave put the bunt sign on in certain situations.

One day Chicago had men on first and second and needed two runs to win. "Turkey comes to bat, and he loves the crowd," Malarcher said. "The crowd's cheering—clap, clap, clap. This is Stearnes, the great slugger, you know."

"Now, Turkey," Dave said, "I want you to lay this right down the third baseline. I want the third baseman to field it, not the pitcher, because then he can't get the man out at third."

"OK, Cap," Stearnes said. He squared to bunt, but let the pitch go by. Malarcher flashed the signal again. Again Stearnes let it go by. Stearnes just knew he'd get the hit sign now, Malarcher said. "He had confidence he could knock it out of the stadium." Turkey looked into the dugout. But instead of the hit sign, Malarcher was waving him out of the game.

"That broke his pride," Dave said. A pinch-hitter did lay the bunt down, and the next man singled the tying run home.

"I didn't say a word to Turkey," Malarcher said.

After a while, Turkey spoke. "Cap, I really was going to lay that next one down."

"I knew you were, Turk," Malarcher answered. And, he said, "I never had to tell him again. He developed into a really diversified player after that. Turkey could bunt, and he could pull them down to first base—and fly. And when his time came to hit, he could really plaster them."

"I thought he never got the recognition he deserved," agreed Jimmy Crutchfield, who played next to Turkey in the Chicago outfield. "Plenty of power, good base runner, good throwing arm, hard to pitch to."

Turkey's home run output dropped to five in 1932, but it was still good enough to lead the league for the seventh time. His average also fell to .299, but he stole 13 bases in 43 games.

The American Giants won the first-half pennant and met the Nashville (later Baltimore) Elite Giants in the play-off. Nashville took the lead two games to one. In game four, Turkey slammed two home runs to help win it, 10–5, and tie the series up. The clubs split the next two games and went into the seventh game with Foster on the mound. Turkey clubbed four hits, including a triple, to win it for Bill, 2–0.

In 1933 Mule Suttles joined the team, bringing together for the first time these two great sluggers. With his speed, Stearnes batted

260

lead-off. "He'd lead off with a home run!" Buck Leonard marveled, "so you knew it was a home run hitting team."

"If Stearnes didn't get a hit his first time up," Rogers said, "you might get him out the rest of the day. But don't let him hit that first one! If he did, he was going to be tough on you all day long."

Leonard said, "I've seen Stearnes hit them out of Chicago through the wind—the wind blows steady in Chicago, especially over to the old American Giants park, but he could hit them through the wind and over the fence." Buck is another who puts Stearnes on his all-time Negro league outfield.

Radcliffe recalled that "I've seen Stearnes hit one in Comiskey Park, hit the facing of the roof in the upper deck. That blow was about 450 feet, and it was still going when it hit."

Only five home runs have been found so far for Turkey in 24 league games in 1933, though that's equal to about 30-plus in 162 games. He batted .323 and led the vote of the fans for the outfield for the first East-West, or All-Star, game.

The Giants won the first-half pennant, one game ahead of Josh Gibson's Pittsburgh Crawfords. The second half was never completed, but the Giants played New Orleans of the Southern League in what was billed as a world series. Turkey hit two home runs, as Chicago won, 6–0. Suttles hit a grand slam in game two to power a 6–1 win.

Turkey went back to California that winter and hit .331. But he hit .385 (15 for 39) against Buck Newsom (30 wins in the Pacific Coast League). Sloppy Thurston (6–8 with Brooklyn), Larry French (18–13 with Pittsburgh), and "Weaver," who may have been either Jim of the Pirates or Monte of the Senators.

We used to beat Buck Newsom all the time in California. He couldn't beat us a game. In fact, wasn't but one big-league pitcher we didn't beat. He didn't pitch often, but we didn't beat him. That was Earl Whitehill. He had plenty of guts, nerve, control. And he could talk too. He'd talk about what he was gonna do to you. He was one of the finest ball players we ever met.

In one game Stearnes homered against Thurston, then made a great catch, as Thurston beat Satchel Paige, 4–1. In the next meeting between the two pitchers, Stearnes got three hits in three at bats, and Paige won, 7–1.

Young Jim Canada, who would later discover Willie Mays, recalled seeing Stearnes in Florida with his odd foot-in-the-bucket stance. "Hit the ball nine miles," Canada whistled. "He was a show, people would go to see him play. He put on a lot of shows out there in the outfield too. Hard chances, he'd make them look easy, and easy chances, he made them look hard."

In 1934 Turkey hit .332 and again won the fans vote for center field on the East-West team. Cum Posey, owner of the Homestead Grays, picked him on his authoritative black all-star team. Stearnes also led the American Giants into the play-offs. In the first game, against Philadelphia's ace lefty, Slim Jones (11–0), Turkey slugged a triple and single to hand Slim his only loss of the season. We have no other box scores, though the Phils won it in seven games.

That year Stearnes and the other American Giants also journeyed to Denver to play in the Denver *Post* semipro tourney, where their main opposition was Satchel Paige's House of David team. Satch was 9–1 in the Negro league that year, and he led his club to victory in Denver, though Turkey hit .444 and was voted the tournament MVP.

The next year, 1935, Stearnes hit a rousing .430 to win his first Negro league batting crown. Again he won the fans' vote to start the East-West game, though the Giants finished deep in the standings.

Turkey Stearnes as an older man standing at bat in Detroit Stadium. Detroit Free Press *photo by John Collier.*

That winter in Los Angeles, Chet Brewer said, Bill "Bojangles" Robinson, the tap dancer, "was winning so much money betting. Those fellows never heard of Negro players. Bojangles just got rich off those boys here, betting on us. They just didn't see how we could beat those big-league players." To increase his odds, Bojangles offered the blacks money for every home run. In one game, Stearnes hit four, "and the fifth one hit the top of the fence." (It was a short fence, Brewer conceded.) Turkey knocked in nine runs that day. "Those guys hit so many home runs, Bojangles cut it down to one dollar and finally knocked it off."

Stearnes jumped to Philadelphia in 1936, where he teamed with Jud "Boojum" Wilson, one of the great hitters of blackball history. But Philadelphia manager Webster McDonald was not happy with the new center fielder. "Ornery!" Mac said—"he was just ornery! I mean *nasty!* Stearnes was always crazy. A good ball player, but he had a one-track mind. A good hitter, but he only thought one way. He wasn't a team man. You couldn't put him with a group of people and let him get along. You can't have your way all the time."

Wilson was also hard to handle, but he and Stearnes got along fine. Turkey remembered:

> *They said he was a mean guy, the same thing they said about Charleston and Beckwith. But I played on the club with him a whole season, I didn't have any trouble with him. I don't think anybody did. One thing about him, he liked to win. That's where a lot of people take the fellow wrong. When a fellow watches you close, and sees the things you're doing wrong and tells you about them, that should be encouragement to you. I'd take advice from anybody. If you thought enough of me to tell me my faults, I'd think just twice as much of you for telling me. I appreciate you watching me that close. I'd tell myself, "I've got to straighten up, I've got to do better." Like young players now, they don't want nobody to tell them anything, they want all the praise. But life doesn't run like that.*

Stearnes is credited with a .350 average. Turkey would probably have hit much higher, but his wife was in the hospital all summer, and his performance fell off in July and August. Philadelphia finished second in the first half but dropped to sixth in the second half, and McDonald let Turkey go.

In 1937 Turkey hooked on with Detroit in the new Negro American, or western, League, then switched to Chicago in time for a thrilling play-off against the Monarchs to decide the first-half title. Stearnes' first inning double drove in two runs, which proved to be Chicago's only runs of the game, against KC's Andy Cooper. In the fifth Turkey made a long throw from center to cut off a run, as the two clubs battled to a 17-inning, 2–2, tie. Kansas City went on to win the title by half a game.

Once again Turkey was voted the starting center fielder for the East-West game. Chicago won the second half though, and the Giants met the Monarchs again in the season play-off, won by Kansas City, four games to three.

The Monarchs and Giants formed a united team to face the Homestead Grays in a special postseason series. Turkey chipped in with two singles, a double, and a homer.

He stayed with Chicago in '38, then moved to Kansas City in 1939, where he finished out his career in 1941.

I enjoyed playing, and when I quit, I went to work. I worked from 1938 to '64, that's 27 years—and I mean there was 27 years put in there too. I was making six dollars a day in 1938, in the rolling mills in Detroit. We were lifting everything, carrying everything. Now they've got these hoists, you can work as fast as you want to or as slow as you want to.

When Stearnes finally earned his retirement, he could be found most afternoons or evenings in the bleachers at Tiger Stadium, arguing baseball with "the boys" and "having a lot of fun."

That's one thing wrong with baseball today: The little fella's trying to keep up with the big one, and he can't do it. If a little man hits a home run, the pitcher ain't got nothing on the ball. If you're not built to produce, you won't do it. They can learn to field, but they can't learn to hit. It's got to be born in you, see, and then everything will come easy.

Baseball's getting greedy for money now. The teams are too weak now. Haven't got the players. They didn't have enough players for eight big league teams, how they going to support 12? Now there are too many players playing big league ball when they're just minor league players. The way they're playing ball now, they couldn't play 15 years ago. Hitting .200, .205! You couldn't play then if you didn't hit .270.

Now they don't have to hit 500 feet to get a home run, they can hit it about 300 feet. That's to show you the difference in baseball now and how it was then. Those old fellows would hit 70 home runs now, with the ball as lively as it is.

Now you won't find three fellows on a team hit 20 home runs a season. You just count 'em. Everybody hitting ten, 12, 14. Why? The ball is lighter, the fences are closer. They used to hit 45–50 home runs. Greenberg hit 58. They used to hit them on Cherry St. here, not into the stands. They used to hit them on Brooklyn St.—that's about a block from the park. Babe Ruth hit them over the Checker Cab. That was Navin Field at the time.

That's the main thing in baseball, hitting.

Turkey was popular with the police too.

I got along with all of them. All of them thought the world of me. I've never been jailed since I been in town, never stole anything, never bothered anybody.

In 1971 the baseball Hall of Fame inducted Satchel Paige, the first of the old Negro leaguers to be admitted, to be followed by eight more through 1977. But Turkey wasn't one of them.

On July 4, 1979, Stearnes, still gaunt and lean, was invited, along with other Negro league greats, to Greenup, Kentucky, to a reunion of black old-timers, a reunion telecast on the NBC News that evening. Instead of sitting on the dais with the other players, he took a seat in the audience with his wife and daughter, absent-mindedly forgetting to remove his hat. His hearing had gone bad, but he wouldn't wear a hearing aid. "Mr. Stearnes isn't sick," chuckled his wife, Nettie, "he's just an old man."

Within two months Turkey was rushed to the hospital with a perforated ulcer, and on September 4 he passed away, still waiting for the phone call from Cooperstown that never came.

Turkey Stearnes vs. White Major Leaguers

Year	AB	H	2B	3B	HR	Pitcher	(W-L)
1923	(4)*	1	1	0	0	Danforth	
	(4)	2	0	0	0	Vangilder	
	(4)	3	1	0	0	Kolp	
1931	3	0	0	0	0	Meine	
1933	2	1	0	0	0	Thurston	(6-8)
	3	0	0	0	0	Thurston	
	3	1	0	0	1	Thurston	
	2	0	0	0	0	Walters	(0-0)
	3	1	0	0	0	French	
	4	0	0	0	0	Weaver	
1934	4	1	0	0	0	Stine	(0-0)
	(4)	2	1	0	1	Stine	
	4	2	0	0	2	Stine, (McDonald)[a]	
	4	1	0	0	0	French	(12-18)
Total 14 games	48	15	3	0	4	Average: .313	

* At bats in parentheses are estimated.

[a] Not a major league pitcher.

Turkey Stearnes

Year	Team	G	AB	H	2B	3B	HR	BA	SA	SB
1923	Detroit	57	232	82	15	13	16*	.353	.737	1
1924	Detroit	58	231	80	7	11	10*	.346	.602	3
	Cuba	—	16	5	—	—	—	.313	—	—
1925	Detroit	84	324	118	20*	10	18*	.364	.654	11
1926	Detroit	82	301	113	24*	10	20	.375	.721	13
1927	Detroit	86	313	106	23	12	21*	.339	.690	11
1928	Detroit	79	310	98	18	7	24*	.316	.652	5
1929	Detroit	63	239	91	14	5	16	.381	.682	10
1930	Detroit-NY	56	215	73	15	12	7	.340	.619	7
1931	Detroit-KC	38	131	47	9	3	8*	.359	.656	5
1932	Chicago	43	137	41	10	4	5*	.299	.540	13
1933	California	39	121	40	—	—	5	.331	—	14
	Chicago	24	96	31	9	2	5	.323	.615	1
1934	Chicago	24	102	34	3	5	6	.332	.637	2
1935	Chicago	33	114	49	6	2	5	.430*	.650	1
1936	Philadelphia	23	93b	32	1	0	3	.350	.452	0
Totals			2866	1010	167	93	160	.352	.643	97

Post-Season

Year	Team	G	AB	H	2B	3B	HR	BA	SA	SB
1930	Play-Offs	6	27	13	4	1	2	.482	.926	0
1933	Play-Offs	—	—	—	—	—	2	—	—	—
1934	Play-Offs	1a	4	2	0	1	0	.500	1.000	1
1937	World Series	2	7	3	1	0	0	.429	.571	0
Totals		9	38	18	5	2	4	.474	.870	1
East-West		4	16	3	1	0	0	.188	.250	0

*Led league.
a Incomplete.
b Estimated.

19

Mule Suttles:
"Kick, Mule"

Hardest hitter? Mule Suttles. Yes, harder than Josh Gibson. In my opinion Mule could hit the ball just as far as anybody—Josh or John Beckwith or Babe Ruth or anybody. He hit a home run one night in Buffalo, hit the house across the street and came back in the ball park. We got the ball and held him to two bases. The ball went out of the park and hit the house so quickly and came back into the park that the umpire said he had to stop at second. The umpire thought it hit the fence, wouldn't let him have a home run.

Walter "Buck" Leonard

Nobody—nobody—hit them farther than the Mule, old-timers say. Josh Gibson hit them more often, they concede, but when Mule Suttles connected, he hit them for miles.

A huge man, about 6'6" and weighing 230 pounds, Suttles stood right-handed in the batter's box, waving a wagon tongue for a bat—the St. Louis *Post-Dispatch* said it weighed over 50 ounces. When the Mule swung it, said Dick Seay, "you could feel the earth quake."

Mule was "the Jimmy Foxx of Negro baseball," Judy Johnson said.

"Josh Gibson hit his homers on a line, Suttles' blows were high and far," said ex-Monarch infielder Othello Renfroe. Renfroe compared the Mule to Harmon Killebrew; former outfielder Ted Page called him stronger than Will Stargell. "He hit them like Ruth," said former Braves outfielder Wally Berger—"towering smashes."

In 1929 Suttles faced Earl Whitehill, George Uhle, Willis Hudlin, and Jake Miller—all 14-game winners or better in the American League—and slugged them for a home run, three triples, and a single in four games for a .389 average. Mule's club won three of the four.

Four years later he clipped Big Jim Weaver for a single, double, and triple in four at bats. The last time he came up, third baseman Dave Malarcher chuckled, Weaver called shortstop Leo Durocher to the mound to ask how to pitch to him. "Don't ask me," Leo grinned, "just pitch and pray."

Altogether, Mule slugged 11 homers in 79 at bats against white big leaguers—that's one every 7.2 at bats. (Babe Ruth averaged one

every 13.7, Hank Aaron one every 16.3.) Mule's batting average
against whites was .392.

In the black leagues, Mule's 150 home runs rank second behind
Turkey Stearnes '160, and ahead of Josh Gibson's 137.

When the Mule hit them, they were gargantuan. The longest
Suttles blow of all may have been struck in Havana's Tropical Park,
famed for its distant fences. Shortstop Willie Wells recalled:

> Suttles hit this ball—I'm telling you the truth, it's no kidding—he hit
> this damn ball so far it looked like we were playing in a lot, it didn't look
> like no ball park. Mule hit that ball into the wind. I bet he hit it 600 feet.
> Easy, easy. They used to have soldiers riding horses along the back of the
> fence to keep people off the fence, and he hit it over their heads. He
> really popped it.

An awestruck rookie, Lenny Pearson, years later visited Tropical
Park to see the plaque marking the spot where Suttle's blow cleared
the fence:

> It was like one that had never been hit before. I think Josh Gibson is
> the only person who ever hit one near it; I believe it was damn near 600
> feet, to tell you the truth. The wall is 500-some feet away there, and it's
> 60 feet high, and they say the ball was still going up when it went over the
> wall.

The plaque may still be there today.

Suttles murdered curve balls. "Hit one off me in St. Louis,"
Chicago pitcher Willie Powell winced. "Over the car barn, completely
over that barn. Curve ball away from him."

Another rookie, Chet Brewer of the Monarchs, said Suttles
"could hit anybody's curve ball but Joe Rogan's—nobody could hit that
successfully. And he could hit that ball just as far as Josh Gibson or
farther."

Mule hit his famous Havana home run against a hurler named
Lastrada. Brewer, who now directs a youth baseball program in Los
Angeles and has sent several players to the majors, was there that day.
"Now, Lastrada," Brewer said, "we play against Mule every summer,
so when he comes up, don't throw him any curve ball. Keep it letter-
high, in on him."

"Lastrada is white," Brewer added. "He's not going to listen to any
colored; figured we didn't know anything about baseball." Lastrada
looked at Chet disdainfully and pitched, and "Mule hit that ball 500-
some feet down left field."

"Lastrada, what did you throw him?" Brewer asked back in the dugout.

"Oh, man," the pitcher moaned, "I never seen a ball hit so far in my life!"

"We *know* that, Lastrada, we could *see* where it went. What did you *throw* him?"

But the pitcher just continued shaking his head and muttering. "I didn't believe any human being could hit a ball so far."

"To this day," Brewer winked, "he hasn't owned up that he threw that man a curve."

Harry Salmon remembered one home run Mule hit in Cuba against Sam Streeter—"out of the park, over a row of houses on the other side of the park, about 450 feet. Broke a car window."

A decade later Newark third baseman Ray Dandridge heard of another Suttles blast in Cienfuegos, Cuba. The locals pointed out just where the ball went—over the fence and into a hospital yard that looked to Ray twice as far from home as the fence was. A strong ocean wind was blowing out, Dandridge said. Still, he asked, "How in the world can a man hit a ball that far?"

Suttles and Wells—the big Mule and the little "Devil"—were sidekicks for 20 years, with St. Louis, Chicago, and Newark. "Mule was the best one-run hitter you want to see," Wells said.

> If the team had a seven- or eight-run lead, he was just another swinger, he didn't care too much about it. But any time you needed one run to win a game or tie a ball game, I don't care how late it was, he'd get it, and that ball would go out of the park. Every time we needed one run, I'd say, "Kick, Mule!" and man, he'd kick it out of there.

Mule—or more properly George—was born in Brockton, Louisiana, in 1901 and developed his muscles in the coal mines of Birmingham. Harry Salmon, a fellow miner who went on to become a good fast ball pitcher, recalled Mule and his older brother, Charles. "Charles was an all-round player," Salmon said. "Did everything but pitch. I couldn't say he hit as hard as Mule, but he was a more consistent hitter than Mule was. He was to go in the league with us, but the same year he got his leg broke in the mine."

Mule played for semipro mining teams before he and Salmon joined the Birmingham Black Barons in the Negro National League in 1923. Mule hit .273 and .317 his first two years, though he hit only three home runs in 148 games. Birmingham's Rickwood Field was one of the toughest home run parks in America.

The next year, 1925, Suttles had a great opening day against the St. Louis Stars with four hits, including a home run, and ended the year hitting .312 with 12 homers. He played first base, third base, outfield, and even pitched.

The Stars didn't forget. In 1926 they brought the big slugger to St. Louis to join Cool Papa Bell and Willie Wells. Bell said Mule held the bat so far at the end that he had two fingers off the bat, thus he couldn't check his swing. Stars manager Candy Jim Taylor told him to shorten his swing and concentrate on striding smoothly into the ball. The Mule rewarded him with a sensational season. The Stars' park at Compton and Laclede Streets had a trolley-car barn jutting into left field, making for a short foul line, but the fence slanted sharply back to about 500 feet in center. Suttles didn't pull the ball, Bell recalled, but even so, he hit 26 homers and batted .418, both tops in the league. He also led the league in triples, 19, and slugging average, .830— Babe Ruth's best was .847. Says SABR's Dick Clark: "The smartest thing Suttles ever did was to get out of that Birmingham park."

Suttles also played a pretty fair first base for a big man. "He wasn't graceful," said Double Duty Radcliffe, "but anything they threw, he could catch."

Mule even stole 11 bases. "Mule outrun me one day," Willie Powell said. "We had a race. And I thought I was pretty fast, which I was."

In 1927 Suttles missed more than half the season with a broken ankle. But he hit .463 for 24 games. His hits included seven homers,

Mule Suttles.

which helped him to a stunning slugging average of exactly 1.000, which means that he averaged one base every time he came to bat. (Some reports credit him with 69 homers that year, presumably against both Negro league and semipro teams. These have not been confirmed, but if the reports are true, they would have been the record for blacks until Josh Gibson's putative 72 in 1932.)

It may have been about this time that Mule smashed another of his home runs against Willie Powell. "Ducked a ball right in his face and got a home run off me," Powell, a double amputee, said in his bed in Three Rivers, Michigan. "Mule said that if he didn't hit the ball, it would have knocked his eyes out."

Suttles was a great low-ball hitter too. If he hit it on the ground, the infielders wouldn't even move—"they'd just spit at it," one old-timer smiled. "One day in St. Louis," Brewer said:

> I threw Mule my overhand drop, broke down around his ankles. He golfed it right by my face about six inches to the right of my face. Just kept on going up, up, up. He hit that ball over the top of that car barn and so high, when it hit the other side of the barn, the ball bounced back in the air. You could see it. Ooh, if that ball had been six inches over, it would have killed me. Just think how hard it was hit!

Brewer said the next time Suttles came up, the fans were drinking beer and yelling, "Kick, Mule, kick!" So "I decided to put the fear of God in him." Brewer shook off a curve sign—"no way for me to throw Mule a curve ball." Instead, he threw a fast ball, about three feet outside. The fans beat on the wooden stands—"they thought they had me all upset." The next pitch was also outside. "Now it was bedlam; those fans going crazy: 'Kick, Mule, kick!' Mule got out of the box, got moisture on his hands, got back in and dug in—and I hit Mule right side of the head." The ball bounced over the grandstand into Compton Avenue, while Suttles collapsed at the plate. One man picked the big hitter up by his shoulders, another by his legs, and they carried him off the field.

Said Brewer: "After that I just had to lean to third base, and back on his heels he went."

In 1928 Suttles fell to .254 with 12 home runs—that's about a 36-homer pace in a 154-game schedule.

The Stars won the first half of the split season and faced the defending champion Chicago American Giants in the play-offs. In the opening game, Mule crashed a double and triple against Chicago's ace, Lefty Bill Foster. Suttles came back in the seventh game finale with 2-for-3 against Foster to give the Stars the pennant.

It's fascinating to speculate how the Stars might have done against the St. Louis Cardinals, their white counterparts, who won the flag in the National League that year and then lost to the Yankees four straight in the World Series. Bell was obviously a better center fielder than the Cards' .295-hitting Taylor Douthit, and Wells was far superior to Rabbit Maranville, the Cards' 36-year-old shortstop, who hit .240. Suttles had more competition from the Cards' first baseman, Sunny Jim Bottomley (.325, 31 homers). Yet in the World Series the Yanks handcuffed both Douthit (.091) and Bottomley (.214). It would have been a thrill to see Suttles in the lineup, trading swings with Lou Gehrig (three homers) and Babe Ruth (three, all in one game).

In 1929 Mule snapped back with 20 homers—second to Wells' 27—a .355 average, and a league-leading 29 doubles in 82 games.

That October in Chicago Suttles got his first look at white big-league pitching, when he faced Charlie Gehringer's club of white all stars, including three future Hall of Famers: Gehringer, Heinie Manush, and Harry Heilmann. Gehringer, now the dean of the Hall of Fame veterans committee, remembers the games, although his memory is faulty on some details. They say Suttles "used the heaviest bat ever swung," Gehringer recalled. "Looking at it, I think it was true." Charlie said Suttles "hit some boomers" against left-hander Earl Whitehill, but he said George Uhle's right-handed curves tied Suttles up. Gehringer also remembered the whites splitting the four-games series. Memory can be a funny thing after more than half a century. Actually, here is how the series went:

Against Cleveland right-hander Willis Hudlin (17–15), Mule cracked out a single and two triples, as his club beat the whites, 12–11. (Wells knocked in the tying run with a triple and scored the winner on a steal of home.)

Left-hander Jake Miller (14–12 with the Indians) held Mule to a single in three at bats, though the blacks won again, 10–1. (Wells got two triples.)

In game three a week later the left-hander Whitehill (14–15 with Detroit), shut Mule out, as the whites won their first game, 1–0.

Finally, Suttles slammed Uhle's (15–11) curves for a triple and homer in three trips, as the blacks won the third game, 7–6. (Wells knocked in the winning run again.)

Will Suttles, Wells, or any additional black old-timers be elected to Cooperstown? Gehringer was asked. No, he replied, he doesn't think any more will be admitted by his committee.

Within a few days of Mule's heroics, the stock market crashed, and the depression had begun.

Mule went to Cuba that winter and hit .289. His home-run total is not recorded. Cuban parks, with their distant fences, were hard on a slugger like Mule. But he smashed some long drives, according to

Chicago American Giants vs. Major League All Stars
Chicago, October 1929

All Stars		AB	H	R	Chicago		AB	H	R
3B	Sweeney	6	4	2	CF	Bell	5	1	1
2B	Gehringer	4	0	1	RF-LF	Gardner	4	2	2
RF-LF	Manush	5	1	1	SS	Wells	5	3	1
1B	Shires	4	4	1	LF-RF	Davis	4	1	2
SS	Kress	5	0	0	1B	Suttles	4	3	2
RF	Heilmann	3	1	0	C	Brown	4	1	0
C	Schang	3	1	0	2B	Williams	4	1	0
CF-LF	Hudlin	5	0	0	3B	Miller	3	1	0
P	Uhle	4	1	1	3B	Jackson	0	0	1
LF	Miller	4	0	0	P	Radcliffe	2	1	0
		43	12	6	P	Harney	2	1	0
							37	15	7

All Stars   001 014 000—6 12
Chicago   200 101 111—7 15

2B: Sweeney, Schang, Radcliffe, Wells
3B: Suttles, Shires
HR: Gehringer, Suttles
SO: Uhle 6, Radcliffe 4, Harney 7
W: Uhle 1, Radcliffe 4

men who saw him. His famous 600-footer may have been struck that winter.

At the start of the 1930 season, Mule jumped to the Baltimore Black Sox. He was like Boog Powell of the 1970 Orioles, pitcher Laymon Yokely said. "He liked that ball away from him. He hit one off me, before I could straighten up, it went through my legs, through Dick Lundy at shortstop, through Pete Washington in center field, and rolled to the fence." Mule hit eight home runs in 14 games and batted .340, before jumping back to St. Louis to finish the year.

In 43 games with the Stars, Suttles hit an even .400 and added 12 more home runs to help lead the Stars into the play-offs. Mule's combined average for the year was .384, and his 20 homers were tops among all hitters. (Wells was the official western league leader, with 14, and a .404 batting average.)

The play-off pitted St. Louis against the Detroit Stars and Turkey Stearnes. It was a seesaw series. Going into game three, the teams were tied one game each, when Mule lashed a three-run home run in the first inning, as St. Louis went on to win the game and eventually the series, four games to three.

There was no black world series against the eastern champion Homestead Grays with their young goliath, 19-year-old Josh Gibson, who had just hit the longest home run in Yankee Stadium history. Thus baseball was denied the chance to compare those two Paul Bunyans in their primes.

It's also a shame that fans could not see Suttles playing side by side with Hack Wilson, the white home-run champ that year with 56. Mule hit 20 homers in 57 games; Hack, 56 in 155 games. Both would have hit less against integrated pitching, but it probably would have been a nip-and-tuck race between them.

(It would also have been fun to watch Wells, the black bat champ at .404, playing against Bill Terry, the white king, with .401.)

Suppose Suttles, Wells, and Cool Papa Bell had played on the Cardinals, who lost to the Athletics in the white world series, four games to two. The Philadelphia pitchers held the Cards to a team batting average of .200. How much difference would the three blacks have made? Their competition: Bottomley (.045 in the series), short-stop Charles Gelbert (.353), and Douthit (.083). On the pitching staff, the Cards' top winner was Wild Bill Hallahan, with 15 victories in the regular season. In the series he won one and lost one, Burleigh Grimes lost two, and dipsomaniacal Flint Rhem lost one. The Stars' Slap Hensley led the Negro league with 17 victories in a 75-game schedule. How many could he have won in the series?

With the depression, the Negro leagues expired. Teams tried to survive by passing the hat and dividing the receipts among the players, but organized leagues disappeared.

Only ten games have been found so far for the Stars against other black teams in 1931. They show Mule hitting .286, with seven home runs.

In October Suttles was playing the white big leaguers again. He faced three more future Hall of Famers—Paul and Lloyd Waner and Bill Terry—plus Babe Herman, and pitchers Heinie Meine of Pittsburgh, the National League's top winner with 19–13, and lefty Bill Walker of the Giants (17–9), the ERA champ. In the first game Terry (.349) struck out three straight times against Ted "Big Florida" Trent. Bill blamed the new-fangled lights. They didn't seem to bother Mule, however: He got two hits in four at bats, as the Stars beat Meine, 10–8. The next night he slugged a homer off Walker, as the blacks won again, 18–1.

In 1932 Suttles played 29 games for the Washington Potomacs and a new club, the Detroit Wolverines, owned by Cum Posey, who also owned the Homestead Grays. Suttles hit .269, with two homers, but Posey picked him on his authoritative black all-star team that year.

That fall Mule exploded against Bobo Newsom (0–0), then a Cub rookie. Suttles socked him for two doubles and a triple. His second double came with two men on in the ninth to win the game, 9–8.

Altogether, Mule got 5-for-9 against Bobo, although Fred Frankhouse (4–6) of the Braves held him to a single in eight trips.

The Wolverines folded in 1933, and Mule and Wells landed with the Chicago American Giants.

Chicago manager Dave Malarcher said he coached Mule on meeting the ball. "He was a great slugger," Dave said, "but he used to swing so hard at St. Louis he'd lose sight of the ball. Smart pitchers like Bill Foster and William Powell just wore him out. When he came to us, I taught him how to meet the ball. After that he would just touch it, and it would ride to the fence."

In 25 games compiled so far, Mule hit .295 with six home runs.

His Chicago teammates recalled him vividly. Nat Rogers, an excellent hitter himself, said Mule weighed 240–250 pounds. He had a knuckle missing off his middle finger, but "when he hit a ball, it looked like it would bend!"

Added Bill Cornelius:

> I didn't see the [tape measure] ball they say Dave Nicholson hit out here [in Comiskey Park], and I didn't see the balls Babe Ruth and Jimmy Foxx hit. Those are supposed to be three of the longest balls hit here. But I saw Mule Suttles on our team hit a spitball one day up in those bleachers, I mean, up there where the crowd sits in center field.

In one contest against the Memphis black team, Mule set a record that will probably never be equalled. Giants center fielder Jimmy Crutchfield explained: "Ted Trent was one of the worst hitters ever put his hands on a bat. But Trent and Suttles both looked alike—both of them big, raw-boned, six-foot-four or five. So they decided to put Trent hitting fourth and Mule hitting fifth." The Memphis club, thinking Trent was Mule and Mule was Trent, walked Trent intentionally to get to Mule, who slugged one over the fence. In fact, he whacked three home runs in one inning. The next time he came to bat, the Memphis club simply walked off the field.

That summer the blacks played their first East-West, or All-Star, game in Comiskey Park. Suttles led all players in the vote of the fans, and started the game at first base. In the game, Suttles went 2-for-4 and slugged a three-run homer off Sam Streeter, the left-handed spitball ace. "He hit a junk ball," said Ted Page. "Streeter threw junkies, but he was a tough son of a gun. Mule picked up the ball from right around his shoe tops and hit it straight on through—not over— the roof, between the decks and out the other side. Streeter always swears he threw him a drop ball that didn't break."

The American Giants sported a formidable line-up. Wells hit

third and Suttles fourth. Young Alec Radcliff played third; Jimmy Crutchfield and Nat Rogers flanked Stearnes in the outfield; Quincy Troupe and Larry Brown split the catching; and the pitching staff boasted Willie Foster, Ted Trent, and Cornelius. At least four men on the team—Suttles, Wells, Stearnes, and Foster—should wind up in Cooperstown. It's a club that could have challenged any team in any league for the pennant. In fact, they did win the first-half pennant in the Negro league, beating the powerful Pittsburgh Crawfords with five Hall of Famers—Satchel Paige, Josh Gibson, Cool Papa Bell, Oscar Charleston, and Judy Johnson.

Again, it's tantalizing to speculate on how the Chicago Cubs, who finished third in the National League, might have done if they had signed Suttles and other American Giant stars. Mule, who hit .295 that year, would have replaced the .247-hitting Charlie Grimm at first. Wells would have ousted Billy Jurges (.269) at short, and Stearnes would have replaced Frank Demaree (six homers) in center. With Foster, Trent, and Cornelius joining Guy Bush (20–12), Lon Warneke (18–13), and Charlie Root (15–10) in the pitching staff, the Cubs would probably have won the pennant instead of finishing six games behind the New York Giants.

That autumn Mule faced Jim Weaver and belted three hits in four at bats (that's when Durocher counseled Jim to "pitch and pray").

Over the winter of 1933–34 Suttles went to the Coast to play in the winter league. The teams played in little Wrigley Field, a hitter's park that was 345 feet down the left-field line. Center field was about 400 feet, said Brewer. "Over behind were some houses. Mule would hit those pitchers over the top of those houses."

He blasted three home runs against French (18–13 with the second-place Pirates). Two came in the same game. Pirate catcher Bill Brubaker recalled the second one vividly. "The game was tied, 1–1," Brubaker said. "Suttles came up with two out, popped one of Larry's screwballs 470 feet over the center-field fence and ended the game right then and there. It was one of the longest balls I've ever seen. It just sailed and sailed. When it went over, our center fielder just looked up and waved at it."

The Mule cracked another against Thurston (6–8 for sixth-place Brooklyn), and one off Bucky Walters, who was struggling to make the change-over from the infield to the pitchers' mound. In two games Suttles went 4-for-5 against Bucky.

Buck Newsom (30–11 in the Coast League), was on his way up to the St. Louis Browns. He "held" Mule to six hits in 20 at bats and no home runs.

Earl Whitehill of the Indians marveled at the Mule's power. "I think he hit a homer in almost every game," Earl said. "He sure could pound that ball." That winter, Suttles slugged the white big leaguers at a .325 clip, with 14 home runs in 157 at bats to lead the league.

The following spring Mule was back in Chicago for the 1934 season, hitting .276. Once again he was a one-man wrecking team in the East-West game, slamming three hits, including a triple, against Slim Jones (11–0), Harry Kincannon (0–2), and Satchel Paige (9–1). Mule was thrown out trying to score from third, as Paige beat Bill Foster, 1–0.

The American Giants swept the first half championship, then lost the play-off to the second-half winners, the Philadelphia Stars, in seven games. No details on the series have yet been found.

Back in California that winter, Suttles bedeviled Newsom, a 30-game winner in the Coast league, lashing a double and single against Bobo. The single came in the eighth inning with Cool Papa on base and won the game, 3–2.

Mule also got four hits in five tries against Bucky Walters (0–0) and three more home runs in two games against French (18–13). The whites were glad to see spring come, when Suttles turned his bat against the black hurlers again.

Mule slumped to .271 in 1935, with a league-leading six home runs.

But that summer was big Mule's most famous home run of all—in the East-West game. Josh Gibson's club, the Crawfords, were shifted to the West for the game, so for the first time the two famous sluggers were hitting back-to-back on the same ball team. Josh hit fourth and Mule fifth. Gibson had a great afternoon, with two doubles and two singles in five at bats. Suttles, playing left field, was frustrated by walks, and after nine innings had no hits, three walks, and one strikeout, though he had scored three runs. The game was tied 4–4. The East scored four times in the top of the tenth. The West came back with four runs in the bottom of the inning. So the score stood at 8–8 in the 11th, when Mule back-tracked 400 feet to pull down Biz Mackey's long fly.

Then in the last of the 11th, the East called in perhaps the greatest all-round player of all time, Martin Dihigo, from center field to pitch to the top of the West's lineup. Cool Papa Bell walked, second baseman Sammy T. Hughes sacrificed, and shortstop Chester Williams struck out. That put Bell on second with two out and Gibson coming to bat. Suttles was itching to hit and concocted a scheme to make sure he got up.

Cornelius was pitching for the West, and, since all-star lineups usually get scrambled after a few innings, Suttles told him, "Go up there and kneel in the on deck circle, Cornelius; they'll think you're up next." Sure enough, Dihigo glanced over, saw Cornelius swinging a bat, and, with first base open, threw four wide ones to Gibson. Imagine Dihigo's disgusted look when he saw Cornelius go back into the dugout, while Suttles advanced to the plate swinging three bats.

As William G. Nunn of the Pittsburgh *Courier* described the scene, the hoarse but resonant voice on the new Comiskey Park PA system announced that "THE MULE" was coming to bat.

Reverberating through the reaches of this historic ballpark and bounding and rebounding through the packed stands comes the chant of some 25,000 frenzied spectators.

They're yelling for blood! They're yelling for their idol, the bronzed Babe Ruth of colored baseball, to come through. . . .

Dihigo, his uniform dripping with perspiration, wiped the sweat out of his eyes, and shot a fast ball across the plate. Ball one, said umpire Craig.

Again, came that blinding fast ball, letter high and splitting the plate. And the count was one and one.

Suttles stepped out of the batter's box, dried his sweating palms in the dust around home plate, tugged his cap, and moved back into position. He looked dangerous as he waggled his big, black club around. But so did Dihigo, who was giving his all.

Another pitch blurred across the plate.

Suttles threw his mighty body into motion. His foot moved forward. His huge shoulder muscles bunched. Came a swish through the air, a crack as of a rifle, and like a projectile hurled from a cannon, the ball started its meteoric flight.

Mule's swing was a bit late, and the ball climbed toward the 400-foot mark in right-center, as the packed crowd rose to its feet and fell silent wondering if it would be caught. It wasn't. In the hush the ball cracked against a seat in the upper stands with a sound that could be heard back in the press box, then bounded upward toward still higher seats.

And then pandemonium broke loose. "Suttles completed his trip home, the third baseline filled with playmates anxious to draw him to their breasts. Over the stands came a surging mass of humanity."

The Chicago *Defender* added that not since the Armistice have Chicagoans gone so wild. "Score cards were torn up and hurled into the air. Men tossed away their summer straw hats, and women screamed."

Years later, as manager of Newark, Mule would tell the story of the home run to wide-eyed youngsters on the long bus rides. One of the rapt listeners was first baseman Lenny Pearson. "Mule was a jovial fellow, always ribbing us about the old days," Pearson said. "He could spin some yarns. One time Suttles was telling us how he won that game in Chicago. After the game they had this dance for him, because he was the hero of the game. He had on a white suit, and he wanted to attract some attention, so he jumped from the balcony to the dance floor, and the band recognized him and struck up a song for him." Mule had his eye on one particular girl, swaggered up to her, and asked for a dance. "She told him, 'If you're strong enough to jump off the balcony, what would you do to my feet if you stepped on them? No *thank* you!'" In later years, after Mule had married, the girl met him and his wife and all the ball players in Newark, Pearson said, and told the story all over again. "Big as he is, and I'm a tiny little woman!" she teased, as the ball players broke up laughing.

In 1936 Suttles and Wells—"the Damon and Pythias of black baseball," owner Cum Posey called them—left Chicago and moved to the Newark Eagles, where Mule raised his batting average to .306.

In 1937 Suttles bounced back with a .357 average and ten home runs, tops in the league—even ahead of Josh Gibson, though the statistics are unconfirmed. Now the easterners had a chance to see that what the westerners had been telling them about Mule all these years was really true, and a new collection of gargantuan Suttles stories grew.

"The longest ball I ever saw anybody hit, I saw Mule hit it out of the old Washington baseball park," Newark pitcher Leon Day said. Griffith Stadium was famous for its wide-open outfield spaces and its 34-foot-high wall. Day said Mule's blast went over the center field fence "over the flagpole and everything"—420 feet from home. Senators owner Clark Griffith "almost swallowed his cigar," writer Ric Roberts said. "It's worth anybody's money to see that man hit," Griff gulped.

Ray Dandridge said he saw Mule hit a 500-foot fly ball into center field in Kansas City, where it was caught for an out.

Little Jake Stephens of the New York Black Yankees and a former teammate of Gibson, saw Josh's two longest drives in Yankee Stadium and insists that Suttles hit them even harder than Josh.

Hall of Famer Buck Leonard, a hard hitter himself and teammate of Josh Gibson in Washington, disagreed with Jake. Buck said Josh hit more homers than Mule, and Mule struck out more. But Mule was still devastating. "Mule was a low-ball hitter," Buck said. "In Hamtramck, Michigan, they used to have some sand pits out there behind the ball park—one behind left field, another behind left-center, and they had a third pit just about in center field. And Mule was hitting that ball in that third sand pit."

Monte Irvin, another Newark teammate, said, "Mule would thrill people even striking out." While Josh Gibson was a graceful swinger, Mule fell down from the force of his swing. "He was a crowd-pleaser.

He used to 'crank up.' We used to say, 'Crank up, Mule, crank up!' I remember him as just a great curve-ball hitter. They used to try to crowd him inside with fast balls, would never throw him a curve ball."

According to Newark's Clarence "Half a Pint" Israel, Suttles told pitcher Lemuel Hooker, "Don't throw me a curve ball." Hooker threw him one in Paterson, New Jersey, and Mule hit it over the center-field fence. "I told you," Mule grinned, "don't ever throw me a slow pitch."

Pitcher Dave Barnhill said he saw Suttles golf a ball up in the air in Toledo, so high—Barnhill swore—that it came down in a smoke stack.

And Effa Manley, the glamorous co-owner of the Eagles, sent the Hall of Fame a clipping to prove that Suttles had hit four home runs over the center-field fence in Newark's Ruppert Stadium, where most of the New York Yankee greats got their minor league training. "In the history of the ball park," she said, "only three white boys had hit them over there."

Judy Johnson, Gibson's discoverer and mentor, said he saw Suttles hit one over deep center field in Newark one night, so high that it disappeared above the lights. "But you'd almost have to carry him to first base," Judy laughed, "because he couldn't run!"

Pitcher Bob Harvey of the Baltimore Elites remembered getting two curve balls over for strikes against Mule: "Then I threw a fast ball on the corner. He hit the ball on the center-field fence. All he got was a single. It hit a brick and bounced back over the center fielder's head. He wasn't too fast. I don't think Josh could hit it farther, but Josh was a much better hitter."

("Mule was a swinger," agreed Newark shortstop Dick Seay, but for all-round hitting, distance plus average, Gibson was best.)

In 1939 the 39-year-old Suttles faced a white big leaguer for the last time. Mule brought a .413 average against whites into the game, but young Bobby Feller, who had won 24 games with the Indians, set him down four times without a hit, giving him a final average against the white stars of .392.

Mule took over as manager of the Eagles. "He wasn't a good manager," Monte Irvin said. "He couldn't relate, especially to the younger players. And he wasn't the teacher that Biz Mackey (another Newark manager) was. But he knew a lot about hitting."

Israel disagreed. Suttles used to take Israel to his home at night, Clarence said. "He was considered my dad." "Suttles was the most gentle person I ever saw," Pearson said:

> If he got angry at an umpire, he would never show his emotions on the field, he'd go into the dugout and shake a towel or something. If you made a mistake—and we were young and always making mistakes—he'd

get you aside and tell you about it instead of embarrassing you in front of your teammates.

He was a tremendous manager too. He knew baseball inside and out. He showed me quite a bit about hitting the curve ball. I couldn't hit the curve. When I first went up I think I was hitting .002. He put some bats in back of me so I wouldn't move away from the pitch or I'd stumble on the bats. He kept me "in the pocket," and I learned to move my body with the curve ball. In later years it was of tremendous value to me, because I got a lot of curve balls thrown at me and I developed into a good curve-ball hitter.

Suttles taught me to play several positions to increase my value. And he had patience. He knew he was in the twilight of his career, and he devoted a lot of time to younger fellows. I guess he foresaw that eventually Negro ball players would be in the majors, because they were developing rapidly. I guess he saw into the future more clearly than most of us.

Suttles stayed with the Eagles until 1944 and lived in Newark until his death, from cancer, in 1968. "His weight fell away to nothing," said Seay. "He was thin as a pencil."

"He was a lonely man when he died," Irvin said.

"We were all pall bearers," Pearson remembered. "He told us, 'When I die, have a little thought for my memory, but don't mourn me too much.'

"I wish you could have known him."

Mule Suttles

Year	Team	G	AB	H	2B	3B	HR	BA	SA	SB
1923	Birmingham	35	132	36	4	3	1	.273	.371	2
1924	Birmingham	83	293	93	23	3	2	.317	.447	1
1925	Birmingham	66	247	77	7	4	12	.312	.518	6
1926	St. Louis	87	342	143	25	19*	26*	.418*	.830	11
1927[a]	St. Louis	24	67	31	7	3	7	.463	1.000	1
1928	St. Louis	52	193	49	9	1	12	.254	.497	1
1929	St. Louis	82	304	108	29*	7	20	.355	.694	3
	Cuba	—	149	43	—	—	—	.289	—	—
1930	St.L.–Baltimore	57	203	78	16	8	20	.384	.832	9
1931	Detroit-Wash.	38	119	34	5	0	7	.286	.504	1
1932	Washington	29	108	29	3	0	2	.269	.352	1
1933	Chicago	25	78	23	2	1	6	.295	.577	3
1934	Chicago	24	98	27	4	1	6	.276	.520	2
	California	—	157	51	—	—	14	.325	.—	—
1935	Chicago	31	85	23	6	0	6*	.271	.553	0
1936	Newark	14	49	15	2	0	6	.306	.714	0
1937	Newark	2	7	1	0	0	0	.143	.143	0
1938	Newark	2	8	1	0	0	0	.125	.125	0
1939	Cuba	—	142	31	—	—	—	.218	—	—
1944	Newark	20	40	10	1	0	3	.250	.500	—
Totals			2875	919	145	491	150	.320	.561	41
	Post-Season									
1930	Play-Offs	9	31	9	0	2	2	.290	.613	0
1934	Play-Offs	1[b]	3	0	0	0	0	.000	.000	0
Totals		10	34	9	0	2	2	.265	.559	0
East-West		6	27	13	4	1	3	.481	1.037	1

* Led league.
[a] Broke ankle.
[b] Incomplete.

Mule Suttles vs. White Big Leaguers

Year	AB	H	2B	3B	HR	Pitcher	(W-L)
1929	4	3	0	1	1	Uhle	(15-11)
	4	0	0	0	0	Whitehill	(14-15)
	3	1	0	0	0	J. Milles	(14-12)
	5	3	0	2	0	Hudlin	(17-15)
1930	4	1	1	0	0	Bayne	(0-0)
	3	1	—	—	—	Fitzsimmons	(8-11)
						Grove	(31-4)
1931	—	—	—	—	1	Walker	(8-12)
	4	2	—	—	—	Meine	(12-9)
1932	5	3	2	1	0	Newsom	(0-0)
	4	2	0	0	1	Newsom	(0-0)
	4	0	0	0	0	Frankhouse	(4-6)
	4	1	0	0	0	Frankhouse	
1933	4	3	1	1	0	Weaver[a]	
1933-34	4	1	0	0	0	Newsom[b]	
	4	2	0	0	0	Newsom	
	4	1	0	0	0	Newsom	
	5	1	0	0	0	Newsom	
	3	1	0	0	0	Newsom	
	—	—	—	—	2	French	(18-13)
	3	1	0	0	1	French	(18-13)
	2	2	1	0	1	Thurston	(6-8)
	4	0	0	0	0	Thurston	(6-8)
	4	1	0	0	0	Thurston	(6-8)
	1	1	0	0	0	Walters	(0-0)
	4	3	0	0	1	Walters	(0-0)
1934-35	4	2	0	0	2	French	(12-18)
	—	—	—	—	1	French	(12-18)
	5	1	0	0	0	Frazier	(1-3)
1939	4	0	0	0	0	Feller	(24-9)
Totals	99	37	4	5	11	Average: .374	

[a] Weaver had been 2-1 with Yankees 1931, would be 13-9 with Browns and Cubs 1934.
[b] Newsom was 0-0 with Cubs in 1932, was 30-11 with Los Angeles in 1933, would be 16-20 with Browns 1934. Without these games, Suttles hit .392 (31 for 79).

20

Red Grier and Luther Farrell: The First Series No-Hitters

He did? *I never heard him say anything about it.*

Outfielder Gene Benson,
informed that Luther Farrell had
pitched a World Series no-hitter

Nineteen eighty-six marked the anniversary of the first no-hit game ever pitched in the World Series. No, it wasn't pitched by Don Larsen. In fact, Don was only the third man to turn the trick.

Larsen threw his perfect game against the Brooklyn Dodgers on October 8, 1956.

Thirty years before that, on October 3, 1926, a light-skinned left-hander named Claude "Red" Grier hurled a hitless classic in the Negro league World Series, defeating the Chicago American Giants, 10–0.

A year later—October 8, 1927—Grier's teammate on the Atlantic City Bacharach Giants, another light-skinned lefty, Luther "Red" Farrell, turned in a seven-inning gem, winning, 3–2.

Like Larsen, Grier and Farrell were among the most unlikely men to achieve immortality. Grier particularly was hardly ranked among the other top black pitchers of his day—Foster, Rogan, Winters, Joe Williams, and others.

In sharp contrast to Larsen's masterpiece, which was seen by 80,000 fans in person and millions more on TV, Grier and Farrell pitched theirs in virtual secrecy. Only a few thousand fans came out in person. The only white newspaper that reported both feats was the Atlantic City *Press*.

Grier's 1926 Masterpiece

Baltimore, October 3, 1926—In New York, Grover Alexander of the Cardinals was defeating the Yankess 6–2 to even the white World Series at one game apiece. Meanwhile, the Atlantic City Bacharachs and Chicago American Giants were facing off at Westport Park, not far from Babe Ruth's birthplace, as Red Grier and the Bacharachs also hoped to even the black World Series at one each.

The facts we know about Grier are scanty. He had reportedly come off the college campus at Virginia A&M and broke in with the last place Washington Potomacs of the Eastern Colored League in 1924. After more than half a century, few men survive who remember him today. One who does is Judy Johnson.

Grier "was a good-size boy, had a very good fastball," Johnson said. "But he was wild, as most young pitchers are. He was wild as the devil. Didn't know where the ball was going."

Bill Foster recalled Grier as "a big red boy" (that is, light-skinned). "He had a good fast ball and a good curve ball. He didn't look to me like he had a change-up, but his fast ball was live, it ran a lot."

Macajah Eggelston, the old-time black catcher, gave Grier the highest praise. "Lefty Grove was one of the best pitchers I ever hit against," Eggelston said. "But Grier was the best left-hand pitcher I ever seen. If Grier had been in the same league with Grove, you'd have to rate him just as high as Grove."

Grier won four and lost seven his rookie year. He split the 1925 season between the Potomacs and the Bacharachs and wound up with a 7–9 record.

In 1926 Grier became a winner, with an 11–6 record, a good total in the abbreviated Negro league season. Farrell was 1–3, but he played mostly outfield and hit .359 to lead the league. Together they helped lead the Bs to the pennant.

The World Series, the third since the two-league structure had been set up in 1923, pitted the Bacharachs against Chicago. It opened in Atlantic City on October 1. The first game ended in a tie.

Grier started game two and was quickly blasted for seven runs in the second inning, as Chicago won, 7–6.

That night the clubs moved to Baltimore for game three. The stage was set for history. Grier came right back from his licking to hook up against Chicago's underhand specialist, Webster McDonald. The game was played in sultry hot weather, Grier was not sharp and was in and out of trouble in almost every inning. He walked five men, including the lead-off man in four innings. But he struck out seven, and only two balls were hit to the outfield, both to Farrell. The

Bacharach infield made two errors behind him, but they also made four sensational plays to rob the Chicagoans of possible hits.

In the first, Grier walked Chicago's speedy lead-off man, Floyd "Jelly" Gardner, a .333-hitter, but struck out Sandy Thompson (.306), as Gardner stole second. Jim Brown (.335) grounded out, Gardner taking third. Then Jimmy Hines (.328) looped a Texas leaguer to left, where Lundy made a beautiful over-the-shoulder catch to end the inning.

The Bs struck for four runs in their half of the inning, giving Grier a good cushion to work with.

The second and third were easy innings. Two Chicagoans struck out; the other four couldn't get the ball out of the infield. Bacharach first baseman Napoleon Cummings (nicknamed "Chance" after Frank Chance) made a second great play to help Grier out.

Grier opened the fourth by walking Thompson, who was gunned down stealing. He ended the inning with a strikeout, a walk, and a ground out.

He opened the fifth by walking "Gentleman Dave" Malarcher, the Chicago manager hitting .255. After two ground outs, Cummings bobbled a ground ball, and Gardner walked to load the bases. But Grier got Thompson on an easy ground ball to end that threat.

Luther Farrell (second from right) with the New York Lincoln Giants at the first black game in Yankee Stadium (1930). Also pictured are Julio Rojo (third from left), Red Ryan (fourth from left), John Beckwith (third from right), and John Henry Lloyd (far right).

Grier got through the sixth on two strikeouts and a fine fielding play by second baseman Garcia.

In the bottom of the inning the Bs struck for six more runs, helped by a single by Grier himself, his third straight hit of the day.

In the seventh Grier got the first two men on ground balls, then Cummings committed his second error before Grier got the third out on a fly to Farrell in right. It was the first ball Chicago had hit to the outfield all day.

Grier walked Gardner to open the eighth—the third time Jelly had gotten on with a pass. But Grier got the next three men easily.

In the ninth Grier would face George "Never" Sweatt (.262), Malarcher, and shortstop Sanford Jackson (.191).

Sweatt, a big schoolteacher from Walter Johnson's hometown of Coffeyville, Kansas, grounded out to Lundy. Two more to go.

Malarcher was next up. He slapped the ball to Marcelle, who came up with a sparkling play, the fourth by the B's infield, and threw Malarcher out.

Now only Jackson could spoil Grier's bid for immortality. Red got him on a ground ball to second, and the first World Series no-hitter was history.

Bacharachs vs. Chicago, October 3, 1926

Bacharachs		AB	H	R		Chicago		AB	H	R
LF	Reid	5	2	2		RF	Gardner	1	0	0
1B	Cummings	5	3	2		LF	Thompson	3	0	0
3B	Marcelle	3	2	1		1B	Brown	4	0	0
CF	White	3	0	1		C	Hines	3	0	0
SS	Lundy	4	1	1		CF	Sweatt	4	0	0
RF	Farrell	3	1	1		3B	Malarcher	3	0	0
C	Jones	5	2	0		SS	Jackson	4	0	0
2B	Garcia	4	0	1		2B	Williams	2	0	0
P	Grier	3	3	1		P	McDonald	3	0	0
						P	Crawford	0	0	0
		34	14	10				27	0	0

Chicago   000 000 000 = 0 0 4
Bacharachs 400 006 00x = 10 14 1

2B: Jones, Grier
SB: Lundy, White, Farrell, Gardner
SO: Grier 8
BB: Grier 6, McDonald 2
HB: McDonald 3

That tied the series at one game each. The Bs won the next game to go one up, but Bill Foster beat them in Chicago to tie it up again. The Bs went ahead again, three games to two, then Grier returned to the mound with a chance to open up a four-to-two lead. Instead, he was defeated, 6–3, to throw the series back into a tie. Chicago then won the last two games to wrap it up.

Grier won only one more game in his life. In 1927 he compiled a 1–2 record before succumbing to some unexplained ailment and was never heard of again. "I think he died young," Johnson said. Red Grier, the Don Larsen of black baseball, remains one of the Negro league's greatest enigmas.

With Grier gone, the Bs were hurting for pitching in 1927. Roy Roberts and Hubert Lockhart were ineffective. So manager Dick Lundy turned to his outfield and called on young Farrell to help out the starting corps, by joining their ace, Arthus "Rats" Henderson, who won 19 games, and Jesse "Mountain" Hubbard.

Farrell was so fair-skinned, said Atlantic City sports editor Henry "Whitey" Gruhler, "you'd think he was a white man." Hence the nickname, "Red." Farrell came from Chicago by way of Gilkerson's semipro Union Giants. One report said he attended Georgetown University in Washington, though this sounds implausible for a Mid-westerner. One old-timer claimed Farrell threw a fast ball, but two players, Clint Thomas of Hilldale and Nat Rogers of Chicago, insisted that he was a spitball and emery ball artist.

Farrell broke in with the second division New York Lincolns in 1925 and compiled an 0–6 record. Traded to the Bacharachs in mid-season, he won five and lost three to end the year at 5–9. He batted .296.

We have no record of Red pitching in 1926, but he hit .369 as an outfielder to help the Bs move up from fourth place to the pennant.

In 1927 Farrell's hitting dropped to .298, but he answered man-ager Dick Lundy's call for pitching help and had a magnificent sea-son—17–8, second highest winning total in the league behind Henderson's 19, as the Bs repeated as champs. Henderson hurt his arm in August and was out for the rest of the year. That meant that in the World Series, Lundy would have to go with a two-man staff, Hubbard and Farrell.

The series opened in Chicago. The American Giants called on their ace, Bill Foster (17–3), who had beaten the Bs, 1–0, in the series finale the year before. Lundy countered with Farrell. Luther was hit hard, giving up 13 hits, and lost by a score of 6–2.

Next Chicago blasted Hubbard 11–1. Jesse came back in game three and was shut out, 7–0. Farrell tried to stop the damage in game four, but he too was knocked around for 11 hits and lost the game, 9–

1, and the two teams entrained for the East, with Chicago needing only one more victory and the Bs needing a near-miraculous five-game sweep.

Luther Farrell's 1927 Gem

Altantic City, October 8, 1927—In New York Wilcy Moore beat the Pirates, 4–3, as the Yankees swept the white World Series in four straight. Chicago sent Bill Foster back to the mound to try to wrap up the black series as well. The beleaguered Bs named Farrell to save them from annihilation.

The day was dark and rainy at the old Bacharach Park, a converted greyhound racetrack out on South Carolina Avenue. The following account is based on material furnished by the Atlantic City Library from the pages of the *Press*.

Like Grier's before him, Farrell's game was far from airtight. He walked four men and struck out three. The Bacharachs made four errors (one by Farrell himself), permitting two runs to score. Two double plays also helped get Farrell out of trouble.

In the first, with one out, Malarcher (hitting .303) walked, bringing up Walter "Steel Arm" Davis (.424). But Farrell got Davis on a grounder to Lundy, who started a fast double play.

The Bs got four hits and three runs off Foster in the second, the only hits Bill gave up all day, as he matched Farrell's hitless efforts in the other six innings.

Farrell went out in the third to protect the lead. With two out, he dropped Jackson's ground ball but struck out Larry Brown to end the inning.

He walked Chicago shortstop Charlie Williams to open the third, but second baseman Speed Wagner turned a quick double play.

In the fourth Farrell quickly got into trouble. He walked Malarcher, and the usually brilliant Marcelle made a wild throw on Davis' grounder to put two men on base. But Luther got clean-up man Pythian Russ on a short fly to center. Little catcher Ed "Yump" Jones made a great peg to second to catch Malarcher off the bag. Davis thereupon stole second, then stole third, and when Jones' throw went wild, Steel Arm came home with the first Chicago run. Right-fielder Smith (first name unknown) then saved Farrell with a great catch to rob Jackson (.281) of a hit.

In the fifth Farrell walked lead-off man Larry Brown, who took second on a sacrifice, third on a ground out, and scored when Wagner booted a grounder at second. That made it 3–2.

Then Farrell settled down. He got the side out in order in the

Bacharachs vs. Chicago, October 8, 1927

	American Giants	AB	R	H	PO	A		Atlantic City	AB	R	H	PO	A
1B	J. Brown	3	0	0	10	0	LF	Reid	3	0	1	1	0
3B	Malarcher	1	0	0	1	2	3B	Marcell	2	0	0	0	1
RF	Davis	3	1	0	0	0	CF	White	3	0	0	1	0
SS	Russ	3	0	0	0	1	1B	Lewis	3	1	1	8	0
LF	Sweatt	2	0	0	2	0	SS	Lundy	3	0	0	2	3
CF	Jackson	3	0	0	0	0	RF	Smith	1	1	1	2	1
C	L. Brown	2	1	0	3	0	C	Jonca	2	1	1	3	2
2B	Williams	1	0	0	2	1	2B	Wagner	3	0	0	3	4
P	Foster	2	0	0	0	5	P	Farrell	2	0	0	1	1
		20	2	0	18	9			22	3	4	21	12

American Giants 000 000 0—2
Atlantic City 030 000 *—3
Errors—Jones, Wagner, Marcell, Farrell, Russ. Two-base hit—Smith. Stolen bases—Davis (2). Struck out—by Foster, 3; by Farrell, 3. Bases on balls—Off Foster, 3; off Farrell, 5. Double plays—Wagner to Lewis; Lundy to Wagner to Lewis. Umpires—McDevitt and Magee.

sixth. In the seventh, as the clouds grew darker, he struck out two men and got the third on a ground ball.

Then the rain pelted down, and the umpires called the game, though the still hitless Chicagoans angrily protested.

Perhaps inspired by Farrell's back-against-the-wall heroics, the Bacharachs came to life. After a rain-out, they battled to a tie in the next game. Farrell himself came back with only two days rest and beat Chicago, 8–1. Farrell won the next game as well, to make it four games to three. But Foster, the Chicago stopper, finally beat Lockhart, 11–4, to give the American Giants their second straight championship.

Incidentally, Jones, the catcher, is, if possible, even less well known than Grier or Farrell. Yet he left a record that will never be broken, the only man ever to catch two World Series no-hitters.

Farrell continued to play in the big time for several years. In 1928 he had another splendid year. Although the league broke up, he compiled a 15–11 record against other top black clubs, the best winning total in the East. He also hit .357, and his eight home runs were second only to Pop Lloyd's 11.

That October Farrell joined a black all-star squad in Baltimore to play Lefty Grove and Max Bishop of the world champion Athletics. Lefty won 24 and lost eight that year, and Bishop hit .316. Spud Davis (.342) of the Phils caught, and Johnny Neunn of the Braves (.213) played first base. The team was fleshed out with Triple-A Baltimore Oriole players, though the outfielders, identified by last names only, might have been any of several Moores from the majors—Randy (.213), or Eddie (.237). At any rate, Lefty that year led the majors in wins and strike-outs. So the game pitted the country's best white left-hander against that year's top black lefty.

Farrell won it, 9–3. He gave up six hits to 11 for Grove and walked only three to seven by Grove. Farrell struck out seven, Grove ten.

The league re-formed in 1929, but Farrell played only two games, presumably because of injury. He didn't get a hit and lost the only game he pitched.

But he came back strong in 1930, with a .529 average in 12 games that have been found so far. One report, unverified, says he was 10–0 on the pitching mound. In the playoff against the Hall of Fame Pittsburgh Crawfords—Josh Gibson, Oscar Charleston, Cool Papa Bell, and Judy Johnson—Farrell was bombed off the mound in the second, though he wasn't charged with the loss. He came right back the next day to hold the four Hall of Famers to a single hit, a double by Gibson, but could only gain a 2–2 tie after nine innings. In the

Baltimore Black Sox vs. Major League All Stars, Baltimore, Oct. 14, 1928

	All Stars	AB	H	R		Baltimore	AB	H	R
2B	Bishop	4	0	0	LF	Holloway	4	0	1
1B	Neunn	4	0	0	RF	Dixon	4	3	3
CF	Porter	2	0	1	3B	Wilson	5	3	1
LF	Moore	4	1	1	1B-CF	Carter	2	1	1
SS	Thomas	4	0	0	C	Mackey	4	0	0
3B	Mooers	3	2	1	SS	Lundy	4	2	0
RF	G. Maisel	4	2	0	1B	Taylor	1	0	0
C	Davis	1	0	0	2B	Warfield	5	2	3
P	Grove	3	0	0	P	Farrell	2	0	0
C	Artigiani	1	0	0	CF	Washington	4	0	0
PH	F. Maisel	1	1	0					
		31	6	3			34	11	9

All Stars   000 200 001— 3   6 5
Baltimore 002 124 00x— 9 11 2

2B: Dixon, Moore, Warfield, Wilson
HR: Dixon
SB: Dixon 2, Warfield 2, Holloway
SO: Farrell 7, Grove 10
W: Farrell 3, Grove 7

tenth Red walked Jake Stephens, who stole and scored on an error to beat him.

After the leagues broke up, little was heard of Farrell until 1934, when he was playing first base for the Bacharachs, a weakened version of the once mighty Bs. He hit .500 in ten known at bats, won one game and lost one. Center fielder Eugene Benson was a rookie then and remembered Farrell well, but as a hitter, not as a pitcher. "He had a very nice swing on the ball," Benson said. "He could hit the ball out of the park easier than anyone you ever saw. It looked like he would just sweep it out, didn't swing hard at all, and that ball would go! That's the way he played first base too—easy. He was a swell fella, a big fella, an easy-going sort of guy. He was very gentle."

Farrell joined the Atlantic City police force, and Gruhler, now 85 years old, recalled playing against him on the police team in the city league. In 1937 Farrell was playing with Lloyd on the Johnson Stars, an Atlantic City semipro team. Max Manning, who would later pitch for the Newark Eagles' great 1946 team, played against Farrell that year. Red still had "a heck of a good curve ball," Manning said.

The left-hander took to drinking heavily, said Ralph Green, former Atlantic City athletic director. After that, "We just sort of lost track of him." Just where or when Farrell died, no one can say. His end, like his great moment of glory, was unremarked by a public that had hardly known him at all.

Luther Farrell

Year	Team	G	AB	H	2B	3B	HR	BA	SB	(W-L)
1925	New York-Atlantic City	29	81	24	3	0	0	.296	0	(5-9)
1926	Atlantic City Bs	47	141	52	6	1	5	.369	—	—
1927	Atlantic City Bs	59	171	51	13	1	4	.298	0	(17-8)
1928	Atlantic City Bs	35	94	33	2	0	8	.351	0	(15-11)
1929	Atlantic City Bs	2	8	0	0	0	0	.000	0	(0-1)
1930	New York Lincolns	12	34	18	2	2	4	.529	0	—
1934	Atlantic City Bs	3	10	5	0	0	0	.500	0	(1-1)
Totals		187	539	183	26	4	21	.340	0	(38-30)
Post-Season										
1926	World Series	11	34	7	0	0	1	.206	2	—
1927	World Series	8	21	4	1	1	0	.190	0	(2-2)
1930	Play-Offs	4	10	1	0	0	0	.100	0	(0-1)
Totals		23	65	12	1	1	1	.185	2	(2-3)

21

Chino Smith:
Black Fists, Black Bat

I've faced two tough hitters. Josh Gibson was one. But the best hitter I think I ever faced was a boy named Chino Smith. That was the best man I ever faced. Smith hit me just like he knew what I was going to throw him. He hit to all fields, and he would spit at the first two pitches then tell me, "Young man, you've got yourself in trouble."

William "Sug" Cornelius,
Pitcher, Chicago American Giants

When Satchel Paige was asked in 1932 to name the toughest hitter he ever faced, he named two: Jud Wilson and Chino Smith. Satch would later put Josh Gibson ahead of both of them. But most old-timers who saw all three, insist that Little Charlie "Chino" Smith was the best pure hitter the Negro leagues produced.

In six meteoric years, Smith's lifetime average was .375, compared to .373 for Wilson.

Old-timers say Chino ("he had Chinese-looking eyes") reminded them of Lloyd Waner or Rod Carew, but with more power. He slapped outside pitches over third base and pulled inside pitches into the right-field seats.

Did Smitty fatten his average on easy pitching in the Negro leagues? Hardly. In ten games against white big leaguers—Dolph Luque, Ed Rommel, and Johnny Ogden—Chino drilled 15 hits in 37 at bats for a .405 average.

Appropriately, Smitty hit in Babe Ruth's number-three spot and patrolled Babe's spot in right field in Yankee Stadium when the Yankees were away. He was out there on July 10, 1930, in the first game ever played by black teams at the Stadium. Eighteen thousand fans showed up for the historic double header between the Lincoln Giants and the defending champion Baltimore Black Sox.

In the first inning Smith walked. In the third with one man on, he whacked a long fly into Ruth's favorite target, the right-field stands. In the fifth, with a man on second, he lined a triple into left field. By the seventh, Baltimore didn't know *where* in the world to pitch him. They tried one down the middle and Smitty lashed it into the right-center-field bleachers for three more runs. It was a day worthy of Ruth himself.

Smitty hit .429 that year, the last season of his young life. He would be dead within a year, still less than 30 years old. Even in an era famous for colorful, pugnacious ball players, both black and white, Chino had a reputation as a fighter.

Johnny Allen, who also had a reputation for a temper, pitched in the Cuban winter league before he went to the New York Yankees. New York Lincoln's pitcher Bill Holland remembered Chino walking up behind Allen, who was warming up, and sneering, "Is that all you gonna throw today?" Allen pretended to ignore him. "If that's all you gonna throw, I'm gonna kill you today."

Holland recalled:

> Sure enough, when Smitty came up, I guess Allen was a little sore at him and threw one at his head, and Smitty had to hit the dirt. Smitty got back up and on the next pitch hit a line drive close to Allen's head. Allen had to duck. Smitty yelled from first base, "I made you duck out there," just like that. Allen stormed over there and they tangled up. The umpire and everybody tried to get them apart. Smitty would hit anybody.

"This guy could do more with the fans down on him." Holland said.

He'd get up to bat and the pitcher would throw one in there and he'd spit at it. The fans would boo him, and he'd come out of the batter's box,

The New York Lincoln Giants at the first black game in Yankee Stadium in 1930. Pictured (left to right) are Nip Winters, Chino Smith, Bill Yancey, Bill Holland, unknown, Larry Brown, and Dick Seay. Photo courtesy Baseball Hall of Fame.

turn around and make like he was going to move toward them, and they'd shout, "Come on." He'd get back in there and hit the ball out of the ball park and go around the bases waving his arms at the stands.

Chino Smith was born in Greenwood, South Carolina, about 1903. He played for Benedict College, which was probably a boarding school for blacks rather than a university-level institution. Like many other black students, he earned money in the summer carrying bags in New York's Pennsylvania Station and playing baseball for the Pennsylvania Redcaps there. He was a second baseman then and teamed with Dick Seay, who would also go on to become a star in the Negro leagues.

In 1924 Smith moved to the Philadelphia Giants and from there, in 1925, to the black big time with the Brooklyn Royal Giants of the Eastern Colored League. Playing third, he hit .315 his rookie year and .326 the next. He wasn't a long-ball hitter yet, but, sighed submarine pitcher Webster McDonald, "those doubles and singles would run you crazy."

Big Jesse "Mountain" Hubbard played with Smitty at Brooklyn. "What I like about Chino, he was a .400 hitter every year," Hubbard said.

> I don't care who he was playing against, he'd go out get two-three hits. And he didn't believe anybody could strike him out. No. And you couldn't strike him out. He was a left-handed hitter, and left-handers looked just like right-handers to him. He'd take two strikes and hit the ball a mile. Spit at two, say, "Now you duck," hit a line drive right through the box. And shoot, man, don't throw one close to his head. Because the next one's going to be right at *your* head: "Now duck!" That's the truth! I'm not lying. He could hit those line drives back through the box just like you were throwing a ball over to first. He could shoot a bullet back through there.

Hubbard recalled one game in Allentown, Pennsylvania, against a semipro team that boasted former Cub pitcher Claude Hendrix, who threw a mean emery ball. "Every colored team that went down there, you know what he'd do? He'd strike out 18–20 of them." Hubbard, who could cut the ball himself when the occasion demanded, volunteered to pitch against him. "Hendrix would go out there and strike out three, and I'd go out there and strike out three. In the seventh inning, Chino Smith told me, 'I'm going to hit a home run off this man.' I said, 'If you hit a home run, Chino, by the time you get back here, here's a $10 bill.' I swear to God, Chino walked up to bat, and the first ball Hendrix threw him, Chino walked up on it and hit it a mile over the right field fence. When he came in I handed him his ten."

Royals outfielder Ted Page also called Chino the greatest hitter the Negro leagues produced. "He looked something like a Chinaman," Page said, "light brown, with a little bit of a slant across his eyes. He and Pop Lloyd were two hitters of the same type, but I would think Chino had better power than Lloyd. His line drives would go farther. Golly, he hit line drives out of the ball park."

Smith was a scrapper. But Page defended him against charges that he was temperamental. "He wasn't the type like Jud Wilson or Oscar Charleston, although he'd fight back if he was riled; he wasn't a pansy by any stretch of the imagination."

In Cuba that winter Chino hit .342, although Dolf Luque, the Cincinnati Reds' star hurler, put a collar on him, holding him to six hits in 21 at bats. But the following winter Chino got a measure of revenge, clipping Luque for three hits in eight tries. "Smitty used to make Luque so mad," Bill Holland chuckled. Luque would uncork his best pitch "and Smitty would spit at it, tell him he didn't have nothing: 'Hit me right here, you couldn't hurt me.' Luque would get two strikes on Smitty and throw one in there, and Smitty was liable to hit a line drive through the pitcher's box. Luque'd have to duck and Smitty would laugh at him. He'd get so mad at Smitty."

"Luque was a mean Cuban," Chet Brewer said. "Smith would curse Luque, Luque would 'low-bridge' him again. Smith would say, 'Come on, you Cuban so-and-so, try and get that ball by me.' Luque had an 'off-the-table' curve ball, but Smith would make him jump rope, hit it back right through his legs."

Said Brewer: "If Smith and those guys had played in the major leagues, they'd have re-written the record books."

Cool Papa Bell shook his head in awe. "He'd go out there, say, 'I guess I'll get me three hits,' and go out there and hit that ball, I don't care who pitched."

Smith's manager, Mike Gonzalez, who also coached for the Cardinals, tried to calm Smitty down. "Cool down," Mike told him.

"Shut up, Mike," Chino shot back. "If I stayed over here a year and learned Spanish, I'd run for Cuban president. You Cubans don't have no sense."

Still Chino was a favorite of the Cuban fans. "He was very *simpatico*" (friendly, popular), insists Pedro Cardona.

Meanwhile, Chino was whacking Negro league pitching mercilessly. He hit a lusty .422 in 1927, second best in the league.

Baltimore fastballer Laymon Yokely faced Jimmy Foxx, Oscar Charleston, and Josh Gibson. "But the greatest hitter I've faced wasn't any of them," he declared. "It was Chino Smith. It seemed like everything I throwed him, he could hit. He wasn't afraid of any pitcher."

No records were published in 1928, which is a pity. Chino was apparently just hitting his stride. Only nine box scores have been uncovered, giving Smith a .271 average. In Havana over the winter he hit .333.

The next summer, 1929, Smith's first with the Royals' cross-town rivals, the Lincoln Giants, Chino really burst into a star. He hit .461, according to research by Paul Doherty and this writer, to lead the league. He came to bat 245 times and smacked 23 home runs, and his 218 total bases gave him the astronomical slugging average of .890! He even stole 17 bases.

Smitty wasn't only a hitter; he played a strong right field as well, Hubbard pointed out. The little left-hander trapped many a man off first by throwing behind the runner making his turn at first.

Chino was still hot in October when he faced the white big leaguers in Baltimore for a double header. He jumped on St. Louis Browns pitcher Johnny Ogden (4–8) for a perfect 4-for-4, including a home run, as his club won, 8–5. In the second game, against the Philadelphia A's Ed Rommel (12–2), Smitty lined out a single and a ground-rule double into the right field bleachers in four times up, as the blacks won again, 5–3.

In 1930 Smith hit .429, with eight home runs in 39 games.

That year the Lincolns challenged the Homestead Grays, with Charleston, Josh Gibson, Smokey Joe Williams, and a host of other stars, to a championship series after the regular season. Chino had a bad series, hitting only .188. In the tenth and final game, won by the Grays, Smitty charged in from right field after a pop fly and smashed into second baseman Rev Cannady going back. Cannady's knee caught Chino in the stomach, and Smith had to be carried from the field.

Chino never played another inning in the United States. He did go to Cuba that winter, but he wasn't his old self at bat. Claude Jonnard, a former National League journeyman, held him hitless in ten trips. It was the end of the line for Chino.

Holland thinks Smith picked up yellow fever. The injury the previous fall might have been a contributing factor. At any rate, when the 1931 season opened, Chino Smith, the greatest hitter in the Negro leagues, was dead. He left a drawer full of medicines in his desk.

Smith was still a young man. He hadn't reached 30 yet. His career had been meteoric, from 1925 to 1930, too short to qualify for the Hall of Fame. "But he played for six years," Hubbard shrugged. "If you can't judge a ball player in six years, you're not much of a judge."

But, oh, what he might have done if he had lived!

Chino Smith

Year	Team	G	EABª	H	2B	3B	HR	BA	SB
1925	Brooklyn	34	126	43	—	—	0	.341	0
1926	Brooklyn	23	89	29	—	—	2	.326	—
	Cuba	—	79	27	—	—	—	.342	—
1927	Brooklyn	42	164	69	16	4	7	.422	2
	Cuba	—	120	41	13	0	0	.342	2
1928	Brooklyn	9	37	10	2	1	0	.271	1
	Cuba	—	135	45	10	7	1	.333	7
1929	New York	—	245	113	28*	4	23*	.461*	17
	Cuba	—	198	67	12	7*	2	.341	—
1930	New York	39	154	66	11	2	8	.429*	2
	Cuba	—	33	9	0	0	0	.273	1
Totals			1380	519	92	25	43	.377	22
World Series									
1930	New York	9	32	6	2	0	0	.188	1

*Led league.
ª Estimated At Bats.

Chino Smith vs. White Big Leaguers

Year	AB	H	2B	3B	HR	Pitcher	(W-L)
1926-27	4	1	0	0	0	Luque	(13-16)
	3	0	0	0	0	Luque	
	3	0	0	0	0	Luque	
	4	2	0	0	0	Luque	
	3	2	0	0	0	Luque (Mendez)*	
	4	1	0	1	0	Luque (Mendez, Gardner)*	
1927-28	4	2	1	0	0	Luque	(13-12)
	4	1	0	0	0	Luque	
1929	4	4	0	0	1	Ogden	(4-8)
	4	2	1	0	0	Rommel	(12-2)
Totals 10 games	37	15	2	1	1	Average: .405	

*Pitched in Negro leagues.

22

Cum Posey and Gus Greenlee:
The Long Gray Line

Cum Posey owned the Grays, and he was as good a baseball man as ever lived. He had gone to college and he could have passed for white. He treated a man like a human being, and he'd look out for his ball players, just like Wilkinson (of the Kansas City Monarchs). The best hotels, the best everything. They operated like big-league teams. They were the only ones treated the ball players half-decent about riding all night. If they didn't go to bed, they gave them their room rent just the same. And Posey paid good salaries. You know he must have been a good man when he was paying Josh Gibson $1,200 a month and Buck Leonard and Sam Bankhead $1,000. Cum Posey was a genius.

Ted "Double Duty" Radcliffe
catcher, Homestead Grays

For 36 years, 1910 through 1945, Cumberland "Cum" Posey was the guiding genius who built one of the finest sports machines ever put together, the Washington Homestead Grays. Led by Josh Gibson and Buck Leonard, they achieved a record probably unequaled by any professional team in U.S. sports history, winning nine straight pennants in the Negro National League, 1937–45. Yet many veterans insist that those were not the best Grays teams of all. Some prefer the 1926 club that won 43 straight games; others hold out for the 1930 squad that swept 11 out of 12 from the proud Kansas City Monarchs. Still others point to the 1931 Grays who won 136 games while losing only 17.

The man who built them all was Cum Posey.

Posey's great rival in the early 1930s was Gus Greenlee and his Pittsburgh Crawfords, which many people regard as the finest black team of all time (maybe the best team, period). It boasted five future Hall of Famers—Satchel Paige, Josh Gibson, Oscar Charleston, Cool Papa Bell, and Judy Johnson. That's one less than the 1927 Yankees.

In fact, said Crawford outfielder Ted Page, it was Greenlee who made Paige into the unparalleled star he became. When Satch came to

Pittsburgh, he was just a hard thrower. Greenlee made him into a media star.

"Cum Posey was the *shrewdest* owner that I played for," Ted Page said, "but Gus was the better promoter between the two."

"Greenlee and Cum Posey didn't get along so good together," said Grays first baseman Buck Leonard. "Posey was a Penn State man and Greenlee a street fellow. Cum was on the school board; he was an educated fellow, liked refined things. Gus was just a run-of-the-mill fellow; liked the numbers business, gambling."

Greenlee almost destroyed the Grays, yet he probably saved black baseball in the depth of the depression. In the end, however, it was Posey who survived and led the way into the Jackie Robinson era.

My own memory of Posey's baseball empire goes back to a humid Tuesday night in May of 1944 in the old, green-painted, ad-studded confines of Washington's Griffith Stadium. I was 14 then.

The park—where Howard University Hospital now stands— seemed a long bus ride from my home in Alexandria to Washington, where we changed from the segregated Virginia bus—whites in front, blacks in back—and boarded the integrated Washington trolley. The stadium also seemed a long ride from downtown then. Today the site is deep within "the inner city."

Josh Gibson, the legendary slugger, was wearing the pin-stripes of the old Grays, who were then working on their eighth of nine straight pennants in the Negro National League. Their bitter rivals, the Kansas City Monarchs of the Negro American League, were in town, and the great Satchel Paige himself would pitch the first two innings to draw a crowd.

And it was a crowd. The *Washington Post* had devoted two paragraphs to the game, more than its usual ration of news about the Grays, since, after all, Paige was in town. But the park was swarming with black fans and every now and then a pink face or two out to watch these two greatest players in black baseball, Josh and Satch, renew their long-standing feud.

I remember crowding against the railing beside the Monarchs' dugout with a swarm of scorecard-waving kids to watch Satchel warm up, his big windmill windup reminiscent of Joe E. Brown's movie, *Elmer the Great*. Across the field, Gibson, warming up his own pitcher, looked round-faced and cheery, a beardless black Santa throwing his head back and chuckling at a dozen things that touched his funny bone.

This was black baseball two years before Jackie Robinson. This was the game that Cum Posey had done so much to shape.

Posey was born June 20, 1890 in Homestead, Pennsylvania. One hundred thirty-five years earlier, in 1755, Homestead had heard the woods ring with the screams of Indians and the crack of muskets when young Colonel George Washington rode into a French and Indian ambush on General Braddock's ill-starred march to Fort Duquesne. But by the twentieth century it was the roar and clang of steel mills that echoed throughout the city.

Posey's grandfather had been a slave who, upon his freedom, moved to Washington, D. C. to become a preacher. Posey's father, C. W. Posey, Sr., was a riverboat engineer on the Ohio river, the first Negro ever so licensed. Later, as general manager of the Delta Coal

Cum Posey.

Company, he would invest in a fleet of coal barges and spread out into banking and real estate. He was well on his way to a modest fortune when Cumberland Willis Posey, Jr. was born.

Posey's mother had a more academic, cultured background. Her father had fought in the Civil War—indeed, she was born in the first year of the war. She became the first Negro to graduate from Ohio State University, as well as the first Negro to teach there. She was also an artist, and her home was covered with her paintings.

Cum was the youngest of three children, and like his mother was very light skinned. He might have been able to pass for white, but his wife, also quite light, insisted that the Poseys were black and all had "good color to them."

Captain Posey could afford to send his son to the best schools, and in 1909 Cum enrolled at Penn State to study chemistry, although his real love seemed to be sports. He stood 5′9″, weighed 145 pounds, and made the freshman basketball team with ease. The following year he was on the varsity.

While Cum was growing up, 1900–1905, the Keystone Giants, starring Emmett Bowman and Booth Wilson, had been the kings of the black clubs in western Pennsylvania. They were supplanted by the Pittsburgh Giants, owned by a saloon-keeper on Wylie Avenue and featuring Dallas Carter, Harvey Pangborn, Mule Armstrong, and pitcher Seth Hall, who was once credited with 95 strikeouts in one five-game stretch.

The semipro Murdock Grays were entertaining steelworkers with games at Homestead Park on weekends. Most of the players came from the Harbison-Walker brickyard and the Carnegie-Illinois steel mills. In 1910 manager Terry Veney changed their name to the Homestead Grays and signed up 19-year-old Cum Posey to play outfield. The players passed the hat and split the receipts, such as they were.

Posey, meanwhile, had quit Penn State. He had been dropped from the basketball squad for low grades and, with his older brother Seward (nicknamed "See"), he organized the Monticello-Delaney semipro basketball team. The following year he was being hailed as the greatest colored basketball player in the country.

Posey played basketball in the winter and baseball in the summer. In 1912 he went to the Grays with a plan: He offered to take charge of booking their games and putting the players on a full-time schedule. Veney took him up on it.

In 1913 the budding entrepreneur married Ethel Truman. They would have five daughters. That year Posey also enrolled at Pitt to resume his aborted academic career. He didn't play on the Pitt team, however. Instead, he formed the first great black basketball team in America, the Loendi Big Five, and turned openly professional. The team starred Posey, James "Stretch" Sessoms, William T. Young, William "Big Greasy" Betts, and James "Pappy" Ricks. They played for $25 a game. Eventually, for a big game, such as one against the famous New York Celtics, they collected $75. In 1919 they would claim the national championship.

The Grays, meanwhile, were also commanding a bigger and bigger reputation. "Brother" Pace and Sell Hall did the pitching. In 1915 they were joined by Charles "Lefty" Williams, who would stay with the club for 21 seasons and might today be considered one of the best black left-handers of all time except for the fact that the Grays were not members of the black leagues. Second baseman Aaron Russell was captain of the club until 1915 when he took over managing and Posey replaced him as captain.

That year Posey returned to academia one more time, to Holy Ghost College (now Duquesne). He enrolled as "Charles W. Cumbert," presumably to disguise his professional extracurricular activities, for he also played on the school's basketball team and became its leading scorer. In addition, he was captain of the golf team.

Meanwhile, in 1917 Posey replaced Russell as manager of the Grays.

In 1918 the new manager picked up little Oscar Owens to join the pitching staff. "We called him Iron Man," said Vic Harris, who joined the team seven years later. "He'd pitch every day if you'd let him." Owens and Williams formed a potent left-right pitching combination.

The 1931 Homestead Grays. Front (left to right) are George Britt, Lefty Williams, Jud Wilson, Vic Harris, Ted Radcliffe, Bill Perkins, Ted Page, and, rear (left to right), Cum Posey, Reed, Jap Washington, Bill Evans, Joe Williams, Josh Gibson, George Scales, Oscar Charleston, and Charlie Walker.

"Owens was about the same size as Williams," said Buck Leonard, recounting a story he was told years later. "Both of them were about the same color, same size. Sometimes Oscar Owens would pitch one day and Lefty Williams the next day, and the people would say the same man pitched one day with his right hand and the next day with his left hand, because they couldn't tell them apart."

The Grays played all around the tristate area—western Pennsylvania, West Virginia, and Ohio. It was practically their private domain until a crisis struck in 1922. Old-time pitching great William "Dizzy" Dismukes brought some hard-muscled coal miners from Birmingham up north, called them the Pittsburgh Keystones, and challenged the Grays' preeminence. The stars of the Keystones were fast-baller Harry Salmon and catcher Larry Brown. Most alarming of all, the Keystones were on salary and were waving contracts at the Grays as well.

Posey decided on a drastic move to save the Grays. He went to Charlie Walker with a request to bankroll the club.

"Charlie was a good businessman," Ted Page said. "Cum just wasted the money."

"Charlie Walker was a great guy," Clint Thomas of Hilldale said, "but I didn't like Cum Posey. He was kind of a greedy guy."

Shortstop Jake Stephens recalled:

> Walker had the money, Posey had the brains. Every fall Walker would buy me a suit of clothes and an overcoat. Cum Posey knew where to go and get the players. They were two good men. Charlie Walker liked the booze—he'd wine and dine, pal. Cum Posey liked the women. Every town he was in he had a woman. He'd say to me, "You don't know, I might be your father; I used to go to York. I may be your pappy."

"Why, you old so-and-so," Jake would retort.

But Posey had the last word. When one of his girlfriends broke a date in order to meet Stephens instead, Posey called his shortstop in for a pointed interview. "To start with, Stephens," he said, "my ball players don't monkey with my women. Or they don't play for me any more. Get the message?"

Jake swallowed. "I get the message, Mr. Posey," he said.

While Posey concentrated on his basketball venture, Walker ran the baseball team—and drove the team bus. They went to the white Pittsburgh Pirates and made a deal to use Forbes Field—though not the locker room—when the Pirates were on the road. Now the Grays played to big crowds and could match the Keystones' salary offers. Before long, they had run the invaders out of town.

In 1923 the Eastern Colored League was formed, but the Grays were doing so well they couldn't afford to give up barnstorming in order to join. "Posey made more money independent," outfielder Vic Harris said. "He could play Beaver Falls, places around Pennsylvania there, and he would get 75% of the gate receipts in some of those towns. They had so many teams around, they kept us playing every day."

Posey even raided the league teams. Spitballer Sam Streeter and second baseman George Scales came from the New York Lincoln Giants; outfielder Dennis Graham came from the Bacharachs; and Harris jumped from the Cleveland Tate Stars. And the biggest catch of all, Smokey Joe Williams, came from the Lincolns.

The Grays had an exciting team, with Jap Washington, an ex-Keystone, on first base, and Moe Harris and Bobby Williams at second and short. Posey himself played outfield with Vic Harris and Graham. The pitching staff was one of the best in the country, white or black— Joe Williams, Lefty Williams, Owens, Streeter, and George Britt.

Posey reportedly offered $10 to his players for every home run they hit, but he soon had to withdraw the offer or he would have gone broke.

In 1926 the Grays claimed they won 43 straight games. Among their victims were some of the better league clubs—the Hilldales, Black Sox, and Lincolns. "A semipro team in Coshocton, Ohio, near Zanesville, ended the streak," Vic Harris said. "The umpire called a balk on Sam Streeter and caused us to lose the ball game. Then we ran it back up to 10–something more wins." Their overall record for the year: a reported 140–13, with 10 ties.

That October the Poseymen felt confident enough to challenge the white big leaguers themselves, including Lefty Grove (13–13), Goose Goslin (.354), George Burns (.358), and the American League batting leader, Heinie Manush (.378). For nine innings the Grays fought to a tie, 6–6, then lost in the tenth, 11–6. In a return match, however, Joe Williams beat the big leaguers, 6–5, before 9,000 fans in Forbes Field. Britt won the third game on a one-hitter 2–1, and finally, Webster McDonald, on loan, pitched the Grays to a 5–1 victory over spitballer Picus Jack Quinn (10–11). If Posey was feeling pretty cocky that winter, he had reason to be.

In 1927, it is said, the Grays were the only black club in the East to make money.

That autumn they met the white big leaguers again and were jolted by four straight defeats, including a humiliating one-hitter by Rube Walburg (17–13) of the Athletics. Finally Joe Williams and Britt salvaged their pride with a double-header victory, 5–0 and 5–1.

A year later the Grays won two straight from the whites, ancient Joe Williams beating Walberg (18–14) and Lefty Williams beating Cleveland's George Uhle (12–17).

At 37, Posey realized he was slowing up afield and benched himself, turning the field captain duties over to Harris, whose style of play he liked. ("Posey played to win," Vic said. "He was fiery, and he knew I was fiery too.") Cum had stopped playing with the Loendis two years earlier. In 1927 he formed a new team, which he also called the Grays. Against the famous New York Celtics, they won three and lost five.

In the spring of 1930 Posey took the Grays to spring training in Hot Springs, Arkansas, a move that may have enticed several stars to jump to the Grays, including the one and only Oscar Charleston, who agreed to play first base.

Another who made the jump was outfielder Ted Page of the Brooklyn Royal Giants. "Cum Posey was the shrewdest owner that I played for," he said. "Billing, booking ball teams, getting good attractions, getting good gate guarantees."

On a sultry night in Pittsburgh that summer Posey pulled off one of the shrewdest coups in the annals of black baseball. He signed a rawboned young catcher named Josh Gibson to a Homestead contract.

Vic Harris called that 1930 club the best Grays team of all time. "That's when we beat the Monarchs when they came out East with their lights. They'd beaten everybody. They were the team out West, the Grays were the team out East. We took them, lights and all. They won one ball game out of the 12 we played." Joe Williams and Kansas City's Chet Brewer hooked up in one unforgettable duel under the lights, Joe winning 1–0 in 12 innings on a one-hitter with 27 strikeouts!

There was no league that year, so in October Posey challenged the Lincoln Giants to a play-off to settle the dispute over who was the best in the East. Lefty Williams won the first game, his 28th straight, and "Samson" Gibson slugged a long homer to help win the second game, 17–16, in 10 innings. Moving to Philadelphia, Gibson smashed a record-breaker in Bigler Field, then, in Yankee Stadium, uncorked the longest ball he ever hit and the longest ever seen in the House that Ruth Built—a blast over the left field roof that fell against the rear of the bull pen and just missed going out of the park completely. By the end of the tenth game, the Grays had won six and claimed the crown. (The tired players staggered into their bus after the final double header and drove to New Jersey for a game against the International League all stars. Back in 1930, even world champions had to make a buck any way they could.)

The 1931 club might have been even better. Gibson was present for the full year and bashed a putative 72 home runs over the fence against all comers, league and semipro, and the team ran up a 136–17 record. That autumn they played Connie Mack's All Stars—Manush, Harry Heilmann, Grove, Walberg, Uhle, Jimmy Dykes, and others. Only two newspaper clippings have been found for those games. They show the Grays winning, 10–7 and 18–0.

According to Vic Harris, they drew 20,000 fans for the first game and 12,000 for the second. The whites clamored for a third game but had already scheduled another team, and Commissioner Kenesaw Mountain Landis wouldn't let them change it.

All in all, 1931 had been a pinnacle year, Posey could look forward to a wonderful future.

Then disaster struck.

Gus Greenlee, the Pittsburgh fight promoter and numbers king, decided to move into the baseball picture, and he did it in a big way. This was far more serious than the Keystone challenge of a decade earlier. Greenlee had big money, and he spent it.

Gus Greenlee (left) with Vic Harris. Photo courtesy Johnny Taylor.

If Greenlee had been white, he would never have passed the scrutiny of Kenesaw Mountain Landis and been allowed to buy a big-league franchise. His financial sources were, frankly, unsavory. Yet almost everyone who speaks of Greenlee liked him and insists that his impact on black baseball was benign.

Greenlee had begun his career high-jacking beer trucks going to Chicago, according to Judy Johnson. Then he and his partner, Joe Vito, "started in the numbers game."

For a penny a bettor could put his money on a "number"—such as the last three digits of the volume on Wall Street that day—and if he was right, he would get back $5, or 500-to-one. (The real odds were 1,000-to-one.) At that time the "numbers" business was illegal and subject to government prosecution. Now of course it is not only legal, most state governments sponsor it themselves under the name of "lottery." (Nevertheless it was one of the excuses given later by Branch Rickey for not paying black owners for Jackie Robinson and other players he took—he sneered that black baseball was "in the zone of a racket.")

The odds, of course, were heavily in the house's favor. But if, by unlucky coincidence, there was a particularly large volume of bets on one number and it happened to come up, it could wipe out the numbers banker. Writing in *The Invisible Men,* historian Donn Rogosin says Greenlee won absolute control of the North Side numbers game when he became the only banker to pay off on one particularly large "hit." It won him a reputation for honesty.

With his profits Gus invested in real estate, including several buildings and the Crawford Grille, a two-story restaurant and dance hall on Wylie Avenue in Pittsburgh's black "Hill" section. Some of the top entertainers of the day performed there—Duke Ellington, Count Basie, Lena Horne, the Mills Brothers, and others. "Everybody who knew everybody used to hang out there," said pitcher Johnny Taylor. Gus himself held court there, surrounded by fawning listeners.

"Greenlee was big, above five-six, about 225 pounds," said second baseman Dick Seay. "He looked like the racketeer that he was. Dressed neat, big expensive hats, always a big crowd around him. I imagine he was something like Diamond Jim Brady, you know, always had a crowd."

"He carried $100-dollar bills all over his pockets," Judy Johnson added. "Gus made a lot of money, he didn't know how much money he had, and only through his wife he saved it."

Ted Page recalled Gus as

a great big man and a fine guy. Not the joking type of fellow, not the humorous type. He was all business. Not an educated man, but he was one of the smart illiterate types—although he wasn't really illiterate by any means, he could read and write. He was the type of man who could see far into possibilities, something that could turn you into some good money. And his heart was as big as his automobile. He'd give you money in the middle of winter. When a player requested money, no problem. Maybe he was too liberal. He was a gambler, made wild investments in sports. Boxers—he had a stable of fighters. Built a home for them. These things cost money.

"Greenlee was the swellest fellow you ever met in your life," nodded pitcher Jesse "Mountain" Hubbard. "You never met a man like him. Didn't care what kind of trouble you were in, he'd do you a favor—any favor you asked. I mean *strangers!* And ball players—he'd give them his heart."

In 1932 Posey and his Grays were hit hard by the Hard Times. "Posey got broke and couldn't pay off," explained Leonard. "That's how Gus Greenlee got half of the players from the Grays." By mid-season Greenlee had bought most of the Grays, lock, stock, and Oscar Charleston! He snatched Posey's top drawing card, Gibson, and the entire Grays infield—Charleston, Pistol Johnny Russell, Jake Stephens, Judy Johnson, Jud Wilson—plus Ted Page, and pitcher-catcher Ted "Double Duty" Radcliffe.

It left the Grays devastated. Only captain Vic Harris, Joe Williams, and the rest of the pitchers remained loyal.

"Of course he had money behind him," shrugged Page. "When a guy got $250 a month, during those years, that was big money. You got

Gus Greenlee (standing, far left) with the Pittsburgh Crawfords in 1932. Also pictured are Satchel Paige (fourth from left) and Oscar Charleston (standing, second from right). Photo courtesy Craig Davidson.

a dollar and a quarter or a dollar and a half a day for your eating money, that was pretty good money."

"The man gave us so much more money," said Radcliffe. "I'll show you how bad he wanted us: He sent us to Hot Springs, Arkansas the next spring—the only time in my life I went to spring training on the 18th of February—went before the big leaguers would go there. He had plenty of money, he didn't care. Greenlee was one of the best."

From the Birmingham Black Barons Greenlee picked up catcher Bill Perkins, pitcher Sam Streeter, and outfielder Jimmy Crutchfield. But his biggest coup of all was signing lanky Satchel Paige from the bankrupt Cleveland club.

Greenlee immediately began capitalizing on his two stars, Josh and Satch. Josh reputedly hit 67 homers for him that year (all games). Whenever the Crawfords went on the road, Gus advertised that Josh would hit at least one home run and Satch would strike out the first nine men.

Greenlee also dug into his pockets for $60,000 to build Greenlee Field, perhaps the only black-owned park in the country. (The grandstand didn't have a top on it, and the sun beat down mercilessly.)

Posey fought back. In September he brashly challenged Greenlee's Crawfords to a four-game city series and annihilated them. Lefty Williams and Joe Williams combined to beat Paige in the first game 13–10. George Britt won the second 6–4. The Craws won the third, 8–1, but the Grays crushed them in the finale, 5–1.

Posey actually fielded two teams that year. He also sponsored the Detroit Wolves, largely made up of ex-St. Louis Stars players such as Cool Papa Bell, Willie Wells, and Mule Suttles. Why he didn't merge the two clubs is not clear; he might very well have built a dynasty that would have endured for decades. Instead, the financial strain of supporting two teams in the depression was too much, and Posey let the Wolves go after one season.

Still, in October, Greenlee felt strong enough to challenge a white National League all-star club—pitchers Larry French (18–16), outfielders Hack Wilson (.297) and Johnny Fredericks (.299), and others. The Craws whipped them five games out of six.

Financially, however, Gus would say later, he lost $30,000 on his baseball venture in 1932.

He could cover his losses from his numbers business, which was thriving. There were no Brinks armored trucks in those days, and Johnson remembered seeing henchmen carrying sacks of coins from Greenlee's office to the cars waiting to take them to the bank. "At that time gang war was on," Judy said, "but they didn't have guards, because everyone was afraid to touch Gus."

Leonard recalled:

The banks used to stay open an extra hour or two every evening to get that numbers money. And everybody knew it was going on—the chief of police, the burgess (mayor), everybody. When the county was going to come in for a raid, Greenlee would get a notice, and everybody would close down. There would be no business that day or night. The police would come in and search and look, search and look, then they'd go away, and it would be a month or so before they came back again. Of course, you know for that kind of protection, you were payin' something. The chief of police was in with them.

Ted Page remembered:

I remember 1932 when I came to the Crawfords, at the end of the season I wasn't going any place to play ball. This year I didn't have any place to go. I was just hanging around the Crawford Grille. This was a real sad time in our baseball. Gus said, "What you gonna do all winter?"

"I don't know, man."

He said, "OK, I got something for you to do." You know, he had the number business. They had an old vacant house or second floor, in Hazlewood at this time, they had a long space up there where they had tables where they turned in all the numbers. This was the headquarters for it. They turned their numbers in like three o'clock in the day. They gave me a chair, my job was to sit right down stairs on the sidewalk and ring a bell. Anybody who was coming in who wasn't supposed to be there, I would just push a button to alert them upstairs to get rid of all that money. That's all I did. I remember so well my pay for each week: $15 a week. I got paid by Gus all winter.

Later I gathered why Gus did this. Because right along about this time I had developed a reputation for jumping around. Whoever treated me the best in my opinion, that's who I was going to play with next year. This is why Gus did this. I sat down in this chair from about one o'clock till about 3:30, when they had finished up counting all the money, sacked it and put it in the bank. That's all I did. I never pushed the button. I did practically nothing all winter for $15 a week. You say, How did you manage? I was getting then from Gus (during the season) $50 a week, which was $200 a month, to play ball. And this was *big* money during those years. I paid for my room and board ten bucks—room *and* board. And I was still five bucks to the good. I had all the rest of the day to hustle whatever I could. I had a very fine winter.

The ball players recognized a soft touch when they saw one. Judy Johnson was paid to chauffeur Greenlee to Chicago. Dick Seay and Jimmy Crutchfield were experts at conning their boss. Seay grinned:

We used to go around the bars. We wanted a little money. Jimmy would say, "Come on, let's go get Gus." So we'd find out where Greenlee was. We'd get him with four or five pretty girls and a gang around him. Jimmy would say, "Hello, Pop, what you doing, boy? How about 50?" Gus

would say, "Man, get out of here, I don't have any time for that." Jimmy
would say, "Boss, you can't do that." He'd be kind of embarrassed and
we'd get our 50. But he wouldn't take it out of our pay. By that time he'd
forgotten all about it. Jimmy out-conned him.

In 1933 Greenlee took two historic steps, as vital to the survival of
black baseball as were Rube Foster's original Negro National League
and J. L. Wilkinson's lights.

First, he took the lead in re-forming the two old leagues into one
new Negro National League of six teams—the Crawfords, Chicago,
Baltimore, Nashville, Detroit, and Columbus.

Posey's Grays stayed out. Posey struggled to keep two teams afloat,
the Grays and the Wolves. To add insult to injury, Greenlee raided the
Wolves and picked up Bell, plus pitcher Leroy Matlock.

That August Greenlee made his second, and perhaps biggest,
contribution to blackball history. He and Tom Wilson of Nashville
organized the first East-West, or All-Star, game, to be played in
Chicago's Comiskey Park about one month after the white leagues had
played their first All-Star game in the same stadium. The fans voted
for their choices to start the game, much as they do now, and the
nation's two leading black papers, the Pittsburgh *Courier* and the
Chicago *Defender,* gave the game good publicity, printed ballots and
tabulated votes. Twenty thousand fans turned out, a good total in the
tough times.

In future years the game would grow into the biggest spectacle of
the Negro League season, eclipsing the World Series as the major
event on the calendar. Crowds grew to 30,000 and even 50,000. The
receipts from that one game were often the difference between red
and black ink for the year for many a team. The game also provided a
stage for the best black talent in the country, and white writers even
dropped in to tell their readers of the stars they saw. The classic, as it
soon was called, may also have been a big factor in the eventual death
of black baseball, as the white owners took a look at the stadium full of
black fans and began to think more seriously of tapping that potential
fan reservoir for themselves.

In the pennant race that year, the Crawfords lost the first-half
pennant to Chicago by one game. No final standings were published
for the second half. Greenlee declared his club the winner, though
Chicago disputed it.

Yet once more Greenlee declared a net loss for the year—
$50,000—which he shrugged off as an "investment."

In 1934 Posey "was still kind of desperate for money," as Buck
Leonard put it. Most of his Players looked for lifeboats to abandon

ship. Even captain Vic Harris, the last of the loyalists, finally listened to Greenlee's blandishments and defected. Joe Williams had retired. The old Grays were no more.

In fact, the club was down to about six players when Williams, tending bar in Harlem, called Charlie Walker with a new recruit, Buck Leonard. "I was wondering why he picked me up," Buck later mused. "I guess it was because he didn't have any money to pay us. I got $125 a month, plus 60 cents a day on which to eat—sixty cents!" That totaled $562 for a four and a half-month season:

> We were supposed to get paid the first and the 15th. The mornin' of the first, the mornin' of the 15th. They cut that *mornin'* of the 15th out. You got to *make* the 15th, you get paid the mornin' of the 16th. Takin' all kind of ticks on you. If you didn't like it, you could just quit and come home. But if you wanted to stay there, then you just had to go along with it.

Posey may have been tight-fisted—he had no alternative—but Leonard said he was popular with the players. "Kind of a quiet guy, but he knew baseball. Taught me two or three things I've never forgotten. Taught me how to hit left-handed pitchers, taught me to use an open stance with left-handers. Taught me how to throw the ball when the pitcher's covering first base. And he told me not to try to steal any bases; told me to quit running, I wasn't fast enough to steal bases."

That July 4 the Grays met the Crawfords at Greenlee Field. Satch took the mound for the Craws and blew the Poseys away with a no-hitter and 17 strikeouts.

In 1934 "we just scraped around and scraped around," Leonard said, until the Grays got together nine able-bodied men. Posey picked up slugging John Beckwith as catcher. Beck reported with his own catching gear and at the end of the season demanded that Posey pay him for it. Cum refused, whereupon the big catcher threatened to punch him in the nose. Leonard and the other players sided with Beckwith, but Posey wouldn't relent.

In 1935 Posey decided to fight fire with fire. He went to another Pittsburgh racketeer with the clout to stand up to Greenlee on even terms—Rufus "Sonnyman" Jackson. "We weren't doing much," Leonard said, "until Rufus Jackson came in there with some fresh money."

Thirty-three years old, Jackson had come out of Columbus, Georgia in 1921 to work in the steel mills. He was soon laid off

however and began living by his wits. By 1934 he was running a
numbers operation in competition with Greenlee. Leonard said:

> They had a "night roll." Jackson had a poolroom, some fellow would
> come in there nine o'clock at night and roll some dice on the table and
> get a number, and they would pay off on that. He had two-three gam-
> bling houses—shoot crap, play poker, black jack, all kinds of games.
> Every time you bet, the man would rake out so much for his cut. Then he
> had a beer tavern called The Skyrocket. Oh, a big place. Sold beer, wine,
> whiskey, and everything. Had a restaurant in the back. He finally ended
> up with a lot of "piccolos"—nickelodeons, jukeboxes. He had about 400
> or 500 up and down the Allegheny and Monongahela rivers. That's
> where his money came from.

Jackson was not above a little strong-arm extortion, Leonard
added. "If you don't do so-and-so, we gonna kill you."

Posey talked Jackson into putting his money into the Grays as a

Rufus "Sonnyman" Jackson, co-owner of the Washington Homestead Grays.

cover-up for his other activities. "The baseball team was covering up for his undercover stuff," Buck said. "Baseball was just a cover-up. Both of them (Jackson and Greenlee) had a baseball team. That was to keep the law off them, see. They weren't making any money with the baseball teams. The numbers business and the rackets, that was their business.

Baseball just sharpened the rivalry between the two gangsters.

When Greenlee bought his team a new bus, a GM Special, Jackson bought the Grays a bus to replace the two Buicks that Posey had been using to transport his players. "It didn't have any back door to it," Leonard remembers. "Of course that's against the law now."

Suddenly, in April 1935 the Pittsburgh *Courier* informed its readers in 72-point headlines:

GRAY'S CO-OWNER DEFIES
GANGLAND DEATH THREAT
Federal Men Set
Trap; Gunmen
Make Escape in
Hail of Bullets
Homestead Bridge Scene of Midnight Warfare As
Attempt Is Made to Capture Men Who Threatened
Life of Rufus Jackson—Extortion Plot Bared

The extortionists, three black men and one white, had demanded $500 on the threat of death. Their note hinted that they wouldn't be too disappointed with the second alternative. The money, they said, should be left on the window sill of an abandoned shack at the end of the Homestead bridge at two A.M.

At five minutes to two, Jackson and his wife drove up to the bridge, Jackson got out and walked alone across the bridge. He deposited the package of bills as directed, while inside the shack 25 FBI agents crouched, guns drawn. Then Jackson turned and walked slowly back across the bridge. In a moment a hail of gunfire cracked in the night behind him and he sprinted for cover as the FBI men poured out of the building firing into the woods at four fleeing men. A fedora hat was all they found.

Jackson's only public statement was that the incident was just an old grudge by certain "business and political enemies."

The headlines created quite a stir down in Florida, where the Grays were training. After the excitement died down, Jackson and Posey resumed their more prosaic struggle to keep the Grays afloat. Jackson tried but failed to incorporate the team, but he and Posey assumed all the debts and ran the team at a loss. It would be seven years before they would be in the black again.

Thereafter, Leonard admitted, "I played with the Homstead Grays 17 years and never missed a payday."

In 1935 Posey and Jackson felt strong enough at last to enter the league. Two other numbers kings, Alejandro Pompez and Abe Manley, both of New York, also sponsored teams, the New York Cubans and the Brooklyn Eagles, giving the league eight clubs. (The numbers, after all, were the best source of black capital in those depression days.)

The Grays played some games in Forbes Field, home of the white Pirates, after the National League clubs finished their double-headers. "After everybody got out of the ball park, we'd start our game at 6:15. We'd call it a twilight game, and we'd play until it got dark. We'd have about an hour and a half, two hours to play. We'd get in about seven innings. We'd charge a dollar, and you could sit anywhere you wanted to in the park. We would have 6,000 or 7,000 even after the Pirates had already played."

Greenlee still operated in Greenlee Field. He had stretched a canvas cover on poles over the grandstand to give some shade. Stymied by the Pennsylvania Blue Laws, the Crawfords couldn't play on Sundays, so Gus scheduled a "milkman's matinee," to begin at 12:01 Monday morning. The team played to empty stands. "People had to go to work Monday morning," Leonard explained. "Drunks were there, but you can't depend on them guys."

Gus was always a high roller. After he bought his bus, he no longer needed the two Lincoln automobiles he had been using to transport the club. So he bet the New York Black Yankees the cars if they could beat the Craws a double-header. New York won the first game, and their big pitcher Jesse "Mountain" Hubbard went out to pitch the second. "You ain't gonna last two innings," Greenlee taunted him.

"Boys, put those license plates on the cars," Jess laughed back. "We're gonna drive them home."

And they did.

Greenlee's fighters were also a drain on his finances, Leonard chuckled:

> He had about eight or ten of them. We were joking about how he was feeding them. He said, "You've got about ten fellows around here, and some of them aren't going to ever box. They're going to eat, but they aren't going to ever box." One time we ran an excursion train from Pittsburgh to Detroit. Everybody was going to Detroit to see John Henry Lewis (the world lightheavyweight champ) fight. John Henry won all right, but he wasn't so impressive. Somebody told Gus, "You can't book John Henry yourself. He can't fight out here in the sticks. John Henry's got to fight in New York if he's going to make any money. He'll make some money, and you'll make some money."
> "I'm not going to turn my boy over to nobody." But he finally did.

John Henry fought Joe Louis (for the heavyweight title) in New York. And that's when he made his best money.

The Crawfords were also riding high. Satchel Paige had walked out to pitch in North Dakota, but Matlock more than filled his place. "I've stayed 17 years in the league," Leonard said, "and I've never seen a team better than that team. No team had two catchers like Gibson and Perkins. And we didn't have the pitching they had." Monte Irvin also calls the 1935 Craws the greatest black team he ever saw. They won the first half of the league, then defeated Pompez' Cubans, four games to three, in the play-offs.

The Grays finished with a respectable .500 average.

Greenlee was riding high. But, like Rube Foster before him, he was finding out that running a league was a thankless job. His fellow owners took some of their frustrations out on him.

It had cost him $2,000 to operate the league since 1933, Greenlee wrote, and his own losses had run into tens of thousands of dollars a year. But "only a few of my associates share that vision. They want immediate results and substantial profits. But until there is a bigger demand, every owner must make sacrifices."

Gus had been accused of taking all the profits from the East-West game for himself. He called such charges "the vilest, meanest kind of ingratitude." Actually, he complained, none of the other teams paid their league dues as promised—money needed to pay umpires and administer the league. Gus could make more money as an independent, he warned. "Up to this time I have been a congenial fellow." But if these rumors of rebellion develop into factual realities, "you'll see a fighting Greenlee equipped with everything needed to win."

In 1936 the Craws won the second half of the league race, but there was no play-off. The Grays finished in the second division. That October Greenlee's stars went south of the border to Mexico to play a powerhouse white lineup that featured Jimmy Foxx (.338), Doc Cramer (.292), Pinky Higgins (.289), Vern Kennedy (21–9), Earl Whitehill (14–11), and 40-year old Rogers Hornsby. They lost two and tied one in extra innings.

Then disaster struck. Greenlee's friends in the county government were swept out of office. And "he had a lot of men around him who didn't have his best interests at heart." One in particular was a janitor, who began tipping the cops off. With their boss on the run, the Crawfords began looking for other work, and when Dominican dictator Rafael Trujillo waved a bankroll, they were ready to jump. Paige (back from the Dakotas) was the first to go, Gibson was next, followed by Bell, Matlock, outfielder Sam Bankhead, and others.

They say Greenlee actually wept when his best players disappeared over the horizon heading south.

Although the players came back later that summer, Bell promptly sprinted to Mexico, Paige shuffled down to Venezuela, and Greenlee was forced to sell Bankhead, plus his last star, Gibson, to Posey for $2,500. Posey jumped at the offer.

Josh "just put new life into everybody," Leonard said. Gibson and Leonard provided a one-two home run punch that would later be compared to Ruth and Gehrig or to Mantle and Maris. Gibson and Posey's son-in-law, Ray Brown, formed a fine battery. The Grays surged to the pennant in 1937. Their overall record against all comers was a reputed 152–11. The Craws meanwhile finished next to last.

The Grays would go on to win nine pennants in a row. Like the Grays, the country's economy was also reviving, though more slowly. Even in the Depression, Homestead, seven miles outside of Pittsburgh, was a bustling steel town. Leonard recalled it:

> I had never seen so much money in all my life 'till I went out there. That's what made me stay out there 17 years. The United States Steel mill was the only thing there. Fifteen to 20,000 people working. When I got there, things were humming. You talkin' about beer taverns! Umm-umm-umm! There was some beer drunk. Slovakians and Italians—everybody was a foreigner out there. (No, we didn't have whites to our games.) Something else they had out there—a red light district. They had 45 women in one block—45 women doin' business with men. And what was so queer about it to me, it was black women doin' business with white men. All the women were colored, but all the men were white. After all, it may have been the best thing for them. What I mean is, they were sure to get their money.

As for the players, Buck said:

> We were always booked somewhere every day. There never came a day when we weren't booked to play a game somewhere. Never. Out of all those 17 years we didn't miss but two ball games, and both of them were during the war when gas was rationed and we missed our train connections. We'd play every day. Go out to Norristown, play a semipro game. Get maybe $75. For the whole *team!* Of course we were on salary. We'd make expenses in the middle of the week. Sundays were our "gettin'-out-of-the-hole days." That's when we'd make enough to pay everybody's salaries.

Another youngster who traveled with the team was writer Ric Roberts of the Pittsburgh *Courier.* "Posey gave black baseball status," he said, recalling his own high school days when his mother refused to let him play baseball, considering it a sport for low-lifes. She insisted that Ric wash windows instead to earn money for college. Now, Roberts discovered, "Posey made his ball players look the part, dress well. These guys [Posey and J. L. Wilkinson of the Monarchs] began to give the game dignity. That took some doing in the depression."

"We thought we could beat anybody," Sam Bankhead said, "but we didn't *play* anybody. I remember one time Mr. Posey offered to play [William] Benswanger, the owner of the Pirates, winner-take-all. But Benswanger just said, 'Can't play you.'"

Benswanger was a shrewd man.

Instead of playing the Grays, Benswanger was reportedly eyeing them enviously for his own Pirates. Alarmed, Posey went to Benswanger and managed to talk him out of assigning any of his Grays, arguing that such a move could break up the Negro leagues.

In 1937 Posey decided to move his Grays to Washington where he could play on Sunday and also take advantage of the growing black population there. They would split their home dates between the two cities, Pittsburgh and the capital, hopping from one to the other by bus. Leonard reported:

> We would play in Washington when the Senators were on the road and in Pittsburgh when the Pirates were away.
> We would leave Pittsburgh after midnight some Sunday morning to play a double header in Washington. That was 263 miles over the Pennsylvania Turnpike. We would get in Washington I would say around a quarter to eleven or eleven o'clock, go out and get a sandwich, and at that time we had to be at the ball park by 11:30. They would say, "If you're not here at 11:30, we're not going to open the gates, unless we're sure you're here." With the traveling we were doing, we weren't sure whether we were going to get there or not. One time I remember our bus broke down out near Hagerstown, Maryland, and we had to call Washington and tell them to send three taxicabs out there to pick us up to get to Washington to start the game at two o'clock.
> We'd play a semipro team, say in Rockville, Maryland, in the after-noon and a league game in Griffith Stadium that night. Or we'd play semipro teams around Pittsburgh. We'd play the Edgar Thomas Steel Mill team, and over in Braddock they had a team. We'd start at 6:30 and play as many innings as we could get in before dark. The Grays would get $75 to $100 to play the game. For the whole team! But Sundays and weekends were the days you really expected to make enough money to pay off your players. Those were the games you played in Forbes Field, Griffith Stadium, Yankee Stadium and those parks.
> Sometimes we'd stay in hotels that had so many bedbugs you had to put a newspaper down between the mattress and the sheets. Other times we'd rent rooms in a YMCA, or we'd go to a hotel and rent three rooms. That way you got the use of the bath, by renting three rooms. All the

ballplayers would change clothes in those three rooms, go to the ball park and play a double header—nine innings the first game, seven innings the second game.

The second game would be over about 6:15. We'd come back to the hotel and take a bath, then go down the street and eat and get back in the bus to go to Pittsburgh. The bus seats would recline—you'd be sitting there, and the drone of the motor would put you to sleep. We'd get back in Pittsburgh 7:30 in the morning, go to bed, get up around three o'clock, go up the river somewhere about twenty-five or thirty miles, play a night game, come back. Next evening the same thing. We logged 30,000 miles one summer. Of course you get tired around July or August. The people didn't know what we went through. They'd see us dragging around, they didn't know we'd ridden all night getting there.

You were tired, you'd ridden 200 miles to get there, rode all night last night maybe, you're going to play here today, and you got a game to play tonight somewhere. You've got to change your sweatshirt after this game, go somewhere maybe 50 miles to play tonight; you're trying to save a little from this evening's game for tonight's game. We used to play at Bushwick in New York on a Sunday evening, and go out to Freeport or out to somewhere on Long Island, and play Sunday night. Man, you're spent when you played a doubleheader at Bushwick or Yankee Stadium or the Polo Grounds. Then you go out there at night to play, you're stiff, tired and you're just forcing yourself.

We didn't have a paid trainer. We rubbed each other. If my back was hurting or my arm was sore, I'd get another player to rub it. And you'd tape yourself up the best you could. I know one time I got scratched on my leg in Washington, and we were going to Boston to play and up in New Hampshire. I needed three stitches in my leg, and they wouldn't put the three stitches in there because I was going to lose some games. I just played until it got well. Now it's got thin skin over it, and it gets inflamed every now and then. That comes from not taking care of it like it should be. Had I been in the major leagues, I would have had proper attention.

Posey shared the long overnight trips.
Ted Radcliffe said:

Posey did something that I didn't know any other club to do as long as I played in Negro baseball. We would play in Pittsburgh on a Saturday night and ride all night to play in Washington Sunday. He would have each man get whatever he ordered: roast beef, barbecue, chicken, whatever he wanted. He'd have his dinner on that bus ready for him when he came out of that ball park, plus he'd have plenty of pop and beer for them to drink. Nobody else ever did that. The three greatest men in Negro baseball were Posey, Wilkinson, and Abe Saperstein of Birmingham. They operated like big-league teams. They were the only ones had four or five sets of uniforms, the rest of them had two, you had to dry your uniform overnight on those other teams.

But the finances of black baseball were still parlous. Said pitcher Wilmer Fields:

Posey'd be up in the front seat of the bus having a fit afraid they were going to rain us out, especially if he thought they were going to have a good crowd. Back in the bus leagues, if you had 20,000 poople, we were going to play four-and-a-half innings of this game somehow.

The winter of 1937–38 Greenlee had left his canvas awning out, and when spring came it was ragged and torn. Greenlee's only gate attraction was catcher Pepper Bassett, whom he had gotten in the Josh Gibson deal. While Bassett had been with the Grays, he caught some exhibition games in a rocking chair. Greenlee capitalized on it to help attract fans. But his luck had run out. The Craws finished fourth, playing .500 ball. It was their last year in the league.

The Grays won the pennant, their second straight.

Pitcher Johnny Taylor remembered bouncing by bus through the mountains of West Virginia to play the Grays. They would wind down a mountainside into a valley that didn't look big enough to fit a ball field and begin going through batting practice and infield drills before empty seats. But as the afternoon went on, miners began to drift in, and by the time the game began, a good crowd was on hand. "They'd been waiting all summer," he said.

At first Posey refused to use booking agents. Buck Leonard explained:

We were gonna try and book ourselves around Philadelphia. There were teams around there in Camdem. Stonehurst had a team, South Philly had a team, the All-Lithuanians had a team, Black Meteors was a team in South Philly, all black boys, and Chester had a team. That was 12 or 15 teams right around Philadelphia. You could stay in Philadelphia in one hotel, go there and play that team, come back, go down there to South Philly, all around. You could stay in Philadelphia two weeks, you wouldn't play the same team.

But now Ed Gottlieb wouldn't book any team. See Posey was our booking agent, said he wasn't gonna pay that ten percent. He was going to book us instead. But now Ed Gottlieb had those teams fixed so that if he didn't book 'em they couldn't get any games. He booked the teams with each other. If one of those teams played us without Ed booking, then Ed wouldn't get that team other games. We didn't know that, so we just stopped letting Ed Gottlieb book us. We stood around there in Philadelphia four or five days, didn't have no games. Well, we finally woke up.

The same way it was in New York. Nat Strong was booking around New York. He owned the Bushwicks team there too. He'd send you a confirmation, where you gonna play, where you gonna change clothes. Out in the Midwest, around Chicago, Abe Saperstein was booking. A lot of our black owners used to think they could get by without doing that. A lot of time you'd sit around doing nothing. That booking agent's getting 10 percent from us, and he's getting 10 percent from the local boys too. He's getting 20 percent. But he's doin' the work. And he's keepin' everybody busy. And it's worth it.

One other thing about Ed Gottlieb: If we get rained out, we still got to pay the hotel bill where we're stayin'. If you need 400 or 500 dollars, go down there to Ed Gottlieb on Broad Street, bam, he'd give it to ya.

Do you remember one time when a circus had a big fire in Hartford? Barnum and Bailey and Ringling Brothers. All them folks got burned up. We played there the next night. Didn't have nobody in the ball park. Now a lot of times whatever money you made tonight to play, you'd have to pay that out tomorrow for gas, oil and eatin' money and hotel bills. We didn't play in no town two days. More or less, you moved every day. And you had to pay your room rent every night. The money you got today, that's the money you lived on tomorrow. So we went back to New York to the booker. He said, "What do you need?" "Three or four hundred dollars"—pretty good money back then. He let us have 300 or 400 dollars, but you know we had to pay him back.

That's how we got along with those bookin' agents.

They're gonna make some money for themselves. But they gonna make *you* some money. You got to have an agent.

Buck Leonard pointed out another problem:

When we played semipro teams they supplied the umpires. The winner would get 60 percent of the dollar and the loser would get 40. So naturally each umpire was trying to make his team get the 60. One time we were playing in a town outside Norfolk, Virginia. Every time we got in front the umpire would fix it so they'd tie the game. In the ninth inning we were leading by a couple of runs; our owner went in there and got the 60 percent. They tied the game in the last of the ninth inning; he went back in there and they split the money. We went out there and we got in front again; he went back in there and we got the 60 percent. They tied us again, and he split the money again. We were getting ready to go back out on the field again when we said, "Wait a minute, there's no way in the world we're going to win." We said, "Let's split it and we'll play no more."

The white Washington Senators were a big help to the Grays, Leonard said:

Clark Griffith said our league wasn't organized. We were organized, but we weren't recognized. If we were going to play a game in Griffith Stadium and got rained out, we're supposed to let the people know when they could come back to another game. We had a problem like this: We used to give the visiting team 30 percent of the gate receipts after expenses. Now if we got rained out with Newark on a Sunday and we were going to play the New York Cubans on a Thursday night, the Cubans didn't feel like we should use the Sunday rain checks on their game. So that's not a good organization. A good organization is where you can establish your home town and be willing and able to redeem your rain checks.

John Morrissey, the Senators' ticket manager, was the biggest help to our team, and to all Negro baseball. He's still in Washington, and I stop by and say hello every time I'm in Washington. When we were playing at Griffith Stadium, he would ask us how many we expected for the game. We'd say, "Well, 18,000." Or if Satchel Paige was coming in to play with Kansas City, we'd say, "30,000." He'd say, "Let us use our ticket sellers and let us have your tickets printed and let us handle everything for you." He even handled the publicity for us. When they announced the Washington Senators' games for the weekend, they would announce our games for the next weekend or for that Thursday night. At that time we were playing in Washington every Sunday that the Senators were away, and Tuesday and Thursday nights.

We would charge $1 for the bleachers, $2 for the grandstand, $2.50 for box seats. During the war when the people couldn't get much gas, that's when our best crowds were. People couldn't travel, so they would have to stay in Washington on weekends. After the war our crowds started dwindling again.

Mr. Morrissey took care of police protection too. If you're expecting 18,000, 25,000 or 30,000 people, you're going to need 12, 16 or 20 policemen. Our crowds were unruly quite a few times. Mr. Morrissey would go along with us. He'd say, "I know how things are now, people can't travel and they're mad, drinking, but we just have to bear with it."

After the game we'd go to the office and Mr. Morrissey had our statement made out, the visiting team's statement was made out, how much went to the revenue man, how much went to the visiting team, how much our end would be. The money was baled up with the statement sheet. Everybody's sheet was separated—our sheet, the visiting team's, the revenue man's. We'd go there, look at our statement, pick up our money, leave. He would even tell the visiting team how to operate their business. Mr. Morrissey was the greatest help, not only for the Homestead Grays but for Negro baseball, period.

"Mr. Posey was held in high esteem by the Senators," Roberts said—"Clark Griffith, Morrissey, everyone. They just thought he was a wonderful man."

Another Posey friend was Art Rooney, owner of the Pittsburgh Steelers football team. When Vic Harris slugged a white umpire, precipitating a racial free-for-all in Forbes Field, it was Rooney who interceded and headed off a lawsuit.

The Grays began to prosper, Leonard said:

By 1941 I was making $500 a month plus 75 cents a day eating money. In 1942 they doubled my pay to $1,000 a month. I wouldn't say Josh and I pulled a double holdout like Koufax and Drysdale. See, both of us had a chance to go to foreign countries to play, and we asked for the same amount of money that we were being offered. I told them what they were going to pay me down in Mexico and asked them would they equal it, and they said they would.

In 1942 the Grays drew 102,000 fans in ten games in Washington's Griffith Stadium. Sometimes they filled the park, especially if

Satchel Paige and the Monarchs were in town for the classic match-up of Paige versus Gibson.

Buck Leonard:

> We were drawing pretty good crowds—20,000, 26,000, 28,000. In 1942, we had 26,000 one night. That same year we played a game with Satchel Paige against Dizzy Dean, and we had 29,000. Cecil Travis of the Senators was in the Service, and he played with Dizzy. And we played another game against the Kansas City Monarchs and had 30,000. At the time Griffith Stadium didn't hold but 30,000. In 1945 we drew more than the Senators, and we weren't playing as many games.
>
> One day about 1942, Clark Griffith had come around and looked at our ball game, and when the game was over he sent word down there for Josh Gibson and me to come see him in his office. He said, "I want to talk to you fellows. You all played a good ball game today," and so on and so on. "You fellows got good size on you and you looked like you were playing to win. There's one thing I want to talk to you about. Sam Lacey [sports editor of the *Afro-American*], Ric Roberts [Pittsburgh *Courier*] and a lot of other fellows have been talking about getting you fellows on the Senators' team." He said, "Well, let me tell you something: If we get you boys, we're going to get the best ones. It's going to break up your league. Now what do you all think of that?" We said, "Well, we haven't given it much thought. We'd be happy to play in the major leagues and believe that we could make the major leagues, but so far as clamoring for it, we'll let somebody else do that." He said, "Well, I just wanted to see how you fellows felt about it." We said, "Well, if we were given the chance, we'd play all right, try to make it. And I believe we could make it." But we never heard from him again.

That was good news for Cum Posey, bad news for Washington's long-suffering white fans. While the Grays had been writing the most impressive winning record in baseball annals, the poor Senators were the butts of jokes. Yet they had a few good players—knuckle baller Dutch Leonard, base-stealer George Case, first baseman Mickey Vernon, second baseman Buddy Myer, and short stop Cecil Travis.

If Griff had added the Grays—Josh and Buck, Ray Brown, outfielders Cool Papa Bell and Bankhead—not only would he have filled Griffith Stadium but would have challenged the mighty Yankees year in and year out. But Griffith didn't seize the chance. He went back to his woeful Senators and empty seats, Gibson and Leonard went back to busting fences and winning pennants for the Grays.

Leonard recalled:

> I always thought the Senators might be first to take a Negro, because Washington was about half Negro then. I figured if half the city boycotted the games, the other half would come. But Griffith was always looking for Cuban ballplayers. He had Joe Cambria down there scouting for him. I guess he didn't have to pay them much money—but he wouldn't have had to pay us much either.

Posey was still a master talent hunter. He found youngsters like pitchers Roy Partlow and Johnny Wright. He also enticed veteran stars like Jud Wilson and Cool Papa Bell. When the black World Series was resumed in 1942, the Grays were in it of course. They lost to Paige and the Monarchs in four straight, but bounced back to beat the Birmingham Black Barons the next two years.

Buck Leonard again:

We used to play ball in Griffith Stadium by the football lights! Remember when they had the football lights? That's what we used to play by. Griffith Stadium had no lights then for baseball. I remember one night we were playing, it was kind of foggy, drizzling rain. The ball would go up and you *just could* see it. You couldn't get a good jump on a good line drive. Or get a good jump on a ground ball. A high fly would go up higher than the lights, go up in the dark. You're standing there waiting for it to come back down.

Then during the war we had portable lights that we put in the parks. We'd install them about six o'clock or 6:30 on poles all around the field. A big dynamo out there in the outfield generated the electricity for the lights. After the game was over, we would take down the poles. We used to have trouble with outfielders running into the poles. Jerry Benjamin ran into a pole up in Niagara, New York, one night and broke his ankle. He ran into one of the guy ropes while chasing a fly ball.

Sometimes we thought the belt was slipping in the dynamo. The lights would dim and then get bright, dim and get bright. We had to stop the game about five minutes so they could pick up a little. We'd put some belt dressing on the belt that turned the wheel, to keep the belt from slipping. Some people said they were giving us about as much light as we were paying for. They said we must have owed them some money, teasing us, you know.

One speedballer had a record strikeout one night under those lights.

During the war we couldn't go but 700 miles a month on the bus, because of gasoline rationing. Now from Pittsburgh to Washington was 263 miles, back to Pittsburgh was 263. Well that was over 500 miles for just one trip. You could ride maybe 100 miles more, then you're through. Had to put your bus up the rest of the month and take the train. One time the conductor told us, "We don't have room on the train for you, and we're not going to let you stand up." So we stayed in the baggage car. That's right. And played that night.

Nineteen forty-four was my biggest payday, $1,100 a month. Josh and I told Posey we were going to Mexico, that's why he raised us to $1,100. Here's my contract: I got $4,500 a season, May first to October first. A little less than $1,000 a month.

In 1945 the young Cleveland Buckeyes—the New York Mets of their day—shocked the Grays by winning the World Series in four straight games.

That winter, 1945, the dramatic announcement was out: The Brooklyn Dodgers had signed Jackie Robinson of the Monarchs. Don

Newcombe of the Newark Eagles, and Campanella of Baltimore were next. The scouts began swarming around every black team, including the Grays. In the big league raids that followed, the Grays would lose Luke Easter, Bob Thurman, and pitchers Wright, Partlow, and Luis Marquez. It decimated the team.

In January 1946 Posey's biggest star, Gibson, bitter at being overlooked by the majors, dropped dead from a drug overdose at the age of 35. The downcast Grays had just reported to spring training when a second shocking telegram arrived on March 28: Cum Posey himself was dead at the age of 54.

Said Roberts: "Posey and Wilkinson and the other owners, those were the guys who had persevered and risked their own personal equity to see that black baseball had some cash credibility. Cum Posey did a hell of a job. And nobody knows it."

A chapter in American history died with Cum Posey that day in Pittsburgh's Mercy Hospital. If he had lived just three weeks more, he would have seen Jackie Robinson play his first historic game in organized ball.

Black fans deserted the black teams, traveling hundreds of miles to see Robinson and the Dodgers. "We'd get 300 people to a game," Leonard said. "We couldn't even draw flies."

In 1948 See (Seymour) Posey sold his last star, Luke Easter, to the Cleveland Indians for $10,000. Leonard said:

> They were going to pay another $5,000 if he went to the majors. But when he went to the majors, Luke wanted the other $5,000 himself. He had an argument with the Homestead Grays' management. At that time Rufus Jackson was dead and his wife was in charge. Luke said he wasn't going if he didn't get the $5,000.

Rick Roberts:

> The last time I talked to See Posey, he was in his office, almost in tears, on his way to the hospital. He gave me hell: "How can you write about my ball players being snatched up by a pirate, didn't need a gun, hiding behind freedom for blacks?" He said it was like coming into a man's store and taking the commodities right off his shelf without paying a dime. "You don't know how much it cost me to build this team. I've been struggling with this damn thing since 1913. I guess I won't live to fight anymore."

In 1948 Gus Greenlee followed Cum Posey to the grave. Greenlee Field was torn down to make a housing project.

An era in baseball history had died.

A new one was about to be born.

23

J. L. Wilkinson:
The Gift of Light

We were the first ball club that ever played under lights. J. L. Wilkinson was the man who started it all, one of the finest men I've ever known. He was one white man who was a prince of a fellow. He loved baseball, and he loved his players. And he traveled right along with us every day, stayed at the same hotels we stayed at. One of the greatest owners I've ever known.

Newt Allen
Kansas City Monarchs

Even if J. L. Wilkinson had not owned one of the first two professional teams to play under lights regularly, he would have earned a high place in baseball history and in the Hall of Fame as the man who gave Satchel Paige his second chance—and Jackie Robinson his first. Without Wilkinson, it is just possible that Robinson might never have been ready for his date with history in 1947, and big league integration might either have failed or most likely been postponed several years longer.

Ironically, Wilkinson grew up in Des Moines, Iowa, the city he would later beat in the race for night baseball. He was born in the little town of Perry, Iowa, in 1874, the son of a college president, and attended Highland Park College in Des Moines, where he pitched for three years, while also playing semipro and professional ball on the side under the name of Joe Green. He played for such towns as Marshalltown, Creston, and Brooklyn, Iowa; in fact, he liked to tell people later, "Why, I pitched for Brooklyn."

Wilkie joined the Hopkins Brothers team, sponsored by a Des Moines sporting goods store. Hank Severeid, who later went on to the Boston Braves, caught him for two years. When the manager ran off with the gate receipts and left the team stranded in Fort Dodge, Iowa, the players elected Wilkinson to manage them.

The Hopkins brothers had two teams; the other one was an all-girls' team. Most of the "girls" were actually men wearing wigs, a common practice then—Rogers Hornsby, for instance, reportedly got his start on a girls' team in Texas.

But the minor leagues kept luring Wilkie's best players, so in 1912 he and J. E. Gall formed a new group, the All Nations, made up of blacks, Cubans, Mexicans, Orientals, and one girl advertised as "Carrie Nation"—ten players in all, including two pitchers: Jose Mendez and John Donaldson, one of the best left-handers in black annals. Either one could have been a big-league star, Wilkinson maintained. Virgil Barnes, who later won 16 games for the New York Giants, also played on the club.

They barnstormed through the little towns of prairie America— Iowa, Missouri, Nebraska, the Dakotas—traveling in a special Pullman, which had cost $25,000. They toured with a wrestling team and a dance band, so at each town they offered a ball game and wrestling match, followed by a dance. They even brought their own bleachers and canvas fence.

Bill Drake joined the pitching staff after Mendez' arm went bad. "I used to make Wilkinson so doggone mad," Drake laughed.

"They tell me that fellow is a pretty good hitter," Wilkie would say, nodding to a local slugger.

"If he's so good, what's he doing out here?" Drake retorted. "He's a white boy. I've *got* to be out here, there's nowhere else I can go. But if he's that good, he'd be in the big leagues. What's he doing out here?"

Still "I have fond memories," Drake said. "We'd go out in the small towns in Iowa, and we would take our tents and put them up, and we would sleep in those tents. And we'd go to restaurants and eat

J. L. Wilkinson (standing, second from left) with the Kansas City Monarchs. Also shown are Joe Rogan (back row, far left), Newt Allen (back row, far right), and Chet Brewer (left of Wilkinson).

during the day, and in the evening, we'd go fish. We just had a dandy good time."

The All Nations also visited the big cities for games against top semipro and black clubs. In 1915 they beat Rube Foster's American Giants two games out of three. The next year they beat the Indianapolis ABCs, starring Oscar Charleston, two straight—and the ABCs claimed the black world championship that year.

The national *Sporting Life* newspaper called them "strong enough to give any major league club a nip-and-tuck battle." But they suddenly met defeat at the hands of the army draft. While playing in remote Caspar, Wyoming, draft notices suddenly arrived for five of the 14 players, leaving exactly nine to finish the tour. Still, they won 34 of their last 35 games—their only loss was 1–0—before Wilkinson finally had to disband them. He revived them briefly for the 1919 season.

That winter Wilkie attended Rube Foster's meeting that founded the Negro National League. Historian Janet Bruce says Rube was reluctant to admit a white owner, but since Wilkinson held the lease to the American Association park in Kansas City, Foster had no choice. But, Bruce points out, as a white man, Wilkinson could make deals with white booking agents that black owners might not be able to. And he could sometimes keep the peace if interracial fights threatened to break out on the field.

Wilkinson immediately set about gathering a top-notch team. Mendez, Donaldson, and Drake came from All Nations. Rogan, Dobie Moore, Heavy Johnson, Andy Cooper, and others came from the black 25th Infantry regiment on the Mexican border, thanks to a timely tip from fellow Kansas Citian Casey (KC) Stengel.

This would be the town's fourth black club. The first one, representing Qyong Fong's Chinese laundry, was formed in 1897. The second, the original Monarchs, represented Jenkins Music Company and operated about 1908, Bruce says. The third, the Kansas City Giants, played in the 1910–1917 era. Bruce says it was Donaldson who suggested reviving the name of "Monarchs."

Wilkie dressed his players in white uniforms with royal maroon letters. He himself stayed in the background, while Quincy J. Gilmore, a black businessman, fronted for him. The team had its office above a pinochle and roulette room on 18th Street in the heart of the black community.

Drake remembered Wilkinson as

an awful good man. He was a white man, and he thought different. He was strictly business. And the man knew baseball. When I first went with the Monarchs, they had an agreement with the Kansas City Blues in the

American Association. They devised a schedule; the Monarchs had an equal amount of home games as the Blues. [The Blues insisted that the grandstand be segregated for all games, whites in front, blacks in back.]

And Wilkinson had something the other fellows didn't have. He had a booking agent [Lee Wilkinson, J. L.'s brother]. He used to go out on the road and book games and look out for the team, find out where you could eat or where you could sleep.

We always had a tourist coach so we could sleep. Wilkinson had a special [railroad] car that we traveled around in, and a cook. We ate and slept right on the car. And we stopped at the best Negro hotels and we ate in the best Negro restaurants.

A ball player is like a contented cow. A contented cow gives good milk, see? And you got to keep your ball players satisfied. If you under-pay a man, he's not satisfied. He's not going to give his best. You couldn't put all those other teams on the same par with the Monarchs, 'cause I remember later I played with a ball club in Nashville, Tennessee, and they didn't allow as much expense money as the Monarchs. Frankly speaking, the Monarchs lived awfully good.

At that time the Monarchs were what you might call the Yankees of Negro baseball.

"They used the park of the white club at 20th and Olive," Newt Allen said. "There's a playground there now. It was a much smaller field than the present one. In right field they had a 25–30-foot screen up there, like you have in Boston. But in left field the bleachers went all around from the railroad track clear around to 21st Street, from left field to center field. At that time the capacity was around 25,000. It was single-deck, all wood, nothing was concrete."

The Kansas City Monarchs during spring training in Little Rock, Arkansas. Photo courtesy Black Archives of Mid-America.

In 1921 Wilkinson challenged the Kansas City Blues, and the Monarchs split two games against them.

"When we played a team like the Blues, we were off salary," Drake said. "We played what you called 'cold' playing: You get a certain percentage of the gate receipts, which would run maybe a hundred or so dollars."

The following year the Blues won the pennant and the two clubs clashed again. It was no contest. The Monarchs won five of six games, whereupon the Blues called the series off.

"Public sentiment was beginning to wonder why these guys couldn't play in organized ball," Chet Brewer said.

Drake agreed. "Everybody was up in arms about us playing the Blues when we beat 'em. A fellow by the name of Hickey was president of the American association, and he wouldn't sanction any more games. We never played them again."

The Kansas City *Star,* the town's white paper, hailed "the new City champions—the Monarchs. There can be little doubt that the best team won. The series speaks for itself, baseball men who saw the set of six games declare. The Monarchs outplayed the Blues in five of the sextet of exhibitions, and so are entitled to their full share of tribute and glory."

The Monarchs' biggest rivals were Foster's American Giants. Foster's men were "racehorses" who could bunt and run the opposition to death; Wilkinson's were sluggers, who could stand up and swing away. Both teams had fine pitching. And both played to win. The threat of a melee was always in the air. In fact, one did break out in Chicago one Sunday when the Monarchs' combative catcher, Frank Duncan, deliberately leaped at Chicago catcher Johnny Hines with his spikes. In an instant the field was engulfed by brawling players and fans until, one player said, the grass almost ran red with blood. The Monarchs, being the visitors, were badly outnumbered, and "were a pretty well beaten bunch," according to young outfielder George Sweatt.

They couldn't wait for Chicago to arrive for its next game in Kansas City. Some of the Giants arrived packing guns for protection, and before the game some Kansas City fans waylaid Chicago catcher Jim Brown under the stands and knocked him cold. Another bloodbath was in the making.

Wilkinson put a stop to it, however. "I'm paying you to play ball," he told the Monarchs, "not fight. Remember that. If you start any fights, you're gone, and I'll see you don't get on any team. I'll blackball you." The Monarchs played the game, sullenly but peacefully.

Infielder Carrol Mothell nodded. "Wilkinson always said, 'Don't give my ball players nothing. Make 'em earn it.' And that's what our umpires'd do. A close play always went against us."

In 1923 the Monarchs moved into a new park, Muehlebach Field, situated in the black neighborhood at 22nd and Brooklyn. It later became the home of the Kansas City Athletics in the American League. The park had 16,000 seats, an electric scoreboard, and the new landlord not only permitted integrated seating for Monarch games (it was still segregated when the Blues were in town), he even let the Monarchs use the dressing room.

Traveling to Dallas that summer, the Monarchs drew enthusiastic crowds. "One would have thought a circus was in town," the Kansas City *Call* reported. Special trains brought blacks from miles around, until the streets of Dallas' black district were filled with crowds waiting to see "the Big Leaguers arrive."

Chicago won the pennant in 1920, 1921, and 1922. But in spite of losing three of their stars—pitcher Rube Currie, first baseman George Carr, and outfielder Heavy Johnson—to the new Eastern Colored League, the Monarchs were tops in 1923, 1924, and 1925.

Rube Foster was still angry at the eastern raids and had refused to consider a world series against them. But in 1924 Wilkinson issued his own challenge to the East, which was accepted, and so that October the Monarchs and the Philadelphia Hilldales met in the first modern black championship. It was a classic battle that went to a marathon ten contests, including one 12-inning tie. Finally, in the tenth game, with the series tied, four games apiece, the Monarchs broke a 0–0 tie with five runs in the ninth inning to take the title.

The next year, with Rogan out with injuries, Hilldale won the rematch, five games to one.

Wilkinson's payroll ran $4,000 a month, the limit set by the league. To earn it, the players traveled all over the Midwest between their league dates. Wilkie said the team lost only one exhibition game in seven years, and country folk drove up to a hundred miles to see them. "The colored ball players play the game with all the spirit of the college athletic teams," Wilkinson said. "I believe that's the main reason the Monarchs are so popular."

Still, the Monarchs were not making money, even when they won the pennants. The world series were not well attended. In 1924 one important weekend game had to be postponed because Muehlebach Stadium was being used for a high school football game.

Series attendance averaged about 5,000 a game in 1924, and each Monarch received $308 as his winning share. In 1925 attendance fell to 3,000 a game for the six games. The losing players' share was $57.64 apiece, a shock to the men, since they were off salary for the games.

The Monarchs were one of the strongest baseball teams in the country, yet their press almost ignored them. The black Kansas City

Call didn't consider baseball worthy of its attention until 1926, and the white *Star* ran box scores of Monarchs games only on Sundays if the Monarchs were home. Attendance was the lowest in the league, and Chicago, St. Louis, and other more affluent teams were reluctant to play in Kansas City.

To increase attendance, Wilkinson instituted Ladies' Day and cut box-seat ticket prices from $1.10 to 75 cents. Grandstand seats remained at 60 cents.

In 1926 he also invested in a new 18-passenger bus with reclining seats, plenty of leg-room, and a place for luggage on top. It was actually an economy move; Wilkinson estimated it would save thousands of dollars a year in railroad fares. The new highway just completed from Kansas City to St. Louis also meant that the bus could cover the distance almost as fast as the train could.

With all his troubles, Wilkinson's players found him a soft touch. Next Allen said they could go to him in the winter and get half of next summer's salary. "He was the swellest guy in the world."

Commented Wilkinson's son, Richard: "I've always said that if Dad had all the money he advanced to the ball players, he'd be a millionaire. But Dad never complained. He was a very gentle man."

Kansas City lost the play-off to Chicago in 1926. It didn't win a pennant again until 1929, though there was no world series that year.

That winter the depression struck.

Was Wilkinson the "Father of Night Baseball"? The debate will rage long and loud. Actually, there were many fathers. Games played after dark, such as they were, were reported as early as September 1890, less than a year after Edison invented the electric light. (Well, why else invent it?) After that first contest outside Boston, games were played in Chambersburg, Pennsylvania, and Fort Wayne, Indiana, in 1883 and in Wilmington, Delaware, in 1896 (Honus Wagner played in that one).

Not until 1909 was there another attempt to duplicate the sun at night. George F. Cahill devised a portable lighting system, says historian Oscar B. Eddelton of the Society for American Baseball Research, and journeyed around the country, trying to interest teams in it. That year, with the Cincinnati Reds looking on, two amateur teams used the lights in Cincinnati. The following year 20,000 fans in Chicago watched a semipro game under Cahill's lights.

Bill Drake said he saw a team called the Nebraska Indians (they really were Indians from Lincoln, Nebraska) playing under a primitive lighting system as early as 1914. They spaced kerosene lamps around the outfield and grandstand.

Newt Allen added that Wilkinson had experimented with a lighting system in Kansas City back before 1920, when he had the All

Nations, but it didn't work. Richard Wilkinson said his father spoke of using arc lamps or kerosene lamps in Algona, Iowa, and around Des Moines in the early 1920s, but the engineers couldn't get the poles high enough.

In 1927 Lynn, Massachusetts, of the New England (white) league played the Salem club under lights, though it is not clear whether the game was an official league contest.

A major question is: Were such primitive systems adequate? Apparently not.

In 1929 E. Lee Keyser, owner of the Des Moines Demons in the white Western League, announced that he would install lights in his

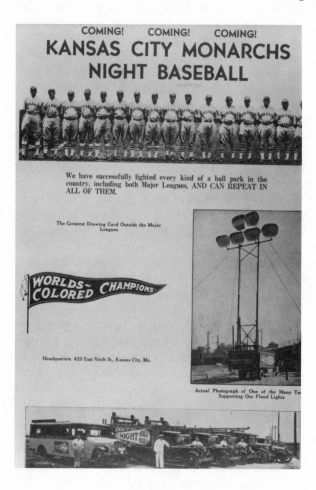

Advertisement in 1930 for Kansas City Monarchs night baseball.

park in 1930. Apparently the idea had been germinating in the mind of Wilkinson as well, and both men set about designing their own systems. "What talkies are to movies," Wilkinson declared, "lights will be to baseball."

To finance his plan, Wilkinson went to Tom Baird, who owned a billiard parlor in Kansas City, Kansas. The two formed a partnership on a handshake. Wilkie himself mortgaged everything he owned— "and probably a little more," his son, Richard, said.

Both Wilkinson and Keyser, who were actually close fiends, went to the same company, the Giant Manufacturing Company of Omaha, to make the lights. But while Keyser's would be permanently installed, Wilkinson was seeking portable lights that he could carry wherever the Monarchs went.

"It was a complete engineered deal," Richard Wilkinson said. "Really quite ingenious. The lights were on cables and telescoped steel poles, and they had a Ford truck under each light, one behind first, one behind third, and the boom truck set up individual poles in the outfield." Each pole supported six big lights. "They were really strong—open-faced lights about four feet across with 1,000-watt bulbs. Could light up a park well. Of course the parks weren't as big then. And they had a 100-kw generator on a big bus" (Wilkinson's prized luxury bus, which had been converted). The 250-hp motor was reportedly as large as a Ford car and drank 15 gallons of gas an hour. "In all it cost around $50,000—that's like one million today."

Meanwhile little Independence, Kansas, was also busy building lights for its park on the shores of the Elk River near the Oklahoma border. Five-hundred-watt lamps were suspended from 50-foot poles. The infield measured 20 foot-candles of illumination, compared to about 150 foot-candles in later big-league parks. The outfield was about half as much. On April 17 Wilkinson traveled to Independence to watch the first test of the lights there in an exhibition against the bearded House of David team. There was a ten-minute delay when a transformer fuse blew and an electrician climbed a pole to repair it. Wilkinson pronounced the test a success but insisted that his own lights would give three times as much power.

The final three-team dash to the finish had begun. Keyser was the victim of bad luck at the starting gate. The schedule makers had his club on the road for the first two weeks. Des Moines would play its home opener under lights May 2. Meanwhile, Independence was readying its lights for a game against Muskogee Saturday, April 26.

Just 80 miles to the east, Wilkinson was on the road with a strange caravan—the bus, the Ford trucks, and four taxi-cabs rented from third baseman Newt Joseph's Monarch Cab Company to carry the players—heading for Arkansas City, Arkansas, for a game the same night. They chugged into town to the fanfare of the local press, which was anticipating the historic night.

And it rained. It rained in Arkansas City, and it rained in Independence. There would be no games anywhere in that part of the Southwest that night. Wilkinson drove to Okmulgee for a Saturday game, but that was also rained out.

Monday, April 28, Wilkinson's caravan drove into Enid, Oklahoma, for a game against Phillips University. The weather was threatening, but 3,000 curious fans showed up. "They came from miles around," said Brewer. The poles were cranked into the air, cables were run to the generator, Wilkinson nodded, the generator chugged, and the lights blazed in the darkness to the oohs of the fans. History had been made.

"When they turned that on, it was light as day out," Brewer said. "Those lights were beautiful. In fact, it was a lot better than a lot of these little minor league teams played under [later]. That was the birth of night baseball."

The Monarchs won the game, incidentally, by a score of 12–3.

Meanwhile, in Independence, 1,000 fans turned out for the equally historic first game there. Muskogee walloped the home team on a soggy field, 13–3. (The losing pitcher was 21-year-old Cy Blanton, who would go on to the major leagues.)

The field in Enid is gone, but Riverside Park in Independence still echoes to the sounds of bat and ball. It carries a marker recalling the historic first night game in organized ball. (Nineteen years after that first night game, the park recorded its second claim to fame. A 17-year-old shortstop named Mickey Mantle hit his first professional home run there.)

Four nights after the games at Enid and Independence, Des Moines staged its own gala opener at night, beneath steel towers 90 feet high that lit up the crowd of 12,000 and started nearby roosters crowing in confusion.

The Monarchs, meanwhile, continued their travels through Texas and Oklahoma, drawing crowds of curious at each stop. "By the time we left Houston, Dallas, and Oklahoma City, Wilkinson had paid for his lights before he even started the season," Allen said.

Houston, Dallas, Fort Worth, Oklahoma City were all in the Texas league and had big parks that would hold 16,000 people. We'd play two nights in each one and draw 25–30,000. The price for baseball wasn't near as steep as it is now, and for the lights they charged a little extra. It was a curiosity; people would come out to see if we could really play ball under lights.

It was hard at first, but when you began to play under them regularly, the only hard part was when a fly ball was hit. You'd have to wait for it to come out of the dark to catch it. Sometimes a fellow would hit it clear out of sight of the lights, then you had to try to find it. But we got used to it later and developed a pretty good judgement of where the ball was.

On Saturday, May 6, at Waco the Monarchs made night baseball history of another kind. Lefty John Markham, a rookie, pitched the world's first night-time no-hitter, beating the Waco Cardinals of the Texas league. The Waco hitters couldn't blame the lights, however. The Monarchs collected 14 hits in winning.

At Memphis 12,000 fans swarmed to the park. The Monarchs stopped at St. Louis in June and played two games under light. The whole Cardinal team turned out to watch, and owner Sam Breadon, an early skeptic, was impressed. He ordered lights installed in the park of his Houston farm club.

Finally the Monarchs reached Kansas City for the first night game in Muehlebach Stadium. Over 12,000 fans bought tickets to see Kansas City win a free-hitting contest, 15–8.

Next Wilkinson journeyed east with his now famous lights. The Monarchs brought the first night games to the Detroit area (Hamtramck) and Pittsburgh's Forbes Field, home of the Pirates. Judy Johnson, third baseman of the Pittsburgh Crawfords, remembered that first game. "When the durn dynamo would die down, the lights would die down," he said. "But we packed the people in." When Pittsburgh pitcher Lefty Williams failed to see the catcher's sign for a fast ball and threw a curve instead, it split the catcher's finger. A high school kid was quickly called in to catch, and that was Josh Gibson's first appearance in a Pittsburgh Crawford uniform.

Richard Wilkinson, still only a child at the time, took away a vivid memory of 10,000 people stampeding the tiny stadium at Hershey, Pennsylvania. "There were 2,000 in the park, 8,000 outside," he said. "They had no money to get in. It was the depression. So they just busted the fence in and stood around and looked."

Wilkinson's lights saved black baseball (as Keyser's saved minor-league ball), permitting it to survive—just barely—through the depths of the hard times. But his own Monarchs were broken up. Mendez was dead, Moore was crippled for life, Heavy Johnson had jumped to Baltimore, Donaldson had retired, and Rogan was getting old.

With the league in a shambles, Wilkinson took his club barnstorming, much as in the old days of the All Nations. They played everybody—the House of David, even the Olympic female star, Babe Didrikson. In 1931 they played two games against a big-league all-star club—Paul and Lloyd Waner, pitcher Heinie Meine, first baseman Joe

Kuhel—and won them both, 4–3 and 6–2. In 1932 they won 43 straight games in one stretch.

But it was still hard times out on the prairies. Newt Allen said the Monarchs met lines of John Steinbeck's Okies, their jalopies piled high with furniture, straggling westward along the highway to escape the Dust Bowl. Sometimes the players and immigrants stopped along the road to share a meal. It was so hot, Allen said, the team cut its games to seven innings. "Even golf balls were melting."

In some ways the itinerant life resembled the fictional barnstormers, the Bingo Long All Stars. But there was no cake-walking or clowning on Main Street before the game to draw a crowd. It wasn't necessary, and the men were too proud. "We were *Monarchs*," said Buck O'Neil.

Bruce said Wilkinson and Baird rented out their lights to the House of David for the first half of each season in order to bring in revenue. In spite of the hard times, they made expenses and then some. While the other teams "wallowed" in red ink, the Chicago *Defender* wrote, the Monarchs were barnstorming across Nebraska and "laughing merrily." Wilkie could even afford to hire Cool Papa Bell, Willie Wells, and other stars away from their clubs, angering the other owners.

In 1934 Wilkinson booked Diz and Paul Dean, fresh from their World Series victory over the Detroit Tigers, to barnstorm against his Monarchs through the Southwest, down into Oklahoma and Texas. The Deans won three games, the Monarchs won one, 9–0, and one was a tie. Said Richard Wilkinson: "Dean said he made more money playing exhibitions with Dad than he did playing the World Series."

In 1935 Dean (28–12) and the Cooper brothers, Mort and Walker, beat the Monarchs, 1–0. But the Monarchs beat two other big-league squads, including Tommy Bridges (21–10), Schoolboy Rowe (19–13), and Charley Gehringer (.371) of the world champion Tigers, 6–0 and 8–2. The following year they lost two to Bobby Feller (9–7), Lon Warneke (18–11), Lou Fette (20–10), and Johnny Mize (.364) by scores of 4–3 and 1–0.

In 1936 Jesse Owens joined the Monarch caravan, fresh from his triumph in the Berlin Olympics. He ran exhibitions against everything—college boys, cars, motorcycles, and horses. The players also mounted donkeys for "donkey ball" games against the House of David.

The Monarchs were slowly recovering from the hard times. In 1937 they rejoined the league and on opening day played host to the American Giants in a gala ceremony that included two 50-piece bands, a contingent of high school cadets, the VFW, and a parade of 50 decorated cars. Twelve thousand fans showed up.

Meanwhile, Wilkinson had gotten a phone call from a lanky pitcher with a sore arm; his name was Satchel Paige. The once golden arm was mysteriously dead, and Paige's career seemed over. "Satchel had a 'whalebone arm,'" said Richard Wilkinson, "all bone, not much muscle. Dad could tell by looking at a ball player whether he could play ball or had potential. They talked, and Dad gave him another chance."

Satch was assigned to the Monarchs' "B" team of rookies and veterans, such as Newt Joseph, which barnstormed the small towns while the main team played the cities. "They can still do some good," Wilkie said of the vets. "They've done a lot for the Negro leagues and made us all some money, so I'm just trying to pay them back a little."

Paige was grateful for the chance. "I'd been dead, now I was alive again," he wrote. "I didn't have my arm, but I had me a piece of work." Then suddenly one day, Paige threw a pitch to Joseph and the arm didn't hurt! Satchel was back!

Wilkinson saved Paige's career. And Paige rejuvenated the Monarchs. Around Satchel, Wilkinson built a second Monarch dynasty. The infield starred Buck O'Neill, Barney Surrell, Newt Allen, and Jewbaby Johnson. O'Neill now scouts for the big leagues. Surrell, in the opinion of many Monarchs, was a better big-league prospect than Jackie Robinson. The outfield boasted Willard Brown, Josh Gibson's rival as the most powerful slugger in black baseball; plus Ted Strong, a Globetrotter basketball star in the winter; and Bill Sims. Duncan and Joe Greene did the catching. Besides Satchel, the pitching corps included Connie Johnson, who would go on to the major leagues with the Orioles and White Sox; and Hilton Smith, who many blackballers insisted was as good as Satchel. The second Monarch team would even outdo the first, winning six pennants in ten years, 1937–1946. Three of their losing seasons came during the war.

The 1941 club was particularly powerful. In the black world series that year they humiliated the great Homestead Grays in four straight games and held the mighty Josh Gibson to a batting average of .125.

Newt Allen remembered:

We used to draw 14–15,000 people during those times, 18–19,000 on Sunday; and ladies' night, my goodness, we'd have lots of people, white and colored. They're good baseball fans here, but you have to have a winner. They don't like a loser here.

In '42 and '44 we made a lot of money with Satchel. We made so much money on a Sunday afternoon ball game against Birmingham that after the ball game, why Mr. Wilkinson would give each man 75 or 100 dollars bonus. From St. Louis all the way into New York, I guess he gave away to ball players $1,000 each night that we played. Of course, he was

smart enough to take that off his income tax. One hundred dollars in
Washington, 75 in St. Louis, 50 apiece in Pittsburgh; in Philadelphia we
got $100 apiece, New York we made $100 apiece. Well, he was making a
world of money with Satchel. Satchel was getting his salary and five
percent of the gate.

As I say, he was one of the best owners ever was in baseball.

Besides a generous percent of the gate—some estimates run to 15
percent off the top—Satchel was often rewarded with an extra special
vase or piece of furniture from Mrs. Wilkinson's antique shop. The
pitcher's home was liberally furnished with these heirlooms.

Wilkinson always kept an eye out for antique bargains for his
wife. "He liked to walk down the street in Chicago," Allen said. "He
once saw four vases in a notion shop and bought them for 50 cents
apiece. When his wife got through doctoring them up, she got $50
apiece for them. She really was an antique dealer."

Wilkinson was a close friend of Abe Saperstein, the owner of the
Harlem Globetrotters and a partner in the Birmingham Black Barons
baseball club. "Dad gave Abe bookings when Abe was just getting
started," Richard Wilkinson said. "He helped give Abe his start. The
Globetrotters started out as a Chicago team playing on weekends. Dad
would help book them in Illinois. Abe never went through town he
didn't jump in a cab and come see Dad. Every month we'd get a
telegram from Abe, from Russia, from everywhere."

As it had in 1917, the military draft destroyed Wilkinson's team in
1942. His best stars were taken from him, and the Monarchs fell to
fourth in 1943 and last in 1944. Ironically, the war brought prosperity
to the country, and fans thronged to the park. Wilkinson scheduled
games for war workers on swing shift, distributed free tickets to GI's,
sold war bonds at games, and played Red Cross benefits.

Catcher Ted "Double Duty" Radcliffe joined the Monarchs from
Saperstein's Barons in 1945. Twelve games later a Barons player slid
into home, rupturing Radcliffe."I had to catch a plane, come on to
Chicago and have an operation," he said. "I hadn't been with Kansas
City but two weeks, but Wilkinson paid the whole hospital bill. So you
know what kind of man he was."

"The three greatest men in Negro baseball were Saperstein, Cum
Posey (of the Homestead Grays), and Wilkinson," Radcliffe declared.

They operated like big-league teams. They were the only ones had
four-five sets of uniforms, the rest of them had two, you had to dry your
uniform overnight, with those other teams. And they were the only ones
treated the ball players half decent about riding all night. They were the
only teams paid the ball players bus riding money. If they didn't go to
bed, they got their room rent just the same. But the rest of the teams
wouldn't do it.

No wonder black kids who could hit and throw dreamed of joining the Monarchs almost as white kids dreamed of becoming Yankees.

Wilkinson made them dress the part. He always wore a coat and tie himself and enforced a dress code on his club.

Said Othello Renfroe:

> They could tell some tall tales about ball players they picked up in these little country towns who would come out and pitch with football shoes on or tennis shoes, and they could throw a ball so hard. The Kansas City Monarchs were very good at that, picking up guys in little small towns in Texas and Arkansas and taking them to town and buying them clothes, you know, guys who didn't even know what a suit of clothes was. But Mr. Wilkinson made sure that you dressed well. That was one of his musts: "Take this guy downtown and buy him a suit of clothes. Let's dress him up." And I tell you, those guys would step out of those clubhouses Sunday sharp as a tack.

Said the Kansas City *Call*: Monarch players met "the most exacting conventions of an English family."

Wilkinson still enforced his "no rough stuff" rule. When third baseman Pat Patterson punched a white fan, Wilkie fined him $50, historian Bruce reports. "You just don't bite the hand that feeds you," he said.

First baseman Buck O'Neil told Bruce, "A Monarch never had a fight on the street. A Monarch never cut anybody. You couldn't shoot craps on our bus. . . . This was the only way to 'open the door.'"

Profound social change was about to come to America: integration. And Wilkinson had helped pioneer it. The Monarchs, wrote the *Call*, "have done more than any other single agent in Kansas City to break down the damnable outrage of prejudice that exists in this city."

Would baseball be integrated across the country? "I think it would be a fine thing for the game," Wilkinson said, "even though we would lose some of our players."

In the winter of 1945 Wilkinson got a tip from pitcher Hilton Smith on an army lieutenant just out of the service. He decided to take a look at the young man, whose name was Jackie Robinson. Jackie hit .345 with the Monarchs, and at the end of the season, the news burst on the baseball world: Wilkinson's discovery had been chosen to open the doors of the major leagues to blacks. In the general jubilation over the news, few thought to remember the man who had made it possible—J. L. Wilkinson.

"Dad never got paid for Jackie," Richard Wilkinson said. "Rickey never paid anybody for anything. Nothing could be done about it in those days. If you'd raised a voice about the money, they'd have said, 'Oh, you're trying to hold a man back,' Dad wasn't like that anyway."

Wilkinson conceded that he had no written contract with Jackie but insisted that he did have a verbal one. Branch Rickey waved it aside. "There is no Negro league as such, as far as I am concerned," he said. He called them "rackets," referring to the several eastern owners who were numbers kings. (Lotteries were then a crime but are now officially sponsored by most state governments.) So, Rickey insisted, the Negro leagues "are not leagues and have no right to expect organized baseball to respect them."

Baird wanted to lodge a formal protest to commissioner Happy Chandler, but Wilkie persuaded him to drop it. "I'm very glad to see Jackie get this chance," he said, "and I'm sure he'll make good."

Robinson wasn't even the best prospect on the team, all authorities agree. Jackie was selected primarily because of his university background at UCLA, where he played with whites. "You go back through the Monarchs' rosters, there were lots of them played better ball than Jackie," Richard Wilkinson said. "Newt Allen could play much better infield than Jackie but couldn't hit as well. There's about ten of them would have been outstanding major league players—Mendez, Rogan, Donaldson, Moore, Paige, Duncan, Smith. They'd have made the major leagues easily. Buck O'Neil would have been a great manager in the majors."

After Robinson, the race was on to raid the Negro leagues, and no black team supplied more talent than the Monarchs—27 men in all—a tribute to Wilkinson's ability to pick players. Besides Jackie, the Monarchs lost Willard Brown, Hank Thompson, Satchel Paige, Connie Johnson, Elston Howard, Ernie Banks, Gene Baker, Lou Johnson, and others.

By 1948 the once great Monarchs were depleted. Fans deserted them for the chance to see the big leagues. Wilkinson was 74 years old, and cataracts had taken away much of his sight. The man who had given light to baseball could no longer see to read or drive. He sold out his interest to Baird.

While the fans applauded Robinson and the other old Monarchs, Wilkinson, the forgotten man, retired to a nursing home. He died there in 1964 at the age of 90. All the Monarchs, going back to John Donaldson and the All Nations, gathered for the funeral.

"That guy was a doll," Hilton Smith recalled fondly.

It was pretty bad how they treated him. They just took Jackie, made all that money off him, and Wilkinson was the man that was responsible for him playing and he didn't get a dime out of it. It was kind of shady, I thought. He had kept Negro baseball alive, you know, all those years. He really had kept it going and developed ball players. All our source of guys being developed was through the Negro league. Yeah, they were taking them, and I don't think any of the clubs got much out of it. When Dan Bankhead went up, I don't know whether Memphis got anything, maybe a little, I don't know. Mrs. Manley in Newark didn't get anything hardly for Larry Doby or Monte Irvin or Don Newcombe. Baltimore lost Roy Campanella, and I don't think they got too much out of it. Same way with the Monarchs. The majors took them all.

24

Leon Day:
A Great Day for Cooperstown

I didn't see anybody in the major leagues that was better than Leon Day. If you want to compare him with Bob Gibson, stuff-wise, Day had just as good stuff. Tremendous curve ball, and a fast ball at least 90–95 miles an hour. You talk about Satchel; I didn't see any better than Day.

Larry Doby

D oby's Newark Eagle teammate, Monte Irvin, vigorously agreed:

People don't know what a great pitcher Leon Day was. He was as good or better than Bob Gibson. He was a better fielder, a better hitter, could run like a deer. And just as good a pitcher. When he pitched against Satchel, Satchel didn't have an edge. You thought Don Newcombe could pitch. You should have seen Day! One of the most complete athletes I've ever seen. If Dwight Gooden can throw as well as Leon for another few years, he'll be in the Hall of Fame.

Leon was also an excellent hitter, Eagles owner Mrs. Effa Manley pointed out. "He could play any position in the field except catch and played them magnificently. It's a shame he was born when he was. He is definitely Hall of Fame caliber."

Ray Dandridge of the Eagles regarded Day as the best all-round player he saw, better than Martin Dihigo, another who is already in the Hall of Fame. If Day was as good as Paige, Gibson and Dihigo—or better—and if they are in the Hall of Fame, one may ask, why isn't Leon Day there with them?

Day is quiet and modest to a fault. In a roomful of black veterans, he sits quietly, smiling and listening to them spin their stories about themselves and about him but rarely volunteers anything. It is not the formula for reaching Cooperstown. If Day had said, "Never look back, someone may be gaining on you," it is just possible that he, and not Satchel Paige, would be in the Hall of Fame today.

But if Paige bested Day in story-telling, Leon bested Satch at least three times on the pitching mound.

In 1942 Day was sent into the East-West game in relief against

Paige with the score tied 2–2. Leon finished the game, struck out five of the seven men he faced, and beat Satchel 5–2.

That September he joined the Homestead Grays to face Satch's Monarchs in the World Series. "He must have struck out 17 of us that day," moaned Monarch first baseman Buck O'Neil, who later scouted Lou Brock and Ernie Banks. "Oh, he was horrible!" Day won the game, 4–1, on a five-hitter, the only game the Grays could win in the Series. (The Monarchs, of course, got it thrown out.)

Four years later, after a tour with the Army in Europe, Day said, he faced Satch a third time and won again, 3–2. "They said I was cuttin' the ball," Leon grinned. "I ain't never threw a cut ball in my life. I said, 'I'm just *blindin'* you.' "

O'Neil nodded: "Hard as that man threw, he didn't have to cut the ball."

If Day was as fast as Paige or Gibson, in stature he couldn't have been more different than the gangling six-footers. "He looked like he was too small to be a batboy," laughed Newark first baseman George Giles. "Little bitty guy, but oh, could he throw hard!" Informed that Day took up bartending after his baseball career, Giles erupted with laughter. "A bartender! Can you picture Leon Day being a bartender! Leon? He couldn't even see over the bar!"

Gibson almost fell off the mound with the force of his delivery. Day was one of the first no-wind-up pitchers—he just cocked his pitching hand at his ear and threw, like Bullet Joe Rogan or Don Larsen. "When I threw overhand, it would hurt my shoulder," Leon said. "But from here [his ear], I'd feel nothing. I threw my fast ball straight up. I couldn't throw overhand, so I jerked it at them. It fooled a lot of hitters."

"Day was a short-arm," said Roy Campanella of the Baltimore Elite Giants. "He used very little motion, but he was very quick, had good control, plus a breaking pitch and a change of speed."

"Day had *smoke!*" said Cool Papa Bell. "And his curve ball would break like that—quick."

It wasn't a big curve, said Irvin, "just a wrinkle, just enough. Good control through. What would get you off-stride was that little hunch just before he threw."

Day holds the Negro league record with 18 strikeouts in one game. (Paige's highest: 17.) Day's came in 1942 against the Elite Giants. Was Campanella playing that day?

"He was three of them," Day chuckled.

"Campanella was a good fast ball hitter, but he was a little weak on the curve. I used to throw him fast balls—I was throwing pretty hard then, you know—and I could sometimes get them by him. Then after I got a couple of strikes on him, I'd throw him a curve. I guess after he

got to the majors someone taught him to hit the curve, because he was
hitting everything up there."

Leon was almost unhittable that day. He gave only one hit and
one walk in addition to the 18 Ks. He even got a hit himself, as he won
it 8–1.

In '46, just back from the war, Day finally got his no-hitter, a
rarity in the hard-hitting Negro leagues.

Three of Leon's younger teammates—Doby, Irvin, and Newcombe—made it to the white majors. Day was just a shade too old to
join them.

Day was born in Alexandria, Virginia, in 1916.

*But I grew up in Baltimore. The Baltimore Black Sox played in a place
called Westport, near where I lived in Mt. Winans. They've torn the park down
now. I think that's where Al Kaline came from, Westport. I pitched against him
one time after he joined the Tigers. He really tagged one on me.*

I used to go "over the fence" to see the Black Sox play the Hilldales and all

Leon Day on the mound.

those old teams when I was a kid. An old guy had made a little gate in the wall and would let people in for 25 or 50 cents. When he opened that gate to let somebody in, we flew through there behind them. The guy couldn't say nothin', because he was cheatin', himself.

Dick Redding, Biz Mackey, Dick Lundy, Boojum Wilson—I imagine I've seen all those guys. And the Black Sox had players like Rap Dixon and his brother Paul, Scrip Lee, Pete Washington—darn, I can't remember all those guys now. My favorite player was Laymon Yokely.

One day the Black Sox were playing a white all-star team that had Lefty Grove and Jimmy Foxx, and Day couldn't get past the guards, until Yokely spotted him and let him in. Yokeley won the game—at one time he had an 8–0 record pitching against white big leaguers, until his arm went dead and he was blasted in his last two starts against them.

Day dropped out of high school after one year.

Ever since I can remember, I wanted to play ball. I started playing with the Mt. Winans AC, a team called the Silver Spoons. I was a second baseman, but if the pitcher got in trouble, I'd say, "Give me the ball." One guy there was messin' around playing a little semipro ball. He knew Rap Dixon, who was managing the Black Sox, and he told Rap about me, and Rap came by and picked me up one spring, took me to spring training. That was 1934. That's when I really started playing professional ball—you know, getting paid. They said they'd give me $50 a month. Heck, that was a lot of money then, so I played. But I never did get all my money. They were playing percentage ball. After every game the players would split the money up, but I didn't know anything about it. The manager'd give me five dollars, ten dollars, something like that. I think I got around $40 the whole season.

Day became the special disciple of Yokely. "I'd tell him what to do, what not to do," the pitcher said. "He was my boy."

In 1935, when Leon was 19, Dixon moved to the Brooklyn Eagles and took Day with him as a second baseman. Candy Jim Taylor was manager. "He'd spit on the feet of young kids," Day recalled. "He waited until I got right in front of him—*ptui*, right on my foot."

Day told Kent Baker of the Baltimore *Sun:*

We didn't have no money, and we'd be riding all night, then get off the bus and play a game. We weren't eatin' right, and my corns would be killin' my feet. The only time I got rubbed down was by myself. You had to love it to go through it.

To ease their troubles, the players sang on the bus. Day may not have been a talker, but he was a great singer. "Golly," said Giles, "him and two or three other guys, when they'd sing 'Marie,' they'd sound just like Tommy Dorsey."

That October, Day came back to Baltimore to pitch against Cliff Melton, who would go on to star with the New York Giants. Leon beat him, 2–1, on a three-hitter.

Then he sailed to Puerto Rico to play winter ball. He hit .307, though his pitching record is not available. But catcher Quincy Trouppe shakes his head over the painful memory. "I used to go up there with that timber and bring it back two straight times against Day—with all my owners sitting on the bench."

In 1935 Day pitched a one-hitter, rare in the free-hitting Negro leagues, and ran up a 9–3 record with Brooklyn, which finished sixth best in the league. He was the ace of the Brooklyn staff (second best was Will Jackman, 5–6). The shoe spitting stopped abruptly.

The next year, 1936, the Eagles moved to Newark. We have no data on Day yet for that season, nor, in fact, for any year thereafter. He himself thinks 1937 was his best year. I think that was my best year. I think I lost one game. I don't know how many I won. We never did keep count.

The next year he pitched in the East-West game again and got a hit in his only at bat.

The Eagles had a powerful club, with Mule Suttles, Dick Lundy, Willie Wells, and Ray Dandridge in the infield. The first three, along with Day, are future Hall of Fame candidates. Dandridge was elected in 1987.

They played in Ruppert Stadium, home of the Newark Bears, one of the greatest clubs in minor-league history. Most of the Bears went on to star with the great Yankee teams of the 1940s—Joe Gordon, Tommy Henrich, Charlie Keller, and so on. The Eagles were pretty popular too.

> We had some good crowds. Sometimes the stadium was packed. I think it held about 18–19,000. We were going to play the Bears after the regular season. The Bears players wanted to play us, but they wouldn't let them. I don't know who said no. We would have made ourselves $700 a game. That was a lot of money.

That winter Leon sailed to Cuba to pitch in the winter league and compiled a 7–3 record. But he got a sore arm and as a result had to sit out the 1938 season at home.

That was the year Satchel Paige, Josh Gibson, Cool Papa Bell, and other black stars jumped to the Dominican Republic, where dictator Trujillo was handing out big pesos to play. Day missed that.

He was always missing the big money. Once, he recalled, the Eagles were giving every player a "day" and presenting the honoree with a suitcase. "They got to my name, and they called it off. I didn't get a suitcase."

Leon returned in 1939 and found a newcomer, Monte Irvin, at short. "We called ourselves 'the Raggedy Nine,'" Irvin laughed. In one game against the Homestead Grays, "I played short, Leon second. In a crucial part of the game somebody hit a ball right over second base. Leon went over there and backhanded the ball and gave it to me for a double play. We beat them, 2–1. We were hoo-rahing Josh and Buck."

Day played second base, shortstop, center field, and pitched. He had the best right-handed move to first base, Eagles infielder Dick Seay said. Irvin agreed.

Some black oldsters, such as Baltimore second baseman Sammy T. Hughes, felt that Day, like Babe Ruth, was too valuable a hitter to be pitching. Hughes would have made him a full-time outfielder to get his bat in the lineup every day.

Israel goes further: "Day was the best athlete I've ever seen in my life. When the second baseman got hurt, he'd go in and play second. You'd say, 'How long you been playin' second?' He'd say, 'I'm a pitcher.' 'What! I hope I never get hurt; you'll go in there and take my job.' He was the most complete ball player I've ever seen."

Negro league statistics were not well kept during the depression, and scholars are only slowly resurrecting them from old box scores. We know that Day pitched three hitless innings in the 1939 East-West game. In Puerto Rico in the winter of 1940–1941 he hit .330.

In the spring of 1941 Day's arm went sore, Irvin reported. It was a boiling hot day in Daytona Beach, and Day declared that "I'm either going to play ball or go back to the farm." Said Monte: "He just threw and threw, as hard as he could, as long as he could, and literally threw the soreness out of his arm." Back in Puerto Rico that winter he compiled a 2.93 ERA (no win-loss figures are available) and hit .351.

"He had plenty of speed and a pretty fair curve," Leonard said. "The best thing he had going for him was he could get it over the plate."

Leon said he got Buck out by pitching him high and tight. "You couldn't hardly shoot the fast ball by him. If you let him see the fast ball, make it bad." One day he told Irvin he was going to see if Leonard really could hit the fast ball. Buck drilled the first one deep against the center-field wall. "That was just luck," Leon said in the dugout. Leonard drilled the second one off the right-field wall. "Well," Day said, throwing his glove down in the dugout later, "I'm convinced."

In 1942 Day racked up his 18-strikeout game. Later that year, before 48,000 people in the East-West game, he and Satchel each entered the game in the seventh with the score tied, 2–2. Leon faced seven batters, struck five of them out, and beat Satchel, 5–2.

That autumn the Homestead Grays went into the World Series against the Kansas City Monarchs and lost the first three games. That's when they sent out a call for help to Leon, who, of course, was under contract to the Eagles. Day responded by whipping Paige, 4–1, on a five-hitter.

Midway through the 1943 season Day got his draft call and was shipped to England with the 818th Amphibian Battalion, driving an Army "Duck," or amphibian landing truck. He drove one onto Normandy Beach six days after D-Day.

After the war was over, Day's unit played General Patton's Third Army team for the ETO (European Theater of Operations) championship. Leon and Willard Brown of the Kansas City Monarchs took on Patton's club—outfielders Harry Walker of the Cardinals and Johnny Wyrostek of the Pirates, second baseman Ben Zientara of the Reds, and pitchers Russ Bauers of the Pirates, Sam Nahem of the Cards, and Ken Heintzelman of the Phils. John Quinn, in peace-time the general manager of the Phils, managed the team. The two clubs met in Nuremburg in the stadium that had once rung with Adolph Hitler's speeches.

Day thought there were "over 100,000 people that day. It was full! It was a big place, you know."

Day took a 2–1 lead into the ninth, when the first batter tripled, with Walker, Wyrostek, and Zientara coming up next. "I pitched Walker high and tight," Day said. "All left-handers, I always went high and tight." Walker went back to the dugout on a strike out. Wyrostek, another left-hander, also saw three fast balls, high and inside, and he too dragged his bat back after three swings and three misses. Zientara, a right-hander, also couldn't touch the ball, and Day walked off the field the winner on a four-hitter.

"I remember Day very well," said Harry Walker.

> I can still see him in Germany, when he was pitching against us. He was maybe five-ten but well built. Had good strong shoulders. Sort of a quiet guy. A real nice guy, sort of a class guy. Just did a job—and a good one. A dedicated, businesslike job. Good control, he didn't overpower you. Nothing flim-flam about him. Would have been a real good pitcher in the major leagues probably. And wasn't too bad a hitter.

The winners were supposed to play the MTO (Mediterranean Theater) champs, the all-black 29th "Buffalo" Division, led by catcher Joe Greene of the Monarchs. Walker and the other Third Army players asked to join Day's club. "They wangled their way on," Leon said. "You know how it is in the army."

After winning the game easily, Day and Brown joined the Buffalos to play Patton's men again before another packed stadium of 50,000 GIs in Marseilles, France. Ewell Blackwell took the mound against Leon. Day won 8–0 on two home runs by Willard Brown of the Monarchs.

"Soon after that, Day returned to the United States. The Eagles' young Don Newcombe had already signed with the Dodgers, and Jackie Robinson talked to Day in Florida about signing with a big-league team too. "But," Leon said, "I was already under contract to Newark."

He was also 30. Could he come back after two and a half years in the service? Leon answered the question on opening day against Philadelphia: He pitched a no-hitter, struck out five, and walked only one.

> Doby tripled and stretched it—kept on running and came home to win it, 2–0. That's got to be the best game I ever pitched.

Day said he went on to beat Paige, 3–2, that year. "But I don't remember how many games I won, I really don't." He hurt his arm at the end of the year, but tried to pitch the opening game of the black World Series against the Monarchs in New York's Polo Grounds with several big-league scouts in the stands. But he lasted only a couple of innings, as Satch came in in relief to win for Kansas City.

Day went to the outfield for the rest of the series. "I hit the ball straight over the center fielder's head," O'Neil recalled. "I felt sure it was gone. Leon Day was playing center field, and he ran that ball down and caught it over his shoulder, and we lost the game. He could play center field!"

The Eagles went on to win the series in seven games. And, said their owner, Mrs. Manley, "I believe we could have gone on and beaten the white champions, the Cardinals, too."

Day's increasing age and his questionable arm kept the scouts leery of him. He went to Mexico in the summers of 1947 and 1948. "I made more money in Mexico than I made here in the States," he said. "I think I played for about four months and made about $5,000."

He returned to the United States in 1949 to play with the Baltimore Elite Giants, who won the Negro league pennant that year. But the black leagues were crumbling under the big-league raids. And "those years in the army had wore me down."

In 1950 Day went to Canada, to the Winnipeg Buffalos.

The next year he finally got an offer from the white leagues to pitch for Toronto in the International League. In 14 games he had a splendid 1.58 ERA, but he could only win one and lose one. He struck out 20 men in 40 innings.

The following year, 1952, Leon was with Scranton in the Red Sox chain, where he had a 13–9 record with a 3.41 ERA.

But the Red Sox weren't interested. That autumn and the next, Day barnstormed with Campanella's All Stars against a white big-league squad that included Whitey Ford and Gil Hodges. But the old smoke was gone. "I don't think I beat them either one of those years."

Today Leon lives in quiet retirement in Baltimore, playing pinochle and taking life easy and watching the modern kids.

> *You can make all the money in the world nowadays if you have any kind of ability. They practically give it to you. I can't understand why they would ruin it all with all the junk they get into.*

Will he ever get to Cooperstown? Leon expressed his hope: "The players from our leagues are dying off. I wish that we could all go in together, while we can still enjoy it."

It will be a great Day for Cooperstown if they do.

Leon Day

Year	Team	G	CG	(W-L)	Pct
1935	Brooklyn Eagles	13	11	(9-3)	.750
1937-38	Cuba	16	6	(7-3)	.700
1947-48	Cuba	3	1	(1-1)	.500
Totals		32	18	(17-7)	.708

Research has not yet been done on the late 1930s and '40s, the period of Day's career. All that is available at this time is the above.

25

Ray Dandridge:
Dandy at Third

Ray Dandridge was fantastic. Best I've ever seen at third. I saw all the greats—Brooks, Nettles—but I've never seen a better third baseman than Dandridge. He had the best hands. In a season he seldom made more than one or two errors. If the ball took a bad hop, his glove took a bad hop. He came in on swinging bunts, grabbed the ball bare-handed and threw to first without looking and got his man. And a good number-two hitter. He was particularly good at hitting behind the runner. He hit like a shot to right field. I never saw Judy in his prime, I never saw Marcelle at all, but a lot of people who saw both would give it to Dandridge because of his hitting, his fielding, and his speed. Once you saw him, you never would forget him.

Monte Irvin

Black veterans who saw him agree: Squat, bow-legged Ray Dandridge played third base like Brooks Robinson and hit like Pie Traynor, a combination that would make Ray, along with Mike Schmidt, the greatest third baseman of all time, black or white.

"The greatest third baseman?" Judy Johnson, the Hall of Famer, asked rhetorically. "I thought I was. But that man could play third base! He should be in the Hall of Fame." Actually, in a vote of old-time black players at Ashland, Kentucky, in 1982, Johnson and Dandridge finished in a dead tie for first place among third basemen.

Finally, in 1987, after years of knocking in vain, Ray was admitted to Cooperstown.

You could drive a train between his legs, the old-timers laughed, "but not a baseball!"

When I first met Ray, at the age of 60-plus, he could still cavort around the living room of his Newark home, charging in to bare-hand imaginary bunts, leaping to his right to spear line drives, racing to his left to cut off slow rollers. "I don't think Robinson could make any plays that I couldn't," he said confidently if immodestly.

Men who played in both the black and white majors—Irvin, Roy Campanella, Larry Doby—agree. Ray was the best they saw, including Campanella's flashy teammate at Brooklyn, Billy Cox.

353

Al Lopez, who managed against Dandridge in the American Association in 1949, recalled that "Ray's arms practically dragged the ground"—Al hunched over in an exaggerated fielders' crouch, knuckles swaying just above the floor. "Funny as hell, but the son of a gun could play ball. He'd throw that ball as soon as he got it. Like Brooks Robinson."

Better than Robinson, corrected Newark Eagles pitcher Bill Harvey. "Ray's arm was much stronger than Brooks'."

"Plus," added another ex-teammate, Doby, "Ray had a tremendous bat. You certainly couldn't put Brooks in there with him in hitting."

Ray's lifetime average was .319 in the Negro leagues (Marcelle hit .310, Johnson .287). Ray would have hit even better if nine winters in Cuba were not included. Ray hit only .282 there, compared to .318 in five seasons in the top U.S. white minors in his late 30s and .347 against white major leaguers. Either Cuba was a pitcher's league, or it was a superior caliber of ball to the U.S. Triple-A.

Ray hit .369 in 1949, his first year with the Minneapolis Millers, and was voted MVP the next year. The Cleveland Indians may have lost two pennants—1949 and 1950—because owner Bill Veeck refused to give Ray a bonus. Several New York Giants—Irvin and pitcher Sal Maglie among them—thought the Giants lost the 1950 pennant because they refused to bring Dandridge up that year.

Ray Dandridge's story is even more poignant than that of most other blackball stars because he just missed the white majors by a year or two. He was 31 when Jackie Robinson signed with the Dodgers, 35 ("I told them I was 30") when he finally got a bid himself. Younger men walked easily through the doors; older men had no expectations. But Dandridge was just young enough to get his hopes up and just old enough to have them dashed.

Dandridge was born in 1913 in Richmond, Virginia, in the Church Hill section, the same neighborhood that gave the world tap dancer Bill "Bojangles" Robinson. In fact, a statue of Robinson stands there today. Ray was born about two blocks from where the dancer lived. Ray was a short, barrel-chested youth, "built like a midget rassler," in one old-timer's phrase, when his family moved to Buffalo.

Ray went to an integrated school and took up all major sports. His basketball coach rejected him as "too rough," but he ran the 100-yard dash on the track team, fought in the Golden Gloves and "got a little banged up," and played quarterback on the football team, where, he remembered, "I got my knee knocked all out of joint." For years the knee would slip out of place on him, and he wore a brace even after he joined the Negro leagues.

I thank my father for making me quit football; he told me to try softball.

I used to hang around the softball team until one day one of the guys don't show up, and they let me play. I made good. A fellow from one of the semipro baseball teams asked me did I play hardball? I said, "Sure." We played in Bison Stadium. The first day out there, I was so nervous I threw the ball up in the stands.

Ray's family moved back to Virginia, where his father, a semipro pitcher, worked in a cigarette factory until he hurt his back and had to get around in a wheelchair.

Ray played all around Virginia and North Carolina, and that's where he first met Dave Barnhill, the little fast-baller who later would go up to Minneapolis with him. Barnhill remembered that Dandridge played first base with a red bandana around his neck like a railroad engineer. Ray nonchalantly scooped low throws out of the dirt seemingly without even looking. At bat he seemed to wield a 4-foot-long club, or so Barnhill thought, because no pitch was too high or too wide for him to hit.

"That was the greatest ball player ever put on a uniform!" Barnhill whistled almost 50 years later. "There's nothing he couldn't do. Oh, that was the most beautiful player I've ever seen! I'll say that the rest of my life. Ray Dandridge was a hell of a ball player—excuse the expression."

We had a team in Richmond named the Paramount All Stars. I was the captain of this team. In 1933 the Detroit Stars came through there on a Saturday, on their way from spring training. We had a scheduled game with them. During that time I was playing outfield. The shortstop didn't show up for the game. We held the game up, waiting for him. I told them, "Let's start the game and I'll play shortstop." That day I had the best day in a long time. Everything I did was right. I was hitting the ball and everything.

The Detroit manager, Candy Jim Taylor, asked me how would I like to go away with them to Detroit? I asked him, "Man, where is Detroit?" I didn't want to go. You know, when you're young like that, you don't know where you're going. I gave him my address and told him he had to talk to my father. Before I could get home from the ball game, they had their bus waiting in front of the house. He was in there talking to my father.

I came around the corner and ducked, turned around and went back to the pool room until the pool room closed. I came back home. The bus was still waiting in front of my house. I didn't go straight in the house. When I peeped around the corner later, the bus had left, and I went in the house.

My father told me the fellows wanted me to go with them. I told him I didn't want to go. My father encouraged me, said, "Why don't you go on with them and try it?" We sat down and talked a long time. We got one of those "straw bags"— suitcases. My father threw a few things in there, and the next morning six o'clock they were knocking at the door. When I went I didn't have enough money to come back home.

Later on I found out he bribed my father. Gave my father $25 for me to go with them.

Ray hit .216 his rookie year.

I used to like to be a home-run hitter. Had a light bat, swung for the fences. Candy got me in practice one day, said, "Kid, come over here. Look, what kind of bat do you have?" He took my bat, threw it away, gave me his bat, weighed 37 ounces.

I said, "Skip, this here is kind of heavy."

He said, "I'm gonna show you how to hit."

With Ray standing behind the batting cage, the lesson began.

He said, "Now, he's gonna throw this ball inside, and I'm gonna hit it to left field. You watch me." Boom. It went to left field. "Now I'm gonna do it again, so you'll see it again." He pulled the ball to left field again.

"Now he's gonna throw it right straight down the middle, and I'm gonna carry it straight back to him." Darned if he didn't. Boom, right through the box. Boom, and there it goes again.

He said, "Watch me, he's gonna throw it outside, I'm gonna take it to right field." Here comes the ball. Boom. Right field it went.

I think to myself, "I'm up there swinging, and he's showing me the moves, how to step into the ball, how to step forward." I stopped swinging for the fences.

That man taught me a lot about hitting.

It's a good thing I listened. I tried it. If he can hit line drives like that—beautiful—I could hit line drives from one side to another too.

For a solid week, Ray said, Taylor drilled the lesson home, how to spray the ball all over the field. From then on, Dandy forgot about home runs. "Ten home runs in one year was tops in my career," he said. "But I had a hell of an average—doubles, singles, and triples."

By season's end Ray was wealthy in hitting instruction but still didn't have enough money to get back to Richmond. Candy Jim had to pawn the team bus to send Ray home.

A year later Dandridge was with the Newark Dodgers and hitting .281. When the club's third baseman was late reporting to spring training, manager Dick Lundy told Dandridge, "Ray, you work out at third." By the time the regular third baseman got there, Lundy told him. "You can go home now. I've *got* a third baseman."

Ray studied hard. He admired Judy Johnson, then winding up his career with the Pittsburgh Crawfords. But he credits Jud Wilson for giving him the secret that made him into a great third baseman. When a batter topped the ball, Ray said, he used to wait for the ball. The hitters consequently were beating them out. Wilson told him,

"Kid, always charge a ball." "I used to listen to old-timers," Ray said, "and I found out Boojum was right. You got to study the man running. If he's a fast man, I've got to fire it. If he's a slow man, I'd lob it, just get him by a step. But when I had to fire, I had to fire."

"Dandridge had plenty of guts," Holland said. "Guys used to fake bunts to draw the third baseman in. Some third basemen wouldn't come in too close. Dandridge would."

Ray was soon playing so close on bunts that "I came near to bumping the catcher."

Black veterans began comparing the fresh young kid with the greatest third sackers in black annals—Johnson and Marcelle. Catcher Larry Brown gave Dandridge the edge over Marcelle. "He was a better hitter, a better fielder, and a better thrower," Brown said. "And he was faster."

"Ray was the flashiest, most exciting third baseman," exoutfielder Jimmy Crutchfield said, but Johnson was steadier and brainier. "Danny just had so much natural ability, he was mechanical. Danny was so fast, sometimes he'd make a play before the second baseman was in position, and the ball would go into the outfield."

Buck Leonard agreed. "Dandridge had the ability, but he didn't study the hitters. But anything he got his hands on, bam! you're out at first base."

Leonard soon learned that when Dandridge was at bat, he was a first-ball hitter. Leonard recalled that, like Davey Lopes or Willie Randolph, when he came to bat he was ready to swing. "You had to open up on him with a curve ball, get something on his mind. If you threw that first ball a fast ball, he'd set it *a-fire!*"

"Dandridge was built close to the ground," laughed Judy Johnson. "They would pitch up in his eyes. Right in his alley. Looked like he was chopping wood."

Ray was a cocky youngster. "When I came up, I was just one of those wild ones," he said. "But I learned."

He liked to tell the story of his first meeting with the great Satchel Paige. His club was in Pittsburgh for a double header and won the first game. In the dressing room between games Ray got a couple of stools and stood on tiptoe to look over the partition into the Craws' dressing room. Satchel was due to pitch the second game. "All right, you're next, you're next," Ray called to Satch. "You just come out here, talkin' 'bout how you can throw hard. We'll see how hard you throw. We're gonna rack you back," and he went on.

On Ray's first trip to the plate, he now admits, he did feel a little nervous and kept wondering what Satchel would throw. Boom! The first pitch exploded under his chin. Ray ducked, and he said he was a lot looser when he stood back up at the plate for pitch number two.

The next pitch was another fast ball, but in the strike zone, and Ray lined it out for a hit. "That's one thing I'll say," he said, "I don't believe any man alive could throw that fast ball by me."

One of the best days I had was playing Bushwick over in New York. During that time we used to play Sunday morning, then go to Bushwick in the afternoon. In 13 times at bat, I got 12 hits.

His average dropped to .268 in 1935, but he was voted to the East-West team and got a single in his only at bat.

In October he was in Philadelphia's Shibe Park facing Dizzy Dean (28–12). He didn't remember how he did against Diz. "I was a young kid," he said, "and they all looked alike to me." Ray may have forgotten, but the box score doesn't. He got two singles and a double in three at bats against Dean, Bill Swift of the Pirates, and Jim Winford of the Cards, as his team beat the big leaguers, 7–1. However, in four other games against these and other white big leaguers that winter, Ray was shut out in 11 at bats.

In the spring of 1935 Ray was selected to an all-star team to play in Puerto Rico. He hit only .196 but teamed with shortstop Perucho Cepeda, Orlando's father, in a game against the Cincinnati Reds. Ray went 1-for-5 against rookie Junie Barnes. Cepeda, incidentally, is regarded by old-timers as better than his more famous son, but Perucho would never play in the United States because of the racial discrimination here.

Back in Newark in 1936 Ray hit .298.

In 1937, Ray played the entire East-West game for the East, which won 7–2. Ray got only one hit in five at bats but stole a base and scored two runs.

That fall he was chosen by the eastern champion Homestead Grays to play a "world series" against a picked squad from Kansas City and Chicago. Ray hit one of his rare home runs in the final game, which was won by Homestead 9–0.

That was also the year Willie Wells and Mule Suttles joined the Eagles.

We had a million-dollar infield. Suttles at first base, Dick Seay at second, Wells at short, and I was playing third. That was our million-dollar infield.

Washington Senators owner Clark Griffith said Wells and Dandridge covered the left side of the infield better than any combination he had ever seen, including Traynor and Glenn Wright of the

October 12, 1935 at Philadelphia

Negro Stars	AB	H	R		Dean Stars	AB	H	R
CF Bell	5	0	0		SS Urbanski	5	0	1
RF Spearman	5	1	1		2B Garbark	4	1	0
3B Wilson	5	1	1		3B Stripp	4	2	0
C Gibson	5	3	2		RF Solters	4	0	0
C Dixon	2	1	1		CF Ripple	3	0	0
LF Patterson	4	1	0		LF Carnegie	2	0	0
1B Thomas	4	1	0		C Ryba	4	0	0
SS Dandridge	4	3	1		1B Roetz	4	2	0
P McDonald	3	2	1		P Dean	2	0	0
LF Page	2	1	0		P Swift	1	0	0
P Stanley	1	0	0		P Winford	1	0	0
	41	14	7			34	5	1

Negro Stars   020 001 400—7 14 2
Dean Stars   000 000 010—1 5 1

2B: Dixon, Dandridge
3B: Gibson
SB: Wilson
DP: Dean 1

	IP	H	R	SO	BB
McDonald	6	3	0	7	1
Stanley	3	2	1	3	2
Dean	5	5	2	3	0
Winford	2	7	5	3	0
Swift	2	1	0	0	0

WP: McDonald, LP: Dean

Pirates. "When are those two bow-legged men coming back?" he used to beg sports writer Ric Roberts. "Please don't let me miss them."

"Nothing could get through that little hole between us," Dandridge nodded, smiling.

Ray, who also played second, had seen Kansas City second baseman Newt Allen field the ball with his left hand, transfer it to his right hand as he went across second base, and backhand it to the shortstop to start a double play. "It can be done!" he exclaimed. "I tried it with Willie Wells one day. It works!" Monte Irvin agreed. He had seen them do it.

"He and Wells worked some plays," whistled Irvin, a kid in East Orange at the time. "Wells would go into the hole, get the ball, toss it to Dandridge, and Dandridge would throw the man out at first."

When the two took their act to Cuba, Mike Gonzalez, who coached the St. Louis Cardinals in the summer, watched in amazement as Wells scooped up a grounder, whipped it to Dandridge, who touched second and whipped it back to Wells for the relay to first. "I never saw guys play like that before," he gulped.

"Well," beamed catcher Larry Brown, "that's the way they play in the States all the time."

Ray hit .299 that winter, his first in Cuba, and led the league in stolen bases. He also picked up a nickname, "Talua," after a character in a popular radio program. (In Mexico he was known as "Mamerto," apparently a nonsense word. Americans called him "Squatty" or "Hooks," because he had a great pair of hands.)

So far we have uncovered only seven games for Ray in 1938—he hit .607 in them. That August he beat out the great Jud Wilson in the vote of the fans for the East-West game (for some reason Rev Cannady actually played in the game itself). At season's end Grays' owner Cum Posey picked Ray for his all-black all-star squad.

Some whites began to sit up and take notice. New York *Post* columnist Jimmy Powers urged the New York Giants to sign Ray, Josh Gibson, Buck Leonard, pitcher Ray Brown, infielder Sammy Bankhead (older brother of later Dodger pitcher Dan), and other black stars. Of course, given the times, the idea was preposterous; the Giants never even considered it. They finished third that year and would not win a pennant until 1951. How much difference might Ray have made if he had been in the lineup all those years, along with Mel Ott, Carl Hubbell, Johnny Mize, and the other Giant stars?

In 1939 Dandridge jumped the Negro league and traveled south of the border to play with Vera Cruz in the Mexican league. His owner at Newark, Mrs. Effa Manley, recalled: "Dandridge came to me one day with this money in his hand and said, 'Well, Mrs. Manley, this is the money they've given me to come play with them. If you'll give me the same amount, I won't go.' At that time we were having such a bad time financially, I decided not to give it to him. But I thought it showed a nice attitude, because he had a family to support."

At Vera Cruz Dandridge teamed with Wells, who also managed the team. "Dandridge depended on his speed and his arm," said Wells, now living in Austin, Texas. But Ray didn't always play the hitters the way Wells thought he should. And, Wells discovered, Dandridge was hard of hearing in his left ear and couldn't hear Willie's instructions. So Wells simply transformed him into a second baseman.

At first Ray couldn't make the pivot. He was taking the toss from short on the run and throwing under his left arm to first base. Many of the throws went wild. Wells taught him to take the throw, pause, pivot, then throw. After that, he said, "we set all kinds of records for double plays."

Ray liked Mexico and played there for eight of the next nine summers. Here is Ray's thumbnail guide to Latin America:

Venezuela—"bad equipment, bad fields. A living."

Cuba—"Beautiful. People who knew the game. Good parks. No money."

Puerto Rico—"I remember the oceans, the way the sun used to do this little dance off it, and how beautiful they treated us. No money."

Vera Cruz players (left to right) Josh Gibson, Ray Dandridge, and Leroy Matlock. Photo Courtesy Johnny Taylor.

Mexico—"Best of all. I set some records down there. I played me some *baseball!*"

The altitude was tough on him. He recalled: "I'd hit a homer and they'd want me to sign autographs, and I'd just huff and puff and say, 'No, let me sit down for a minute.'"

He hit .346 in 1940 and .367 in 1941, as Josh Gibson joined him and Wells on the Vera Cruz club. "We finished about 12–13 games ahead," he said.

Many other American blacks were going south of the border. One was Roy Campanella, who caught for Monterrey. Campy spiked Ray going into base one time, and Ray told Donn Rogosin he bided his time for revenge. At last he had his chance, as he raced around third on a hit and steamed for home, where Campy was waiting for the throw. "I got you now," Dandridge cried triumphantly as he leaped, spikes first. Roy "practically ended up in the stands," Ray beamed.

Dandridge hit .310 and .354 in Mexico for the next two years, 1942 and 1943.

Returning to Newark in 1944, Ray hit .370 and led the Negro league in runs and hits.

Then it was back to Mexico to manage Vera Cruz for Jorge Pasquel, the wealthy baseball impressario. First baseman Lenny Pearson related:

> Ray was a stickler as a manager. He wanted perfection, complete perfection. That's the way he played baseball, he was a dedicated ball player. He just expected discipline from everybody: "If they're going to play baseball, they're going to win or I don't want them on the ball field." He spoke Spanish very well and had damn good results. He helped them become better ball players, and they won the championship behind him. Maybe they hated him while he was teaching them, maybe he was a little stern, but he got results.

Dandridge also batted .366, stole 20 bases, and set a record by hitting in 29 straight games. At the end of the year the president of Mexico presented Ray with a trophy inscribed in Spanish, "He came, he conquered." A photo of that moment hangs on Ray's living room wall.

The next spring, in Montreal Jackie Robinson played his first game in white organized ball. And in Mexico Pasquel opened his checkbook and bought half a dozen U.S. major league players—Max Lanier, Sal Maglie, Ace Adams, Mickey Owens, Harry Feldman, and Danny Gardella.

Ray hit .323 that year with 24 stolen bases, his personal high. Box scores for five games against the white big leaguers show Ray hitting

.455 (10-for-22) against them. He slugged Maglie for four hits in nine at bats.

On opening day, Ray said, he hit two Lanier fast balls. Max called time and came off the mound. "Who the hell are you?" he demanded. "I never heard of you. I never heard of any of you black guys down here. Where the hell have you been?"

"Right here, man," Ray replied cheerfully. "We been here for a while now. We were just waiting for guys like you to find out about us so we could get together and do a little rasslin'."

Thereafter Lanier held him to 1-for-5 by jamming him with inside pitches. But in the field, "you couldn't hit one through him," Max said. "He could play in the big league with his glove, I guarantee."

> *Lanier, all those guys were coming down, making all that money, getting $5,000 bonuses. We were making nothing, we were making chicken feed, $350 a month. I told Pasquel, "I want more money." I went to his office. "Look, I'm getting my family up and going back home if I don't get some more money." He said he couldn't give me more money, so we packed up our things and were down in the station ready to get on the train. All of a sudden, here comes the chauffeur— oh man, a lot of people.*

Pasquel had met Rays' terms—$10,000. The Dandridges got into the limousine and rode back to the city. "They asked me how I did it. I told them, 'You just have to ask for it.' "

In the spring of 1947 Ray was called to Caracas, Venezuela, to join an all-star team to play the Yankees, who were destined to win the World Series that year. He tripled off Bill Bevens, who would pitch a one-hitter against the Dodgers in October, and scored on Phil Rizzuto's error, as Monarch pitcher Hilton Smith beat the Yanks, 4–3.

Ray had come down on a one-game contract.The promoters hastily renewed it for the second game the next day. This time Ray got two singles against Al Lyons, Frank Hiller, and Vic Raschi, who would win his first seven American League games that season.

In Mexico that summer Ray hit .329 with 23 steals, then sailed to Cuba for the winter season. Pasquel sent his brother to Havana to sign players for the 1948 campaign, but he didn't broach the subject with Dandridge. "I ain't going to Mexico next year?" Ray finally asked.

> *Next day he put me on the plane to Mexico, gave me $100 spending money in my pocket. His other brother met the plane, gave me $100 pocket money, put me in a hotel. The next morning Pasquel's chauffeur came, and I went to his house. I said, "Look, if you want me to come back, you have to give me a bonus. What I want to do is buy me a house. I want some money in advance." I was talking about $10,000. A two-family house cost $7,500 back during that time.*

> *He said, "How you going to pay me back?"*
> *I said, "How you want to be paid?"*
> *He called his secretary up, said, "Make out a certified check for Ray for $10,000 and put him on the plane to Newark." He gave me another $100 for my pocket. I never got to spend nothing of it, because they paid all the expenses in Mexico. So that was pretty good: I still had $2,500 profit and $300 pocket money too.*
> *He took out money for two pay days and then told his secretary to forget it.*
> *I was Pasquel's number-one boy.*

Ray rewarded Pasquel by hitting .373 to lead the league.

Bill Veeck of the Cleveland Indians, who had just signed Satchel Paige and Larry Doby, was also making overtures to Ray.

> *That was during the time I was in my playing season. I had a contract with the Mexican club. I asked Bill Veeck what was in it for me? Because I had my family down in Mexico. They didn't want to give me no bonus to go. I wasn't going to lose my job with Pasquel; I had a good salary down there.*

Veeck won the 1948 pennant without Ray in a last-ditch play-off, as two veterans, second baseman Joe Gordon and third baseman Ken Keltner, had the best years of their lives. But the next year Gordon's hitting fell off to .251, and Keltner, in his final year, hit only .232, while the Indians finished eight games behind New York. In 1950 Keltner was gone and Gordon was down to .236; the Indians came in fourth, six games behind New York. How might they have done with Dandridge? If Veeck had taken a gamble and sent Ray an advance, or if Ray had gambled and reported to Cleveland anyway, the Indians might have won two more pennants, and Ray just might have gotten into the Hall of Fame long before he finally did.

(Not only might Ray be in—Casey Stengel might be out. If the Indians had beaten Stengel's Yanks for the pennants in 1949–1950, Casey would not have won five in a row. In fact, if he had finished second his first two years with New York, he might not have even been hired back for the third year. Ol' Case could well have ended with no pennants in a very undistinguished managing career that included second division finishes for many years with the Dodgers and Braves. No one would even remember him today. Does Casey owe his bust in Cooperstown to the fact that Ray Dandridge did not play third base for Cleveland in 1949?)

In the winter of 1948 Dandridge was back in Cuba, still trying to cash in on the big money being thrown around.

> *I jumped from Luque's team over to a new league. All the boys were jumping, about six or seven of us. They wanted to put us in jail. I happened to be out of the*

hotel during that time. I got back, asked, "Where all the guys at?" They said, "The cops got 'em." I got in a taxicab, went down to the police station, walk in there. All the cops look around, say, "Talua! We been lookin' for you. Where you been?"

The guy with the (new) team came with his lawyer, got us all out. The team we jumped to didn't last but about six weeks. But we all got our money up front before we played. After that they barred me out of the league in Cuba, so I went to the Sonora Mexico winter league.

In Sonora Ray was named to the all-star team, along with a kid pitcher named Whitey Ford. Dandridge allowed as how he hit Ford "pretty well." Dave Barnhill, who was also there, is more emphatic. "He hit Ford like he owned him," Dave exclaimed.

I made an appearance on the "Good Morning America" show. [The announcer] said, "You know Whitey Ford had a good curve ball."

I told him, "I know Whitey had one of the best curve balls. But I had one of the best bats."

Ray returned home in 1949 to manage the New York Cubans, whose third baseman, Orestes Minoso, worshipped "Ray Dondreedge." Larry Doby, who had gone from Newark to the Indians, also came to Ray for help. Larry was having trouble relating to his new teammates. Ray said he told Larry to pay no attention, to go out and do his job. The advice seemed to work. Dandridge remembered, "Next year, he said, 'Ray, now I can't get those ball players away from me.'"

The Cubans played their home games in the Polo Grounds, home of the New York Giants. Their farm director was former pitching great Carl Hubbell. He approached Cuban owner Alexander Pompez, who agreed to sell his two best players, Barnhill and Dandridge.

Pompez called me on the road one day and asked me if I wanted to play in the big leagues before I quit. I told him, "Sure!" So he said, "Pack up your bag and get on the plane to Minneapolis."

Had the big chance come too late? "I was 35," Ray said, "but I told them I was 30."

Dave and Ray caught the plane and hustled straight to the Millers' stadium, suitcases and all. The game was already in progress as they suited up. Wild Mickey McDermott, a left-handed fast-baller who later went to the Red Sox, was on the mound and had already struck out about 17 or 18 men, Ray said, when he and Barnhill walked into the dugout and shook hands with manager Tommy Heath and then took seats at the end of the bench.

"Ray, when was the last time you played?" Heath asked.

"Last time I played? Are you kidding? I played yesterday."

"Well, do you think you can play today?" Heath wanted to know.

"I came here to play," Ray told him, "I didn't come here to look around."

"Well, how'd you like to go up and hit against him?" Heath asked, jerking his head toward McDermott.

"I'll go up and try," Ray shrugged. He went to the bat rack, shook several models, picked out "one to my balance," and walked up to the plate.

The first pitch whistled in under Ray's chin. But he was used to those and on the next pitch shot a line drive toward right field, which the second baseman leaped and grabbed. And that, Ray remembers, was his debut in organized ball.

Barnhill started and won his first game, and Ray made some good plays in the field. After that, Barnhill said, when the players took their seats, the dugout was integrated, there were no more blacks on one end, whites on the other. "They treated me and Ray like we were on the ball club. Well, we *were* on the club. It wasn't who was white or

Ray Dandridge at the plate.

who was black. Oh man, I had some experiences with that club—good experiences." The Minneapolis *Tribune* headline read:

Minneapolis Welcomes
Barnhill and Dandridge

The two blacks stayed in white hotels with the team everywhere but Louisville and Kansas City. In those towns they stayed at black hotels or boarded with the wife of Kansas City Monarch outfielder Willard Brown. "There was no problem at all," Barnhill said. "Everything was lovely. Yes it was. Lovely."

Heath installed Dandridge at second base. When the Giants sent second baseman Davey Williams down to Minneapolis for more seasoning, Dandridge was hitting like a terror. Heath asked Ray to move to the outfield. "I don't want to play no damn outfield," Dandridge retorted, so Heath shrugged and decided he had no choice but to keep Williams on the bench.

When the Millers' third baseman got spiked, Heath asked Dandridge, "Ray, ever play third before?"

"I'll go over there and try," Ray said modestly.

"They bunted a ball," Ray recalled. "I tossed him out right easy. A ball over the pitcher's head, I went over and got that."

"What the hell is he doing?" the Millers asked in awe.

On the bench, Barnhill just winked. "You done threw the rabbit in the briar patch," he said.

That year Ray played first base, second base, shortstop, and third base, hit .362, and just missed winning the batting title. He was voted Rookie of the Year—at the age of 35.

Why didn't the Giants bring him up that year? It was Leo Durocher's first full season with the team, and he complained that he had inherited a muscle-bound team of sluggers who couldn't run. Sid Gordon on third hit 26 home runs but was slow afield and afoot.

The Giants made their first tentative experiment in race relations that year, bringing Monte Irvin, Ray's old teammate at Newark, up to play a few games at outfield and third base; Monte hit .224. Twenty-three-year-old Hank Thompson, a product of the Kansas City Monarchs, played second base for half the season and hit .280. In all, the Giants led the league in home runs but were next to last in fielding average, lost more games than they won, and finished fifth, 24 games behind the Dodgers. Leo swore he would rebuild the team in his own aggressive image in 1950. Would he cast his eyes toward Minneapolis and Dandridge?

Instead, Leo brought Eddie Stanky over from Brooklyn to play second and shifted Thompson to third. Ray would have to stay in Minneapolis in 1950.

He had another splendid year there, hitting .311.

The biggest thrill of his career came in Minneapolis, he said. Ray had already knocked in three runs in one game but the Millers were still losing, 7–3, when he came up for his last at bat with the bases loaded and two out. Even the other Miller players had given up hope and were on the top step of the dugout waiting to trot across the field to the locker room, when Ray socked a home run to tie it back up. Seven RBI's in one game, for the former banjo hitter! He said that day in Minneapolis was tops in his memory book.

Ray was also sparkling afield. "He had great hands," said Miller second baseman Roy Hughes, a veteran of the Chicago Cubs. "If he got ahold of anything, he never turned loose with it. Of course, he was built close to the ground, didn't have to get down very far for a ground ball."

"He wore his pants almost to the shoes, because his legs were so short," remembered writer Joel Hoeger. "He one-handed the ball on topped balls. You never saw the ball, he was so quick." Hoeger added, "He personally filled the stands."

The fans had all his plays catalogued, said sports writer Ric Roberts of the black Pittsburgh *Courier*. If he scooped up a bunt with one hand, they'd yell "number-one!" Taking a hard smash on the line was "number-two," and so on.

One Minnesotan who saw Ray play was a young lawyer named Warren Burger. Some 35 years later, as chief justice of the United States, he spent 20 minutes at a Washington cocktail party rhapsodizing to authors Donn Rogosin and Craig Davidson about Ray.

"That's what you call a folk hero," Roberts said. "There are ball players' ball players, the media pick their players, but when the fans pick one, you've got something special."

When the votes for league most valuable player were counted, Ray Dandridge received more than anyone else.

The Giants, meanwhile, were making a dash for the pennant, in pursuit of the Phillies and Dodgers. Sal Maglie, who had seen Ray in Mexico, pleaded with the Giants' top scout to bring him up.

"He's too old," the scout protested.

"That's not the question," Sal replied. "We have a month to play. Bring him up for a month."

Recently looking back, Maglie shook his head. The scout didn't have the authority, he said; it was up to Giants' owner Horace Stoneham. "But we could have won the pennant. I know damn well, with Dandridge playing third, we'd have won that pennant in '50."

In Durocher's defense, it is hard to see where Ray could have fit into the team, with Stanky hitting .300 at second and Al Dark, a .279-hitter, at short. The weak spot of the infield was first baseman Tookie Gilbert, who batted only .220. Could Dandridge have handled that position? At least he could have provided back-up insurance at the other three positions, and he could have given Durocher a ninth bat in emergencies.

Irvin blames the quota system, still in effect on those few teams that had integrated. Then too, the Millers won the American Association flag that year. "They were going to call me and Ray to finish the season with the Giants," Barnhill said, "but we had to play in the play-offs instead. I could have had a cup of coffee and a cookie in the big leagues. You never saw a man as mad as I was! Man, was I mad!"

Another theory is that Dandridge was too good a drawing card at Minneapolis, so the Millers resisted sending him up to New York.

For whatever reason, it is hard to justify a pennant contender's deliberately ignoring a star of Dandridge's ability. But the Giants did ignore him, and they may have paid a heavy price. They just couldn't generate the extra oomph to overtake the leaders and finished third. Like Maglie, Irvin thinks the decision on Dandridge cost the Giants the 1950 flag.

That winter Ray returned to Cuba, hitting .299. The next year, the fateful 1951 season, the Giants had high hopes but began miserably. Thompson, a moody, unpopular man, was not doing the job at third. His batting average fell to .264, his home run production from 20 to eight. By August the Giants were far behind the Dodgers and were counted out of the race.

Meanwhile, the Giants had sent a kid outfielder to Minneapolis from their Trenton farm club, a youngster by the name of Willie Mays. "Did you know I was part of the cause of Willie going to the Giants?" Dandridge asked. He had seen Mays, then 19, play in Cuba, and a few days later, as Ray knelt in the on-deck circle, a spectator caught his eye. "Damn," he said to himself, "that looks like Rosey Ryan sitting there." Ryan was Minneapolis general manager, and as Ray trotted back to the dugout after his at bat, he stopped at Ryan's box. "What are you doing here, Rosey?" he asked.

"What you think of this boy, Mays?" Ryan replied. "How do you think he'd do at Minneapolis?"

"Are you kidding?" Ray said. "If you came here to get him, then *get* him!"

When Mays reported to Minneapolis, he hit right ahead of Dandridge in the batting order. "Every time Willie came up and hit one over the center-field fence, it seemed like I came up and hit one over the left-field fence," Dandridge grinned. Pretty soon, every time Willie hit a homer, Ray would hit the dirt as the pitcher aimed the next one at his head. Ruefully he dusted himself off and told Heath, "You better get that man out from in front of me or you're going to get me killed!"

Willie recalled: "Ray Dandridge was like my father: a bow-legged guy. But they said nobody could hit a ball between his legs. He would knock it down some kind of way and throw you out."

Once, Mays said, a pitcher named Ray Atkins with Louisville threw three straight beanballs at him. While Willie lay sprawled on the ground, he looked up to see Dandridge advancing on Atkins. Atkins was built like Wilt Chamberlain, about six-four or six-five, Willie says; Dandridge was about five-seven or five-eight. "Now I'm on the ground, I'm looking up, and I'm looking at Ray saying something to Atkins, and I'm saying to myself, 'My God, don't let this guy hit Ray.' "

Back in the dugout Mays asked Dandridge what he had said. Ray replied: "I told the guy, 'Back home I have two dogs. I have a dog that will go right to your spot if I say bite! Then I got another one that just sits back until the first one gets through, and then I will say 'Bite!' again."

Atkins told Ray, "Well, Ray, I like you, but I don't like that little black worm over there."

And Ray replied, "You call him that again and I'll sic my *third* dog at you!"

One day, before an exhibition game at Sioux City, Iowa, Willie and Ray were sitting in a movie when a message flashed on the screen: "Willie Mays, report to the box office." In a moment Mays returned and whispered, "Ray, I've got to go to the hotel." Ray stayed for the end of the show, then joined his teammates.

"Heh, Skip, where the hell is Willie at?" he asked Heath.

"Didn't you know?" Heath replied. "He's already on a plane. He's half-way to New York now."

Dandridge went back to the room, gathered Mays' belongings, and mailed them to the Polo Grounds.

But again there was no plane ticket for Ray, although he hit .324. In fact, the Giants had to dismiss second baseman Artie Wilson, ironically Mays' old tutor with the Birmingham Black Barons, to maintain the quota when Willie joined the team.

Instead of calling Dandridge, Durocher moved outfielder Bobby Thomson to third. Thomson was no Dandridge with the glove, but he hit with power, and the rest is history. Yet it's fascinating to speculate how history might have been changed if the Giants had put Ray on third. Would he have meant an extra victory or two? If so, there would not have been a play-off and Thomson would not have hit his "Shot heard round the world."

Judy Johnson, scouting for the Philadelphia Athletics, urged

Connie Mack to buy Ray, but, he said, "Minneapolis wouldn't sell him for no money." Johnson then urged a trade, As' pitcher Lou Brissie for Ray, "but Mr. Mack wouldn't do it. He said he'd rather see Brissie rot on the bench before he'd trade him." Brissie had a 7–19 record in 1950 as the As finished last. The next year Brissie was 0–2 when Mack finally traded him to Cleveland. Bobby Shantz won 18 games as the As rose to sixth. In 1952 Shantz won 24 and the As climbed to fourth. But third baseman Billy Hitchcock, a .246 hitter, held them down. They had a good team, Johnson said; all they needed was a third baseman and they might have won the pennant.

The Giants wouldn't bring Ray up to the Polo Grounds either. Davey Williams, a journeyman second baseman, replaced Stanky in 1952 but hit only .254. Irvin broke his ankle, Mays was drafted, Hank Thompson was moved to the outfield, and Bobby Thomson continued to struggle with the unfamiliar hot corner. The Giants finished second, four and a half games behind the Dodgers. And Dandridge, one of the greatest third baseman of all time, stayed in Minneapolis, hitting .292.

Finally, in 1953, the Giants let Ray go, to Oakland in the Pacific Coast league. But Ray, by then 40 years old, ran into the catcher chasing a foul ball, hurt his elbow, hit only .268, and was given his release at the end of the year.

He was out of the game in 1954, but the arm came around in 1955 and he played with Bismarck, North Dakota, where he hit .320. But he was 42 years old. At last he realized that the big league doors would never open for him. He called it a career.

Cum Posey, owner of the Homestead Grays and perhaps the leading authority on black baseball history, named him to his all-time all-black team. "There never was a smoother master at third," he wrote.

Dandridge returned to Newark to the house that Pasquel had bought for him. He tended bar and scouted part-time for the Giants.

"I met Horace Stoneham, the Giants' owner, at an old-timers' game," Ray said. "I cussed him out. My ambition was to go from the lowest to the highest. They could have called me up. I asked him, 'Gee, couldn't you at least have brought me up even for one week, just so I could say I've actually put my foot in a major league park?'

"But no use getting mad about something you can't control," Dandridge shrugged. As for his career,

I've enjoyed it, and I think I've been a lucky fellow. Didn't make no money, but I think I went a long ways. I have no regrets. None at all.

Ray Dandridge

Year	Team	G	AB	H	2B	3B	HR	BA	SB
1933	Nashville-Detroit	11	37	8	1	2	0	.216	0
1934	Newark	9	32	9	2	1	0	.281	0
1935	Newark	22	83	21	3	3	0	.253	0
	Puerto Rico	12	51	10	—	—	—	.196	
1936	Newark	14	47	14	0	0	0	.298	
1937	Newark	5	19	6	0	0	0	.316	
	Cuba	—	211	63	5	1	0	.299	11*
1938	Newark	(not yet compiled)							
	Cuba	—	182	58	5	2	1	.319	3
1939	Mexico	(not available)							
	Cuba	—	116	36	4	1	1	.310	1
1940	Mexico	27	127	44	8	3	1	.346	6
	Cuba	—	158	29	2	1	0	.184	4
1941	Mexico	101	430	158	32	5	8	.367	12
1942	Mexico	35	142	44	7	1	4	.310	8
	Newark								
1943	Mexico	90	370	131*	24	4	8	.354	17
1944	Newark	47	189	70*	12	5	2	.370	8
1945	Mexico	83	344	126	29	4	1	.366	20
	Cuba	—	173	55	5	2	0	.318	2
1946	Mexico	98	418	135	24	0	7	.323	24
	Cuba	—	101	30	—	—	—	.297	—
1947	Mexico	122	514	169*	24	6	2	.329	23
	Cuba	66	14	2	0	0	1	.212	1
1948	Mexico	88	370	138*	22	6	3	.373*	10

Year	Team									
1949	New York Cubans	—	—	—	—	—	—	—	—	
	Minneapolis	99	398	144	.362	8	5	22	4	rookie of the year
1950	Cuba	—	318	84	.264	2	3	15	10	
	Minneapolis	150	627*	195*	.311	1	1	24	—	MVP
1951	Cuba	—	278	83	.299	2	1	12	—	
	Minneapolis	107	423	137	.324	8	1	24	1	
1952	Cuba	—	221	64	.290	3	2	8	2	
	Minneapolis	145	618	180	.291	10	1	7	3	
1953	Cuba	—	305	85	.279	1	1	10	—	
	Sacramento/Oakland	87	254	68	.268	0	1	10	1	
1955	Bismarck	—	328	118*	.320	—	—	—	—	
Totals			7879	2527	.320	74	63	337	171	

Recap

Negro Leagues	86	408	103	.319	2	10	16	8	
Cuba	—	2129	601	.282	10	14	68	34	
Mexico	644	2715	945	.348	34	29	170	120	
Minneapolis	501	2066	656	.318	27	9	77	8	
Other^a	99	633	196	.310	0	1	10	1	
White Big Leagues	13	49	17	.347	0	1	1	—	

Post-Season

Year										
1937	World Series	2	8	3	.375	1	0	0	0	
	East-West	3	11	5	.455	0	0	1	1	

* Led league.
a Puerto Rico, Sacramento, Oakland, Bismarck.

Ray Dandridge vs. White Major Leaguers

Year	AB	H	2B	3B	HR	Pitcher	(W-L)
1935	2	0	0	0	0	Bill Swift	(15-8)
	4	3	1	0	0	Dizzy Dean	(28-12)
						Bill Swift	(15-8)
						Jim Winford	(0-0)
	3	0	—	—	—	Swift, Dean, Winford	
	3	0	0	0	0	Tony Freitas	(5-10)
						Whitey Hilcher	(2-0)
	3	0	0	0	0	Gene Schott	(8-11)
						Hermann	—
1936	5	1	0	0	0	Barnes	(0-0)
1946	4	3	—	—	0	Ace Adams	*
	4	2	0	0	0	Adams, Harry Feldman	*
	5	1	—	—	—	Feldman, Max Lanier	*
	5	2	0	0	0	Sal Maglie	*
	4	2	0	0	0	Sal Maglie	*
	4	1	0	1	0	Bill Berens	(7-13)
						Don Johnson	(4-3)
						Allie Reynolds	(19-8)
						Cuddles Marshall	—
	3	2	0	0	0	Vic Raschi	(7-2)
						Al Lyons	(2-2)
						Frank Hiller	(5-2)
Total 13 Games	49	17	1	1	0	Average: .347	

*Mexican league. Adams had been 11-9 in 1945, Feldman 12-13, Maglie 5-4. Lanier was 6-0 in 1946 before jumping to Mexico.

Statistical Appendix

Lifetime Batting Leaders

Player	BA
*Josh Gibson	.379[a]
Chino Smith	.375
Jud Wilson	.370
Dobie Moore	.359
Dewey Creacy	.359
Willie Wells	.358
*Oscar Charleston	.353
Valentin Dreke	.353
Turkey Stearnes	.352
*Cool Papa Bell	.343
*Pop Lloyd	.342
Joe Rogan	.341
Ed Wesley	.341
Cristobal Torriente	.339
*Monte Irvin	.338
Buck Leonard	.336
*Frog Redus	.336
John Beckwith	.323
Dick Lundy	.321
Mule Suttles	.320
*Ray Dandridge	.320[b]
Biz Mackey	.318
Hurley McNair	.317
Orville Riggins	.312
Oliver Marcelle	.310
Gene Benson	.310
Martin Dihigo	.304
Louis Santop	.303

* Hall of Famers.
[a] Gibson hit .328 in Negro league, .415 in Mexico, Puerto Rico, and Santo Domingo.
[b] Dandridge hit .321 in Negro league, .319 in minor leagues.

Lifetime Home Run Leaders

Player	HR	AB	AB/HR
Turkey Stearnes	160	2866	17.9
Mule Suttles	150	2775	19.2
*Josh Gibson	137	1676	12.2[a]
*Oscar Charleston	136	3479	25.6
*Martin Dihigo	134	5496	40.7
Willie Wells	111	3677	33.1
*Cool Papa Bell	88	4679	53.2
Ed Wesley	82	1439	17.5
*Ray Dandridge	74[b]	7879	106.5[b]
Jud Wilson	71	2879	40.5
John Beckwith	66	1445	21.9
Cristobal Torriente	57	3233	56.7
Dick Lundy	54	2757	51.1
Chino Smith	46	1346	29.3
Joe Rogan	46	1517	33.0
*Buck Leonard	45	1212	26.9
Biz Mackey	44	2377	54.0

* Hall of Famers.
[a] Gibson hit 64 homers (1 per 18.0 at bats) in Negro league, 73 homers (1 per 8.6 at bats) in Latin America.
[b] Dandridge had 28 home runs in Negro league and Latin America, 46 in white minor leagues.

Lifetime Pitching Leaders

Player	(W-L)	
*Satchel Paige	143–78[a]	.647
Joe Rogan	109–46	.703
Nip Winters	89–32	.736
Bill Drake	83–60	.580
Bill Foster	79–41	.658
Webster McDonald	65–27	.706
Chet Brewer	51–22	.700
Ted Radcliffe	49–33	.598

[a] Paige was 80-37, .684, in Negro league; 63-43, .594, in white minors and majors.
NOTE: All statistics are incomplete and subject to updating. Data for 1940s, particularly, are under-represented.

Vs. White Big Leaguers

Player	Years	G	AB	H	HR	BA
Spotswood Poles	1913–17	10	41	25	—	.610
Josh Gibson	1931–46	16	66	28	5	.424
Clint Thomas	1924–26	4	12	5	—	.417
Chino Smith	1926–31	10	37	15	1	.405
Cool Papa Bell	1929–48	46	169	67	4	.395
Mule Suttles	1929–39	23	79	31	11	.392
Sammy T. Hughes	1934–36	10	41	16	—	.390
Larry Brown	1923–35	5	18	7	—	.390
Barney Serrell	1946	4	18	7	—	.389
Ted Page	1930–35	13	48	18	—	.375
Ted Radcliffe	1929–46	8	29	11	—	.376
Bill Wright	1933–46	27	89	33	—	.375
Rap Dixon	1926–35	26	86	32	—	.372
Willie Wells	1929–45	31	115	46	6	.369
Joe Rogan	1920–37	18	57	21	2	.368
Oliver Marcelle	1918–28	17	63	23	0	.365
Jud Wilson	1924–36	25	86	31	3	.360
Ray Dandridge	1935–47	13	49	17	0	.347
Sam Bankhead	1933–48	21	79	27	—	.342
Dick Seay	1933–36	15	47	16	—	.340
Buck Leonard	1936–43	7	24	8	—	.333
Dave Malarcher	1917–23	5	15	5	0	.333
Pop Lloyd	1906–25	29	106	34	0	.327
Biz Mackey	1921–42	14	49	16	0	.326
Bill Perkins	1928–48	8	28	9	—	.321
Vic Harris	1926–43	12	44	14	—	.319
Oscar Charleston	1915–36	53	195	62	11	.318
Turkey Stearnes	1923–36	14	48	15	4	.313
Cristobal Torriente	1918–28	28	90	28	3	.311
John Beckwith	1922–34	29	119	37	—	.311
Louis Santop	1913–20	15	58	18	0	.310
Bunny Downs	1917–19	5	20	6	—	.300

League Leaders, East

Year	Player	BA	Player	HR	Pitcher	(W–L)
1923	Jud Wilson	.464	Charlie Mason	5	Rats Henderson	(7–9)
1924	George Scales	.422	Dick Lundy	13	Nip Winters	(26–4)
1925	Oscar Charleston	.418	Oscar Charleston	16	Nip Winters	(21–10)[a]
1926	Luther Farrell	.359	Martin Dihigo	11	Nip Winters	(18–6)
1927	Jud Wilson	.412	Oscar Charleston	12	Rats Henderson	(19–7)
1928	Pop Lloyd	.564	Pop Lloyd	11	Luther Farrell	(15–11)
1929	Chino Smith	.461	Chino Smith	23	Connie Rector	(18–1)
1930	Chino Smith	.429	John Beckwith	9	Pud Flournoy	(11–1)
1931	Jud Wilson	.358	John Beckwith	6	Porter Charleston	(14–3)
1934	Jud Wilson	.355	Josh Gibson	8	Satchel Paige	(16–2)[b]
1935	Turkey Stearnes	.430	Martin Dihigo	9	Leroy Matlock	(17–0)
			Josh Gibson	9		
1936	Martin Dihigo	.391	Martin Dihigo	13	Satchel Paige	(8–1)
					Webster McDonald	(8–1)
1938	Bill Perkins	.341	Bill Perkins	4	Bob Griffith	(4–0)
					Bill Byrd	(4–0)
1939	Buck Leonard	.492	Buck Leonard	7	Henry McHenry	(6–2)
1940	Pee Wee Butts	.411*				
1941	Monte Irvin	.395*				
1942	Josh Gibson	.452*	Josh Gibson	20*		
1943	Josh Gibson	.503*				
1944	Fred Austin	.390	Gibson, Leonard	6	Bill Ricks	(10–4)
1945	Josh Gibson	.393	Josh Gibson	8	Roy Welmaker	(12–4)
1946	Monte Irvin	.394*				
1947	Luis Marquez	.417*				
1948	Buck Leonard	.395*				

* Unconfirmed.

[a] Rats Henderson was 21–17.

[b] Slim Jones was 13–1 in 1934.

League Leaders, West

Year	Player	BA	Player	HR	Pitcher	(W–L)
1920	Jimmy Lyons	.399	Edgar Wesley	11	Bill Gatewood	(14–4)
1921	Charles Blackwell	.448	Oscar Charleston	15	Bill Drake	(20–10)
1922	Charles Blackwell	.387	Oscar Charleston	15	Bill Holland	(16–13)*
1923	Cristobal Torriente	.389	Wesley-Stearnes	17	Andy Cooper	(15–8)
1924	Dobie Moore	.470	Turkey Stearnes	10	Joe Rogan	(15–5)
1925	Edgar Wesley	.440	Wesley-Stearnes	18	Joe Rogan	(12–2)
1926	Mule Suttles	.418	Mule Suttles	26	Slap Hensley	(17–7)
1927	Red Parnell	.438	Turkey Stearnes	21	Bill Foster	(18–3)
1928	Pythian Russ	.406	Turkey Stearnes	24	Ted Trent	(17–4)
1929	Clarence Smith	.390	Willie Wells	27	John Williams	(19–7)
1930	Willie Wells	.404	Mule Suttles	20	Slap Hensley	(17–6)
1931	Nat Rogers[a]	.424	Turkey Stearnes	8	Nelson Dean	(8–3)
1932	Willie Scott[a]	.385	Turkey Stearnes	5	Bill Foster	(14–6)
	Leroy Taylor[b]	.500	Josh Gibson	6	Bertram Hunter	(16–6)
1933	Leroy Morney	.419	Oscar Charleston	9	Bertram Hunter	(7–1)
1944	Sam Jethroe	.353	Alec Radcliff	5	Alfred Saylor	(14–5)
1945	Sam Jethroe	.393	Alec Radcliff	7	Gentry Jessup	(15–10)
1946	Buck O'Neil	.353[c]				
1947	Hank Thompson	.344[c]				
1948	Artie Wilson	.402[c]				

Except for 1921, 1926, 1929, and 1930, all data are incomplete and may be updated.

* John Meyers had a record of 15–1.

[a] Southern League.

[b] East-West League.

[c] Unconfirmed.

Cuban League Champions

Year	Player	BA	Player	HR	Pitcher	(W-L)
1920-21	Pelayo Chacon	.344	Torriente, M. Gonzalez,		Cheo Hernandez	4-1
			B. Jimenez, M. Guerra	1		
1921*	Bienvenido Jimenez	.619	Manuel Cueto	1	Julio Leblanc	2-0
1922-23	Bernardo Baro	.401	C. Torriente	4	Lucas Boada	10-4
1923-24	Oliver Marcelle	.393	Bienvenido Jimenez	4	Bill Holland	10-2
1924-25	Alejandro Oms	.393	Estaban Montalvo	5	Jose Acosta	4-1
1925-26	Jud Wilson	.430	J.H. Lloyd, Jud Wilson	3	Cesar Alvarez	10-2
1926-27	Manuel Cueto	.398	J. Hernandez	4	Juan Olmo	3-0
1927-28	Jud Wilson	.424	Oscar Charleston	5	Oscar Levis	7-2
1928-29	Alejandro Oms	.432	Cool Papa Bell	5	Adolfo Luque	9-2
1929-30	Alejandro Oms	.380	Mule Suttles	7	Heliodoro Diaz	13-3
1930*	Oscar Charleston	.373	Ernest Smith,		Martin Dihigo	2-0
			Jose Fernandez	1		
1931-32	Ramon Couto	.400	Oms, Ismael Morales	3	Juan Eckelson	5-1
1932-33	Mike Gonzalez	.432	Roberto Estalella	3	Jesus Lorenzo	3-0
1933-34	(Season was suspended)					
1934-35	Lazaro Salazar	.407	11 players tied with	1	Lazaro Salazar	6-1
1935-36	Martin Dihigo	.358	W. Wells, Jacinto Roque	5	Martin Dihigo	11-2
1936-37	Harry Williams	.339	Herman Andrews,		Raymond Brown	21-4
			Estalella	5		
1937-38	Sam Bankhead	.366	Wells, Estalella,		Raymond Brown	12-5
			R. Brown	4		
1938-39	Tony Castaño	.371	Josh Gibson	11	Martin Dihigo	14-2
1939-40	Tony Castaño	.340	Mule Suttles	4	Rodolfo Fernandez	7-4
1940-41	Lazaro Salazar	.316	Alejandro Crespo	3	Gilberto Torres	10-3
1941-42	Silvio Garcia	.351			Macon A. Mayor	6-2
1942-43	Alejandro Crespo	.337	R. Ortiz, S. Hernandez	2	Cocaina Garcia	10-3
1943-44	Roberto Ortiz	.337	Saguita Hernandez		Martin Dihigo	8-1
1944-45	Claro Duany	.340	Claro Duany	3	Oliverio Ortiz	10-4
1945-46	Lloyd Davenport	.332	Dick Sisler	9	Adrian Zabala	9-3
1946-47	Lou Klein	.330	Roberto Ortiz	11	Cocaina Garcia	10-3
1947-48	Henry Kimbro	.346	Chanquilon Diaz	7	Conrado Marrero	12-2
	Roland Gladu	.330	Danny Gardella	10	Adrian Zabala	13-7
1948-49	Alejandro Crespo	.326	Monte Irvin	10	Octavio Rubert	8-1
1949-50	Pedro Formental	.336	R. Ortiz, Don Lenhardt	15	Octavio Rubert	5-1

* Short Season.

Mexican League Champions

Year	Player	BA	Player	HR	Player	RBI
1938	Martin Dihigo	.387	Angel Castro	9	Angel Castro	40
1939	Lazaro Salazar	.374	Angel Castro	9	Angel Castro	50
1940	Cool Papa Bell	.437	Cool Papa Bell	12	Cool Papa Bell	79
1941	Bill Wright	.390	Josh Gibson	33	Josh Gibson	124
1942	Monte Irvin	.397	Monte Irvin	20	Silio Garcia	83
1943	Bill Wright	.366	Bill Wright	13	Wright Dandridge	
					Alexandro Crespo	70
1944	Sagua Hernandez	.395	Sagua Hernandez	13	Sagua Hernandez	97
1945	Claro Duany	.375	Roberto Ortiz	26	Claro Duany	100
1946	Claro Duany	.364	Roberto Ortiz	25	Roberto Ortiz	108
1947	Roberto Avila	.346	Roberto Ortiz	22	Alejandro Crespo	96
1948	Ray Dandridge	.373	Roberto Ortiz	19	Roberto Ortiz	74

Year	Pitcher	ERA	Pitcher	(W-L)	Pitcher	SO
1938	Martin Dihigo	0.90	Martin Dihigo	(18-2)	Martin Dihigo	184
1939	Johnny Taylor	1.19	B. Brown, Salazar	(16-5)	Martin Dihigo	202
1940	Ramon Bragana	2.58	Bill Jefferson	(22-9)	Pullman Porter	232
1941	Cochihuila Valenzuela	3.12	Barney Brown	(16-5)	Pullman Porter	133
1942	Martin Dihigo	2.53	Martin Dihigo	(22-7)	Martin Dihigo	211
1943	Vidal Lopez	2.08	Manuel Fortes	(18-6)	Martin Dihigo	134
1944	Adrian Zabala	2.74	Lazaro Salazar	(14-8)	Ramon Bragana	144
1945	Juan Guerrerro	2.87	Cocaina Garcia	(18-11)	Agapito Mayor	156
1946	Max Lanier	1.94	Cocaina Garcia	(14-10)	Booker McDaniel	171
1947	Santiago Ulrich	2.65	Indian Torres	(14-6)	Booker McDaniel	127
1948	Meno Lopez	2.37	Charrascas Ramirez	(9-2)	Agapito Mayor	92

Negro Baseball Yearbook
All-Star Teams

	1944	1945
1B	Buck Leonard	Buck Leonard
2B	Ray Dandridge	Jesse Douglas
SS	Frank Austin	Avelino Canalares
3B	Parnell Woods	Parnell Woods
LF	Cool Papa Bell	Gene Benson
CF	Charlie Davis	Sam Jethroe
RF	Ed Steele	Bill Wright
C	Roy Campanella	Josh Gibson
P	George Jefferson	George Jefferson
	Gendry Jessup	Willie Jefferson
	Ray Brown	Roy Welmaker
	Alfred Saylor	

All Star Teams

	1924 (Cum Posey)	1925 (All East)*	1929 (East)[a]
1B	Rev Cannady	George Carr	Jud Wilson
2B	Frank Warfield	Frank Warfield	George Scales
SS	Dobie Moore	Dick Lundy	Dick Lundy
3B	Dave Malarcher	Judy Johnson	Judy Johnson[b]
LF	Cristobal Torriente	Chaney White	Vic Harris
CF	Oscar Charleston	Oscar Charleston	Rap Dixon
RF	Hurley McNair	Rap Dixon	Chino Smith
C	John Beckwith	Biz Mackey	Buck Ewing
	Biz Mackey	Julio Rojo	Biz Mackey
P	Army Cooper	Rats Henderson	Laymon Yokely
	Joe Rogan	Nip Winters	Porter Charleston
	Rats Henderson	Phil Cockrell	Roswell
	Joe Williams	Rube Currie	Connie Rector
	George Harney	Oscal Lewis	Pud Flournoy
			Sam Streeter
Util IF	Orvil Riggins	George Britt	John Beckwith
Util OF	Crush Holloway	Fats Jenkins	Martin Dihigo
MGR	—	John Lloyd	John Lloyd

* Chosen by fans in Pittsburgh *Courier*.
[a] Chosen by Rollo Wilson, sports editor, Pittsburgh *Courier*.
[b] Wilson's choice for MVP.

All Star Teams (Cum Posey)

	1931	1932	1933
1B	Charleston	Suttles	Charleston
2B	Allen	Wells	Cannady
SS	Lundy	Lundy	Wells
3B	Wilson	Wilson	Wilson
LF	Dihigo	Jenkins	Harris
CF	Bell	Bell	Bell
RF	Mothel	Parnell	Dixon
C	Gibson, Mackey	Young	Gibson, Mackey
P	Foster	Foster	Holland
	Radcliffe	Hunter	Britt, Brown
	Streeter		Paige, Jones
Util	Suttles	C. Williams	Scales, Stearnes

	1934	1935
1B	Leonard	Leonard
2B	Hughes	Hughes
SS	Stephens	C. Williams
3B	Scales	Wilson
LF	Benjamin	Harris
CF	R. Brown	Stearnes
RF	Stearnes	Dixon
C	Gibson, Young	Gibson, Clarke
P	Paige	Paige
	Jones	Matlock
	Tiant	
Util		Dihigo, Crutchfield

	1936	(2nd Team)	1938
1B	Leonard	(Wilson)	Leonard
2B	Hughes	(Cannady)	Hughes
SS	Wells	(C. Williams)	
3B	Dandridge	(Patterson)	Dandridge
LF	Wright	(Parnell)	Jenkins
CF	Bankhead	(Bell)	Wright
RF	Harris	(Stone)	N. Robinson
C	Gibson	(Duncan)	Gibson
P	Paige	(Stanley)	R. Brown
	Dihigo	(Day)	B. Brown
	Matlock	(Holland)	Smith
MGR	Taylor		Harris

Pittsburgh *Courier* All-Time All-Star Team, 1952

1B	*Buck Leonard	Ben Taylor	Jŭd Wilson
2B	*Jack Robinson	Bingo DeMoss	Bill Monroe
SS	*Pop Lloyd	Willie Wells	Dick Lundy
3B	Oliver Marcelle	*Judy Johnson	Jud Wilson
LF	*Monte Irvin	Pete Hill	Rap Dixon
CF	*Oscar Charleston	*Cool Papa Bell	Larry Doby
RF	Cristobal Torriente	Chino Smith	Fats Jenkins
C	*Josh Gibson	*Roy Campanella	Ted Radcliffe
	Biz Mackey	Bruce Petway	Louis Santop
P	Joe Williams	Dave Brown	Slim Jones
	*Satchel Paige	Dick Redding	Bill Holland
	Bullet Rogan	Nip Winters	Phil Cockrell
	John Donaldson	Dizzy Dismukes	Webster McDonald
	Bill Foster	Don Newcombe	Bill Byrd
Util	*Martin Dihigo	John Beckwith	Emmett Bowman
	Sam Bankhead	Newt Allen	Dick Wallace
Mgr	*Rube Foster	Cum Posey	Ed Bolden
Coach	Dizzy Dismukes	C.I. Taylor	
	Danny McClellan	Dave Malarcher	

1B	Ed Douglas	George Carr
2B	George Scales	Bunny Downs
SS	Doby Moore	Pelayo Chacon
3B	*Ray Dandridge	Dave Malarcher
LF	Jimmy Lyons	Frank Duncan
CF	Mule Suttles	Turkey Stearnes
RF	Spotswood Poles	Jelly Gardner
C	Frank Duncan	Doc Wiley
	Bill Perkins	Speck Webster
P	Ted Radcliffe	Stringbean Williams
	Frank Wickware	Ray Brown
	Danny McClellan	Rats Henderson
	Leon Day	Luis Tiant
	Bill Jackman	Leroy Matlock
Util	Rev Cannady	
	Jose Mendez	
Mgr	Vic Harris	

Others:
1B: Leroy Grant, Mule Suttles.
2B: Nate Harris, Sammy T. Hughes, Frank Warfield, Ray Dandridge, George Wright, Harry Williams.
SS: Gerard Williams, Bobby Williams, Morton Clark.
3B: Bill Francis, Jim Taylor.
OF: Minnie Minoso, Jap Payne, Blaine Hall, Ted Strong, Ted Page, Vic Harris.
P: Jose Mendez, Laymon Yokely.
*   Hall of Famers.

All-Star Teams (by vote of the fans)

West

Position	1933	1934	1935	1936	1937	1938	1939
1B	Suttles	Suttles	Charleston	St. Taylor	Mayweather	Strong	Strong
2B	Allen	Allen	Hughes	Allen	Allen	Bibbs	Horne
SS	Wells	Wells	Wells	Strong	Easterling	Johnson	Morney
3B	Radcliff	Radcliff	Radcliff	Patterson	Radcliff	Robinson	Radcliff
OF	Stearnes	Stearnes	Harris	Robinson	W. Brown	Whatley	Owens
	Rogers	Barnell	Stearnes	Dial	Stearnes	W. Brown	Robinson
	Davis	Bankhead	Z. Wright	Redus	Davenport	Trouppe	Milton
C	Brown	Brown	Brown	Bias	Radcliffe	Duncan	Bassett
P	Foster	Foster	R. Brown	Trent	Trent	Cornelius	Smith
	Brewer	Brewer	Matlock	Cornelius	Moss	Smith	Radcliffe
	Cornelius	Trent	Trent	Cooper	Smith	McAllister	Henry

East

Position	1933	1934	1935	1936	1937	1938	1939
1B	Charleston	Charleston	Wilson	West	Leonard	West	Leonard
2B	Russell	C. Williams	Seay	Hughes	Hughes	Hughes	Hughes
SS	Lundy	Lundy	Stephens	C. Williams	Jackson	C. Williams	Wells
3B	Wilson	Wilson	Creacy	Johnson	Dandridge	J. Wilson	Patterson
OF	Harris	Harris	Jenkins	Bankhead	Jenkins	Wilson (Pit)	Parnell
	Bell	Bell	Arnold	Bell	B. Wright	Jenkins	Wright
	Dixon	Dixon	Dihigo	Crutchfield	Benjamin	Bankhead	Curry
C	Mackey	Gibson	Hayes	Gibson	Bassett	Bassett	Gibson
P	Streeter	Paige	Tiant	Paige	Morris	Taylor	Byrd
	Britt	Jones	Jones	Matlock	Davis	Porter	Partlow
	Paige	Holland	Evans	Griffith	T. Smith	B. Brown	Day

All-Star Teams (by vote of the fans)

West

Position	1940	1941	1942	1943
1B	Mayweather	Taylor	O'Neil	O'Neil
2B	Bibbs	Horne	Sampson	F. Bankhead
SS	Morney	Allen	T.J. Brown	Wyatt
3B	Woods	Woods	Woods	Woods
OF	Rieves	Robinson	W. Brown	Robinson
	Milton	D. Wilson	Strong	W. Brown
	Sims	Brown	Jethroe	Davenport
C	Greene	Bassett	Greene	Hardy
P	Smith	Paige	Paige	Paige
	Bowe	Smith	Smith	Moss
	Wright	Henry	Mathis	McKinnis

East

Position	1940	1941	1942	1943
1B	Leonard	Leonard	West	Leonard
2B	Hughes	Seay	Hughes	S. Bankhead
SS	Clarkson	Butts	Wells	Martinez
3B	Easterling	Easterling	Patterson	Spearman
OF	Hoskins	Parnell	Wright	Stone
	Benjamin	Hoskins	Benjamin	Benjamin
	Whatley	Vargas	Wilson (N.Y.)	Vargas
C	Perkins	Mackey	Gibson	Gibson
P	J. Taylor	Barnhill	Barnhill	Barnhill
	R. Brown	McHenry	B. Brown	Day
	Adams	McDuffie	R. Brown	Wright

All-Time All-Star Team
By Cum Posey

1B	Buck Leonard
2B	Martin Dihigo
SS	John Henry Lloyd
3B	Ray Dandridge
LF	Pete Hill
CF	Oscar Charleston
RF	Cristobal Torriente
C	Josh Gibson
	Biz Mackey
RHP	Joe Williams
	Dick Redding
	Satchel Paige
	Joe Rogan
LHP	Dave Brown
	Bill Foster

Suggestions for Further Reading

Bruce, Janet. *The Kansas City Monarchs: Champions of Black Baseball*, University Press of Kansas, 1985. Details of one of the great teams, with emphasis on its impact on the city's black culture.

Holway, John B. *Voices From the Great Black Baseball Leagues*, Dodd Mead, 1975. Interviews with eighteen veterans, many now deceased. Subjects include Cool Papa Bell and Buck Leonard.

Peterson, Robert. *Only the Ball Was White*, Prentice-Hall, 1970; McGraw-Hill, 1984. The pioneer book in black baseball research. Good overview and starting point for information on Negro league players.

Riley, Jim. *Negro League Allstars*. TK Publishers, 1983. Thumbnail sketches of the top players of the Negro leagues.

Rogosin, Donn. *Invisible Men: Life in Baseball's Negro Leagues*, Atheneum, 1983. A look at the sociological context of the Negro leagues.

Trouppe, Quincy. *Twenty Years Too Soon*, S&S Enterprises, Los Angeles, 1977. Colorful recollections of life in the black leagues by a man who lived it.

Tygiel, Jules. *Baseball's Great Experiment: Jackie Robinson and His Legacy*, Oxford University Press, 1985. Definitive history of the signing of Jackie Robinson and the events surrounding the early integration of the Major Leagues.

Index